BIBLICAL COMMENTARY

ON

THE BOOK OF JOB

BIBLICAL COMMENTARY

ON

THE BOOK OF JOB

BY

F. DELITZSCH, D.D.,

PROFESSOR OF THEOLOGY.

TRANSLATED FROM THE GERMAN

BY THE

REV. FRANCIS BOLTON, B.A.,

ELLAND.

VOL. II.

TRANSLATOR'S PREFACE

It is with no ordinary feeling of relief and satisfaction that I am at length able to send forth the second and concluding volume of this Commentary. And I am confident that the trifling delay in this year's issues of the Foreign Theological Library will be readily pardoned, when the tedious toil involved in carrying such a work through the press amidst the pressure of other duties is considered. No pains have been spared to render the work worthy its position; and the care bestowed upon the work by myself has been fully seconded by the attention of the printers.

The duties of translation have been carefully discharged, and it has been my aim to preserve the complexion of the original as far as possible, even sometimes at the expense of an easy flow of language. Conscious of imperfection in the working out of my design, I have nevertheless sought to put the reader in the position of a student of the original volume. The task which I imposed upon myself has not been confined to *mere* translation; but close attention has been given to the accurate reproduction of the critical portions, with the hope of contributing in some small degree to the diffusion of sound exegetical knowledge for the elucidation of one of the

grandest and most practical books of the Old Testament
Scriptures, and from a conviction of the need there is for the
cultivation of the cognate Semitic languages. This latter
branch of study is specially applicable and necessary in the
interpretation of the book of Job, and the established scholar-
ship of Dr Delitzsch eminently qualifies him for the effective
execution of the work.

Further explanation need scarcely be added, except in
reference to the retention of the word *Chokma,* and the
character of the translation of the text. As to the former,
I regret that I did not append a note to vol. i. p. 5, to the
effect that the word *Chokma* (חָכְמָה, *Wisdom*) was reproduced
because used technically by the author. I presumed that
students of the volume would at once recognise the word ;
but from the consideration that the Commentary may also
be used, so far as the practical parts are concerned, even by
readers unacquainted with Hebrew, this explanation has been
deemed needful.

And it may further suffice, in connection with the second
section of the Introduction, to define *Chokma* as the one
word for the lofty spirit of wisdom which dwelt in the minds
of the wise men of Israel in the Salomonic age,—a wisdom
taught, inspired, by the Holy Spirit of God—the culmination
of which is found in Solomon himself. In brief, the *Chokma*
is the divine philosophy of the Jewish church.

With reference to the new rendering of the text : it aims
at a literal and faithful reproduction of Dr Delitzsch's translation, as representing his " sense and appreciation of the
original," and as the embodiment of the results of the critical
notes. Therefore I have not felt at liberty to use that

freedom of expression which I regard as most desirable in adapting the translation of the original text to the requirements of the general reader. This portion of my undertaking has not been free from difficulty; and occasionally an amount of stiffness has seemed unavoidable, owing to the different structure of the Hebrew and English languages, while, from the plastic nature of the German language, the author is enabled to mould his translation closely after the original text, and still render it elegant, and at times rhythmical.

A note on the transcription of Arabic words will be found at the end of the Appendix. The references have been verified, so far as the means of verification have been accessible; and I believe I may speak with confidence of those that I have not been able to verify, from the general accuracy I found in the others.

To clear up the misapprehension which has been manifested in many quarters, I would add that this Commentary forms a part of the *Biblical Commentary on the Old Testament* by Drs Keil and Delitzsch. But the name of the latter only is appended to these volumes, because Dr Delitzsch is the writer of this portion, just as Dr Keil only is the author of the *Commentary on the Pentateuch,* and all the other volumes that have appeared to this date.

I have still to acknowledge the kind promptitude with which my esteemed friend Dr Delitzsch has, in more than one instance, given me an explanation of a difficult point, and favoured me with an additional amendment of the original work during the progress of this translation through the press.

In the hope that the usefulness of Dr Delitzsch's valuable contribution to Biblical Exegesis may be extended beyond his original design, I commend it to all earnest students of the Holy Word, with the prayer that the blessing of the Spirit of Jehovah may rest upon the labours of *our* hands.

F. B.

ELLAND, *November* 2, 1866.

TABLE OF CONTENTS

THE BOOK OF JOB

---◆---

SECOND PART.—THE ENTANGLEMENT

CHAP. IV.–XXVI.

THE THIRD COURSE OF THE CONTROVERSY.— CHAP. XXII.–XXVI.

(CONTINUED.)

Job's First Answer.—Chaps. xxiii. xxiv.

Schema: 8. 8. 8. 8. | 8. 9. 9. 9. 5. 10. 9.

[Then began Job, and said :]

2 *Even to-day my complaint still biddeth defiance,*
  My hand lieth heavy upon my groaning.
3 *Oh that I knew where I might find Him,*
  That I might come even to His dwelling-place!
4 *I would lay the cause before Him,*
  And fill my mouth with arguments :
5 *I should like to know the words He would answer me,*
  And attend to what He would say to me.

SINCE מְרִי (for which the LXX. reads ἐκ τοῦ χειρός μου, מִידִי; Ew. מִידוֹ, from his hand) usually elsewhere signifies obstinacy, it appears that ver. 2a ought to be explained : My complaint is always accounted as rebellion (against God) ; but by this rendering ver. 2b requires some sort of expletive, in order to furnish a connected thought: *although* the hand which is upon me stifles my groaning (Hirz.); or, according to another rendering of the עַל: *et pourtant mes gémissements n'égalent pas mes souffrances* (Renan, Schlottm.). These interpretations are objectionable on account of the artificial restoration of the connection between the two members of the verse, which they require; they lead one to expect וְיָדִי (as a circumstantial clause; LXX., *Cod. Vat.* καὶ ἡ χεὶρ αὐτοῦ). As the words stand, it is to be supposed that the definition of time, גַּם־הַיּוֹם (even to-day still, as Zech. ix. 12), belongs to both divisions of the verse. How, then, is מרי to be understood? If we compare ch. vii. 11, x. 1, where מר, which is combined with שִׂיחַ, signifies *amarum = amaritudo*, it is natural to take מרי also in the signification *amaritudo, acerbitas* (Targ., Syr., Jer.); and this is also possible, since, as is evident from Ex. xxiii. 21, comp. Zech. xii. 10, the verbal forms מרר and מרה run into one another, as they are really cognates.[1] But it is more satisfactory, and more in accordance with the relation of the two divisions of the verse, if we keep to the usual signification of מְרִי; not, however, understanding it of ob-

---

[1] מרר and מרה both spring from the root מר [*vid. supra*, i. p. 279, note], with the primary signification *stringere*, to beat, rub, draw tight. Hence مَرّ, to touch lightly, smear upon (to go by, over, or through, to move by, etc.), but also *stringere palatum*, of an astringent taste, strong in taste, to be bitter, *opp.* حَلّ, soft and mild in taste, to be sweet, as in another direction חלה, to be loose, weak, sick, both from the root حل in حَلّ, *solvit, laxavit*. From the signification to be tight come *amarra*, to stretch tight, *istamarra*, to stretch one's self tight, to draw one's self out in this state of tension—of things in time, to continue unbroken; *mirreh*, string, cord; מרה, to make and hold one's self tight against any one, *i.e.* to be obstinate: originally of the body, as تَمَارَّ، مَارَّ, to strengthen themselves in the contest against one another; then of the mind, as تَمَارَى، مَارَى, to struggle against anything, both outwardly by contradiction and disputing, and inwardly by doubt and unbelief.—Fl.

stinacy, revolt, rebellion (viz. in the sense of the friends), but, like מָרָה, 2 Kings xiv. 26 (which describes the affliction as stiff-necked, obstinate), of stubbornness, defiance, continuance in opposition, and explain with Raschi : My complaint is still always defiance, *i.e.* still maintains itself in opposition, viz. against God, without yielding (Hahn, Olsh. : unsubmitting) ; or rather : against such exhortations to penitence as those which Eliphaz has just addressed to him. In reply to these, Job considers his complaint to be well justified even to-day, *i.e.* even now (for it is not, with Ewald, to be imagined that, in the mind of the poet, the controversy extends over several days,—an idea which would only be indicated by this one word).

In ver. 2*b* he continues the same thought under a different form of expression. My hand lies heavy on my groaning, *i.e.* I hold it immoveably fast (as Fleischer proposes to take the words) ; or better : I am driven to a continued utterance of it.[1] By this interpretation יִדִי retains its most natural meaning, *manus mea*, and the connection of the two members of the verse without any particle is best explained. On the other hand, all modern expositors, who do not, as Olsh., at once correct יִדִי into יָדוֹ, explain the suffix as objective : the hand, *i.e.* the destiny to which I have to submit, weighs upon my sighing, irresistibly forcing it out from me. Then ver. 2*b* is related to ver. 2*a* as a confirmation ; and if, therefore, a particle is to be supplied, it is כִּי (Olsh.) and no other. Thus, even the Targ. renders it מְחָתִי, *plaga mea*. Job's affliction is frequently traced back to the hand of God, ch. xix. 21, comp. i. 11, ii. 5, xiii. 21 ; and on the suffix used objectively (pass.) we may compare ver. 14, חֻקִּי ; ch. xx. 29, אִמְרוֹ ; and

---

[1] The idea might also be : My hand presses my groaning back (because it would be of no use to me) ; but ver. 2*a* is against this, and the Arab. *kamada*, to restrain inward pain, anger, etc. by force (*e.g. mât kemed*, he died from suppressed rage or anxiety), has scarcely any etymological connection with כבד.

especially xxxiv. 6, חָצִי. The interpretation : the hand upon
me is heavy above my sighing, *i.e.* heavier than it (Ramban,
Rosenm., Ges., Schlottm., Renan), also accords with the connection. עַל can indeed be used in this comparative meaning,
Ex. xvi. 5, Eccl. i. 16 ; but כבדה יד על is an established
phrase, and commonly used of the burden of the hand upon
any one, Ps. xxxii. 4 (comp. ch. xxxiii. 7, in the division
in which Elihu is introduced; and the connection with אֶל,
1 Sam. v. 6, and שָׁם, 1 Sam. v. 11); and this usage of the
language renders the comparative rendering very improbable.
But it is also improbable that " my hand" is = the hand [that
is] upon me, since it cannot be shown that יד was directly
used in the sense of *plaga;* even the Arabic, among the
many turns of meaning which it gives to يَد, does not support
this, and least of all would an Arab conceive of يدى passively,
plaga quam patior. Explain, therefore : his complaint now,
as before, offers resistance to the exhortation of the friends,
which is not able to lessen it, his (Job's) hand presses upon
his lamentation so that it is forced to break forth, but —
without its justification being recognised by men. This
thought urges him on to the wish that he might be able to
pour forth his complaint directly before God. מִי־יִתֵּן is at
one time followed by an accusative (ch. xiv. 4, xxix. 2, xxxi.
31, 35, to which belongs also the construction with the inf.,
ch. xi. 5), at another by the *fut.*, with or without *Waw* (as
here, ver. 3*b*, ch. vi. 8, xiii. 5, xiv. 13, xix. 23), and at
another by the *perf.*, with or without *Waw* (as here, ver. 3*a* :
utinam noverim, and Deut. v. 26). And יָדַעְתִּי is, as in ch.
xxxii. 22, joined with the *fut.*: *scirem (noverim) et invenirem*
instead of *possim invenire eum* (לְמָצְאוֹ), Ges. § 142, 3, *c.* If
he but knew [how] to reach Him (God), could attain to His
throne; תְּכוּנָה (everywhere from כּוּן, not from תָּכַן) signifies
the setting up, *i.e.* arrangement (Ezek. xliii. 11) or establish-
ment (Nah. ii. 10) of a dwelling, and the thing itself which is

set out and established, here of the place where God's throne
is established. Having attained to this, he would lay his
cause (*instruere causam*, as ch. xiii. 18, comp. xxxiii. 5) before
Him, and fill his mouth with arguments to prove that he has
right on his side (תּוֹכָחוֹת, as Ps. xxxviii. 15, of the grounds of
defence, or proof that he is in the right and his opponent in
the wrong). In ver. 5 we may translate: I would, or: I
should like (to learn); in the Hebrew, as in *cognoscerem*,
both are expressed; the substance of ver. 5*a* makes the
optative rendering more natural. He would like to know
the words with which He would meet him,[1] and would give
heed to what He would say to him. But will He condescend?
will He have anything to do with the matter?—

6 *Will He contend with me with great power?*
   No, indeed; He will only regard me!
7 *Then the upright would be disputing with Him,*
   And I should for ever escape my judge.
8 *Yet I go eastward, He is not there,*
   And westward, but I perceive Him not;
9 *Northwards where He worketh, but I behold Him*
    not;
   He turneth aside southwards, and I see Him not.

The question which Job, in ver. 6*a*, puts forth: will He
contend with me in the greatness or fulness of His strength,
i.e. (as ch. xxx. 18) with a calling forth of all His strength?
he himself answers in ver. 6*b*, hoping that the contrary may
be the case: no, indeed, He will not do that.[2] לֹא is here

---

[1] אֶדְעָה is generally accented with *Dechi*, מִלִּים with *Munach*, according
to which Dachselt interprets: *scirem, quæ eloquia responderet mihi Deus,*
but this is incorrect. The old editions have correctly אֶדְעָה *Munach*,
מלים *Munach* (taking the place of *Dechi*, because the *Athnach*-word
which follows has not two syllables before the tone-syllable; *vid. Psalter,*
ii. 104, § 4).

[2] With this interpretation, לֹא should certainly have *Rebia mugrasch;*

THE BOOK OF JOB.

followed not by the כִּי, which is otherwise customary after a
negation in the signification *imo*, but by the restrictive ex-
ceptive אַךְ, which never signifies *sed*, sometimes *verum tamen*
(Ps. xlix. 16; comp. *supra*, ch. xiii. 15, vol. i. p. 215), but
here, as frequently, *tantummodo*, and, according to the hyper-
baton which has been mentioned so often (vol. i. pp. 72, 238,
and also 215), is placed at the beginning of the sentence,
and belongs not to the member of the sentence immediately
following it, but to the whole sentence (as in Arabic also
the restrictive force of the اِنَّمَا never falls upon what immediately follows it): He will do nothing but regard me
(יָשִׂים, *scil.* לֵב, elsewhere with עַל of the object of regard or
reflection, ch. xxxiv. 23, xxxvii. 15, Judg. xix. 30, and without an ellipsis, ch. i. 8; also with אֶל, ch. ii. 3, or לְ, 1 Sam. ix.
20; here designedly with בְּ, which unites in itself the significations of the Arab. بِ and فِي, of seizing, and of plunging
into anything). Many expositors (Hirz., Ew., and others)
understand ver. 6*b* as expressing a wish: "Shall He contend
with me with overwhelming power? No, I do not desire that;
only that He may be a judge attentive to the cause, not a
ruler manifesting His almighty power." But ver. 6*a*, taken
thus, would be purely rhetorical, since this question (shall
He, etc.) certainly cannot be seriously propounded by Job;
accordingly, ver. 6*b* is not intended as expressing a wish, but
a hope. Job certainly wishes the same thing in ch. ix. 34,
xiii. 21; but in the course of the discussion he has gradually
acquired new confidence in God, which here once more
breaks through. He knows that God, if He could but be
found, would also condescend to hear his defence of himself,

its accentuation with *Mercha* proceeds from another interpretation, probably *non utique ponet in mé* (*manum suam*), according to which the
Targ. translates. Others, following this accentuation, take לֹא in the
sense of הֲלֹא (*vid.* in Dachselt), or are at pains to obtain some other
meaning from it.

that He would allow him to speak, and not overwhelm him with His majesty.

Ver. 7. The question arises here, whether the שָׁם which follows is to be understood locally (ثَمَّ) or temporally (ثُمَّ); it is evident from ch. xxxv. 12, Ps. xiv. 5, lxvi. 6, Hos. ii. 17, Zeph. i. 14, that it may be used temporally; in many passages, e.g. Ps. xxxvi. 13, the two significations run into one another, so that they cannot be distinguished. We here decide in favour of the temporal signification, against Rosenm., Schlottm., and Hahn; for if שָׁם be understood locally, a "then" must be supplied, and it may therefore be concluded that this שָׁם is the expression for it. We assume at the same time that נוכח is correctly pointed as part. with Kametz; accordingly it is to be explained: then, if He would thus pay attention to me, an upright man would be contending with Him, i.e. then it would be satisfactorily proved that an upright man may contend with Him. In ver. 7b, פַּלֵּט, like מַלֵּט, ch. xx. 20 (comp. פָּתַח, to have open, to stand open), is intensive of Kal: I should for ever escape my judge, i.e. come off most completely free from unmerited punishment. Thus it ought to be if God could be found, but He cannot be found. The הֵן, which according to the sense may be translated by "yet" (comp. ch. xxi. 16), introduces this antithetical relation: Yet I go towards the east (הֵן with Mahpach, קֶדֶם with Munach), and He is not there; and towards the west (אָחוֹר, comp. אחרנים, occidentales, ch. xviii. 20), and perceive Him not (expressed as in ch. ix. 11; בִּין לְ elsewhere: to attend to anything, ch. xiv. 21, Deut. xxxii. 29, Ps. lxxiii. 17; here, as there, to perceive anything, so that לוֹ is equivalent to אֹתוֹ). In ver. 9 the left (שְׂמֹאול, Arab. shemâl, or even without the substantival termination, on which comp. Jesurun, pp. 222–227, sham, shâm) is undoubtedly an appellation of the north, and the right (יָמִין, Arab. jemîn) an appellation of the south; both words are locatives which outwardly are undefined. And if the usual signification of עשׂה and עטף are retained, it is to be explained thus: northwards or in the north, if He should be active—I behold not; if He veil himself southwards or in the south—I see not. This explanation is also satisfactory so far as ver. 9*a* is concerned, so that it is unnecessary to understand בַּעֲשֺׂתוֹ other than in ch. xxviii. 26, and with Blumenfeld to translate according to the phrase עָשָׂה דַרְכּוֹ, Judg. xvii. 8: if He makes His way northwards; or even with Umbr. to call in the assistance of the Arab. غشى (to cover), which neither here nor ch. ix. 9, xv. 27, is admissible, since even then שׂמאול בעשׂתו cannot signify: if He hath concealed himself on the left hand (in the north). Ewald's combination of עשׂה with עטה, in the assumed signification "to incline to" of the latter, is to be passed over as useless. On the other hand, much can be said in favour of Ewald's translation of ver. 9*b*: "if He turn to the right hand—I see Him not;" for (1) the Arab. عطف, by virtue of the radical notion,[1] which is also traceable in the Heb. עטף, signifies both trans. and intrans. to turn up, bend aside; (2) Saadia translates: "and if He turns southwards ('atafa 'gunûban);" (3) Schultens correctly observes: עטף *significatione operiendi commodum non efficit sensum, nam quid mirum si quem occultantem se non conspiciamus.* We therefore give the preference to this Arabic rendering of יעטף. If יעטף, in the sense of *obvelat se,* does not call to mind the חַדְרֵי תֵמָן, *penetralia austri,*

ch. ix. 9 (comp. خدر, *velamen, adytum*), neither will בעשׂתו

---

[1] The verb عطف signifies trans. to turn, or lay, anything round, so that it is laid or drawn over something else and covers it; hence عطاف, a garment that is cast round one, تعطّف with ب of a garment: to cast it or wrap it about one. Intrans. to turn aside, depart from, of deviating from a given direction, *deflectere, declinare;* also, to turn in a totally opposite direction, to turn one's self round and to go back.—FL.

point to the north as the limit of the divine dominion. Such conceptions of the extreme north and south are nowhere found among the Arabs as among the Arian races (*vid.* Isa. xiv. 13);[1] and, moreover, the conception of the north as the abode of God cannot be shown to be biblical, either from ch. xxxvii. 22, Ezek. i. 4, or still less from Ps. xlviii. 3. With regard to the syntax, יַעְטֹף is a hypothetical *fut.*, as ch. xx. 24, xxii. 27 sq. The use of the *fut. apoc.* אָחַז, like אָשׂם, ver. 11, without a voluntative or aoristic signification, is poetic. Towards all quarters of the heavens he turns, *i.e.* with his eyes and the longing of his whole nature, if he may by any means find God. But He evades him, does not reveal Himself in any place whatever.

The כִּי which now follows does not give the reason of Job's earnest search after God, but the reason of His not being found by him. He does not allow Himself to be seen anywhere; He conceals Himself from him, lest He should be compelled to acknowledge the right of the sufferer, and to withdraw His chastening hand from him.

10 *For He knoweth the way that is with me :*
   If He should prove me, I should come forth as gold.
11 *My foot held firm to His steps ;*
   His way I kept, and turned not aside.
12 *The command of His lips—I departed not from it ;*
   More than my own determination I kept the words of His
   mouth.
13 *Yet He remaineth by one thing, and who can turn Him ?*
   And He accomplisheth what His soul desireth.

That which is not merely outwardly, but inwardly with

---

[1] In contrast to the extreme north, the abode of the gods, the habitation of life, the extreme south is among the Arians the abode of the prince of death and of demons, *Jama* (*vid.* vol. i. p. 325) with his attendants, and therefore the habitation of death.

(עָם) any one, is that which he thinks and knows (his consciousness), ch. ix. 35, xv. 9, or his willing and acting, ch.
x. 13, xxvii. 11 : he is conscious of it, he intends to do it ;
here, ver. 10, עָם is intended in the former sense, in ver. 14 in
the latter. The " way with me" is that which his conscience
(συνείδησις) approves (συμμαρτυρεῖ) ; comp. *Psychol.* S. 134.
This is known to God, so that he who is now set down as a
criminal would come forth as tried gold, in the event of God
allowing him to appear before Him, and subjecting him to
judicial trial. בְּחָנַנִי is the *præt. hypotheticum* so often mentioned, which is based upon the paratactic character of the
Hebrew style, as Gen. xliv. 22, Ruth ii. 9, Zech. xiii. 6 ;
Ges. § 155, 4, *a*. His foot has held firmly[1] to the steps of
God (אָשׁוּר, together with אָשׁוּר, ch. xxxi. 7, from אשר *Piel*, to
go on), so that he was always close behind Him as his predecessor (אָחַז synon. תָּמַךְ, Ps. xvii. 5, Prov. v. 5). He guarded,
i.e. observed His way, and turned not aside (אָט *fut. apoc.*
Hiph. in the intransitive sense of *deflectere*, as *e.g.* Ps. cxxv. 5).

In ver. 12*a*, מִצְוַת שְׂפָתָיו precedes as *cas. absolutus* (as respects the command of His lips) ; and what is said in this
respect follows with *Waw apod.* (= Arab. ﻑ) without the
retrospective pronoun מִמֶּנָּה (which is omitted for poetic
brevity). On this prominence of a separate notion after the
manner of an antecedent, comp. vol. i. p. 91, note 1. The
Hiph. הֵמִישׁ, like הִפָּה, ver. 11, and הַלִּיז, Prov. iv. 21, is not
causative, but simply active in signification. In ver. 12*b* the
question arises, whether צָפַן מִן is one expression, as in ch.
xvii. 4, in the sense of " hiding from another," or whether מִן
is comparative. In the former sense Hirz. explains : I removed the divine will from the possible ascendancy of my own.

---

[1] On אָחַז, Carey correctly observes, and it explains the form of the
expression : The oriental foot has a power of grasp and tenacity, because
not shackled with shoes from early childhood, of which we can form but
little idea.

But since צָפַן is familiar to the poet in the sense of preserving and laying by (צְפוּנִים, treasures, ch. xx. 26), it is more natural to explain, according to Ps. cxix. 11 : I kept the words (commands) of Thy mouth, *i.e.* esteemed them high and precious, more than *my* statute, *i.e.* more than what my own will prescribed for me.[1] The meaning is substantially the same ; the LXX., which translates ἐν δὲ κόλπῳ μου (בְּחֻקִּי), which Olsh. considers to be "perhaps correct," destroys the significance of the confession. Hirz. rightly refers to the "law in the members," Rom. vii. 23 : חֻקִּי is the expression Job uses for the law of the sinful nature which strives against the law of God, the wilful impulse of selfishness and evil passion, the law which the apostle describes as ἕτερος νόμος, in distinction from the νόμος τοῦ Θεοῦ (*Psychol.* S. 379). Job's conscience can give him this testimony, but He, the God who so studiously avoids him, remains in one mind, viz. to treat him as a criminal ; and who can turn Him from His purpose? (the same question as ch. ix. 12, xi. 10) ; His soul wills it (*stat pro ratione voluntas*), and He accomplishes it. Most expositors explain *permanet in uno* in this sense ; the *Beth* is the usual בְּ with verbs of entering upon and persisting in anything. Others, however, take the בְּ as *Beth essentiæ* : He remains one and the same, viz. in His conduct towards me (Umbr., Vaih.), or : He is one, is alone, viz. in absolute majesty (Targ. Jer. ; Schult., Ew., Hlgst., Schlottm.), which is admissible, since this *Beth* occurs not only in the comple-

---

[1] Wetzstein arranges the significations of צפן as follows :—1. (Beduin) *intr. fut. i,* to contain one's self, to keep still (hence in Hebr. to lie in wait), to be rapt in thought ; conjug. II. *c. acc. pers.* to make any one thoughtful, irresolute. 2. (Hebr.) *trans. fut. o,* to keep anything to one's self, to hold back, to keep to one's self ; *Niph.* to be held back, *i.e.* either concealed or reserved for future use. Thus we see how, on the one hand, צפן is related to טמן, *e.g.* ch. xx. 26 (Arab. *itmaanna,* to be still) ; and, on the other, can interchange with צפה in the signification *designare* (comp. ch. xv. 22 with xv. 20, xxi. 19), and to spy, lie in wait (comp. Ps. x. 8, lvi. 7, Prov. i. 11, 18, with Ps. xxxvii. 32).

ments of a sentence (Ps. xxxix. 7, like a shadow ; Isa. xlviii.
10, after the manner of silver; Ps. lv. 19, in great number;
Ps. xxxv. 2, as my help), but also with the predicate of a
simple sentence, be it verbal (ch. xxiv. 13 ; Prov. iii. 26) or
substantival (Ex. xviii. 4 ; Ps. cxviii. 7). The same construction is found also in Arabic, where, however, it is more
frequent in simple negative clauses than in affirmative (vid.
Psalter, i. 272). The assertion : He is one (as in the primary
monotheistic confession, Deut. vi. 4), is, however, an expression
for the absoluteness of God, which is not suited to this connection ; and if באחד הוא is intended to be understood of the
unchangeable uniformity of His purpose concerning Job, the
explanation : versatur (perstat) in uno, Arab. hua fi wáhidin, is
not only equally, but more natural, and we therefore prefer it.

Here again God appears to Job to be his enemy. His
confidence towards God is again overrun by all kinds of
evil, suspicious thoughts. He seems to him to be a God of
absolute caprice, who punishes where there is no ground for
punishment. There is indeed a phase of the abiding fact
which he considers superior to God and himself, both being
conceived of as contending parties; and this phase God
avoids, He will not hear it. Into this vortex of thoughts, as
terrible as they are puerile, Job is hurried forward by the
persuasion that his affliction is a decree of divine justice.
The friends have greatly confirmed him in this persuasion ;
so that his consciousness of innocence, and the idea of God
as inflicting punishment, are become widely opposite extremes,
between which his faith is hardly able to maintain itself.
It is not his affliction in itself, but this persuasion, which pre-
cipitates him into such a depth of conflict, as the following
strophe shows.

14 *For He accomplisheth that which is appointed for me,
And much of a like kind is with Him.*

15 *Therefore I am troubled at His presence;*
If I consider it, I am afraid of Him.
16 *And God hath caused my heart to be dejected,*
And the Almighty hath put me to confusion;
17 *For I have not been destroyed before darkness,*
And before my countenance, which thick darkness covereth.

Now it is the will of God, the absolute, which has all at once turned against him, the innocent (ver. 13); for what He has decreed against him (חָקִּי) He also brings to a complete fulfilment (הִשְׁלִים, as *e.g.* Isa. xliv. 26); and the same troubles as those which he already suffers, God has still more abundantly decreed for him, in order to torture him gradually, but surely, to death. Job intends ver. 14*b* in reference to himself, not as a general assertion: it is, in general, God's way of acting. Hahn's objection to the other explanation, that Job's affliction, according to his own previous assertions, has already attained its highest degree, does not refute it; for Job certainly has a term of life before him, though it be but short, in which the wondrously inventive (ch. x. 16) hostility of God can heap up ever new troubles for him. On the other hand, the interpretation of the expression in a general sense is opposed by the form of the expression itself, which is not that God delights to do this, but that He purposes (עִמּוֹ) to do it. It is a conclusion from the present concerning the future, such as Job is able to make with reference to himself; while he, moreover, abides by the reality in respect to the mysterious distribution of the fortunes of men. Therefore, because he is a mark for the enmity of God, without having merited it, he is confounded before His countenance, which is so angrily turned upon him (comp. פנים, Ps. xxi. 10, Lam. iv. 16); if he considers it (according to the sense *fut. hypothet.*, as ver. 9*b*), he trembles before Him, who recompenses faithful attachment by such torturing pain. The following connection with וֹ and the mention of God twice at the beginning of the affirmations, is intended to mean : (I tremble before Him), and He it is who has made me faint-hearted (הֵרַךְ *Hiph.* from the *Kal,* Deut. xx. 3, and freq., to be tender, soft, disconcerted), and has troubled me ; which is then supported in ver. 17.

His suffering which draws him on to ruin he perceives, but it is not the proper ground of his inward destruction ; it is not the encircling darkness of affliction, not the mysterious form of his suffering which disconcerts him, but God's hostile conduct towards him, His angry countenance as he seems to see it, and which he is nevertheless unable to explain. Thus also Ew., Hirz., Vaih., Hlgst., and Schlottm. explain the passage. The only other explanation worthy of mention is that which finds in ver. 17 the thought already expressed in ch. iii. 10 : For I was not then destroyed, in order that I might experience such mysterious suffering ; an interpretation with which most of the old expositors were satisfied, and which has been revived by Rosenm., Stick., and Hahn. We translate : for I have not been destroyed before darkness (in order to be taken away from it before it came upon me), and He has not hidden darkness before my face ; or as an exclamation : that I have not been destroyed! which is to be equivalent to : Had I but been . . . ! Apart from this rendering of the *quod non = utinam,* which cannot be supported, (1) It is doubly hazardous thus to carry the לֹא forward to the second line in connection with verbs of different persons. (2) The darkness in ver. 17*b* appears (at least according to the usual interpret. *caliginem*) as that which is being covered, whereas it is naturally that which covers something else ; wherefore Blumenfeld explains : and darkness has not hidden, viz. such pain as I must now endure, from my face. (3) The whole thought which is thus gained is without point, and meaningless, in this connection. On the other hand, the antithesis between מִפָּנָיו and מִפְּנֵי, מִמֶּנּוּ and מִפְּנֵי־חֹשֶׁךְ, is at once obvious; and this antithesis, which forces itself upon the attention, also furnishes the thought which might be expected from the context. It is unnecessary to take נִצְמַת in a different signification from ch. vi. 17; in Arabic صمت signifies *conticescere*; the idea of the root, however, is in general a constraining depriving of free movement. חֹשֶׁךְ is intended as in the question of Eliphaz, ch. xxii. 11: "Or seest thou not the darkness?" to which it perhaps refers. It is impossible, with Schlottm., to translate ver. 17b: and before that darkness covers my face; מִן is never other than a *præp.*, not a conjunction with power over a whole clause. It must be translated: *et a facie mea quam obtegit caligo.* As the absolute פנים, ch. ix. 27, signifies the appearance of the countenance under pain, so here by it Job means his countenance distorted by pain, his deformed appearance, which, as the attributive clause affirms, is thoroughly darkened by suffering (comp. ch. xxx. 30). But it is not this darkness which stares him in the face, and threatens to swallow him up (comp. מפני־חשך, ch. xvii. 12); not this his miserable form, which the extremest darkness covers (on אֹפֶל, *vid.* ch. x. 22), that destroys his inmost nature; but the thought that God stands forth in hostility against him, which makes his affliction so terrific, and doubly so in connection with the inalienable consciousness of his innocence. From the incomprehensible punishment which, without reason, is passing over him, he now again comes to speak of the incomprehensible connivance of God, which permits the godlessness of the world to go on unpunished.

Ch. xxiv. 1 *Wherefore are not bounds reserved by the Almighty,*
    And they who honour Him see not His days?
  2 *They remove the landmarks,*
    They steal flocks and shepherd them.

3 *They carry away the ass of the orphan,*
 And distrain the ox of the widow.
4 *They thrust the needy out of the way,*
 The poor of the land are obliged to slink away together.

The supposition that the text originally stood מַדּוּעַ לְרְשָׁעִים מִשַּׁדַּי is natural; but it is at once destroyed by the fact that ver. 1*a* becomes thereby disproportionately long, and yet cannot be divided into two lines of comparatively independent contents. In fact, לרשעים is by no means absolutely necessary. The usage of the language assumes it, according to which עֵת followed by the genitive signifies the point of time at which any one's fate is decided, Isa. xiii. 22, Jer. xxvii. 7, Ezek. xxii. 3, xxx. 3; the period when reckoning is made, or even the *terminus ad quem*, Eccl. ix. 12; and יוֹם followed by the gen. of a man, the day of his end, ch. xv. 32, xviii. 20, Ezek. xxi. 30, and freq.; or with יהוה, the day when God's judgment is revealed, Joel i. 15, and freq. The boldness of poetic language goes beyond this usage, by using עִתִּים directly of the period of punishment, as is almost universally acknowledged since Schultens' day, and יָמָיו of God's days of judgment or of vengeance;[1] and it is the less ambiguous, since צָפַן, in the sense of the divine predetermination of what is future, ch. xv. 20, especially of God's storing up merited

---

[1] On עתים, in the sense of times of retribution, Wetzstein compares the Arab. عَدَات, which signifies predetermined reward or punishment; moreover, עֵת is derived from עֶדֶת (from וָעַד), and עִתִּים is equivalent to עֶדְתִּים, according to the same law of assimilation, by which now-a-days they say לִתִּי instead of לִדְתִּי (one who is born on the same day with me, from لِدَة, *lida*), and רִתִּי instead of רִדְתִּי (my drinking-time), since the assimilation of the ד takes place everywhere where ת is pronounced. The ת of the feminine termination in עִתִּים, as in שִׁקְתוֹת and the like, perhaps also in בתים (*bâttim*), is amalgamated with the root.

punishment, ch. xxi. 19, is an acknowledged word of our poet. On מִן with the passive, *vid*. Ew. § 295, *c* (where, however, ch. xxviii. 4 is erroneously cited in its favour); it is never more than equivalent to ἀπό, for to use מִן directly as ὑπό with the passive is admissible neither in Hebrew nor in Arabic. ידעו (*Keri* יְדָעָיו, for which the Targ. unsuitably reads יִדְעֵי) are, as in Ps. xxxvi. 11, lxxxvii. 4, comp. *supra*, ch. xviii. 21, those who know God, not merely superficially, but from experience of His ways, consequently those who are in fellowship with Him. לֹא חָזוּ is to be written with *Zinnorith* over the לֹא, and *Mercha* by the first syllable of חזו. The *Zinnorith* necessitates the retreat of the tone of חזו to its first syllable, as in כִּי־חֲרָה, Ps. xviii. 8 (Bär's *Psalterium*, p. xiii.); for if חזו remained *Milra*, לֹא ought to be connected with it by *Makkeph*, and consequently remain toneless (*Psalter*, ii. 507).

Next follows the description of the moral abhorrence which, while the friends (ch. xxii. 19) maintain a divine retribution everywhere manifest, is painfully conscious of the absence of any determination of the periods and days of judicial punishment. Fearlessly and unpunished, the oppression of the helpless and defenceless, though deserving of a curse, rages in every form. They remove the landmarks; comp. Deut. xxvii. 17, " Cursed is he who removeth his neighbour's landmark " (מַסִּיג, here once written with שׂ, while otherwise הִשִּׂיג from נָשַׂג signifies *assequi*, on the other hand הִפִּיג from סוג signifies *dimovere*). They steal flocks, וַיִּרְעוּ,·*i.e.* they are so barefaced, that after they have stolen them they pasture them openly. The ass of the orphans, the one that is their whole possession, and their only beast for labour, they carry away as prey (נָהַג, as *e.g.* Isa. xx. 4); they distrain, *i.e.* take away with them as a pledge (on חָבַל, to bind by a pledge, *obstringere*, and also to take as a pledge, *vid*. on ch. xxii. 6, and Köhler on Zech. xi. 7), the yoke-ox of the widow (this is the exact meaning of

שׁוֹר, as of the Arab. *thôr*). They turn the needy aside from the way which they are going, so that they are obliged to wander hither and thither without home or right: the poor of the land are obliged to hide themselves altogether. The *Hiph.* הִטָּה, with אֶבְיוֹנִים as its obj., is used as in Amos v. 12; there it is used of turning away from a right that belongs to them, here of turning out of the way into trackless regions. אֶבְיוֹן (*vid.* on ch. xxix. 16) here, as frequently, is the parallel word with עָנִי, the humble one, the patient sufferer; instead of which the *Keri* is עָנָו, the humbled, bowed down with suffering (*vid.* on Ps. ix. 13). עַנְוֵי־אֶרֶץ occurs without any *Keri* in Ps. lxxvi. 10, Zeph. ii. 3, and might less suitably appear here, where it is not so much the moral attribute as the outward condition that is intended to be described. The *Pual* חֻבָּאוּ describes that which they are forced to do.

The description of these unfortunate ones is now continued; and by a comparison with ch. xxx. 1–8, it is probable that aborigines who are turned out of their original possessions and dwellings are intended (comp. ch. xv. 19, according to which the poet takes his stand in an age in which the original relations of the races had been already disturbed by the calamities of war and the incursions of aliens). If the central point of the narrative lies in Haurân, or, more exactly, in the Nukra, it is natural, with Wetzstein, to think of the عرب الحَجَر or اهل الوَكْر, *i.e.* the (perhaps Ituræan) "races of the caves" in Trachonitis.

> 5 *Behold, as wild asses in the desert,*
>   *They go forth in their work seeking for prey,*
>   *The steppe is food to them for the children.*
> 6 *In the field they reap the fodder for his cattle,*
>   *And they glean the vineyard of the evil-doer.*
> 7 *They pass the night in nakedness without a garment,*

And have no covering in the cold.

8 *They are wet with the torrents of rain upon the mountains,*
And they hug the rocks for want of shelter.

The poet could only draw such a picture as this, after having himself seen the home of his hero, and the calamitous fate of such as were driven forth from their original abodes to live a vagrant, poverty-stricken gipsy life. By ver. 5, one is reminded of Ps. civ. 21–23, especially since in ver. 11 of this Psalm the פְּרָאִים, *onagri* (Kulans), are mentioned,— those beautiful animals[1] which, while young, are difficult to be broken in, and when grown up are difficult to be caught; which in their love of freedom are an image of the Beduin, Gen. xvi. 12: their untractableness an image of that which cannot be bound, ch. xi. 12; and from their roaming about in herds in waste regions, are here an image of a gregarious, vagrant, and freebooter kind of life. The old expositors, as also Rosenm., Umbr., Arnh., and Vaih., are mistaken in thinking that *aliud hominum sceleratorum genus* is described in vers. 5 sqq. Ewald and Hirz. were the first to perceive that vers. 5–8 is the further development of ver. 4*b*, and that here, as in ch. xxx. 1 sqq., those who are driven back into the wastes and caves, and a remnant of the ejected and oppressed aborigines who drag out a miserable existence, are described.

The accentuation rightly connects פראים במדבר; by the omission of the *Caph similit.*, as *e.g.* Isa. li. 12, the comparison (like a wild ass) becomes an equalization (as a wild ass). The *perf.* יָצְאוּ is a general uncoloured expression of that which is usual: they go forth בְּפָעֳלָם, in their work (not: to

---

[1] Layard, *New Discoveries*, p. 270, describes these wild asses' colts. The Arabic name is like the Hebrew, *el-ferâ*, or alsc *himâr el-wahsh, i.e.* wild ass, as we have translated, whose home is on the steppe. For fuller particulars, *vid.* Wetzstein's note on ch. xxxix. 5 sqq.

their work, as the Psalmist, in Ps. civ. 23, expresses himself, exchanging בְּ for (לְ). מְשַׁחֲרֵי לַטָּרֶף, searching after prey, *i.e.* to satisfy their hunger (Ps. civ. 21), from טָרַף, in the primary signification *decerpere* (*vid.* Hupfeld on Ps. vii. 3), describes that which in general forms their daily occupation as they roam about; the *constructivus* is used here, without any proper genitive relation, as a form of connection, according to Ges. § 116, 1. The idea of waylaying is not to be connected with the expression. Job describes those who are perishing in want and misery, not so much as those who themselves are guilty of evil practices, as those who have been brought down to poverty by the wrongdoing of others. As is implied in משחרי (comp. the morning Psalm, lxiii. 2, Isa. xxvi. 9), Job describes their going forth in the early morning; the children (נְעָרִים, as ch. i. 19, xxix. 5) are those who first feel the pangs of hunger. לוֹ refers individually to the father in the company: the steppe (with its scant supply of roots and herbs) is to him food for the children; he snatches it from it, it must furnish it for him. The idea is not: for himself and his family (Hirz., Hahn, and others); for ver. 6, which has been much misunderstood, describes how they, particularly the adults, obtain their necessary subsistence. There is no MS. authority for reading בְּלִי־לוֹ instead of בְּלִילוֹ; the translation "what is not to him" (LXX., Targ., and partially also the Syriac version) is therefore to be rejected. Raschi correctly interprets יבולו, as a general explanation, and Ralbag תבואתו: it is, as in ch. vi. 5, mixed fodder for cattle, *farrago*, consisting of oats or barley sown among vetches and beans, that is intended. The meaning is not, however, as most expositors explain it, that they seek to satisfy their hunger with the food for cattle grown in the fields of the rich evil-doer; for קָצַר does not signify to sweep together, but to reap in an orderly manner; and if they meant to steal, why did they not seize the better portion of the produce? It is correct to take the suff. as referring to the רָשָׁע which is mentioned in the next clause, but it is not to be understood that they plunder his fields *per nefas;* on the contrary, that he hires them to cut the fodder for his cattle, but does not like to entrust the reaping of the better kinds of corn to them. It is impracticable to press the *Hiph.* יקצירו of the *Chethib* to favour this rendering; on the contrary, הקציר stands to קצר in like (not causative) signification as הנחה to נחה (*vid.* on ch. xxxi. 18). In like manner, ver. 6*b* is to be understood of hired labour. The rich man prudently hesitates to employ these poor people as vintagers; but he makes use of their labour (whilst his own men are fully employed at the wine-vats) to gather the straggling grapes which ripen late, and were therefore left at the vintage season. The older expositors are reminded of לֶקֶשׁ, late hay, and explain יְלַקֵּשׁוּ as *denom.* by יכרתו לקשו (Aben-Ezra, Immanuel, and others) or יאכלו לקשו (Parchon); but how unnatural to think of the second mowing, or even of eating the after-growth of grass, where the vineyard is the subject referred to! On the contrary, לְקֵשׁ signifies, as it were, *serotinare, i.e. serotinos fructus colligere* (Rosenm.) :[1] this is the work which the rich man assigns to them, because he gains by it, and even in the worst case can lose but little.

Vers. 7 sq. tell how miserably they are obliged to shift for themselves during this autumnal season of labour, and also at other times. Naked (עָרוֹם, whether an adverbial form or not, is conceived of after the manner of an accusative : in

---

[1] In the idiom of Hauran, לְקַשׁ, *fut. i,* signifies to be late, to come late ; in *Piel,* to delay, *e.g.* the evening meal, return, etc.; in *Hithpa. telaqqas,* to arrive too late. Hence *laqîs* לְקִישׁ and *loqsî* לְקְשִׁי, delayed, of any matter, *e.g.* לָקִישׁ and זֶרַע לִקְשִׁי, late seed (= לְקֵשׁ, Amos vii. 1, in connection with which the late rain in April, which often fails, is reckoned on), וְלֶד לִקְשִׁי, a child born late (*i.e.* in old age) ; *bakîr* בָּכִיר and *bekrî* בָּכְרִי are the opposites in every signification.—WETZST.

a naked, stripped condition, Arabic ʿurjânan) they pass the night, without having anything on the body (on לְבוּשׁ, vid. on Ps. xxii. 19), and they have no (אֵין supply לָהֶם) covering or veil (corresponding to the notion of בֶּגֶד) in the cold.[1] They become thoroughly drenched by the frequent and continuous storms that visit the mountains, and for want of other shelter are obliged to shelter themselves under the overhanging rocks, lying close up to them, and clinging to them,—an idea which is expressed here by חֻבְּקוּ, as in Lam. iv. 5, where, of those who were luxuriously brought up on purple cushions, it is said that they "embrace dunghills;" for in Palestine and Syria, the forlorn one, who, being afflicted with some loathsome disease, is not allowed to enter· the habitations of men, lies on the dunghill (mezâbil), asking alms by day of the passers-by, and at night hiding himself among the ashes which the sun has warmed.[2] The usual accentuation, מזרם with Dechî, הרים with Munach, after which it should be translated ab in-

---

[1] All the Beduins sleep naked at night. I once asked why they do this, since they are often disturbed by attacks at night, and I was told that it is a very ancient custom. Their clothing (kiswe, כְּסוּה), both of the nomads of the steppe (bedû) and of the caves (waʿr), is the same, summer and winter; many perish on the pastures when overtaken by snow-storms, or by cold and want, when their tents and stores are taken from them in the winter time by an enemy.—WETZST.

[2] Wetzstein observes on this passage: In the mind of the speaker, מחסה is the house made of stone, from which localities not unfrequently derive their names, as El-hasa, on the east of the Dead Sea; the well-known commercial town El-hasâ, on the east of the Arabian peninsula, which is generally called Lahsâ; the town of El-hasja (אֶלְחַסְיָה), north-east of Damascus, etc.: so that חבקו צור forms the antithesis to the comfortable dwellings of the حَضَرِي, hadarî, i.e. one who is firmly settled. The roots חבק, חבך, seem, in the desert, to be only dialectically distinct, and like the root עבק, to signify to be pressed close upon one another. Thus חֲבָקָה (pronounced hibtsha), a crowd = zahme, and asâbiʿ mahbûke (מַחְבּוּכָה), the closed fingers, etc. The locality, hibikke (Beduin pronunciation for habáka, חֲבָכָה with the Beduin Dag. euphonicum), de-

undatione montes humectantur, is false ; in correct Codd. זרם
has also *Munach ;* the other *Munach* is, as in ch. xxiii. 5*a,* 9*a,*
xxiv. 6*b,* and freq., a substitute for *Dechî.* Having sketched
this special class of the oppressed, and those who are abandoned to the bitterest want, Job proceeds with his description
of the many forms of wrong which prevail unpunished on
the earth :

> 9 *They tear the fatherless from the breast,*
>   *And defraud the poor.*
> 10 *Naked, they slink away without clothes,*
>   *And hungering they bear the sheaves.*
> 11 *Between their walls they squeeze out the oil;*
>   *They tread the wine-presses, and suffer thirst.*
> 12 *In the city vassals groan,*
>   *And the soul of the oppressed crieth out—*
>   *And Eloah heedeth not the anomaly.*

The accentuation of ver. 9*a* (יגזלו with *Dechî,* מִשֹּׁד with

scribed in my *Reisebericht,* has its name from this circumstance alone,
that the houses have been attached to (fastened into) the rocks.   Hence
חָבַק in this passage signifies to press into the fissure of a rock, to seek
out a corner which may defend one (*dherwe*) against the cold winds and
rain-torrents (which are far heavier among the mountains than on the

plain).   The *dherwe* (from دَرَأَ, to afford protection, shelter, a word frequently used in the desert) plays a prominent part among the nomads ;
and in the month of March, as it is proverbially said the *dherwe* is better
than the *ferwe* (the skin), they seek to place their tents for protection
under the rocks or high banks of the wadys, on account of the cold
strong winds, for the sake of the young of the flocks, to which the cold
storms are often very destructive.   When the sudden storms come on, it
is a general thing for the shepherds and flocks to hasten to take shelter

under overhanging rocks, and the caverns (*mughr* مغر) which belong to
the troglodyte age, and are *e.g.* common in the mountains of Hauran ;
so that, therefore, ver. 8 can as well refer to concealing themselves only
for a time (from rain and storm) in the clefts as to troglodytes, who
constantly dwell in caverns, or to those dwelling in tents who, during
the storms, seek the *dherwe* of rock sides.

Munach) makes the relation of שֹׁד יָתוֹם genitival. Heidenheim
(in a MS. annotation to Kimchi's *Lex*.) accordingly badly interprets: they plunder from the spoil of the orphan; Ramban
better: from the ruin, *i.e.* the shattered patrimony; both
appeal to the Targum, which translates מביזת יתום, like the
Syriac version, *men bezto de-jatme* (comp. Jerome: *vim fece-
runt deprædantes pupillos*). The original reading, however, is
perhaps (*vid.* Buxtorf, *Lex*. col. 295) מִבִּיזָא, ἀπὸ βυζίου, from
the mother's breast, as it is also, with LXX. (ἀπὸ μαστοῦ),
to be translated contrary to the accentuation. Inhuman
creditors take the fatherless and still tender orphan away
from its mother, in order to bring it up as a slave, and so to
obtain payment. If this is the meaning of the passage, it is
natural to understand יַחְבֹּלוּ, ver. 9*b*, of distraining; but (1)
the poet would then repeat himself tautologically, *vid.* ver. 3,
where the same thing is far more evidently said; (2) חָבַל,
to distrain, would be construed with עַל, contrary to the logic
of the word. Certainly the phrase חבל על may be in some
degree explained by the interpretation, "to impose a fine"
(Ew., Hahn), or "to distrain" (Hirz., Welte), or "to oppress
with fines" (Schlottm.); but violence is thus done to the
usage of the language, which is better satisfied by the explanation of Ralbag (among modern expositors, Ges., Arnh.,
Vaih., Stick., Hlgst.): and what the unfortunate one possesses they seize; but this עַל = עַל אֲשֶׁר directly as object is
impossible. The passage, Deut. vii. 25, cited by Schultens in
its favour, is of a totally different kind.

But throughout the Semitic dialects the verb חָבַל also
signifies "to destroy, to treat injuriously" (*e.g.* Arab. *el-
châbil*, a by-name of Satan); it occurs in this signification in
ch. xxxiv. 31, and according to the analogy of הֵרַע עַל, 1 Kings
xvii. 20, can be construed with עַל as well as with לְ. The poet,
therefore, by this construction will have intended to distinguish the one חבל from the other, ch. xxii. 6, xxiv. 3; and it

is with Umbreit to be translated: they bring destruction upon the poor; or better: they take undue advantage of those who otherwise are placed in trying circumstances.

The subjects of ver. 10 are these עֲנִיִּים, who are made serfs, and become objects of merciless oppression, and the poet here in ver. 10a indeed repeats what he has already said almost word for word in ver. 7a (comp. ch. xxxi. 19); but there the nakedness was the general calamity of a race oppressed by subjugation, here it is the consequence of the sin of *merces retenta laborum,* which cries aloud to heaven, practised on those of their own race: they slink away (הִלְּכוּ, as ch. xxx. 28) naked (*nude*), without (מִבְּלִי = בְּלִי, as perhaps *sine = absque*) clothing, and while suffering hunger they carry the sheaves (since their masters deny them what, according to Deut. xxv. 4, shall not be withheld even from the beasts). Between their walls (שׁוּרֹת like שֵׁרֹת, Jer. v. 10, Chaldee שׁוּרַיָּא), *i.e.* the walls of their masters who have made them slaves, therefore under strict oversight, they press out the oil (יַצְהִירוּ, ἅπ. γεγρ.), they tread the wine-vats (יְקָבִים, *lacus*), and suffer thirst withal (*fut. consec.* according to Ew. § 342, *a*), without being allowed to quench their thirst from the must which runs out of the presses (גִּתּוֹת, *torcularia,* from which the verb דָּרַךְ is here transferred to the vats). Böttch. translates: between their rows of trees, without being able to reach out right or left; but that is least of all suitable with the olives. Carey correctly explains: "the factories or the garden enclosures of these cruel slaveholders." This reference of the word to the wall of the enclosure is more suitable than to walls of the press-house in particular. From tyrannical oppression in the country,[1] Job now passes over to the abominations of discord and war in the cities.

Ver. 12a. It is natural, with Umbr., Ew., Hirz., and others,

---

[1] Brentius here remarks: *Quantum igitur judicium in eos futurum est, qui in homines ejusdem carnis, ejusdem patriæ, ejusdem fidei, ejusdem Christi*

to read מְתִים like the Peschito; but as *mîte* in Syriac, so also מתים in Hebrew as a noun everywhere signifies the dead (Arab. *mauta*), not the dying, mortals (Arab. *maïtûna*); wherefore Ephrem interprets the *præs.* " they groan" by the *perf.* " they have groaned." The pointing מְתִים, therefore, is quite correct; but the accentuation which, by giving *Mehupach Zinnorith* to מעיר, and *Asla legarmeh* to מתים, places the two words in a genitive relation, is hardly correct: in the city of men, *i.e.* the inhabited, thickly-populated city, they groan; not: men (as Rosenm. explains, according to Gen. ix. 6, Prov. xi. 6) groan; for just because מְתִים appeared to be too inexpressive as a subject, this accentuation seems to have been preferred. It is also possible that the signification fierce anger (Hos. xi. 9), or anguish (Jer. xv. 8), was combined with עִיר, comp.

غَيْرَة, jealousy, fury (=קִנְאָה), of which, however, no trace is anywhere visible.[1]   With Jer., Symm., and Theod., we take מתים as the sighing ones themselves; the feebleness of the subject disappears if we explain the passage according to such passages as Deut. ii. 34, iii. 6, comp. Judg. xx. 48: it

committunt quod nec in bruta animalia committendum est, quod malum in Germania frequentissimum est.   Væ igitur Germaniæ!

[1] Wetzstein translates Hos. xi. 9 : I will not come as a raging foe, with בְ of the attribute = بِصَفَةِ الغَيُّورِ (comp. Jer. xv. 8, עִיר, parall. שֹׁדֵד) after the form קִים, to which, if not this עִיר, certainly the עִיר, ἐγρήγορος, occurring in Dan. iv. 10, and freq., corresponds. What we remarked above, vol. i. p. 440, on the form קִים, is cleared up by the following observation of Wetzstein: "The form קִים belongs to the numerous class of segolate forms of the form פְּעָל, which, as belonging to the earliest period of the formation of the Semitic languages, take neither plural nor feminine terminations; they have often a collective meaning, and are not originally *abstracta*, but *concreta* in the sense of the Arabic *part. act.* مَفَاعِل.   This inflexible primitive formation is frequently found in the present day in the

is the male inhabitants that are intended, whom any conqueror would put to the sword; we have therefore translated
men (men of war), although "people" (ch. xi. 3) also would
not have been unsuitable according to the ancient use of the
word. נָאַק is intended of the groans of the dying, as Jer. li.
52, Ezek. xxx. 24, as ver. 12b also shows: the soul of those
that are mortally wounded cries out. חֲלָלִים signifies not
merely the slain and already dead, but, according to its etymon, those who are pierced through, those who have received
their death-blow; their soul cries out, since it does not leave
the body without a struggle. Such things happen without
God preventing them. לֹא־יָשִׂים תִּפְלָה, He observeth not the
abomination, either = לֹא ישׂים בלבו, ch. xxii. 22 (He layeth it
not to heart), or, since the phrase occurs nowhere elliptically,
= לֹא ישׂים לבו על, ch. i. 8, xxxiv. 23 (He does not direct His
heart, His attention to it), here as elliptical, as in ch. iv. 20,
Isa. xli. 20. True, the latter phrase is never joined with the
acc. of the object; but if we translate after שִׂים בְּ, ch. iv. 18:
non imputat, He does not reckon such תפלה, *i.e.* does not
punish it, בָּם (בָּהֶם) ought to be supplied, which is still somewhat liable to misconstruction, since the preceding subject

idiom of the steppe, which shows that the Hebrew is essentially of primeval antiquity (*uralt*). Thus the Beduin says: *hû qitlî* (הוּא קְטְלִי), he
is my opponent in a hand-to-hand combat; *nithî* (נְטְחִי), my opponent
in the tournament with lances; *chilfî* (חִלְפִי) and *diddî* (צִדְּי), my adversary; thus a step-mother is called *dîr* (צִיר), as the oppressor of
the step-children, and a concubine *dirr* (צָרַר), as the oppressor of her
rival. The Kamus also furnishes several words which belong here, as *tilb*
(טָלֵב), a persecutor." Accordingly, קִים is derived from קוּם, as also עָיר,
a city, from עוּר (whence, according to a prevalent law of the change of
letters, we have עָיר first of all, *plur.* עָיָרִים, Judg. x. 4), and signifies the
rebelling one, *i.e.* the enemy (who is now in the idiom of the steppe
called *qômâni*, from *qôm*, a state of war, a feud), as עָיר, a keeper,
and צָיר, a messenger; עָיר (קִיר) is also originally concrete, a wall
(enclosure).

is not the oppressors, but those who suffer oppression. תִּפְלָה
is properly insipidity (comp. Arab. *tafila*, to stink), absurdity,
self-contradiction, here the immorality which sets at nought
the moral order of the world, and remains nevertheless
unpunished. The Syriac version reads תְּפִלָּה, and translates,
like Louis Bridel (1818) : *et Dieu ne fait aucune attention à
leur prière.*

> 13 *Others are those that rebel against the light,*
> *They will know nothing of its ways,*
> *And abide not in its paths.*
> 14 *The murderer riseth up at dawn,*
> *He slayeth the sufferer and the poor,*
> *And in the night he acteth like a thief.*
> 15 *And the eye of the adulterer watcheth for the twilight;*
> *He thinks : " no eye shall recognise me,"*
> *And he putteth a veil before his face.*

With הֵמָּה begins a new turn in the description of the moral
confusion which has escaped God's observation ; it is to be
translated neither as retrospective, "since they" (Ewald), nor
as distinctive, "they even" (Böttch.), *i.e.* the powerful in distinction from the oppressed, but "those" (for המה corresponds
to our use of "those," אֵלֶּה to "these"), by which Job passes
on to another class of evil-disposed and wicked men. Their
general characteristic is, that they shun the light. Those
who are described in vers. 14 sq. are described according to
their general characteristic in ver. 13 ; accordingly it is not
to be interpreted : those belong to the enemies of the light,
but : those are, according to their very nature, enemies of the
light. The *Beth* is the so-called *Beth essent.; הָיוּ* (comp. Prov.
iii. 26) affirms what they are become by their own inclination,
or as what they are fashioned, viz. as ἀποστάται φωτός
(Symm.) ; מָרַד (on the root מר, *vid.* on ch. xxiii. 2) signifies
properly to push one's self against anything, to lean upon, to

rebel; מֹרֵד therefore signifies one who strives against another, one who is obstinate (like the Arabic *mârid, merîd*, comp. *mumâri*, not conformable to the will of another). The improvement מֹרְדֵי אוֹר (not with *Makkeph*, but with *Mahpach* of *Mercha mahpach.* placed between the two words, *vid.* Bär's *Psalterium*, p. x.) assumes the possibility of the construction with the *acc.*, which occurs at least once, Josh. xxii. 19. They are hostile to the light, they have no familiarity with its ways (הִכִּיר, as ver. 17, Ps. cxlii. 5, Ruth ii. 19, to take knowledge of anything, to interest one's self in its favour), and do not dwell (יָשְׁבוּ, Jer. *reversi sunt,* according to the false reading יָשֻׁבוּ) in its paths, *i.e.* they neither make nor feel themselves at home there, they have no peace therein. The light is the light of day, which, however, stands in deeper, closer relation to the higher light, for the vicious man hateth τὸ φῶς, John iii. 20, in every sense; and the works which are concealed in the darkness of the night are also ἔργα τοῦ σκότους, Rom. xiii. 12 (comp. Isa. xxix. 15), in the sense in which light and darkness are two opposite principles of the spiritual world. It need not seem strange that the more minute description of the conduct of these enemies of the light now begins with לָאוֹר. It is impossible that this should mean: still in the darkness of the night (Stick.), prop. towards the light, when it is not yet light. Moreover, in biblical Hebrew, אוֹר does not signify evening, in which sense it occurs in Talmudic Hebrew (*Pesachim* 1*a*, *Seder olam rabba,* c. 5, אוֹר שְׁבִיעִי, *vespera septima*), like אוֹרְתָּא (= נֶשֶׁף) in Talmudic Aramaic. The meaning, on the contrary, is that towards daybreak (comp. הבקר אור, Gen. xliv. 3), therefore with early morning, the murderer rises up, to go about his work, which veils itself in darkness (Ps. x. 8–10) by day, viz. to slay (comp. on יָקוּם ... יִקְטֹל, Ges. § 142, 3, *c*) the unfortunate and the poor, who pass by defenceless and alone. One has to supply the idea of the ambush in which the waylayer lies in wait; and it is certainly inconvenient that it is not expressed. The antithesis וּבַלַּיְלָה, ver. 14c, shows that nothing but *primo mane* is meant by לָאוֹר. He who in the day-time goes forth to murder and plunder, at night commits petty thefts, where no one whom he could attack passes by. Stickel translates : to slay the poor and wretched, and in the night to play the thief ; but then the *subjunctivus* וִיהִי ought to precede (*vid. e.g.* ch. xiii. 5), and in general it cannot be proved without straining it, that the voluntative form of the future everywhere has a modal signification. Moreover, here יְהִי does not differ from ch. xviii. 12, xx. 23, but is only a poetic shorter form for יִהְיֶה : in the night he is like a thief, *i.e.* plays the part of the thief. And the adulterer's eye observes the darkness of evening (*vid.* Prov. vii. 9), *i.e.* watches closely for its coming on (שָׁמַר, in the usual signification *observare*, to be on the watch, to take care, observe anxiously), since he hopes to render himself invisible ; and that he may not be recognised even if seen, he puts on a mask. סֵתֶר פָּנִים is something by which his countenance is rendered unrecognisable (LXX. ἀποκρυβὴ προσώπου), like the Arab. *sitr, sitâreh,* a curtain, veil, therefore a veil for the face, or, as we say in one word borrowed from the Arabic

مَسْخَرَة, a farce (masquerade): the mask, but not in the proper sense.[1]

> 16 *In the dark they dig through houses,*
> *By day they shut themselves up,*
> *They will know nothing of the light.*

[1] The mask was perhaps never known in Palestine and Syria ; סתר פנים is the *mendíl* or women's veil, which in the present day (in *Hauran* exclusively) is called *sitr,* and is worn over the face by all married women in the towns, while in the country it is worn hanging down the back, and is only drawn over the face in the presence of a stranger. If this explanation is correct, the poet means to say that the adulterer, in order to

17 *For the depth of night is to them even as the dawn of the*
   morning,
   For they know the terrors of the depth of night.

The handiwork of the thief, which is but slightly referred
to in ver. 14c, is here more particularly described. The
indefinite subj. of חָתַר, as is manifest from what follows, is
the band of thieves. The בְּ, which is elsewhere joined with
חתר (to break into anything), is here followed by the *acc.*
בָּתִּים (to be pronounced *bâttim*, not *bottim*),[1] as in the Talmudic, חָתַר שִׁנּוֹ, to pick one's teeth (and thereby to make
them loose), *b. Kidduschin,* 24 *b.* According to the Talmud,
Ralbag, and the ancient Jewish interpretation in general,
ver. 16*b* is closely connected to בתים : houses which they
have marked by day for breaking into, and the mode of its
accomplishment ; but חָתַם nowhere signifies *designare,* always
obsignare, to seal up, to put under lock and key, ch. xiv. 17,
ix. 7, xxxvii. 7 ; according to which the *Piel,* which occurs
only here, is to be explained : by day they seal up, *i.e.* shut
themselves up for their safety (לָמוֹ is not to be accented with
Athnach, but with *Rebia mugrasch*) : they know not the light,
i.e. as Schlottm. well explains : they have no fellowship with
it ; for the biblical יָדַע, γινώσκειν, mostly signifies a knowledge which enters into the subject, and intimately unites

remain undiscovered, wears women's clothes [comp. Deut. xxii. 5] ; and,
in fact, in the Syrian towns (the figure is taken from town-life) women's
clothing is always chosen for that kind of forbidden nocturnal undertaking, *i.e.* the man disguises himself in an *izâr,* which covers him from head
to foot, takes the *mendil,* and goes with a lantern (without which at night
every person is seized by the street watchman as a suspicious person) un-
hindered into a strange house.—WETZST.

[1] *Vid.* Aben-Ezra on Ex. xii. 7. The main proof that it is to be pronounced *bâttim* is, that written exactly it is בָּֽתִּים, and that the *Metheg,*
according to circumstances, is changed into an accent, as Ex. viii. 7, xii. 7,
Jer. xviii. 22, Ezek. xlv. 4, which can only happen by *Kametz,* not by
Kometz (K. *chatûph*); comp. Köhler on Zech. xiv. 2.

itself with it. In ver. 17 one confirmation follows another.
Umbr. and Hirz. explain : for the morning is to them at
once the shadow of death ; but יַחְדָּו, in the signification at the
same time, as we have taken יַחַד in ch. xvii. 16 (nevertheless
of simultaneousness of time), is unsupportable : it signifies
together, ch. ii. 11, ix. 32 ; and the arrangement of the words
יַחְדָּו . . . לָמוֹ (to them together) is like Isa. ix. 20, xxxi. 3,
Jer. xlvi. 12.   Also, apart from the erroneous translation of
the יחדו, which is easily set aside, Hirzel's rendering of ver.
17 is forced : the morning, *i.e.* the bright day, is to them all
as the shadow of death, for each and every one of them
knows the terrors of the daylight, which is to them as the
shadow of death, viz. the danger of being discovered and
condemned.   The interpretation, which is also preferred by
Olshausen, is far more natural : the depth of night is to them
as the dawn of the morning (on the precedence of the predicate, comp. Amos iv. 13 and v. 8 : walking in the darkness
of the early morning), for they are acquainted with the terrors
of the depth of night, *i.e.* they are not surprised by them,
but know how to anticipate and to escape them.   Ch. xxxviii.
15 also, where the night, which vanishes before the rising of
the sun, is called the "light" of the evil-doer, favours this
interpretation (not the other, as Olsh. thinks).   The accentuation also favours it ; for if בקר had been the subj., and
were to be translated : the morning is to them the shadow of
death, it ought to have been accented בקר למו צלמות, *Dechî*,
Mercha, Athnach.   It is, however, accented *Munach, Munach,
Athnach*, and the second *Munach* stands as the deputy of
Dechî, whose value in the interpunction it represents ; therefore בקר למו is the predicate : the shadow of death is morning
to them.   From the *plur.* the description now, with יַכִּיר, passes
into the *sing.*, as individualizing it.   בַּלְהוֹת, constr. of בַּלָּהוֹת, is
without a *Dagesh* in the second consonant.   Mercier admir-
ably remarks here : *sunt ei familiares et noti nocturni terrores,*

neque eos timet aut curat, quasi sibi cum illis necessitudo et familiaritas intercederet et cum illis ne noceant fœdus aut pactum inierit. Thus by their skill and contrivance they escape danger, and divine justice allows them to remain undiscovered and unpunished,—a fact which is most incomprehensible.

It is now time that this thought was once again definitely expressed, that one may not forget what these accumulated illustrations are designed to prove. But what now follows in vers. 18–21 seems to express not Job's opinion, but that of his opponents. Ew., Hirz., and Hlgst. regard vers. 18–21, 22–25, as thesis and antithesis. To the question, What is the lot that befalls all these evil-doers? Job is thought to give a twofold answer: first, to ver. 21, an ironical answer in the sense of the friends, that those men are overtaken by the merited punishment; then from ver. 22 is his own serious answer, which stands in direct contrast to the former. But (1) in vers. 18–21 there is not the slightest trace observable that Job does not express his own view: a consideration which is also against Schlottman, who regards vers. 18–21 as expressive of the view of an opponent. (2) There is no such decided contrast between vers. 18–21 and 22–25, for vers. 19 and 24 both affirm substantially the same thing concerning the end of the evil-doer. In like manner, it is also not to be supposed, with Stick., Löwenth., Böttch., Welte, and Hahn, that Job, outstripping the friends, as far as ver. 21, describes how the evil-doer certainly often comes to a terrible end, and in vers. 22 sqq. how the very opposite of this, however, is often witnessed; so that this consequently furnishes no evidence in support of the exclusive assertion of the friends. Moreover, ver. 24 compared with ver. 19, where there is nothing to indicate a direct contrast, is opposed to it; and ver. 22, which has no appearance of referring to a direct contrast with what has been previously said, is opposed to

such an antithetical rendering of the two final strophes. Ver.
22 might more readily be regarded as a transition to the
antithesis, if vers. 18–21 could, with Eichh., Schnurr., Dathe,
Umbr., and Vaih., after the LXX., Syriac, and Jerome, be
understood as optative : " Let such an one be light on the
surface of the water, let . . . be cursed, let him not turn
towards," etc., but ver. 18*a* is not of the optative form ; and
18*c*, where in that case אל־יפנה would be expected, instead of
לא־יפנה, shows that 18*b*, where, according to the syntax, the
optative rendering is natural, is nevertheless not to be so
rendered. The right interpretation is that which regards
both vers. 18–21 and 22 sqq. as Job's own view, without
allowing him absolutely to contradict himself. Thus it is interpreted, *e.g.* by Rosenmüller, who, however, as also Renan,
errs in connecting ver. 18 with the description of the thieves,
and understands ver. 18*a* of their slipping away, 18*b* of their
dwelling in horrible places, and 18*c* of their avoidance of the
vicinity of towns.

> 18 *For he is light upon the surface of the water ;*
>   *Their heritage is cursed upon the earth ;*
>   *He turneth no more in the way of the vineyard.*
> 19 *Drought, also heat, snatch away snow water—*
>   *So doth Sheól those who have sinned.*
> 20 *The womb forgetteth him, worms shall feast on him,*
>   *He is no more remembered ;*
>   *So the desire of the wicked is broken as a tree—*
> 21 *He who hath plundered the barren that bare not,*
>   *And did no good to the widow.*

The point of comparison in ver. 18*a* is the swiftness of
the disappearing : he is carried swiftly past, as any light
substance on the surface of the water is hurried along by
the swiftness of the current, and can scarcely be seen ; comp.
ch. ix. 26 : " My days shoot by as ships of reeds, as an eagle

which dasheth upon its prey," and Hos. x. 7, " Samaria's
king is destroyed like a bundle of brushwood (LXX.,
Theod., φρύγανον) on the face of the water," which is
quickly drawn into the whirlpool, or buried by the approaching wave.[1]   But here the idea is not that of being swallowed
up by the waters, as in the passage in Hosea, but, on the
contrary, of vanishing from sight, by being carried rapidly
past by the rush of the waters.   If, then, the evil-doer dies
a quick, easy death, his heritage (חֶלְקָה, from חָלַק, to divide)
is cursed by men, since no one will dwell in it or use it,
because it is appointed by God to desolation on account of
the sin which is connected with it (vid. on ch. xv. 28) ;
even he, the evil-doer, no more turns the way of the vineyard (פָּנָה, with דֶּרֶךְ, not an acc. of the obj., but as indicating
the direction = אֶל־דֶּרֶךְ ; comp. 1 Sam. xiii. 18 with ver. 17 of
the same chapter), proudly to inspect his wide extended domain, and overlook the labourers.   The curse therefore does
not come upon him, nor can one any longer lie in wait for
him to take vengeance on him ; it is useless to think of venting upon him the rage which his conduct during life pro-
voked ; he is long since out of reach in Sheôl.

    That which Job says figuratively in ver. 18a, and in ch.
xxi. 13 without a figure : " in a moment they go down to
Sheôl," he expresses in ver. 19 under a new figure, and,
moreover, in the form of an emblematic proverb (vid.
Herzog's Real-Encyklopädie, xiv. 696), according to the
peculiarity of which, not בְּ, but either only the copulative
Waw (Prov. xxv. 25) or nothing whatever (Prov. xi. 22), is

---

[1] The translation : like foam (spuma or bulla), is also very suitable here.
Thus Targ., Symm., Jerome, and others ; but the signification to foam
cannot be etymologically proved, whereas קָצַף in the signification confringere is established by קְצָפָה, breaking, Joel i. 7, and قصف ; so that consequently קֶצֶף, as synon. of אַף, signifies properly the breaking forth, and
is then allied to עֶבְרָה.

to be supplied before שָׁאוּל חטאו. חָטָאוּ is virtually an object:
eos qui peccarunt. Ver. 19*b* is a model-example of extreme
brevity of expression, Ges. § 155, 4, *b.* Sandy ground (צִיָּה,
arid land, without natural moisture), added to it (גַּם, not:
likewise) the heat of the sun—these two, working simultaneously from beneath and above, snatch away (גָּזְלוּ, cogn. גָּזַר,

root גז, to cut, cut away, tear away; Arab. جزر, *fut. i,* used
of sinking, decreasing water) מֵימֵי שֶׁלֶג, water of (melted)
snow (which is fed from no fountain, and therefore is
quickly absorbed), and Sheôl snatches away those who have
sinned (= גָּזְלָה אֶת־אֲשֶׁר חָטָאוּ). The two incidents are alike:
the death of those whose life has been a life of sin, follows
as a consequence easily and unobserved, without any painful
and protracted struggle. The sinner disappears suddenly;
the womb, *i.e.* the mother that bare him, forgets him (רֶחֶם,
matrix = mater; according to Ralbag: friendship, from רָחַם,
to love tenderly; others: relationship, in which sense رَحِم =
רֶחֶם is used), worms suck at him (מְתָקוֹ for מְתָקַתּוּ, according
to Ges. § 147, *a, sugit eum,* from which primary notion of
sucking comes the signification to be sweet, ch. xxi. 33: Syriac,
metkat ennun remto; Ar. *imtasahum,* from the synonymous
مَصّ = מצץ, מצה, מזה), he is no more thought of, and thus
then is mischief (*abstr. pro concr.* as ch. v. 16) broken like a
tree (not: a staff, which עֵץ never, not even in Hos. iv. 12,
directly, like the Arabic ʿasa, ʿasât, signifies). Since עֻלָּה is
used personally, רֹעֶה וגו', ver. 21, can be connected with it as
an appositional permutative. His want of compassion (as is
still too often seen in the present day in connection with the
tyrannical conduct of the executive in Syria and Palestine,
especially on the part of those who collect the taxes) goes the
length of eating up, *i.e.* entirely plundering, the barren, child-

less (Gen. xi. 30; Isa. liv. 1), and therefore helpless woman, who has no sons to protect and defend her, and never showing favour to the widow, but, on the contrary, thrusting her away from him. There is as little need for regarding the verb רָעָה here, with Rosenm. after the Targ., in the signification *confringere*, as cognate with רָעַע, רָצַץ, as conversely to change תִּרֹעֵם, Ps. ii. 9, into תִּרְעֵם; it signifies *depascere*, as in ch. xx. 26, here in the sense of *depopulari*. On the form יֵיטִיב for יֵיטִיב, *vid.* Ges. § 70, 2, rem.; and on the transition from the *part.* to the *v. fin.*, *vid.* Ges. § 134, rem. 2. Certainly the memory of such an one is not affectionately cherished; this is equally true with what Job maintains in ch. xxi. 32, that the memory of the evil-doer is immortalized by monuments. Here the allusion is to the remembrance of a mother's love and sympathetic feeling. The fundamental thought of the strophe is this, that neither in life nor in death had he suffered the punishment of his evil-doing. The figure of the broken tree (broken in its full vigour) also corresponds to this thought; comp. on the other hand what Bildad says, ch. xviii. 16: "his roots dry up beneath, and above his branch is lopped off" (or: withered). The severity of his oppression is not manifest till after his death.

In the next strophe Job goes somewhat further. But after having, in vers. 22, 23, said that the life of the ungodly passes away as if they were the favoured of God, he returns to their death, which the friends, contrary to experience, have so fearfully described, whilst it is only now and then distinguished from the death of other men by coming on late and painlessly.

22 *And He preserveth the mighty by His strength;*
   Such an one riseth again, though he despaired of life.
23 *He giveth him rest, and he is sustained,*
   And His eyes are over their ways.

24 *They are exalted—a little while,—then they are no more,*
   And they are sunken away, snatched away like all others,
   And as the top of the stalk they are cut off.—
25 *And if it is not so, who will charge me with lying,*
   And make my assertion worthless?

Though it becomes manifest after their death how little
the ungodly, who were only feared by men, were beloved,
the form of their death itself is by no means such as to reveal
the retributive justice of God. And does it become at all
manifest during their life? The *Waw*, with which the
strophe begins, is, according to our rendering, not adversative,
but progressive. God is the subject. מָשַׁךְ, to extend in
length, used elsewhere of love, Ps. xxxvi. 11, cix. 12, and
anger, Ps. lxxxv. 6, is here transferred to persons: to prolong, preserve long in life. אַבִּירִים are the strong, who bid
defiance not only to every danger (Ps. lxxvi. 6), but also to
all divine influences and noble impulses (Isa. xlvi. 12).
These, whose trust in their own strength God might smite
down by His almighty power, He preserves alive even in
critical positions by that very power: he (the אַבִּיר) stands up
(again), whilst he does not trust to life, *i.e.* whilst he believes
that he must succumb to death (הֶאֱמִין as Ps. xxvii. 13, comp.
Genesis, S. 368; חַיִּין, Aramaic form, like מִלִּין, ch. iv. 2,
xii. 11; the whole is a contracted circumstantial clause for
והוּא לֹא וגו'). He (God) grants him לָבֶטַח, in security, viz.
to live, or even directly: a secure peaceful existence, since
לבטח is virtually an object, and the לְ is that of condition
(comp. לָרֹב, ch. xxvi. 3). Thus Hahn, who, however, here is
only to be followed in this one particular, takes it correctly:
and that he can support himself, which would only be possible
if an *inf.* with לְ had preceded. Therefore: and he is supported, or he can support himself, *i.e.* be comforted, though
this absolute use of נִשְׁעָן cannot be supported; in this instance

we miss עַל־טוּבוֹ, or some such expression (ch. viii. 15). God
sustains him and raises him up again : His eyes (עֵינָיו = עֵינֵיהוּ)
are (rest) on the ways of these men, they stand as it were
beneath His special protection, or, as it is expressed in ch.
x. 3 : He causes light to shine from above upon the doings of
the wicked. "They are risen up, and are conscious of the
height (of prosperity)—a little while, and they are no more."
Thus ver. 24a is to be explained. · The accentuation רוֹמּוּ
with *Mahpach*, מְעַט with *Asla legarmeh* (according to which
it would have to be translated : they stand on high a short
time), is erroneous. The verb רוּם signifies not merely to be
high, but also to rise up, raise one's self, *e.g.* Prov. xi. 11,
and to show one's self exalted, here *extulerunt se in altum* or
exaltati sunt; according to the form of writing רוֹמּוּ, רֻם is
treated as an *Ayin Waw* verb *med. O*, and the *Dagesh* is a
so-called *Dag. affectuosum* (Olsh. § 83, *b*), while רֹמּוּ (like רֹבּוּ,
Gen. xlix. 23) appears to assume the form of a double *Ayin*
verb *med. O*, consequently רָמַם (Ges. § 67, rem. 1). מְעַט,
followed by *Waw* of the conclusion, forms a clause of itself,
as more frequently עוֹד מְעַט וְ (yet a little while, then . . .),
as, *e.g.* in an exactly similar connection in Ps. xxxvii. 10;
here, however, not expressive of the sudden judgment of the
ungodly, but of their easy death without a struggle (εὐθα-
νασία) : a little, then he is not (again a transition from the
plur. to the distributive or individualizing *sing.*). They are,
viz. as ver. 24b further describes, bowed down all at once (an
idea which is expressed by the *perf.*), are snatched off like all
other men. הֻמְּכוּ is an Aramaizing *Hophal*-form, approaching
the *Hoph.* of strong verbs, for הוּמַכּוּ (Ges. § 67, rem. 8), from
מָכַךְ, to bow one's self (Ps. cvi. 43), to be brought low (Eccl.
x. 18); comp. ملك, to cause to vanish, to annul. יִקָּפְצוּן (for
which it is unnecessary with Olsh. to read יִקָּבְצוּן, after Ezek.
xxix. 5) signifies, according to the primary signification of

קפץ, *comprehendere, constringere, contrahere* (cogn. קבץ, קמץ, קמט, comp. *supra,* i. 437): they are hurried together, or snatched off, *i.e.* deprived of life, like the Arabic قبضه الله (קפצו אלהים) and passive قُبِضَ, equivalent to, he has died. There is no reference in the phrase to the *componere artus,* Gen. xlix. 33; it is rather the figure of housing (gathering into the barn) that underlies it; the word, however, only implies seizing and drawing in. Thus the figure which follows is also naturally (comp. קֹמֶץ, قُبْضَة, *manipulus*) connected with what precedes, and, like the head of an ear of corn, *i.e.* the corn-bearing head of the wheat-stalk, they are cut off (by which one must bear in mind that the ears are reaped higher up than with us, and the standing stalk is usually burnt to make dressing for the field; *vid.* Ges. *Thes. s.v.* קַשׁ [1]).

On יִמָּלוּ (*fut. Niph.* = יִמָּלוּ), *vid.* on ch. xiv. 2, xviii. 16; the signification *præciduntur,* as observed above, is more suitable here than *marcescunt* (in connection with which signification ch. v. 26 ought to be compared, and the form regarded as *fut. Kal*). Assured of the truth, in conformity with experience, of that which has been said, he appeals finally to the friends: if it be not so (on אֵפוֹ = אֵפוֹא in conditional clauses, *vid.* ch. ix. 24), who (by proving the opposite) is able to charge me with lying and bring to nought

---

[1] Another figure is also presented here. It is a common thing for the Arabs (Beduins) in harvest-time to come down upon the fields of standing corn—especially barley, because during summer and autumn this grain is indispensable to them as food for their horses—of a district, chiefly at night, and not unfrequently hundreds of camels are laden at one time. As they have no sickles, they cut off the upper part of the stalk with the ʿaqfe (a knife very similar to the Roman *sica*) and with sabres, whence this theft is called qard קְרִץ, *sabring off;* and that which is cut off, as well as the uneven stubble that is left standing, is called qarid.— WETZST.

(לְאַל = לְאֵין, Ew. § 321, *b*, perhaps by אַל being conceived of as originally *infin.* from אָלַל (comp. אֱלִיל), in the sense of non-existence, العَدَم) my assertion?

The bold accusations in the speech of Eliphaz, in which the uncharitableness of the friends attains its height, must penetrate most deeply into Job's spirit. But Job does not answer like by like. Even in this speech in opposition to the friends, he maintains the passionless repose which has once been gained. Although the misjudgment of his character has attained its height in the speech of Eliphaz, his answer does not contain a single bitter personal word. In general, he does not address them, not as though he did not wish to show respect to them, but because he has nothing to say concerning their unjust and wrong conduct that he would not already have said, and because he has lost all hope of his reproof taking effect, all hope of sympathy with his entreaty that they would spare him, all hope of understanding and information on their part.

In the first part of the speech (ch. xxiii.) he occupies himself with the mystery of his own suffering lot, and in the second part (ch. xxiv.) with the reverse of this mystery, the evil-doers' prosperity and immunity from punishment. How is he to vindicate himself against Eliphaz, since his lament over his sufferings as unmerited is accounted by the friends more and more as defiant obstinacy (מרי), and consequently tends to bring him still deeper into that suspicion which he is trying to remove? His testimony concerning himself is of no avail; for it appears to the friends more self-delusive, hypocritical, and sinful, the more decidedly he maintains it; consequently the judgment of God can alone decide between him and his accusers. But while the friends accuse him by word of mouth, God himself is pronouncing sentence against him by His acts,—his affliction is a *de facto* accusation of

God against him. Therefore, before the judgment of God can become a vindication of his affliction against the friends, he must first of all himself have defended and proved his innocence in opposition to the Author of his affliction. Hence the accusation of the friends, which in the speech of Eliphaz is become more direct and cutting than heretofore, must urge on anew with all its power the desire in Job of being able to bring his cause before God.

At the outset he is confident of victory, for his consciousness does not deceive him; and God, although He is both one party in the cause and judge, is influenced by the irresistible force of the truth. Herein the want of harmony in Job's conception of God, the elevation of which into a higher unity is the goal of the development of the drama, again shows itself. He is not able to think of the God who pursues him, the innocent one, at the present time with suffering, as the just God; on the other hand, the justice of the God who will permit him to approach His judgment throne, is to him indisputably sure: He will attend to him, and for ever acquit him. Now Job yields to the arbitrary power of God, but then he will rise by virtue of the justice and truth of God. His longing is, therefore, that the God who now afflicts him may condescend to hear him: this seems to him the only way of convincing God, and indirectly the friends, of his innocence, and himself of God's justice. The basis of this longing is the desire of being free from the painful conception of God which he is obliged to give way to. For it is not the darkness of affliction that enshrouds him which causes Job the intensest suffering, but the darkness in which it has enshrouded God to him,—the angry countenance of God which is turned to him. But if this is sin, that he is engaged in a conflict concerning the justice of the Author of his affliction, it is still greater that he indulges evil thoughts respecting the Judge towards whose throne of judgment he presses forward. He thinks that God designedly avoids him, because He is well aware of his innocence; now, however, he will admit no other thought but that of suffering him to endure to the end the affliction decreed. Job's suspicion against God is as dreadful as it is childish. This is a profoundly tragic stroke. It is not to be understood as the sarcasm of defiance; on the contrary, as one of the childish thoughts into which melancholy bordering on madness falls. From the bright height of faith to which Job soars in ch. xix. 25 sqq. he is here again drawn down into the most terrible depth of conflict, in which, like a blind man, he gropes after God, and because he cannot find Him thinks that He flees before him lest He should be overcome by him. The God of the present, Job accounts his enemy; and the God of the future, to whom his faith clings, who will and must vindicate him so soon as He only allows himself to be found and seen—this God is not to be found! He cannot get free either from his suffering or from his ignominy. The future for him is again veiled in a twofold darkness.

Thus Job does not so much answer Eliphaz as himself, concerning the cutting rebukes he has brought against him. He is not able to put them aside, for his consciousness does not help him; and God, whose judgment he desires to have, leaves him still in difficulty. But the mystery of his lot of affliction, which thereby becomes constantly more torturing, becomes still more mysterious from a consideration of the reverse side, which he is urged by Eliphaz more closely to consider, terrible as it may be to him. He, the innocent one, is being tortured to death by an angry God, while for the ungodly there come no times of punishment, no days of vengeance: greedy conquerors, merciless rulers, oppress the poor to the last drop of blood, who are obliged to yield to them, and must serve them, without wrong being helped by the right; murderers, who shun the light, thieves, and adulterers, carry on their evil

courses unpunished; and swiftly and easily, without punishment overtaking them, or being able to overtake them, Sheôl
snatches them away, as heat does the melted snow; even
God himself preserves the oppressors long in the midst of
extreme danger, and after a long life, free from care and
laden with honour, permits them to die a natural death, as a
ripe ear of corn is cut off.   Bold in the certainty of the truth
of his assertion, Job meets the friends: if it is not so, who
will convict me as a liar?!   What answer will they give?
They cannot long disown the mystery, for experience out-
strips them.   Will they therefore solve it?   They might, had
they but the key of the future state to do it with!   But
neither they nor Job were in possession of that, and we shall
therefore see how the mystery, without a knowledge of the
future state, struggled through towards solution; or even if
this were impossible, how the doubts which it excites are
changed to faith, and so are conquered.

Bildad's Third Speech.—Chap. xxv.

Schema: 10.

[Then began Bildad the Shuhite, and said:]
2 *Dominion and terror are with Him,*
  He maketh peace in His high places.
3 *Is there any number to His armies,*
  And whom doth not His light surpass?
4 *How could a mortal be just with God,*
  And how could one born of woman be pure?
5 *Behold, even the moon, it shineth not brightly,*
  And the stars are not pure in His eyes.
6 *How much less mortal man, a worm,*
  And the son of man, a worm!

Ultimum hocce classicum, observes Schultens, *quod a parte triumvirorum sonuit, magis receptui canentis videtur, quam prœlium renovantis.* Bildad only repeats the two common-places, that man cannot possibly maintain his supposedly per-verted right before God, the all-just and all-controlling One, to whom, even in heaven above, all things cheerfully submit, and that man cannot possibly be accounted spotlessly pure, and consequently exalted above all punishment before Him, the most holy One, before whom even the brightest stars do not appear absolutely pure. הַמְשֵׁל is an *inf. abs.* made into a substantive, like הַשְׁקֵט; the *Hiph.* (to cause to rule), which is otherwise causative, can also, like *Kal,* signify to rule, or properly, without destroying the *Hiphil*-signification, to exer-cise authority (*vid.* on ch. xxxi. 18) ; המשל therefore signifies sovereign rule. עֹשֶׂה, with הוא to be supplied, which is not unfrequently omitted both in participial principal clauses (ch. xii. 17 sqq., Ps. xxii. 29, Isa. xxvi. 3, xxix. 8, xl. 19, comp. Zech. ix. 12, where אני is to be supplied) and in partic. subor-dinate clauses (Ps. vii. 10, lv. 20, Hab. ii. 10), is an expression of the simple *prœs.,* which is represented by the *partic.* used thus absolutely (including the personal pronoun) as a proper tense-form (Ew. § 168, *c,* 306, *d*). Schlottman refers עשׂה to המשל ופחד; but the analogy of such attributive descriptions of God is against it. Umbreit and Hahn connect בִּמְרוֹמָיו with the subject: He in His heights, *i.e.* down from His throne in the heavens. But most expositors rightly take it as descriptive of the place and object of the action expressed : He establishes peace in His heights, *i.e.* among the celestial beings immediately surrounding Him. This, only assuming the abstract possibility of discord, might mean : *facit majestate sua ut in summa pace et promptissima obedientia ipsi ministrent angeli ipsius in excelsis* (Schmid). But although from ch. iv. 18, xv. 15, nothing more than that even the holy ones above are neither removed from the possibility of sin nor the necessity of a judicial authority which is high above them, can be inferred; yet, on the other hand, from ch. iii. 8, ix. 13 (comp. xxvi. 12 sq.), it is clear that the poet, in whose conception, as in Scripture generally, the angels and the stars stand in the closest relation, knows of actual, and not merely past, but possibly recurring, instances of hostile dissension and titanic rebellion among the celestial powers; so that עֹשֶׂה שָׁלוֹם, therefore, is intended not merely of a harmonizing reconciliation among creatures which have been contending one against another, but of an actual restoration of the equilibrium that had been disturbed through self-will, by an act of mediation and the exercise of judicial authority on the part of God.

Ver. 3. Instead of the appellation מְרוֹמָיו, which reminds one of Isa. xxiv. 21,—where a like peacemaking act of judgment on the part of God is promised in reference to the spirit-host of the heights that have been working seductively among the nations on earth,—גְּדוּדָיו, of similar meaning to צְבָאָיו, used elsewhere, occurs in this verse. The stars, according to biblical representation, are like an army arrayed for battle, but not as after the Persian representation—as an army divided into troops of the *Ahuramazdâ* and *Angramainyus* (Ahriman), but a standing army of the children of light, clad in the armour of light, under the guidance of the one God the Creator (Isa. xl. 26, comp. the anti-dualistic assertion in Isa. xlv. 7). The one God is the Lord among these numberless legions, who commands their reverence, and maintains unity among them; and over whom does not His light arise? Umbr. explains: who does not His light, which He communicates to the hosts of heaven, vanquish (קוּם עַל in the usual warlike meaning: to rise against any one); but this is a thought that is devoid of purpose in this connection. אוֹרֵהוּ with the emphatic suff. *êhu* (as ch. xxiv. 23, עֵינֵיהוּ) at any rate refers directly to God: *His* light in distinction from the derived light of the hosts of heaven. This distinction is better brought out if we interpret (Merc., Hirz., Hahn,

Schlottm., and others) : over whom does (would) not His light arise? *i.e.* all receive their light from His, and do but reflect it back. But יְזְרַח = יָקוּם cannot be justified by ch. xi. 17. Therefore we interpret with Ew. and Hlgst. thus : whom does not His light surpass, or, literally, over whom (*i.e.* which of these beings of light) does it not rise, leaving it behind and exceeding it in brightness (יָקוּם as synon. of יָרוּם)? How then could a mortal be just with God, *i.e.* at His side or standing up before Him ; and how could one of woman born be spotless! How could he (which is hereby indirectly said) enter into a controversy with God, who is infinitely exalted above him, and maintain before Him a moral character faultless, and therefore absolutely free from condemnation! In the heights of heaven God's decision is revered ; and should man, the feeble one, and born flesh of flesh (*vid.* ch. xiv. 1), dare to contend with God? Behold, עַד־יָרֵחַ (עַד, as usually when preceded by a negation, *adeo, ne . . . quidem, e.g.* Ex. xiv. 28, comp. Nah. i. 10, where J. H. Michaelis correctly renders: *adeo ut spinas perplexitate æquent,* and אֶל used in the same way, ch. v. 5, Ew. § 219, *c*), even as to the moon, it does not (וְלֹא with *Waw apod.,* Ges. § 145, 2, although there is a reading לֹא without וְ) shine bright, יַהֵל = יֶהֱלִ, from הָלַל = אָהַל.[1] Thus LXX., Targ. Jer., and Gecatilia translate; whereas Saadia translates: it turns not in (لا يدخل), or properly, it does not pitch its tent, fix its habitation. But to pitch one's tent is אָהַל or אֹהֶל, whence יָהֵל, Isa. xiii. 20, = יֶאֱהָל; and what is still more decisive, one would naturally expect יַאֲהִיל שָׁם in connection with this thought. We therefore render אהל as a form for once boldly used in the scriptural language for הלל, as in Isa. xxviii. 28 אָדָשׁ once occurs for דּוּשׁ. Even the moon is only a feeble light before

---

[1] It is worthy of observation, that *hilâl* signifies in Arabic the new moon (comp. *Genesis,* S. 307); and the Hiphil *ahalla,* like the Kal *halla,* is used of the appearing and shining of the new moon.

God, and the stars are not clean in His eyes; there is a vast distance between Him and His highest and most glorious creatures—how much more between Him and man, the worm of the dust!

The friends, as was to be expected, are unable to furnish any solution of the mystery, why the ungodly often live and die happily; and yet they ought to be able to give this solution, if the language which they employ against Job were authorized. Bildad alone speaks in the above speech, Zophar is silent. But Bildad does not utter a word that affects the question. This designed omission shows the inability of the friends to solve it, as much as the tenacity with which they firmly maintain their dogma; and the breach that has been made in it, either they will not perceive or yet not acknowledge, because they think that thereby they are approaching too near to the honour of God. Moreover, it must be observed with what delicate tact, and how directly to the purpose in the structure of the whole, this short speech of Bildad's closes the opposition of the friends. Two things are manifest from this last speech of the friends : First, that they know nothing new to bring forward against Job, and nothing just to Job's advantage; that all their darts bound back from Job; and that, though not according to their judgment, yet in reality, they are beaten. This is evident from the fact that Bildad is unable to give any answer to Job's questions, but can only take up the one idea in Job's speech, that he confidently and boldly thinks of being able to approach God's throne of judgment; he repeats with slight variation what Eliphaz has said twice already, concerning the infinite distance between man and God, ch. iv. 17–21, xv. 14–16, and is not even denied by Job himself, ch. ix. 2, xiv. 4. But, secondly, the poet cannot allow us to part from the friends with too great repugnance; for they are Job's friends notwithstanding, and at the close we see them willingly obedient to God's instruction, to go to

Job that he may pray for them and make sacrifice on their behalf. For this reason he does not make Bildad at last repeat those unjust incriminations which were put prominently forward in the speech of Eliphaz, ch. xxii. 5–11. Bildad only reminds Job of the universal sinfulness of the human race once again, without direct accusation, in order that Job may himself derive from it the admonition to humble himself; and this admonition Job really needs, for his speeches are in many ways contrary to that humility which is still the duty of sinful man, even in connection with the best justified consciousness of right thoughts and actions towards the holy God.

Job's Second Answer.—Chap. xxvi.

Schema: 6. 6. 6. 6. 3.

[Then Job began, and said:]
2 *How hast thou helped him that is without power,*
   Raised the arm that hath no strength!
3 *How hast thou counselled him that hath no wisdom,*
   And fully declared the essence of the matter!
4 *To whom hast thou uttered words,*
   And whose breath proceeded from thee?

Bildad is the person addressed, and the exclamations in vers. 2, 3 are ironical: how thy speech contains nothing whatever that might help me, the supposedly feeble one, in conquering my affliction and my temptation; me, the supposedly ignorant one, in comprehending man's mysterious lot, and mine!   לְלֹא־כֹחַ, according to the idea, is only equivalent to בה לו (אין) לַאֲשֶׁר לֹא, and זְרוֹעַ לֹא־עֹז equivalent to זרוע בלא־עז (לֹא עֹז לוֹ); the former is the *abstr. pro concreto*, the latter the genitival connection—the arm of the no-power, *i.e.* powerless (Ges. § 152, 1). The powerless one is Job himself, not God (Merc., Schlottm.), as even the choice of the verbs, vers.

50 THE BOOK OF JOB.

2*b*, 3*a*, shows. Respecting תוּשִׁיָּה, which we have translated essentiality, duration, completion, we said, on ch. v. 12, that it is formed from יֵשׁ (*vid.* Prov. viii. 21), not directly indeed, but by means of a verb יָשִׁי (וְשָׁה), in the signification *subsistere* (comp. كان, and Syriac קוּם[1]) ; it is a *Hophal*-formation (like תּוּגָה), and signifies, so to speak, durability, *subsistentia*, *substantia*, ὑπόστασις, so that the comparison of וְשׁי with אֲשִׁישׁ

اُس (whence אֲשִׁישׁ, Arab. *asîs, asâs*, etc., *fundamentum*) is forced upon one, and the relationship to the Sanskrit *as* (*asmi* = εἰμί) can remain undecided. The observation of J. D. Michaelis[2] to the contrary, *Supplem.* p. 1167 : *non placent in linguis ejusmodi etyma metaphysica nimis a vulgari sensu remota ; philosophi in scholis ejusmodi vocabula condunt, non plebs*, is removed by the consideration that תושיה, which out of Prov. and Job occurs only in Isa. xxviii. 29, Mic. vi. 9, is a Chokma-word : it signifies here, as frequently, *vera et realis sapientia* (J. H. Michaelis). The speech of Bildad is a proof of poverty of thought, of which he himself gives the evidence. His words—such is the thought of ver. 4—are altogether inappropriate, inasmuch as they have no reference whatever to the chief point of Job's speech ; and they are, moreover, not his own, but the suggestion of another, and that not God, but Eliphaz, from whom Bildad has borrowed the substance of his brief declamation. Since this is the meaning of ver. 4*b*, it might seem as though אֶת־מִי were

---

[1] Comp. also Spiegel, *Grammatik der Huzvâresch-Sprache*, S. 103.

[2] Against the comparison of the Arab. وَاسَى, *solari*, by Michaelis, Ges., and others (who assume the primary significations *solatium, auxilium*), Lagarde (*Anmerkungen zur griech. Uebersetzung der Proverbien*, 1863, S. 57 f.) correctly remarks that وَاسَى is only a change of letters of the common language for اَسَى ; but وَشَى, to finish painting (whence تَوْشِيَة, decoration), or וְשָׁה as a transposition from שָׁוָה, to be level, simple (Hitzig on Prov. iii. 21), leads to no suitable sense.

intended to signify by whose assistance (Arnh., Hahn); but as the poet also, in ch. xxxi. 37, comp. Ezek. xliii. 10, uses הִגִּיד seq. *acc.*, in the sense of explaining anything to any one, to instruct him concerning anything, it is to be interpreted : to whom hast thou divulged the words (LXX., τίνι ἀνήγγειλας ῥήματα), *i.e.* thinking and designing thereby to affect him ?

In what follows, Job now continues the description of God's exalted rule, which Bildad had attempted, by tracing it through every department of creation ; and thus proves by fact, that he is wanting neither in a recognition nor reverence of God the almighty Ruler.

> 5 —*The shades are put to pain*
> *Deep under the waters and their inhabitants.*
> 6 *Sheôl is naked before him,*
> *And the abyss hath no covering.*
> 7 *He stretched the northern sky over the emptiness ;*
> *He hung the earth upon nothing.*

Bildad has extolled God's majestic, awe-inspiring rule in the heights of heaven, His immediate surrounding ; Job continues the strain, and celebrates the extension of this rule, even to the depths of the lower world. The operation of the majesty of the heavenly Ruler extends even to the realm of shades ; the sea with the multitude of its inhabitants forms no barrier between God and the realm of shades ; the marrowless, bloodless phantoms or shades below writhe like a woman in travail as often as this majesty is felt by them, as, perhaps, by the raging of the sea or the quaking of the earth. On רְפָאִים, which also occurs in Phœnician inscriptions, *vid. Psychol.* S. 409 ; the book of Job corresponds with Ps. lxxxviii. 11 in the use of this appellation. The *sing.* is not רְפָאִי (whence רפאים, as the name of a people), but רָפָא (רָפָה), which signifies both giants or heroes of colossal stature (from רפה = رَفِعَ, to be high), and the relaxed (from רפה, to be loose, like نَفَى, to soften, to soothe), *i.e.* those who are bodiless in the state after death (comp. חָלָה, Isa. xiv. 10, to be weakened, *i.e.* placed in the condition of a *rapha*). It is a question whether יְחוֹלָלוּ be *Pilel* (Ges.) or *Pulal* (Olsh.); the *Pul.*, indeed, signifies elsewhere to be brought forth with writhing (ch. xv. 7); it can, however, just as well signify to be put in pain. On account of the reference implied in it to a higher causation here at the commencement of the speech, the *Pul.* is more appropriate than the *Pil.;* and the pausal *â*, which is often found elsewhere with *Hithpael* (*Hithpal.*), ver. 14, ch. xxxiii. 5, but never with *Piel* (*Pil.*), proves that the form is intended to be regarded as passive.

Ver. 6*a.* שְׁאוֹל is seemingly used as *fem.*, as in Isa. xiv. 9*b;* but in reality the *adj.* precedes in the primitive form, without being changed by the gender of שְׁאוֹל. אֲבַדּוֹן alternates with שְׁאוֹל, like קֶבֶר in Ps. lxxxviii. 12. As Ps. cxxxix. 8 testifies to the presence of God in Sheôl, so here Job (comp. ch. xxxviii. 17, and especially Prov. xv. 11) that Sheôl is present to God, that He possesses a knowledge which extends into the depths of the realm of the dead, before whom all things are γυμνὰ καὶ τετραχηλισμένα (Heb. iv. 13). The following *partt.*, ver. 7, depending logically upon the chief subject which precedes, are to be determined according to ch. xxv. 2; they are conceived as present, and indeed of God's primeval act of creation, but intended of the acts which continue by virtue of His creative power.

Ver. 7. By צָפוֹן many modern expositors understand the northern part of the earth, where the highest mountains and rocks rise aloft (accordingly, in Isa. xiv. 13, ירכתי צפון are mentioned parallel with the starry heights), and consequently the earth is the heaviest (Hirz., Ew., Hlgst., Welte, Schlottm., and others). But (1) it is not probable that the poet would first have mentioned the northern part of the earth, and then in ver. 7*b* the earth itself—first the part, and then the whole; (2) נטה is never said of the earth, always of the heavens, for the expansion of which it is the stereotype word (נֹטֶה, ch. ix. 8, Isa. xl. 22, xliv. 24, li. 13, Zech. xiv. 1, Ps. civ. 2; נוטיהם, Isa. xlii. 5; נטה, Jer. x. 12, li. 15; יָדִי נטו, Isa. xlv. 12); (3) one expects some mention of the sky in connection with the mention of the earth; and thus is צפון,[1] with Rosenm., Ges., Umbr., Vaih., Hahn, and Olsh., to be understood of the northern sky, which is prominently mentioned, because there is the pole of the vault of heaven, which is marked by the Pole-star, there the constellation of the Greater Bear (עָשׁ, ch. ix. 9) formed by the seven bright stars, there (in the back of the bull, one of the northern constellations of the ecliptic) the group of the Pleiades (כִּימָה), there also, below the bull and the twins, Orion (כְּסִיל). On the derivation, notion, and synonyms of תֹּהוּ, *vid.* *Genesis*, S. 93; here (where it may be compared with the Arab. *tehij-un*, empty, and *tîh*, desert) it signifies nothing more than the unmeasurable vacuum of space, parall. בְּלִימָה, not anything = nothing (comp. modern Arabic *lâsh*, or even *mâsh*, compounded of لَا or مَا and شَيء, a thing, *e.g.* *bilâs*, for nothing, *ragul mâsh*, useless men). The sky which vaults the earth from the arctic pole, and the earth itself, hang free without support in space. That which is elsewhere (*e.g.* ch. ix. 6) said of the pillars and foundations of the earth, is intended of the internal support of the body of the earth, which is, as it were, fastened together by the mountains, with their roots extend-

---

[1] The name צפון signifies the northern sky as it appears by day, from its beclouded side in contrast with the brighter and more rainless south; comp. old Persian *apâkhtara,* if this name of the north really denotes the "starless" region, Greek ζόφος, the north-west, from the root *skap*, σκεπᾶν, σκεπανός (Curtius, *Griech. Etymologie*, ii. 274), *aquilo*, the north wind, as that which brings black clouds with it.

ing into the innermost part of the earth; for the idea that
the earth rests upon the bases of the mountains would be,
indeed, as Löwenthal correctly observes, an absurd inversion.
On the other side, we are also not justified in inferring from
Job's expression the laws of the mechanism of the heavens,
which were unknown to the ancients, especially the law of
attraction or gravitation. The knowledge of nature on the
part of the Israelitish Chokma, expressed in ver. 7, however,
remains still worthy of respect. On the ground of similar
passages of the book of Job, Keppler says of the yet un-
solved problems of astronomy : *Hæc et cetera hujusmodi
latent in Pandectis ævi sequentis, non antea discenda, quam
librum hunc Deus arbiter seculorum recluserit mortalibus.*
From the starry heavens and the earth Job turns to the
celestial and sub-celestial waters.

> 8 *He bindeth up the waters in His clouds,*
> *Without the clouds being rent under their burden.*
> 9 *He enshroudeth the face of His throne,*
> *Spreading His clouds upon it.*
> 10 *He compasseth the face of the waters with bounds,*
> *To the boundary between light and darkness.*

The clouds consist of masses of water rolled together,
which, if they were suddenly set free, would deluge the
ground; but the omnipotence of God holds the waters together in the hollow of the clouds (צֹרֵר, *Milel,* according to a
recognised law, although it is also found in Codd. accented
as *Milra,* but contrary to the Masora), so that they do not
burst asunder under the burden of the waters (תִּחְתָּם); by
which nothing more nor less is meant, than that the physical
and meteorological laws of rain are of God's appointment.
Ver. 9 describes the dark and thickly-clouded sky that showers
down the rain in the appointed rainy season. אָחַז signifies to
take hold of, in architecture to hold together by means of

beams, or to fasten together (*vid.* Thenius on 1 Kings vi. 10,
comp. 2 Chron. ix. 18, מְאֻחָזִים, *coagmentata*), then also, as
usually in Chald. and Syr., to shut (by means of cross-bars,
Neh. vii. 3), here to shut off by surrounding with clouds:
He shuts off פְּנֵי־כִסֵּה, the front of God's throne, which is
turned towards the earth, so that it is hidden by storm-clouds
as by a סֻכָּה, ch. xxxvi. 29, Ps. xviii. 12. God's throne,
which is here, as in 1 Kings x. 19, written כִּסֵּה instead of
כִּסֵּא (comp. Arab. *cursi*, of the throne of God the Judge, in
distinction from العَرْش, the throne of God who rules over
the world[1]), is indeed in other respects invisible, but the
cloudless blue of heaven is His reflected splendour (Ex.
xxiv. 10) which is cast over the earth. God veils this His
radiance which shines forth towards the earth, פַּרְשֵׁז עָלָיו עֲנָנוֹ,
by spreading over it the clouds which are led forth by Him.
פַּרְשֵׁז is commonly regarded as a Chaldaism for פִּרְשֵׁז (Ges.
§ 56, Olsh. § 276), but without any similar instance in favour
of this vocalization of the 3 *pr. Piel* (*Pil.*). Although רַעֲנָן and
שַׁאֲנָן, ch. xv. 32, iii. 18, have given up the *i* of the *Pil.*, it
has been under the influence of the following guttural; and
although, moreover, *i* before *Resh* sometimes passes into *a*,
e.g. וַיֵּרָא, it is more reliable to regard פַּרְשֵׁז as *inf. absol.* (Ew.
§ 141, *c*): *expandendo*. Ges. and others regard this פַּרְשֵׁז as
a mixed form, composed from פרשׂ and פרז; but the verb פרשׂ
(with *Shin*) has not the signification to expand, which is
assumed in connection with this derivation; it signifies to
separate (also Ezek. xxxiv. 12, *vid.* Hitzig on that passage),

---

[1] According to the more recent interpretation, under Aristotelian influence, العَرْش is the outermost sphere, which God as πρῶτον κινοῦν
having set in motion, communicates light, heat, life, and motion to the
other revolving spheres; for the *causæ mediæ* gradually descend from God
the Author of being (*muhejji*) from the highest heaven into the sub-
lunary world.

whereas פרשׂ certainly signifies to expand (ch. xxxvi. 29, 30);
wherefore the reading פָּרְשֵׂז (with *Sin*), which some Codd.
give, is preferred by Bär, and in agreement with him by
Luzzatto (*vid.* Bär's *Leket zebi*, p. 244), and it seems to
underlie the interpretation where פרשז עליו is translated by
פרש (פָּרַשׂ) עליו, He spreadeth over it (*e.g.* by Aben-Ezra,
Kimchi, Ralbag). But the Talmud, *b. Sabbath*, 88 *b* (פירש
שׁדי מזיו שׁבינתו ועננו עליו, the Almighty separated part of the
splendour of His Shechina and His cloud, and laid it upon
him, *i.e.* Moses, as the passage is applied in the Haggada),
follows the reading פָּרְשֵׁז (with *Shin*), which is to be retained
on account of the want of naturalness in the consonantal
combination שֵׁז; but the word is not to be regarded as a
mixed formation (although we do not deny the possibility of
such forms in themselves, *vid. supra*, i. 411), but as an intensive form of פרשׂ formed by Prosthesis and an Arabic change
of *Sin* into *Shin*, like فرشط, فرشد, فرشم, which, being formed
from فرش = פָּרַשׂ (פְּרַשׂ), to expand, signifies to spread out
(the legs).

Ver. 10 passes from the waters above to the lower waters.
תַּכְלִית signifies, as in ch. xi. 7, xxviii. 3, Neh. iii. 21, the
extremity, the extreme boundary; and the connection of
תַּכְלִית אוֹר is genitival, as the *Tarcha* by the first word correctly
indicates, whereas אוֹר with *Munach*, the substitute for *Rebia
mugrasch* in this instance (according to *Psalter*, ii. 503, § 2),
is a mistake. God has marked out (חג, LXX. ἐγύρωσεν) a
law, *i.e.* here according to the sense: a fixed bound (comp.
Prov. viii. 29 with Ps. civ. 9), over the surface of the waters
(*i.e.* describing a circle over them which defines their circuit)
unto the extreme point of light by darkness, *i.e.* where the
light is touched by the darkness. Most expositors (Rosenm.,
Hirz., Hahn, Schlottm., and others) take עד־תכלית adverbially:
most accurately, and refer חָג to אוֹר as a second object, which
is contrary to the usage of the language, and doubtful and

unnecessary. Pareau has correctly interpreted: *ad lucis usque tenebrarumque confinia;* עַם in the local sense, not *æque ac,* although it might also have this meaning, as *e.g.* Eccl. ii. 16. The idea is, that God has appointed a fixed limit to the waters, as far as to the point at which they wash the *terra firma* of the extreme horizon, and where the boundary line of the realms of light and darkness is; and the basis of the expression, as Bouillier, by reference to Virgil's *Georg.* i. 240 sq., has shown, is the conception of the ancients, that the earth is surrounded by the ocean, on the other side of which the region of darkness begins.

11 *The pillars of heaven tremble*
   And are astonished at His threatening.
12 *By His power He rouseth up the sea,*
   And by His understanding He breaketh Rahab in pieces.
13 *By His breath the heavens become cheerful;*
   His hand hath formed the fugitive dragon.

The mountains towering up to the sky, which seem to support the vault of the sky, are called poetically "the pillars of heaven." יְרוֹפְפוּ is *Pulal,* like יְחוֹלָלוּ, ver. 5; the signification of violent and quick motion backwards and forwards is secured to the verb רוּף by the Targ. אִתְרוֹפַף = הִתְפַּלֵּץ, ch. ix. 6, and the Talm. רִפְרֵף of churned milk, blinking eyes (comp.

הֶרֶף עַיִן, the twinkling of the eye, and رَفَّ, *fut. i. o. nictare*),

flapping wings (comp. رَفَّ and رَفْرَفَ, *movere, motitare alas*), of wavering thinking. גְּעָרָה is the divine command which looses or binds the powers of nature; the astonishment of the supports of heaven is, according to the radical signification of תָּמַהּ (cogn. שָׁמֵם), to be conceived of as a torpidity which follows the divine impulse, without offering any resistance whatever. That רָגַע, ver. 12*a*, is to be understood transitively, not like ch. vii. 5, intransitively, is proved by the dependent (borrowed) passages, Isa. li. 15, Jer. xxxi. 35, from which it is also evident that רגע cannot with the LXX. be translated κατέπαυσεν. The verb combines in itself the opposite significations of starting up, *i.e.* entering into an excited state, and of being startled, from which the significations of stilling (*Niph.*, *Hiph.*), and of standing back or retreat (رَجَعَ), branch off. The conjecture גָּעַר after the Syriac version (which translates, *goʻar bᵉjamo*) is superfluous. רַהַב, which here also is translated by the LXX. τὸ κῆτος, has been discussed already on ch. ix. 13. It is not meant of the turbulence of the sea, to which מָחַץ is not appropriate, but of a sea monster, which, like the crocodile and the dragon, are become an emblem of Pharaoh and his power, as Isa. li. 9 sq. has applied this primary passage : the writer of the book of Job purposely abstains from such references to the history of Israel. Without doubt, רהב denotes a demoniacal monster, like the demons that shall be destroyed at the end of the world, one of which is called by the Persians *akomano*, evil thought, another *taromaiti*, pride. This view is supported by ver. 13, where one is not at liberty to determine the meaning by Isa. li. 9, and to understand נָחָשׁ בָּרִחַ, like תַּנִּין in that passage, of Egypt. But this dependent passage is an important indication for the correct rendering of חֹלְלָה. One thing is certain at the outset, that שִׁפְרָה is not *perf. Piel* = שִׁפְּרָה, and for this reason, that the *Dagesh* which characterizes *Piel* cannot be omitted from any of the six *mutæ* ; the translation of Jerome, *spiritus ejus ornavit cœlos*, and all similar ones, are therefore false. But it is possible to translate : "by His spirit (creative spirit) the heavens are beauty, His hand has *formed* the flying dragon." Thus, in the signification to bring forth (as Prov. xxv. 23, viii. 24 sq.), חללה is rendered by Rosenm., Arnh., Vaih., Welte, Renan, and others, of whom Vaih. and Renan, however, do not understand ver. 13*a* of the creation of the heavens, but of their illumination. By this rendering vers. 13*a* and 13*b* are severed, as being without connection; in general, however, the course of thought in the description does not favour the reference of the whole or half of ver. 13 to the creation. Accordingly, חֹלְלָה is not to be taken as *Pilel* from חוּל (חִיל), but after Isa. lvii. 9, as *Poel* from חלל, according to which the idea of ver. 13*a* is determined, since both lines of the verse are most closely connected.

נָחָשׁ בָּרִחַ (בָּרִיחַ) is, to wit, the constellation of the Dragon,[1] one of the most straggling constellations, which winds itself between the Greater and Lesser Bears almost half through the polar circle.

> " *Maximus hic plexu sinuoso elabitur Anguis*
> *Circum perque duas in morem fluminis Arctos.*"
> VIRGIL, *Georg.* i. 244 sq.

Aratus in Cicero, *de nat. Deorum*, ii. 42, describes it more graphically, both in general, and in regard to the many stars of different magnitudes which form its body from head to tail. Among the Arabs it is called *el-hajje*, the serpent, *e.g.* in Firuzabâdi: the *hajje* is a constellation between the Lesser Bear (*farqadân*, the two calves) and the Greater Bear (*benât en-na'sch*, the daughters of the bier), " or *et-tanîn*, the dragon, *e.g.* in one of the authors quoted by Hyde on Ulugh Beigh's *Tables of the Stars*, p. 18 : the *tanîn* lies round about the north pole in the form of a long serpent, with many bends and windings." Thus far the testimony of the old expositors is found in Rosenmüller. The Hebrew name טְלִי (the quiver) is perhaps to be distinguished from טָלִי and דְלִי, the Zodiac constellations Aries and Aquarius.[2] It is questionable how בָּרִחַ is to be understood. The LXX. translates δράκοντα ἀποστάτην in this passage, which is certainly in-

---

[1] Ralbag, without any ground for it, understands it of the milky way (הָעִגּוּל הַחֲלָבִי), which, according to Rapoport, Pref. to Slonimski's *Toledoth ha-schamajim* (1838), was already known to the Talmud *b. Berachoth*, 58*b*, under the name of נְהַר דְנוּר.

[2] Vid. *Wissenschaft, Kunst, Judenthum* (1838), S. 220 f.

correct, since בריח beside נחש may naturally be assumed
to be an attributive word referring to the motion or form
of the serpent. Accordingly, Isa. xxvii. 1, ὄφιν φεύγοντα is
more correct, where the Syr. version is חִוְיָא חַרְמָנָא, the fierce
serpent, which is devoid of support in the language; in the
passage before us the Syr. also has חִוְיָא דַעֲרַק, the fleeing
serpent, but this translation does not satisfy the more neuter
signification of the adjective. Aquila in Isaiah translates
ὄφιν μόχλον, as Jerome translates the same passage *serpentem
vectem* (whereas he translates *coluber tortuosus* in our passage),
as though it were בְּרִיחַ; Symm. is better, and without doubt a
substantially similar thought, ὄφιν συγκλείοντα, the serpent
that joins by a bolt, which agrees with the traditional Jewish
explanation, for the dragon in Aben-Ezra and Kimchi (in
Lex.)—after the example of the learned Babylonian teacher of
astronomy, Mar-Samuel (died 257), who says of himself that
the paths of the heavens are as familiar to him as the places
of Nehardea[1]—is called נחש עקלתון, because it is as though
it were wounded, and בריח, because it forms a bar (מבריח)
from one end of the sky to the other; or as Sabbatai Donolo
(about 940), the Italian astronomer,[2] expresses it: "When God
created the two lights (the sun and moon) and the five stars
(planets) and the twelve מזלות (the constellations of the Zodiac),
He also created the תלי (dragon), to unite these heavenly
bodies as by a weaver's beam (מנור אורגים), and made it
stretch itself on the firmament from one end to another as a
bar (כבריח), like a wounded serpent furnished with head and
tail." By this explanation בְּרִיחַ is either taken directly as
בְּרִיחַ, *vectis*, in which signification it does not, however, occur
elsewhere, or the signification *transversus* (*transversarius*) is

---

[1] *Vid.* Grätz, *Geschichte der Juden*, iv. 324. On Isa. xxvii. 1 Kimchi
interprets the מבריח differently : he scares (pushes away).

[2] *Vid.* extracts from his ספר המזלות in Joseph Kara's *Comm. on Job*,
contributed by S. D. Luzzatto in *Kerem Chemed*, 7th year, S. 57 ff.

assigned to the בְּרִיחַ (=*barrîah*) with an unchangeable *Kametz*, —a signification which it might have, for ברח بَرَخَ signifies properly to go through, to go slanting across, of which the meanings to unite slanting and to slip away are only variations. בְּרִיחַ, notwithstanding, has in the language, so far as it is preserved to us, everywhere the signification *fugitivus*, and we will also keep to this: the dragon in the heavens is so called, as having the appearance of fleeing and hastening away. But in what sense is it said of God, that He pierces or slays it? In Isa. li. 9, where the תנין is the emblem of Egypt (Pharaoh), and xxvii. 1, where נחש בריח is the emblem of Assyria, the empire of the Tigris, the idea of destruction by the sword of Jehovah is clear. The present passage is to be explained according to ch. iii. 8, where לִוְיָתָן is only another name for נחש בריח (comp. Isa. xxvii. 1). It is the dragon in the heavens which produces the eclipse of the sun, by winding itself round about the sun; and God must continually wound it anew, and thus weaken it, if the sun is to be set free again. That it is God who disperses the clouds of heaven by the breath of His spirit, the representative of which in the elements is the wind, so that the azure becomes visible again; and that it is He who causes the darkening of the sun to cease, so that the earth can again rejoice in the full brightness of that great light,—these two contemplations of the almighty working of God in nature are so expressed by the poet, that he clothes the second in the mythological garb of the popular conception.

In the closing words which now follow, Job concludes his illustrative description: it must indeed, notwithstanding, come infinitely short of the reality.

14 *Behold, these are the edges of His ways,*
   And how do we hear only a whisper thereof!
   But the thunder of His might—who comprehendeth it?

These (אֵלֶּה retrospective, as in ch. xviii. 21) are only קְצוֹת, the extremest end-points or outlines of the ways of God, which Job has depicted; the wondrous fulness of His might, which extends through the whole creation, transcends human comprehension; it is only שֵׁמֶץ דָּבָר therefrom that becomes audible to us men. שֵׁמֶץ (שֶׁמֶץ) is translated by Symm. here

ψιθύρισμα, ch. iv. 12, ψιθυρισμός; the Arab. شَمَص (to speak very quickly, mutter) confirms this idea of the word; Jerome's translation, *vix parvam stillam sermonis ejus* (comp. ch. iv. 12, *venas*, tropical for parts), is doubly erroneous: the rendering of the שמץ has the antithesis of רַעַם against it, and דָּבָר is not to be understood here otherwise than in עֶרְוַת דָּבָר, Deut. xxiii. 15, xxiv. 1: shame of something = something that excites a feeling of shame, a whisper of something = some whisper. The notion "somewhat," which the old expositors attribute to שמץ, lies therefore in דבר. מה is exclamatory in a similar manner as in Ps. lxxxix. 48 : how we hear (נִשְׁמַע, not נִשְׁמָע) only some whisper thereof (בּוֹ partitive, as *e.g.* Isa. x. 22), *i.e.* how little therefrom is audible to us, only as the murmur of a word, not loud and distinct, which reaches us !

As in the speech of Bildad the poet makes the opposition of the friends to fade away and cease altogether, as incapable of any further counsel, and hence as conquered, so in Job's closing speech, which consists of three parts, ch. xxvi., xxvii.–xxviii., xxix.–xxxi., he shows how Job in every respect, as victor, maintains the field against the friends. The friends have neither been able to loose the knot of Job's lot of suffering, nor the universal distribution of prosperity and misfortune. Instead of loosing the knot of Job's lot of suffering, they have cut it, by adding to Job's heavy affliction the invention of heinous guilt as its ground of explanation; and the knot of the contradictions of human life in general with divine justice they have ignored, in order that they may not

be compelled to abandon their dogma, that suffering everywhere necessarily presupposes sin, and sin is everywhere
necessarily followed by suffering. Even Job, indeed, is not
at present able to solve either one or other of the mysteries;
but while the friends' treatment of these mysteries is untrue,
he honours the truth, and keenly perceives that which is
mysterious. Then he proves by testimony and an appeal to
facts, that the mystery may be acknowledged without therefore being compelled to abandon the fear of God. Job
firmly holds to the objective reality and the testimony of his
consciousness; in the fear of God he places himself above
all those contradictions which are unsolvable by and perplexing to human reason; his faith triumphs over the rational-
ism of the friends, which is devoid of truth, of justice, and
of love.

Job first answers Bildad, ch. xxvi. He characterizes his
poor reply as what it is: as useless, and not pertinent in
regard to the questions before them: it is of no service to
him, it does not affect him, and is, moreover, a borrowed
weapon. For he also is conscious of and can praise God's
exalted and awe-inspiring majesty. He has already shown
this twice, ch. ix. 4–10, xii. 13–25, and shows here for the
third time: its operation is not confined merely to those
creatures that immediately surround God in the heavens;
it extends, without being restrained by the sea, even down
to the lower world; and as it makes the angels above to
tremble, so there it sets the shades in consternation. From
the lower world, Job's contemplation rises to the earth, as a
body suspended in space without support; to the clouds above,
which contain the upper waters without bursting, and veil the
divine throne, of which the sapphire blue of heaven is the reflection; and then he speaks of the sea lying between Sheôl
and heaven, which is confined within fixed bounds, at the
extreme boundaries of which light passes over into darkness;

—he celebrates all this as proof of the creative might of God. Then he describes the sovereign power of God in the realm of His creation, how He shakes the pillars of heaven, rouses the sea, breaks the monster in pieces, lights up the heavens by chasing away the clouds and piercing the serpent, and thus setting free the sun. But all these—thus he closes—are only meagre outlines of the divine rule, only a faint whisper, which is heard by us as coming from the far distance. Who has the comprehension necessary to take in and speak exhaustively of all the wonders of His infinite nature, which extends throughout the whole creation? From such a profound recognition and so glorious a description of the exaltation of God, the infinite distance between God and man is most clearly proved. Job has adequately shown that his whole soul is full of that which Bildad is anxious to teach him; a soul that only requires a slight impulse to make it overflow with such praise of God, as is not wanting in an universal perception of God, nor is it full of wicked devices. When therefore Bildad maintains against Job that no man is righteous before such an exalted God, Job ought indeed to take it as a warning against such unbecoming utterances concerning God as those which have escaped him; but the universal sinfulness of man is no ground of explanation for his sufferings, for there is a righteousness which avails before God; and of this, Job, the suffering servant of God, has a consciousness that cannot be shaken.

THIRD PART.—THE TRANSITION TO THE UNRAVELMENT.

CHAP. XXVII.–XXXI.

Job's Final Speech to the Friends.—Chap. xxvii. xxviii.

Schema: 12. 10. 12. 10. | 10. 8. 8. 8. 8. 8. 10.

[Then Job continued to take up his proverb, and said :]
2 *As God liveth, who hath deprived me of my right,*
  And the Almighty, who hath sorely saddened my soul—
3 *For still all my breath is in me,*
  And the breath of Eloah in my nostrils—
4 *My lips do not speak what is false,*
  And my tongue uttereth not deceit!
5 *Far be it from me, to grant that you are in the right :*
  Till I die I will not remove my innocence from me.
6 *My righteousness I hold fast, and let it not go :*
  My heart reproacheth not any of my days.
7 *Mine enemy must appear as an evil-doer,*
  And he who riseth up against me as unrighteous.

The friends are silent, Job remains master of the discourse, and his continued speech is introduced as a continued שָׂאֵת מְשָׁלוֹ (after the analogy of the phrase נשׂא קוֹל), as in Num. xxiii. 7 and further on, the oracles of Balaam. מָשָׁל is speech of a more elevated tone and more figurative character; here, as frequently, the unaffected outgrowth of an elevated solemn mood. The introduction of the ultimatum, as מִשׁל, reminds one of "the proverb (*el-methel*) seals it" in the mouth of the Arab, since in common life it is customary to use a pithy saying as the final proof at the conclusion of a speech.

Job begins with an asseveration of his truthfulness (*i.e.*

the agreement of his confession with his consciousness) by
the life of God. From this oath, which in the form *bi-hajât
allâh* has become later on a common formula of assurance,
R. Josua, in his tractate *Sota*, infers that Job served God
from love to Him, for we only swear by the life of that which
we honour and love; it is more natural to conclude that the
God by whom, on the one hand, he believes himself to be so
unjustly treated, still appears to him, on the other hand, to
be the highest manifestation of truth. The interjectional
clause: living is God! is equivalent to, as true as God liveth.
That which is affirmed is not what immediately follows: He
has set aside my right, and the Almighty has sorely grieved
my soul (Raschi); but הסיר משפטי and המר נפשי are attributive
clauses, by which what is denied in the form of an oath introduced by אִם (as Gen. xlii. 15, 1 Sam. xiv. 45, 2 Sam. xi. 11,
Ges. § 155, 2, *f*) is contained in ver. 4; his special reference
to the false semblance of an evil-doer shows that semblance
which suffering casts upon him, but which he constantly
repudiates as surely not lying, as that God liveth. Among
moderns, Schlottm. (comp. Ges. § 150, 3), like most of the
old expositors, translates: so long as my breath is in me, . . .
my lips shall speak no wrong, so that vers. 3 and 4 together
contain what is affirmed. But (1) כִּי indeed sometimes introduces that which shall happen as affirmed by oath, Jer. xxii. 5,
xlix. 13; but here that which shall not take place is affirmed,
which would be introduced first in a general form by כִּי
explic. s. recitativum, then according to its special negative
contents by אִם,—a construction which is perhaps possible
according to syntax, but it is nevertheless perplexing; (2) it
may perhaps be thought that "the whole continuance of my
breath in me" is conceived as accusative and adverbial, and is
equivalent to, so long as my breath may remain in me (בל עוד,
as long as ever, like the Arab. *cullama*, as often as ever); but
the usage of the language does not favour this explanation,

for 2 Sam. i. 9, בָל־עוֹד נפשׁי בי, signifies my whole soul (my full life) is still in me; and we have a third instance of this prominently placed כל *per hypallagen* in Hos. xiv. 3, כל־תשׂא עון, *omnem auferas iniquitatem*, Ew. § 289, *a* (comp. Ges. § 114, rem. 1). Accordingly, with Ew., Hirz., Hahn, and most modern expositors, we take ver. 3 as a parenthetical confirmatory clause, by which Job gives the ground of his solemn affirmation that he is still in possession of his full consciousness, and cannot help feeling and expressing the contradiction between his lot of suffering, which brands him as an evil-doer, and his moral integrity. The נִשְׁמָתִי which precedes the רוח signifies, according to the prevailing usage of the language, the intellectual, and therefore self-conscious, soul of man (*Psychol.* S. 76f). This is in man and in his nostrils, inasmuch as the breath which passes in and out by these is the outward and visible form of its being, which is in every respect the condition of life (*ib.* S. 82f.). The suff. of נשמתי is unaccented; on account of the word which follows being a monosyllable, the tone has retreated (נסוג אחור, to use a technical grammatical expression), as *e.g.* also in ch. xix. 25, xx. 2, Ps. xxii. 20. Because he lives, and, living, cannot deny his own existence, he swears that his own testimony, which is suspected by the friends, and on account of which they charge him with falsehood, is perfect truth.

Ver. 4 is not to be translated: "my lips shall never speak what is false;" for it is not a resolve which Job thus strongly makes, after the manner of a vow, but the agreement of his confession, which he has now so frequently made, and which remains unalterable, with the abiding fact. Far be from me —he continues in ver. 5—to admit that you are right (חָלִילָה לִי with unaccented *ah*, not of the *fem.*, comp. ch. xxxiv. 10, but of direction: for a profanation to me, *i.e.* let it be profane to me, Ew. § 329, *a*, Arab. hâshâ li, in a like sense); until I expire (prop.: sink together), I will not put my innocence

(תֻּמָּה, perfection, in the sense of purity of character) away from me, *i.e.* I will not cease from asserting it. I will hold fast (as ever) my righteousness, and leave it not, *i.e.* let it not go or fall away; my heart does not reproach even one of my days. מִיָּמָי is virtually an obj. in a partitive sense: *mon cœur ne me reproche pas un seul de mes jours* (Renan). The heart is used here as the seat of the conscience, which is the knowledge possessed by the heart, by which it excuses or accuses a man (*Psychol.* S. 134); חָרַף (whence חֹרֶף, the season in which the fruits are gathered) signifies *carpere*, to pluck = to pinch, lash, inveigh against. Jos. Kimchi and Ralbag explain: my heart draws not back (from the confession of my innocence) my whole life long (as Maimonides explains נחרפת, Lev. xix. 20, of the female slave who is inclined to, *i.e.* stands near to, the position of a free woman), by comparison with the Arabic اِنْحَرَفَ, *deflectere*; it is not, however, حَرَفَ, but خَرَفَ, *decerpere*, that is to be compared in the tropical sense of the prevailing usage of the Hebrew specified. The old expositors were all misled by the misunderstood partitive מימי, which they translated *ex* (= *inde a*) *diebus meis*. There is in ver. 7 no ground for taking יְהִי, with Hahn, as a strong affirmative, as supposed in ch. xviii. 12, and not as expressive of desire; but the meaning is not: let my opponents be evil-doers, I at least am not one (Hirz.). The voluntative expresses far more emotion: the relation must be reversed; he who will brand me as an evil-doer, must by that very act brand himself as such, inasmuch as the מרשיע of a צדיק really shows himself to be a רשע, and by recklessly judging the righteous, is bringing down upon himself a like well-merited judgment. The כְּ is the so-called *Caph veritatis*, since כְּ, *instar*, signifies not only similarity, but also equality. Instead of קִימִי, the less manageable, primitive form, which the poet used in ch. xxii. 20 (comp. vol. i. 440), and beside which קָם (קוֹם, 2 Kings xvi. 7) does not occur in the book, we here find the more usual form מִתְקוֹמְמִי (comp. ch. xx. 27).[1]

The description of the misfortune of the ungodly which now follows, beginning with כִּי, requires no connecting thought, as for instance : My enemy must be accounted as ungodly, on account of his hostility ; I abhor ungodliness, for, etc. ; but that he who regards him as a רֹשָׁע is himself a רֹשָׁע, Job shows from the fact of the רֹשָׁע having no hope in death, whilst, when dying, he can give no confident hope of a divine vindication of his innocence.

8 *For what is the hope of the godless, when He cutteth off,*
   When Eloah taketh away his soul?
9 *Will God hear his cry*
   When distress cometh upon him?
10 *Or can he delight himself in the Almighty,*
   Can he call upon Eloah at all times?
11 *I will teach you concerning the hand of God,*
   I will not conceal the dealings of the Almighty.
12 *Behold, ye have all seen it,*
   Why then do ye cherish foolish notions?

In comparing himself with the רֹשָׁע, Job is conscious that he has a God who does not leave him unheard, in whom he delights himself, and to whom he can at all times draw near ; as, in fact, Job's fellowship with God rests upon the freedom of the most intimate confidence. He is not one of the godless ; for what is the hope of one who is estranged from God, when he comes to die ? He has no God on whom his hope

---

[1] In Beduin the enemy is called *qômâni* (*vid. supra*, on ch. xxiv. 12, p. 26), a denominative from *qôm* قوم, war, feud ; but *qôm* has also the signification of a collective of *qômâni*, and one can also say: *entum wa-ijânâ qôm*, you and we are enemies, and *bênâtna qôm*, there is war between us.—Wetzst.

might establish itself, to whom it could cling. The old expositors err in many ways respecting ver. 8, by taking בצע, *abscindere* (root בץ), in the sense of (*opes*) *corradere* (thus also more recently Rosenm. after the Targ., Syr., and Jer.), and referring יֵשֶׁל to שָׁלָה in the signification *tranquillum esse* (thus even Blumenfeld after Ralbag and others). נַפְשׁוֹ is the object to both verbs, and בצע נפש, *abscindere animam*, to cut off the thread of life, is to be explained according to ch. vi. 9, Isa. xxxviii. 12. שלה נפש, *extrahere animam* (from

שָׁלָה, whence سَلَا שִׁלְיָה, the after-birth, cogn. שָׁלַל سل نشل نسل,

نثل، نشل), is of similar signification, according to another figure, since the body is conceived of as the sheath (נְדְנֶה,

Dan. vii. 15) of the soul[1] (comp. سل in the universal signification *evaginare ensem*). The *fut. apoc. Kal* יֵשֶׁל (= יִשֹׁל) is therefore in meaning equivalent to the intrans. יִשַּׁל, Deut. xxviii. 40 (according to Ew. § 235, *c*, obtained from this by change of vowel), *decidere;* and Schnurrer's supposition that יִשֹׁל, like the Arab. يسل, is equivalent to יִשְׁאַל (when God demands it), or such a violent correction as De Lagarde's[2] (when he is in distress יצק, when one demands his soul with a curse יִשָּׁאֵל בְּאָלָה), is unnecessary.

The ungodly man, Job goes on to say, has no God to hear his cry when distress comes upon him; he cannot delight himself (יִתְעַנָּג, pausal form of יִתְעַנֵּג, the primary form of יִתְעַנֵּג) in the Almighty; he cannot call upon Eloah at any

---

[1] On the similar idea of the body, as the *kosha* (sheath) of the soul, among the Hindus, *vid. Psychol.* S. 227.

[2] *Anm. zur griech. Uebers. der Proverbien* (1863), S. VI. f., where the first reason given for this improvement of the text is this, that the usual explanation, according to which יִשֹׁל and יבצע have the same subj. and obj. standing after the verb, is altogether contrary to Semitic usage. But this assertion is groundless, as might be supposed from the very beginning. Thus, *e.g.* the same obj. is found after two verbs in ch. xx. 19, and the same subj. and obj. in Neh. iii. 20.

time (*i.e.* in the manifold circumstances of life under which
we are called to feel the dependence of our nature). Torn
away from God, he cannot be heard, he cannot indeed pray
and find any consolation in God. It is most clearly manifest
here, since Job compares his condition of suffering with that
of a חָנֵף, what comfort, what power of endurance, yea, what
spiritual joy in the midst of suffering (הִתְעַנֵּג, as ch. xxii. 26,
Ps. xxxvii. 4, 11, Isa. lv. 2, lviii. 13 sq.), which must all
remain unknown to the ungodly, he can draw from his
fellowship with God; and seizing the very root of the distinction between the man who fears God and one who is
utterly godless, his view of the outward appearance of the
misfortune of both becomes changed; and after having
allowed himself hitherto to be driven from one extreme to
another by the friends, as the heat of the controversy gradually cools down, and as, regaining his independence, he stands
before them as their teacher, he now experiences the truth of
docendo discimus in rich abundance. I will instruct you,
says he, in the hand, *i.e.* the mode of action, of God (בְ just
as in Ps. xxv. 8, 12, xxxii. 8, Prov. iv. 11, of the province
and subject of instruction); I will not conceal אֲשֶׁר עִם־שַׁדַּי,
i.e. according to the sense of the passage : what are the principles upon which He acts; for that which is with (עִם) any
one is the matter of his consciousness and volition (*vid.* on
ch. xxiii. 10, p. 10).

Ver. 12*a* is of the greatest importance in the right interpretation of what follows from ver. 13 onwards. The instruction which Job desires to impart to the friends has
reference to the lot of the evil-doer; and when he says :
Behold, ye yourselves have beheld (learnt) it all,—in connection with which it is to be observed that אַתֶּם כֻּלְּכֶם does
not signify merely *vos omnes*, but *vosmet ipsi omnes*,—he
grants to them what he appeared hitherto to deny, that the
lot of the evil-doer, certainly in the rule, although not with-

out exceptions, is such as they have said. The application, however, which they have made of this abiding fact of experience, is and remains all the more false: Wherefore then (זֶה makes the question sharper) are ye vain (blinded) in vanity (self-delusion), viz. in reference to me, who do not so completely bear about the characteristic marks of a רֹשָׁע? The verb הָבַל signifies to think and act vainly (without ground or connection), 2 Kings xvii. 15 (comp. ἐματαιώθησαν, Rom. i. 21); the combination הָבַל הֶבֶל is not to be judged of according to Ges. § 138, rem. 1, as it is also by Ew. § 281, a, but הֶבֶל may also be taken as the representative of the gerund, as e.g. עֶרְיָה, Hab. iii. 9.

In the following strophe Job now begins as Zophar (ch. xx. 29) concluded. He gives back to the friends the doctrine they have fully imparted to him. They have held the lot of the evil-doer before him as a mirror, that he may behold himself in it and be astounded; he holds it before them, that they may perceive how not only his bearing under suffering, but also the form of his affliction, is of a totally different kind.

13   *This is the lot of the wicked man with God,*
     And the heritage of the violent which they receive from the
      Almighty :
14   *If his children multiply, it is for the sword,*
     And his offspring have not bread enough.
15   *His survivors shall be buried by the pestilence,*
     And his widows shall not weep.
16   *If he heapeth silver together as dust,*
     And prepareth garments for himself as mire :
17   *He prepareth it, and the righteous clothe themselves,*
     And the innocent divide the silver among themselves.
18   *He hath built as a moth his house,*
     And as a hut that a watchman setteth up.

We have already had the combination אָדָם רָשָׁע for אִישׁ רָשָׁע in ch. xx. 29; it is a favourite expression in Proverbs, and reminds one of ἄνθρωπος ὁδίτης in Homer, and ἄνθρωπος σπείρων, ἐχθρός, ἔμπορος, in the parables Matt. xiii. *Psik* (*Pasek*) stands under רשׁע, to separate the wicked man and God, as in Prov. xv. 29 (Norzi). לָמוֹ, exclusively peculiar to the book of Job in the Old Testament (here and ch. xxix. 21, xxxviii. 40, xl. 4), is לְ rendered capable of an independent position by means of מו = מה, Lᵉ. The sword, famine, and pestilence are the three punishing powers by which the evil-doer's posterity, however numerous it may be, is blotted out; these three, חֶרֶב, רָעָב, and מָוֶת, appear also side by side in Jer. xv. 2; מָוֶת, instead of מְמוֹתֵי, *diris mortibus*, is (as also Jer. xviii. 21) equivalent to דֶּבֶר in the same trio, Jer. xiv. 12; the plague is personified (as when it is called by an Arabian poet *umm el-farit*, the mother of death), and Vavassor correctly observes: *Mors illos sua sepeliet, nihil præterea honoris supremi consecuturos.* Böttcher (*de inferis*, § 72) asserts that במות can only signify *pestilentiæ tempore*, or better, *ipso mortis momento;* but since בְּ occurs by the passive elsewhere in the sense of *ab* or *per, e.g.* Num. xxxvi. 2, Hos. xiv. 4, it can also by נקבר denote the efficient cause. Olshausen's correction במות לֹא יקברו, they will not be buried when dead (Jer. xvi. 4), is still less required; "to be buried by the pestilence" is equivalent to, not to be interred with the usual solemnities, but to be buried as hastily as possible. Ver. 15*b* (common to our poet and the psalm of Asaph, lxxviii. 64, which likewise belongs to the Salomonic age) is also to be correspondingly interpreted: the women that he leaves behind do not celebrate the usual mourning rites (comp. Gen. xxiii. 2), because the decreed punishment which, stroke after stroke, deprives them of husbands and children, prevents all observance of the customs of mourning, and because the shock stifles the feeling of pity. The treasure in gold which his avarice has heaped up, and in garments which his love of display has gathered together, come into the possession of the righteous and the innocent, who are spared when these three powers of judgment sweep away the evil-doer and his family. Dust and dirt (*i.e.* of the streets, חוצות) are, as in Zech. ix. 3, the emblem of a great abundance that depreciates even that which is valuable. The house of the ungodly man, though a palace, is, as the fate of the fabric shows, as brittle and perishable a thing, and can be as easily destroyed, as the fine spinning of a moth, עָשׁ (according to the Jewish proverb, the brother of the סָס), or even the small case which it makes from remnants of gnawed articles, and drags about with it; it is like a light hut, perhaps for the watchman of a vineyard (Isa. i. 8), which is put together only for the season during which the grapes are ripening.[1]

> 19 *He lieth down rich, and doeth it not again,*
> *He openeth his eyes and—is no more.*
> 20 *Terrors take hold of him as a flood;*
> *By night a tempest stealeth him away.*

[1] The watchman's hut, for the protection of the vineyards and melon and maize fields against thieves, herds, or wild beasts, is now called either *'arîshe* and *mantara* (מְנְטָרה) if it is only slightly put together from branches of trees, or *chême* (חֵימָה) if it is built up high in order that the watcher may see a great distance. The *chême* is the more frequent; at harvest it stands in the midst of the threshing-floors (*bejâdir*) of a district, and it is constructed in the following manner :—Four poles (*'awâmîd*) are set up so as to form the corners of a square, the sides of which are about eight feet in length. Eight feet above the ground, four cross pieces of wood (*'awârid*) are tightly bound to these with cords, on which planks, if they are to be had, are laid. Here is the watcher's bed, which consists of a litter. Six or seven feet above this, cross-beams are again bound to the four poles, on which boughs, or reeds (*qasab*), or a mat (*hasîra*, חֲצִירָה) forms a roof (*sath*, שֶׂטַח), from which the *chême* has its name; for the *Piel*-forms עָרִשׁ, חִים, and שָׂטַח signify, " to be stretched over anything after the manner of a roof." Between the roof and the bed, three sides of the *chême* are hung round with a mat, or with

21 *The east wind lifteth him up, that he departeth,*
   And hurleth him forth from his place.
22 *God casteth upon him without sparing,*
   Before His hand he fleeth utterly away.
23 *They clap their hands at him,*
   And hiss him away from his place.

The pointing of the text וְלֹא יֶאֱסֹף is explained by Schnurr., Umbr., and Stick.: He goes rich to bed and nothing is taken as yet, he opens his eyes and nothing more is there; but if this were the thought intended, it ought at least to have been וְאֵין נֶאֱסָף, since לֹא signifies *non*, not *nihil;* and Stickel's translation, "while nothing is carried away," makes the *fut.* instead of the *prœt.*, which was to be expected, none the more tolerable; also אסף can indeed signify to gather hastily together, to take away (*e.g.* Isa. xxxiii. 4), when the connection favours it, but not here, where the first impression is that רָשָׁע is the subj. both to וְלֹא יֶאֱסֹף and to וְאֵינֶנּוּ. Böttcher's translation, "He lieth down rich and cannot be displaced," gives the words a meaning that is ridiculed by the usage of the language. On the other hand, וְלֹא יֶאֱסֹף can signify: and he

reeds or straw (*qashsh*, קַשׁ) bound together, in order both to keep off the cold night-winds, and also to keep the thieves in ignorance as to the number of the watchers. A small ladder, *sullem* (סֻלָּם), frequently leads to the bed-chamber. The space between the ground and this chamber is closed only on the west side to keep off the hot afternoon sun, for through the day the watcher sits below with his dog, upon the ground. Here is also his place of reception, if any passers-by visit him; for, like the village shepherd, the field-watcher has the right of showing a humble hospitality to any acquaintances. When the fruits have been gathered in, the *chême* is removed. The field-watchman is now called *nâtûr* (ناطور), and the verb is *natar,* נָטַר, "to keep watch," instead of which the quadriliteral *nôtar,* נוֹטַר (from the *plur.* نواطير, "the watchers"), has also been formed. In one part of Syria all these forms are written with צ (d) instead of ט, and pronounced accordingly. The נֹצֵר in this passage is similarly related to the נֹטֵר in Cant. i. 6, viii. 11, 12.—WETZST.

is not conveyed away (comp. *e.g.* Jer. viii. 2, Ezek. xxix. 5;
but not Isa. lvii. 1, where it signifies to be swept away, and
also not Num. xx. 26, where it signifies to be gathered to the
fathers), and is probably intended to be explained after the
pointing that we have, as Rosenm. and even Ralbag explain
it: "he is not conveyed away; one opens his eyes and he is
not;" or even as Schlottm.: "he is not conveyed away; in
one moment he still looks about him, in the next he is no
more;" but the relation of the two parts of the verse in this
interpretation is unsatisfactory, and the preceding strophe
has already referred to his not being buried. Since, therefore, only an unsuitable, and what is more, a badly-expressed
thought, is gained by this reading, it may be that the expression should be regarded with Hahn as interrogative: is he
not swept away? This, however, is only a makeshift, and
therefore we must see whether it may not perhaps be susceptible of another pointing. Jerome transl.: *dives cum dor-
mierit, nihil secum auferet;* the thought is not bad, but מְאוּמָה
is wanting, and לֹא alone does not signify *nihil.* Better
LXX. (Ital., Syr.): πλούσιος κοιμηθήσεται καὶ οὐ προσ-
θήσει. This translation follows the form of reading יֵאָסֵף =
יוֹסִיף, gives a suitable sense, places both parts of the verse in
the right relation, and accords with the style of the poet
(*vid.* ch. xx. 9, xl. 5); and accordingly, with Ew., Hirz., and
Hlgst., we decide in favour of this reading: he lieth down to
sleep rich, and he doeth it no more, since in the night he is
removed from life and also from riches by sudden death; or
also: in the morning he openeth his eyes without imagining
it is the last time, for, overwhelmed by sudden death, he
closes them for ever. Vers. 20*a* and 20*b* are attached cross-
wise (*chiastisch*) to this picture of sudden destruction, be it
by night or by day: the terrors of death seize him (*sing. fem.*
with a *plur.* subj. following it, according to Ges. § 146, 3)
like a flood (comp. the floods of Belial, Ps. xviii. 5), by night

a whirlwind (גְּנָבַתּוּ סוּפָה, as ch. xxi. 18) carrieth him away. The Syriac and Arabic versions add, as a sort of interpolation: as a fluttering (large white) night-moth,—an addition which no one can consider beautiful.

Ver. 21 extends the figure of the whirlwind. In Hebrew, even when the narrative has reference to Egyptian matters (Gen. xli. 23), the קָדִים which comes from the Arabian desert is the destructive, devastating, and parching wind κατ᾽ ἐξοχήν.[1] וַיֵּלַךְ signifies peribit (ut pereat), as ch. xiv. 20, xix. 10. שָׂעַר (comp. סֹעֲרָה, O storm-chased one) is connected with the accus. of the person pursued, as in Ps. lviii. 10. The subj. of וַיַּשְׁלֵךְ, ver. 22, is God, and the verb stands without an obj.: to cast at any one (shoot), as Num. xxxv. 22 (for the figure, comp. ch. xvi. 13); LXX. correctly: ἐπιρρίψει (whereas ch. xviii. 7, σφάλαι = ותכשׁילהו). The gerundive with יִבְרָח lays stress upon the idea of the exertion of flight: whithersoever he may flee before the hand of God, every attempt is in vain. The suff. êmo, ver. 23a, both according to the syntax and the matter, may be taken as the plural suff.; but the fact that כַּפֵּימוֹ can be equivalent to כַּפֵּיו (comp.

---

[1] In Syria and Arabia the east wind is no longer called qadîm, but exclusively sharqîja, i.e. the wind that blows from the rising of the sun (sharq). This wind rarely prevails in summer, occurring then only two or three days a month on an average; it is more frequent in the winter and early spring, when, if it continues long, the tender vegetation is parched up, and a year of famine follows, whence in the Lebanon it is called semûm (שְׁמוּם), which in the present day denotes the "poisonous wind" (= nesme musimme), but originally, by alliance with the Hebr. שׁמם, denoted the " devastating wind." The east wind is dry; it excites the blood, contracts the chest, causes restlessness and anxiety, and sleepless nights or evil dreams. Both man and beast feel weak and sickly while it prevails. Hence that which is unpleasant and revolting in life is compared to the east wind. Thus a maid in Hauran, at the sight of one of my Damascus travelling companions, whose excessive ugliness struck her, cried: billâh, nahâr el-jôm aqshar (اقشر), wagahetni (وجهتني) sharqîja, " by God, it is an unhealthy day to-day: an east wind blew upon me." And in a festive dance song of the Merg district, these words occur: wa rudd

Ps. xi. 7), עָלֵימוֹ to עָלָיו (comp. ch. xx. 23, xxii. 2), as לָמוֹ is equivalent to לוֹ (*vid.* Isa. xliv. 15, liii. 8), is established, and there is no reason why the same may not be the case here. The accumulation of the terminations *êmo* and *ômo* gives a tone of thunder and a gloomy impress to this conclusion of the description of judgment, as these terminations frequently occur in the book of Psalms, where moral depravity is mourned and divine judgment threatened (*e.g.* in Ps. xvii. xlix. lviii. lix. lxxiii.). The clapping of hands (שָׂפַק כַּפַּיִם = סָפַק, Lam. ii. 15, comp. תְּקַע, Nah. iii. 19) is a token of malignant joy, and hissing (שָׁרַק, Zeph. ii. 15, Jer. xlix. 17) a token of scorn. The expression in ver. 23*b* is a pregnant one. Clapping of hands and hissing accompany the evil-doer when merited punishment overtakes him, and chases him forth from the place which he hitherto occupied (comp. ch. viii. 18).

Earlier expositors have thought it exceedingly remarkable that Job, in ch. xxvii. 13–23, should agree with the assertions of the three friends concerning the destiny of the ungodly and his descendants, while he has previously opposed them

lî nômet hodênik | *seb' lejâlî bi-'olîja* | *wa berd wa sherd wa sharqîja* . . .
   "And grant me again to slumber on thy bosom,
      Seven nights in an upper chamber,
      And (I will then endure) cold, drifting snow, and east wind."
During the harvest, so long as the east wind lasts, the corn that is already threshed and lying on the threshing-floors cannot be winnowed; a gentle, moderate draught is required for this process, such as is only obtained by a west or south wind. The north wind is much too strong, and the east wind is characterized by constant gusts, which, as the Hauranites say, "*jôchotû tibn wa-habb*, carries away chaff and corn." When the wind shifts from the west to the east, a whirlwind (*zôba'a*, זוֹבְעָה) not unfrequently arises, which often in summer does much harm to the threshing-floors and to the cut corn that is lying in swaths (unless it is weighted with stones). Storms are rare during an east wind; they come mostly with a west wind (never with a south or north wind). But if an east wind does bring a storm, it is generally very destructive, on account of its strong gusts; and it will even uproot the largest trees.—WETZST.

on this point, ch. xii. 6, xxi. xxiv.   Kennicott thinks the confusion is cleared away by regarding ch. xxvi. 2–xxvii. 12 as
Job's answer to the third speech of Bildad, xxvii. 13 sqq. as
the third speech of Zophar, and xxviii. (to which the super-
scription xxvii. 1 belongs) as Job's reply thereto; but this
reply begins with ‏כִּי‎, and is specially appropriate as a striking
repartee to the speech of Zophar.   Stuhlmann (1804) makes
this third speech of Zophar begin with xxvii. 11, and imagines
a gap between xxvii. 10 and xxvii. 11; but who then are
the persons whom Zophar addresses by "you"?   The three
everywhere address themselves to Job, while here Zophar,
contrary to custom, would address himself not to him, but,
according to Stuhlmann's exposition, to the others with reference to Job.   Ch. xxviii. Stuhlmann removes and places
after ch. xxv. as a continuation of Bildad's speech; Zophar's
speech therefore remains unanswered, and Zophar may thank
this critic not only for allowing him another opportunity of
speaking, but also for allowing him the last word.   Bernstein
(Keil-Tzschirner's *Analekten*, Bd. i. St. 3) removes the contradiction into which Job seems to fall respecting himself in a
more thorough manner, by rejecting the division ch. xxvii. 7–
xxviii. 28, which is certainly indissolubly connected as a
whole, as a later interpolation; but there is no difference of
language and poetic spirit here betraying an interpolator;
and had there been one, even he ought indeed to have proceeded on the assumption that such an insertion should be
appropriate to Job's mouth, so that the task of proving its
relative fitness, from his standpoint at least, remains.   Hosse
(1849) goes still further: he puts ch. xxvii. 10, xxxi. 35–37,
xxxviii. 1, etc., together, and leaves out all that comes between
these passages.   There is then no transition whatever from
the entanglement to the unravelment.   Job's final reply, ch.
xxvii. xxviii., with the monologue ch. xxix.–xxxi., in which
even a feeble perception must recognise one of the most

essential and most beautiful portions of the dramatic whole,
forms this transition.

Eichhorn (in his translation of Job, 1824), who formerly
(*Allgem. Bibliothek der bibl. Lit.* Bd. 2) inclined to Kennicott's view, and Böckel (2d edition, 1804) seek another explanation of the difficulty, by supposing that in ch. xxvii. 13–23
Job reproduces the view of the friends. But in ver. 11 Job
announces the setting forth of his own view ; and the supposition that with זה חלק אדם רשׁע he does not begin the enun-
ciation of his own view, but that of his opponents, is refuted
by the consideration that there is nothing by which he
indicates this, and that he would not enter so earnestly into
the description if it were not the feeling of his heart. Feeling the worthlessness of these attempted solutions, De Wette
(*Einleitung*, § 288), with his customary spirit of criticism
with which he depreciates the sacred writers, turns against
the poet himself. Certainly, says he, the division ch.
xxvii. 11–xxviii. 28 is inappropriate and self-contradictory
in the mouth of Job; but this want of clearness, not to say
inconsistency, must be brought against the poet, who, despite
his utmost endeavour, has not been able to liberate himself
altogether from the influence of the common doctrine of
retribution.

This judgment is erroneous and unjust. Umbreit (2d
edition, S. 261 [Clark's edition, 1836, ii. 122]) correctly
remarks, that "without this apparent contradiction in Job's
speeches, the interchange of words would have been endless ;"
in other words : had Job's standpoint been absolutely immoveable, the controversy could not possibly have come to a
well-adjusted decision, which the poet must have planned,
and which he also really brings about, by causing his hero
still to retain an imperturbable consciousness of his innocence,
but also allowing his irritation to subside, and his extreme
harshness to become moderated. The latter, in reference to

the final destiny of the godless, is already indicated in ch. xxiv., but is still more apparent here in ch. xxvii., and indeed in the following line of thought: "As truly as God lives, who afflicts me, the innocent one, I will not incur the guilt of lying, by allowing myself to be persuaded against my conscience to regard myself as an evil-doer. I am not an evil-doer, but my enemy who regards me and treats me as such must be accounted wicked; for how unlike the hopelessness and estrangement from God, in which the evil-doer dies, is my hope and entreaty in the midst of the heaviest affliction! Yea, indeed, the fate of the evil-doer is a different one from mine. I will teach it you; ye have all, indeed, observed it for yourselves, and nevertheless ye cherish such vain thoughts concerning me." What is peculiar in the description that then follows—a description agreeing in its substance with that of the three, and similar in its form—is therefore this, that Job holds up the end of the evil-doer before the friends, that from it they may infer that *he is not an evil-doer*, whereas the friends held it up before Job that he might infer from it that *he is an evil-doer*, and only by a penitent acknowledgment of this can he escape the extreme of the punishment he has merited. Thus in ch. xxvii. Job turns their own weapon against the friends.

But does he not, by doing so, fall into contradiction with himself? Yes; and yet not so. The Job who has become calmer here comes into contradiction with the impassioned Job who had, without modification, placed the exceptional cases in opposition to the exclusive assertion that the evil-doer comes to a fearful end, which the friends advance, as if it were the rule that the prosperity of the evil-doer continues uninterrupted to the very end of his days. But Job does not come into collision with his true view. For how could he deny that in the rule the retributive justice of God is manifest in the case of the evil-doer! We can only perceive his true opinion when we compare the views he here expresses with his earlier extreme antitheses: hitherto, in the heat of the controversy, he has opposed that which the friends one-sidedly maintained by the direct opposite; now he has got upon the right track of thought, in which the fate of the evil-doer presents itself to him from another and hitherto mistaken side,—a phase which is also but imperfectly appre-ciated in ch. xxiv.; so that now at last he involuntarily does justice to what truth there is in the assertion of his opponent. Nevertheless, it is not Job's intention to correct himself here, and to make an admission to the friends which has hitherto been refused. Hirzel's explanation of this part inclines too much to this erroneous standpoint. On the contrary, our rendering accords with that of Ewald, who observes (S. 252 f. 2d edition, 1854) that Job here maintains *in his own favour*, and against them, what the friends directed *against* him, since the hope of not experiencing such an evil-doer's fate becomes strong in him: "Job is here on the right track for more confidently anticipating his own rescue, or, what is the same thing, the impossibility of his perishing just as if he were an evil-doer." Moreover, how well designed is it that the descrip-tion vers. 13 sqq. is put into Job's mouth! While the poet allows the friends designedly to interweave lines taken from Job's misfortunes into their descriptions of the evil-doer's fate, in Job's description not one single line is found which coincides with his own lot, whether with that which he has already experienced, or even with that which his faith pre-sents to him as in prospect. And although the heavy lot which has befallen him looks like the punitive suffering of the evil-doer, he cannot acknowledge it as such, and even denies its bearing the marks of such a character, since even in the midst of affliction he clings to God, and confidently hopes for His vindication. With this rendering of ch. xxvii. 13 sqq. all doubts of its genuineness, which is indeed admitted by all modern expositors, vanish; and, far from charging the poet with inconsistency, one is led to admire the undiminished skill with which he brings the idea of the drama by concealed ways to its goal.

But the question still comes up, whether ch. xxviii. 1, opening with כִּי, does not militate against this genuineness. Hirzel and others observe, that this כִּי introduces the confirmation of ch. xxvii. 12*b*: " But wherefore then do ye cherish such vain imaginations concerning me ? For human sagacity and perseverance can accomplish much, but the depths of divine wisdom are impenetrable to man." But how is it possible that the כִּי, ch. xxviii. 1, should introduce the confirmation of ch. xxvii. 12*b*, passing over ch. xxvii. 13–23 ? If it cannot be explained in any other way, it appears that ch. xxvii. 13–23 must be rejected. There is the same difficulty in comprehending it by supplying some suppressed thought, as *e.g.* Ewald explains it: *For*, as there may also be much in the divine dealings that is dark, etc.; and Hahn : Because evil-doers perish according to their desert, it does not necessarily follow that every one who perishes is an evil-doer, and that every prosperous person is godly, *for*—the wisdom of God is unsearchable. This mode of explanation, which supposes, between the close of ch. xxvii. and the beginning of ch. xxviii., what is not found there, is manifestly forced; and in comparison with it, it would be preferable, with Stickel, to translate כִּי " because," and take ch. xxviii. 1, 2 as the antecedent to ver. 3. Then after ch. xxvii. a dash might be made; but this dash would indicate an ugly blank, which would be no honour to the poet. Schlottmann explains it more satisfactorily. He takes ch. xxvii. 13 sqq. as a warning addressed to the friends, lest they bring down upon themselves, by their unjust judgment, the evil-doer's punishment which they have so often proclaimed. If this rendering of ch. xxvii. 13 sqq. were correct, the description of the fate of the evil-doer would be influenced by an underlying thought, to which the following statement of the exalted nature of the divine wisdom would be suitably connected as a confirmation. We cannot, however, consider this rendering as correct. The picture ought to have been differently drawn, if it had been designed to serve as a warning to the friends.

It has a different design. Job depicts the revelation of the divine justice which is exhibited in the issue of the life of the evil doer, to teach the friends that they judge him and his lot falsely. To this description of punishment, which is intended thus and not otherwise, ch. xxviii. with its confirmatory כי must be rightly connected. If this were not feasible, one would be disposed, with Pareau, to alter the position of ch. xxviii., as if it were removed from its right place, and put it after ch. xxvi. But we are cautioned against such a violent measure, by the consideration that it is not evident from ch. xxvi. why the course of thought in ch. xxviii., which begins with כי, should assume the exact form in which we find it; whereas, on the other hand, it was said in ch. xxvii. that the ungodly heaps up silver, כסף, like dust, but that the innocent who live to see his fall divide this silver, כסף, among themselves; so that when in ch. xxviii. 1 it continues : כי יש לכסף מוצא, there is a connection of thought for which the way has been previously prepared.

If we further take into consideration the fact of ch. xxviii. being only an amplification of the one closing thought to which everything tends, viz. that the fear of God is man's true wisdom, then ch. xxviii., also in reference to this its special point, is suitably attached to the description of the evil-doer's fate, ch. xxvii. 13 sqq. The miserable end of the ungodly is confirmed by this, that the wisdom of man, which he has despised, consists in the fear of God; and Job thereby at the same time attains the special aim of his teaching, which is announced at ch. xxvii. 11 by אורה אתכם ביד־אל: viz. he has at the same time proved that he who retains the

fear of God in the midst of his sufferings, though those sufferings are an insoluble mystery, cannot be a רשׁע. This design
of the confirmation, and that connection of thought, which
should be well noted, prove that ch. xxviii. stands in its original
position. And if we ponder the fact, that Job has depicted
the ungodly as a covetous rich man who is snatched away by
sudden death from his immense possession of silver and other
costly treasures, we see that ch. xxviii. confirms the preceding
picture of punitive judgment in the following manner: silver
and other precious metals come out of the earth, but wisdom,
whose value exceeds all these earthly treasures, is to be found
nowhere within the province of the creature; God alone possesses it, and from God alone it comes; and so as man can
and is to attain to it, it consists in the fear of the LORD, and
the forsaking of evil. This is the close connection of ch.
xxviii. with what immediately precedes, which most expositors
since Schultens have missed, by transferring the central point
to the unsearchableness of the divine wisdom which rules in
the world; whereas Bouiller correctly observes that the whole
of ch. xxviii. treats not so much of the wisdom of God as of
the wisdom of man, which God, the sole possessor of wisdom,
imparts to him: *omnibus divitiis, fluxis et evanidis illis possessio
præponderat sapientiæ, quæ in pio Dei cultu et fuga mali est
posita.* The view of von Hofmann (*Schriftbeweis,* i. 96, 2d
edit.) accords with this: "If ch. xxviii. 1, where a confirmatory
or explanatory כִּי forms the transition, is taken together with
xxviii. 12, where another part of the speech is introduced with
a *Waw*, and finally with ch. xxviii. 28, where this is rounded
off, as forming the unity of one thought: it thus proves that
the final destruction of the godless, who is happy and prosperous in worldly things, is explained by the fact that man can
obtain every kind of hidden riches by his own exertion and
courage, but not the wisdom which is not indigenous to this
outward world, but is known to God alone, and is to be learned

from Him only; and the teaching concerning it is: behold, the fear of God, that is wisdom, and to depart from evil is understanding."

Before we now pass on to the detailed exposition of ch. xxviii., we may perhaps here, without anticipating, put the question, Whence has the poet obtained the knowledge of the different modes of mining operations which is displayed in ch. xxviii. 1 sqq., and which has every appearance of being the result of personal observation? Since, as we have often remarked already, he is well acquainted with Egypt, it is most natural that he derived this his knowledge from Egypt and the Sinaitic peninsula. The ruins of mines found there show that the Sinaitic peninsula has been worked as a mining district from the earliest times. The first of these mining districts is the *Wadi Nasb*, where Lepsius (*Briefe*, S. 338) found traces of old smelting-places, and where also Graul and his companions, having their attention drawn to it by Wilkinson's work, searched for the remains of a mine, and found at least traces of copper slag, but could see nothing more (*Reise*, ii. 202). E. Rüppell explored the spot at the desire of the Viceroy Mehemed Ali, and Russegger with less successful result (*vid.* the particulars in Ritter's *Erdkunde*, xiv. 784–788).[1] A second mining district is denoted by the ruins of a temple of *Hathor*, on the steep terrace of the rising

---

[1] The valley is not called *Wadi nahas* (Copper valley), which is only a supposition of Rüppell, but *Wadi nasb*, نصب, which, according to Reinaud, signifies valley of statues or columns. Thirty hours' journey from Suez, says a connoisseur in the *Historisch-politische Blätter*, 1863, S. 802 f., lies the *Wadi nesb* [a pronunciation which assumes the form of writing نسب]; it is rare that the ore is so easy to get, and found in such abundance, for the blocks containing the copper are in many places 200 feet in diameter, and the ore is almost in a pure state. The mineral (the black earth containing the copper) abounds in the metal. . . . . Besides this, iron-ore, manganese, carbonate of lead, and also the exceeding precious cinnabar, have been discovered on Sinai.

ground *Sarbut* (*Serâbît*) *el-châdim,* which stretches out into
a spacious valley. This field of ruins, with its many lofty
columns within the still recognisable area of a temple, and
round about it, gives the impression of a large burying-ground,
and it is described and represented as such by Carsten Niebuhr
(*Reise,* 235, Tafel xliv.). In February 1854, Graul (*Reise,*
ii. 203) and Tischendorf spent a short time upon this eminence
of the desert, which is hard to climb, and abounds in monuments. It produced a strong impression upon us—says the
latter (*Aus dem heiligen Lande,* S. 35)—as we tarried in the
midst of the grotesque forms of these monuments, while the
setting sun cast its deep red gleam over the wild terrific-
looking copper rocks that lay around in their varied shades,
now light, now dark. That these copper rocks were worked
in ancient days, is proved by the large black heaps of slag
which Lepsius (*Briefe,* S. 338) discovered to the east and
west of the temple. Moreover, in the inscriptions *Hathor*
bears the by-name "Queen of *Mafkat,*" *i.e.* the copper country
(*mafka,* copper, with the feminine post-positive article *t*). It
even bears this name on the monuments in the *Wadi maghâra,*
one of the side-gorges of the *Wadi mucatteb* (*i.e.* the Written
Valley, valley full of inscriptions). These signs of another
ancient mining colony belong almost entirely to the earliest
Egyptian antiquity, while those on *Sarbut el-châdim* extend
back only to *Amenemha* III., consequently to the last dynasty
of the old kingdom. Even the second king of the fifth
dynasty, *Snefru,* and indeed his predecessor (according to
Lepsius, his successor) *Chufu*—that Χέοψ who built the
largest pyramid—appear here as conquerors of foreign peoples,
and the mountainous district dedicated to *Hathor* is also
called *Mafka·t.* The remains of a mine, discovered by J.
Wilson, at the eastern end of the north side of the *Wadi
mucatteb,* also belongs to this copper country : they lie near
the road, but in back gorges; there is a very high wall of

rock of granite or porphyry, which is penetrated by dark seams of metal, which have been worked out from above downwards, thus forming artificial caverns, pits, and shafts; and it may be inferred that the yield of ore was very abundant, and, from the simplicity of the manner of working, that it is of very great antiquity. This art of mining thus laid open, as Ritter says,[1] furnishes the most important explanation of Job's remarkable description of mining operations.

As to Egypt itself, it has but few places where iron-ore was obtained, and it was not very plentiful, as iron occurs much more rarely than bronze on the tombs, although Wilkinson has observed important copper mines almost as extensive as the copper country of Sinai: we only, however, possess more exact information concerning the gold mines on the borders of Upper Egypt. Agatharchides mentions them in his *Periplus;* and Diodorus (iii. 11 sqq.) gives a minute description of them, from which it is evident that mining in those days was much the same as it was with us about a hundred years ago: we recognise in it the day and night relays, the structure of shafts, the crushing and washing apparatus, and the smelting-place.[2] There are the gold mines of Nubia, the name of which signifies the gold country, for *NOYB* is the old Egyptian name for gold. From the time of *Sethoshi* I., the father of *Sesostris*, we still possess the plan of a gold mine, which Birch (*Upon a historical tablet of Rameses* II. *of the* XIX. *dynasty, relating to the gold mines of Æthiopia*) has first of all correctly determined. Moreover, on monuments of all ages frequent mention is made of other metals (silver, iron, lead), as of precious stones, with which *e.g.* harps were ornamented; the diamond can also be

---

[1] In the essay on the Sinaitic peninsula in *Piper's Ev. Jahrbuch*, 1852. The mining district that J. Wilson saw (1843–44) is not one that was unknown up to that time, but one of the places of the *Wadi maghâra* recognised as favouring the ancient Egyptian system of excavation.

[2] Thus Klemm, *Allgem. Cultur-Geschichte*, v. 304.

traced. In the *Papyrus Prisse,* which Chabas has worked up under the title *Le plus ancien livre du monde, Phtha-hotep,* the author of this moral tractate, iv. 14, says : " Esteem my good word more highly than the (green) emerald, which is found by slaves under the pebbles." [1] The emerald-hills near Berenice produced the emerald.

But if the scene of the book of Job is to be sought in Idumæa proper ('Gebal) or in Hauran,. there were certainly mines that were nearer than the Egyptian. In *Phunon* (*Phinon*), between Petra and Zoar, there were pits from which copper (χαλκοῦ μέταλλα, *æris metalla*) was obtained even to the time of Moses, as may be inferred from the fact of Moses having erected the brazen serpent there (Num. xxi. 9 sq., comp. xxxiii. 42 sq.), and whither, during the persecutions of the Christians in the time of the emperors, many witnesses for the faith were banished, that they might fall victims to the destructive labour of pit life (Athanasius extravagantly says : ἔνθα καὶ φονεὺς καταδικαζόμενος ὀλίγας ἡμέρας μόγις δύναται ζῆσαι).[2] But Edrîsi also knew of gold and silver mines in the mountains of Edom, the *'Gebel esh-Sherâ* (الشرى), *i.e.* הַר שֵׂעִיר. According to the *Onomasticon,* דִּי זָהָב, Deut. i. 1 (LXX. καταχρύσεα), indicates such gold mines in Arabia Petræa ; and Jerome (under *Cata ta chrysea* [3]) observes on that passage : *sed et metallo æris Phæno, quod nostro tempore corruit, montes venarum auri plenos olim fuisse vicinos existimant.* Eupolemus' account (in Euseb. *præp.* ix. 30) of an island Οὐρφῆ, rich in gold, in

---

[1] According to a contribution from Prof. Lauth of Munich.

[2] *Vid. Genesis,* S. 512 ; Ritter, *Erdkunde,* xiv. 125–127 ; as also my *Kirchliches Chronikon des peträischen Arabiens* in the *Luth. Zeitschr.* 1840, S. 133.

[3] *Opp. ed. Vallarsi,* iii. 183. The text of Eusebius is to be amended according to that of Jerome ; *vid.* Ugolini, *Thes.* vol. v. col. cxix. sq. What Ritter says, *Erdkunde,* xiv. 127, is disfigured by mischievous mistakes.

the Red Sea, does not belong here; for by the red sea, ἐρυθρὰ θάλασσα,[1] it is not the Arabian Gulf that is meant; and the reference of the name of the range of hills *Telûl ed-dhahab* in ancient Gilead to gold mines rests only on hearsay up to the present time. But it is all the more worthy of mention that traces of former copper mines are still found on the Lebanon (*vid.* Knobel on Deut. viii. 9); that Edrîsi (*Syria,* ed. *Rosenm.* p. 12) was acquainted with the existence of a rich iron mine near Beirut; and that, even in the present day, the Jews who dwell in *Deir el-kamar,* on the Lebanon, work the iron on leases, and especially forge horse-shoes from it, which are sent all over Palestine.[2]

The poet of the book of Job might therefore have learned mining in its diversified modes of operation from his own observation, both in the kingdom of Egypt, which he had doubtless visited, and also in Arabia Petræa and in the Lebanon districts, so as to be able to put a description of them into the mouth of his hero. It is unnecessary, with Stickel, to give the preference to the mining of Arabia proper, where iron and lead are still obtained, and where, according to ancient testimony, even gold is said to have been worked at one time. " Since he places his hero in the country east of Jordan, the poet may in ver. 2 have thought chiefly of the mines of the Iron mountain (τὸ σιδηροῦν καλούμενον ὄρος, Jos. *Bell.* iv. 8, 2), which is also called the 'cross mountain,' *el-mi῾râd,* because it runs from west to east, while the *Gebel ῾Aglûn* stretches from north to south. It lies between the gorges of the *Wâdî Zerkâ* and *Wâdî ῾Arabûn,* begins at the mouths of the two *Wâdîs* in the *Ghôr,* and ends in the east with a precipitous descent towards the town of *Gerash,* which from its

---

[1] On the meaning of this appellation, *vid. Genesis,* S. 630.

[2] Schwarz, *Das h. Land* (1852), S. 323. The Egyptian monuments mention a district by the name of *Asj,* which paid native iron as tribute; *vid.* Brugsch, *Geogr. der Nachbarländer Ægyptens,* S. 52.

height, and being seen from afar, is called the *Negde* (נֶגְדָּה).
The ancient worked-out iron mines lie on the south declivity
of the mountain south-west of the village of *Burmâ*, and
about six miles from the level bed of the *Wâdî Zerkâ.* The
material is a brittle, red, brown, and violet sandstone, which
has a strong addition of iron. It also contains here and there
a large number of small shells, where it is then considerably
harder. Of these ancient mines, some which were known in
Syria under the name of the 'rose mines,' *maʿâdin el-ward,*
were worked by Ibrahim Pasha from 1835 till 1839; but
when, in 1840, Syria reverted to Turkey, this mining, which
had been carried on with great success, because there was an
abundance of wood for the smelting furnaces, ceased. A
large forest, without a proprietor, covers the back and the
whole north side of this mountain down to the bed of the
Wâdî ʿArabûn; and as no tree has been cut down in it for
centuries, the thicket, with the fallen and decaying stems,
gives one an idea of a primeval forest. We passed through
the forest from *Kefrengi* to *Burmâ* in June 1860. Except
North Gilead, in which the Iron mountain is situated, no
other province of *Basan* admits of a mine; they are exclusively volcanic, their mountains are slag, lava, and basalt;
and probably the last-mentioned kind of stone owes its name
to the word Βασάλτις, the secondary form of Βασάντις
(= *Basan*)."—WETZST.

Ch. xxviii. 1 *For there is a mine for the silver,*
    And a place for gold which they fine.
        2 *Iron is taken out of the dust,*
    And he poureth forth stone as copper.
        3 *He hath made an end of darkness,*
    And he searcheth all extremities
    For the stone of darkness and of the shadow of
        death.

4 *He breaketh away a shaft from those who tarry above :*
There, forgotten by every foot,
They hang and swing far from men.[1]

According to the most natural connection demonstrated by
us, Job desires to show that the final lot of the rich man is
well merited, because the treasures which he made the object
of his avarice and pride, though ever so costly, are still
earthy in their nature and origin. Therefore he begins with
the most precious metals, with silver, which has the precedence in reference to ch. xxvii. 16 sq., and with gold. מוֹצָא
without any secondary notion of fulness (Schultens) signifies
the issuing place, *i.e.* the place from which anything naturally
comes forth (ch. xxxviii. 27), or whence it is obtained (1 Kings
x. 28) ; here in the latter sense of the place where a mineral
is found, or the mine, as the parall. מָקוֹם, the place where the
gold comes forth, therefore a gold mine. According to the
accentuation (*Rebia mugrasch, Mercha, Silluk*), it is not to be
translated : and a place for the gold where they refine it ; but :
a place for the gold which they refine. זָקַק, to strain, filter,
is the technical expression for purifying the precious metals
from the rock that is mingled with them (Mal. iii. 3) by
washing. The pure gold or silver thus obtained is called
מְזֻקָּק (Ps. xii. 7 ; 1 Chron. xxviii. 18, xxix. 4). Diodorus, in
his description of mining in Upper Egypt (iii. 11 sqq.), after
having described the operation of crushing the stone to small

---

[1] Among the expositors of this and the two following strophes, are two
acquainted with mining : The director of mines, von Veltheim, whose
observations J. D. Michaelis has contributed in the *Orient. u. exeg.
Bibliothek*, xxiii. 7–17 ; and the inspector of mines, Rudolf Nasse, in
Studien und Krit. 1863, 105–111. Umbreit's Commentary contains some
observations by von Leonhard ; he understands ver. 4*c* as referring to
the descent upon a cross bar attached to a rope, ver. 5*b* of the lighting
up by burning poles, ver. 6 of the lapis lazuli, and ver. 10*a* of the earliest
mode of " letting off the water."

fragments,[1] proceeds: "Then artificers take the crushed stone and lay it on a broad table, which is slightly inclined, and pour water over it; this washes away the earthy parts, and the gold remains on the slab. This operation is repeated several times, the mass being at first gently rubbed with the hand; then they press it lightly with thin sponges, and thus draw off all that is earthy and light, so that the gold dust is left quite clean. And, finally, other artificers take it up in a mass, shake it in an earthen crucible, and add a proportionate quantity of lead, grains of salt, and a little tin and barley bran; they then place a close-fitting cover over the crucible, and cement it with clay, and leave it five days and nights to seethe constantly in the furnace. After this they allow it to cool, and then finding nothing of the flux in the crucible, they take the pure gold out with only slight diminution." The expression for the first of these operations, the separation of the gold from the quartz by washing, or indeed sifting (straining, *Seihen*), is זָקַק; and for the other, the separation by exposure to heat, or smelting, is צָרַף.

Ver. 2. From the mention of silver and gold, the description passes on to iron and ore (copper, *cuprum = æs Cyprium*). Iron is called בַּרְזֶל, not with the noun-ending *el* like כַּרְמֶל (thus Ges., Olsh., and others), but probably expanded from בֻּזֶל (Fürst), like שַׁרְבִּיט from שַׁבִּיט = שֶׁבֶט, סַמְפִּיר from סַפִּיר, βάλσαμον from בֶּשֶׂם, since, as Pliny testifies, the name of basalt (iron-marble) and iron are related,[2] and copper is called נְחֹשֶׁת,

---

[1] *Vid.* the whole account skilfully translated in Klemm's *Allgem. Cultur-Geschichte*, v. 503 f.

[2] *Hist. nat.* xxxvi. 7, 11 : *Invenit eadem Ægyptus in Æthiopia quem vocant basalten (basaniten) ferrei coloris atque duritiæ, unde et nomen ei dedit* (*vid.* von Raumer, *Palästina*, S. 96, 4th edition). Neither Seetzen nor Wetzstein has found proper iron-ore in Basan. Basalt is all the more prevalent there, from which Basan may have its name. For there is no special Semitic word for basalt ; Bocthor calls in the aid of نوع رخام أسود, "a kind of black marble ;" but, as Wetzstein informs me, this is

for which the book of Job (ch. xx. 24, xxviii. 2, xl. 18, xli. 19; comp. even Lev. xxvi. 19) always has נְחוּשָׁה (æreum = æs, Arab. *nuhás*). Of the iron it is said that it is procured from the עָפָר, by which the bowels of the earth are meant here, as the surface of the earth in ch. xli. 25; and of copper it is said that they pour out the stone into copper (*vid.* Ges. § 139, 2), *i.e.* smelt copper from it: יָצוּק as ch. xxix. 6, *fundit*, here with a subj. of the most general kind: one pours; on the contrary, ch. xli. 15 sq. *partic.* of יָצַק. Ver. 3 distinctly shows that it is the bowels of the earth from which these metals are obtained: he (man) has made an end of the darkness, since he turns out and lights up the lightless interior of the earth; and לְכָל־תַּכְלִית, to every extremity, *i.e.* to the remotest depths, he searches out the stone of deep darkness and of the shadow of death, *i.e.* hidden in the deepest darkness, far beneath the surface of the earth (*vid.* on ch. x. 22;

only a translation of the phrase of a French dictionary which he had, for the general name of basalt, at least in Syria, is *hagar aswad* (black stone). Iron is called *hadîd* in Arabic (literally a pointed instrument, with the not infrequent transference of the name of the tool to the material from which it is made). בַּרְזֶל (פרזל) is known in Arabic only in the form *firzil*, as the name for iron chains and great smith's shears for cutting iron; but it is remarkable that in Berber, which is related to Egyptian, iron is called even in the present day *wazzâl; vid. Lex. geographicum* ed. *Juynboll, tom.* iv. (*adnot.*) p. 64, l. 16, and Marcel, *Vocabulaire Français-arabe de dialectes vulgaires africains*, p. 249: " *Fer* حديد, *hadyd* (*en berbere* وزال, *ouezzâl*; اوزال, *ôouzzâl*)." The Coptic name of iron is *benipi* (dialect. *penipe*), according to Prof. Lauth perhaps, as also *barôt*, ore, connected with *ba*, the hieroglyph name of a very hard mineral; the black basalt of an obelisk in the British Museum is called *bechenen* in the inscription. If it really be so, that iron and basalt are homonymous in Semitic, the reason could only be sought for in the dark iron-black colour of basalt, in its hardness, and perhaps also its weight (which, however, is only about half the specific gravity of pure iron), not in the magnetic iron, which has only in more modern times been discovered to be a substantial component part of basalt, the grains of which cannot be seen by the naked eye, and are only detected with the magnetic needle, or by chemical analysis.

and comp. Pliny, *h. n.* xxxiii. *prooem.* of mining: *imus in viscera ejus [terrœ] et in sede Manium opes quœrimus).* Most expositors (Hirz., Ew., Hahn, Schlottm., and others) take לְבָל־תַּכְלִית adverbially, " to the utmost" or "most closely," but *vid.* on ch. xxvi. 10; לְתַכְלִית might be used thus adverbially, but לְבָל־תַּכְלִית is to be explained according to לְבָל־רוּחַ, Ezek. v. 10 (to all the winds).

Ver. 4. Job now describes the operation of mining more minutely; and it is worthy of observation that the last-mentioned metal, with which the description is closely connected, is copper. נַחַל, which signifies elsewhere a valley, the bed of a river, and the river itself, like the Arab. وَاٍل (not from נָחַל = נָהַל, to flow on, as Ges. *Thes.* and Fürst, but from נַחַל, root חל to hollow, whence נְחִילָה = חָלִיל, a flute, as being a hollowed musical instrument), signifies here the excavation made in the earth, and in fact, as what follows shows, in a perpendicular direction, therefore the shaft. Nasse contends for the signification " valley," by which one might very well conceive of "the working of a surface vein:" " By this mode of working, a small shaft is made in the vein (consequently in a perpendicular direction), and the ore is worked from both sides at once. At a short distance from the first shaft a second is formed, and worked in the same way. Since thus the work progresses lengthwise, a cutting becomes formed in the mountain which may well be compared to a deep valley, if, as is generally the case where the stone is firm and the ways are almost perpendicular, the space that is hewn out remains open (that is, not broken in or filled in)." But if נחל everywhere else denotes a valley with its watercourse, it has not necessarily a like signification in mining technology. It signifies, perhaps not without reference to its usual signification, the shafts open above and surrounded by walls of rock (in distinction from the more or less horizontal galleries or pit-ways, as they were cut through the excavated rocks in the gold mines of Upper Egypt, often so crooked that, as Diodorus relates, the miners, provided with lights on their forehead, were always obliged to vary the posture of the body according to the windings of the galleries) ; and מֵעִם־גָּר, away from him who remains above, shows that one is to imagine these shafts as being of considerable depth ; but what follows even more clearly indicates this : there forgotten (הַנִּשְׁכָּחִים with the demonstrative *art.* as ch. xxvi. 5, Ps. xviii. 31, xix. 11, Ges. § 109 *ad init.*) of (every) foot (that walks above), they hang (comp. Rabb. מְדֻלְדָּל, *pendulus*[1]) far from men, hang and swing or are suspended ; comp. Pliny, *h. n.* xxxiii. 4, 21, according to Sillig's text : *is qui cædit funibus pendet, ut procul intuenti species ne ferarum quidem sed alitum fiat. Pendentes majori ex parte librant et linias itineri præducunt.* דָּלַל has here the primary signification proper also to the Arab. دَلّ,

deorsum pendēre; and נוּעַ is related to נוּד, as *nuere, νεύειν,* to *nutare.* The מִנִּי of מִנִּי־רָגֶל, taken strictly, does not correspond to the Greek ὑπό, neither does it form an adverbial secondary definition standing by itself : far away from the foot ; but it is to be understood, as מִן is also used elsewhere after נִשְׁכַּח, Deut. xxxi. 21, Ps. xxxi. 13 : forgotten out of the mouth, out of the heart ; here : forgotten away from the foot, so that this advances without knowing that there is a man beneath ; therefore : totally vanished from the remembrance of those who pass by above. מֵאֱנוֹשׁ is not to be connected with נָעוּ (Hahn, Schlottm.), but with דַּלּוּ, for *Munach* is the representative of *Rebia mugrasch,* according to *Psalter,* ii. 503, § 2 ; and דלו is regularly *Milel,* whereas Isa. xxxviii. 14 is *Milra*

---

[1] *Vid.* Luzzatto on Isa. xviii. 5, where זַלְזַלִּים, of the trembling and quivering twigs, is correctly traced to דָּלַל = זָלַל ; on the other hand, Isa. xiv. 19, אַבְנֵי־בוֹר is wrongly translated *fundo della fossa,* by comparison with Job xxviii. 3. אֶבֶן does not signify a shaft, still less the lowest shaft, but stone (rock).

without any evident reason. The accentuation here follows no fixed law with equally regulated exceptions (*vid.* Olsh. § 233, *c*).

Moreover, the perception that ver. 4 speaks of the shaft of the mine, and the descent of the miners by a rope, is due to modern exegesis; even Schultens, who here exclaims: *Cimmeriæ tenebræ, quas me exsuperaturum vix sperare ausim,* perceived the right thing, but only imperfectly as yet. By נחל he understands the course or vein of the metal, where it is embedded; and, since he understands גר after the Arab. *'garr,* foot of the mountain, he translates: *rumpit (homo) alveum de pede montis.* Rosenm., on the other hand, correctly translates: *canalem deorsum actum ex loco quo versatur homo.* Schlottm. understands by גר the miner himself dwelling as a stranger in his loneliness; and if we imagine to ourselves the mining districts of the peninsula of Sinai, we might certainly at once conceive the miners' dwellings themselves which are found in the neighbourhood of the shaft in connection with מעם־גר. But in and for itself גר signifies only those settled (above), without the secondary idea of strangers.

5 *The earth—from it cometh forth bread,*
  And beneath it is turned up like fire.
6 *The place of the sapphire are its stones,*
  And it containeth gold ore.
7 *The way, that no bird of prey knoweth,*
  And the eye of the hawk hath not gazed at,
8 *Which the proud beast of prey hath not trodden,*
  Over which the lion hath not walked.

Ver. 5 is not to be construed as Rosenm.: *ad terram quod attinet, ex qua egreditur panis, quod subtus est subvertitur quasi igne;* nor with Schlottm.: (they swing) in the earth, out of which comes bread, which beneath one turns about with fire;

for ver. 5a is not formed so that the *Waw* of וְתַחְתֶּיהָ could be *Waw apod.*, and אֶרֶץ cannot signify "in the interior of the earth" as *locativus;* on the contrary, it stands in opposition to תחתיה, that which is beneath the earth, as denoting the surface of the earth (the proper name of which is אֲדָמָה, from the root דם, with the primary notion of a flat covering). They are two grammatically independent predicates, the first of which is only the foil of the other: the earth, out of it cometh forth bread (לֶחֶם as Ps. civ. 14), and beneath it (the surface of the earth) = that which lies beneath it (ותחתיה only virtually a subj. in the sense of וְתַחְתִּיּתֶיהָ, since תַּחְתֵּי occurs only as a preposition), is turned about (comp. the construction of the *sing.* of the verb with the *plur.* subj., ch. xxx. 15) as (by) fire (*instar ignis, scil. subvertentis*) ; *i.e.* the earth above furnishes nourishment to man, but that not satisfying him, he also digs out its inward parts (comp. Pliny, *h. n.* xxxiii. *proœm.: in sede Manium opes quærimus, tanquam parum benigna fertilique quaqua calcatur*), since this is turned or tossed about (comp. מַהְפֵּכָה, the special word for the overthrow of Sodom by fire) by mining work, as when fire breaks out in a house, or even as when a volcanic fire rumbles within a mountain (Castalio: *agunt per magna spatia cuniculos et terram subeunt non secus ac ignis facet ut in Ætna et Vesuvio*). The reading במו (Schlottm.) instead of כמו is natural, since fire is really used to blast the rock, and to separate the ore from the stone ; but, with the exception of Jerome, who has arbitrarily altered the text (*terra, de qua oriebatur panis in loco suo, igni subversa est*), all the old translations reproduce כמו, which even Nasse, in opposition to von Veltheim, thinks suitable: Man's restless search, which rummages everything through, is compared to the unrestrainable ravaging fire.

Ver. 6 also consists of two grammatically independent assertions: the place (bed) of the sapphire is its rock. Must we refer לו to סַפִּיר, and translate: "and it contains fine dust

of gold" (Hirz., Umbr., Stick., Nasse)? It is possible, for
Theophrastus (p. 692, *ed. Schneider*) says of the sapphire it
is ὥσπερ χρυσόπαστος, as it were covered with gold dust or
grains of gold; and Pliny, *h. n.* xxxvii. 9, 38 sq.: *Inest ei
(cyano) aliquando et aureus pulvis qualis in sapphiris, in iis
enim aurum punctis conlucet,* which nevertheless does not hold
good of the proper sapphire, but of the azure stone (*lapis
lazuli*) which is confounded with it, a variegated species of
which, with gold, or rather with iron pyrites glittering like
gold, is specially valued.[1] But Schultens rightly observes:
*vix crediderim, illum auratilem pulvisculum sapphiri peculiari
mentione dignum;* and Schlottm.: such a collateral definition
to ספיר, expressed in a special clause (not a relative one), has
something awkward about it. On the other hand, עֲפְרֹת זָהָב
is a perfectly suitable appellation of gold ore. "The earth,
which is in itself black," says Diodorus in the passage quoted
before, "is interspersed with veins of marble, which is of such
pre-eminent whiteness, that its brilliance surpasses everything
that glitters, and from it the overseers of the mine prepare
gold with a large number of workmen." And further on, of
the heating of this gold ore he says: "the hardest auriferous
earth they burn thoroughly in a large fire; thus they make it
soft, so that it can be worked by the hand." עפרת זהב is a
still more suitable expression for such auriferous earth and
ore than for the nuggets of ἄπυρος χρυσός (*i.e.* unsmelted)
of the size of a chestnut, which, according to Diodorus, ii. 50,
are obtained in mines in Arabia (μεταλλεύεται). But it is
inadmissible to refer לוֹ to man, for the clause would then
require to be translated: and gold ore is to him = he has,
while it is the rather intended to be said that the interior of
the earth has gold ore. לוֹ is therefore, with Hahn and
Schlottm., to be referred to מָקוֹם: and this place of the

---

[1] Comp. Quenstedt, *Handbuch der Mineralogie* (1863), S. 355 and
302.

sapphire, it contains gold. The poet might have written לָהּ, but לֹ implies that where the sapphire is found, gold is also found. The following נָתִיב (with *Dechî*), together with the following relative clause, is connected with אֲבָנֶיהָ, or even with מָקוֹם, which through ver. 6*b* is become the chief subj. : the place of the sapphire and of the gold is the rock of the bowels of the earth,—a way, which, etc., *i.e.* such a place is the interior of the earth, accessible to no living being of the earth's surface except to man alone. The sight of the bird of prey, the עַיִט, ἀετός, and of the אַיָּה, *i.e.* the hawk or kite, reaches from above far and wide beneath;[1] the sons of pride, שָׁחַץ (also Talmud. arrogance, *ferocia*, from שָׁחַץ = شَخَصَ, to raise one's self, not : fatness, as Meier, after شَخُصَ, to be fat, thick), *i.e.* the beasts of prey, especially the lion, שַׁחַל (*vid.* on ch. iv. 10, from שַׁחַל, سَحَلَ, to roar, Arab. of the ass, comp. the Lat. *rudere* used both of the lion and of the ass), seek the most secret retreat, and shun no danger ; but the way by which man presses forward to the treasures of the earth is imperceptible and inaccessible to them.

> 9 *He layeth his hand upon the pebbles ;*
> *He turneth up the mountains from the root.*
> 10 *He cutteth canals through the rocks ;*
> *And his eye seeth all kinds of precious things.*
> 11 *That they may not leak, he dammeth up rivers ;*
> *And that which is hidden he bringeth to light.*
> 12 *But wisdom, whence is it obtained ?*
> *And where is the place of understanding ?*

Beneath, whither no other being of the upper world penetrates, man puts his hand upon the quartz or rock. חַלָּמִישׁ (perhaps from חלם, to be strong, firm ; Arabic, with the re-

---

[1] The אַיָּה—says the Talmud *b. Chullin*, 63*b*—is in Babylon, and seeth a carcase in the land of Israel.

duplication resolved, *chalnubûs*, like עַכָּבִישׁ, Arab. 'ancabûth, vid. *Jesurun*, p. 229) signifies here the quartz, and in general the hard stone ; בְּ יָד שָׁלַח something like our "to take in hand" of an undertaking requiring strong determination and courage, which here consists in blasting and clearing away the rock that contains no ore, as Pliny, *h. n.* xxxiii. 4, 21, describes it: *Occursant . . . silices; hos igne et aceto rumpunt, sæpius vero, quoniam id cuniculos vapore et fumo strangulat, cædunt fractariis CL libras ferri habentibus egeruntque umeris noctibus ac diebus per tenebras proxumis tradentes; lucem novissimi cernunt.* Further : he (man, devoted to mining) overturns (*subvertit* according to the primary signification of הפך, أَفَلَ, أَفَتَ, to turn, twist) mountains from the roots. The accentuation הפך with *Rebia mugrasch*, מִשֹּׁרֶשׁ with *Mercha*, is false ; it is, according to Codd. and old editions, to be accented הפך with *Tarcha*, מִשֹּׁרֶשׁ with *Munach*, and to be translated accordingly : *subvertit a radice montes* (for *Munach* is the transformation of a *Rebia mugrasch*), not *a radice montium*. Blasting in mining which lays bare the roots (the lowest parts) of the mountains is intended, the conclusion of which—the signal for the flight of the workmen, and the effective crash—is so graphically described by Pliny in the passage cited above : *Peracto opere cervices fornicum ab ultumo cadunt ; dat signum ruina eamque solus intellegit in cacumine ejus montis vigil. Hic voce, nutu evocari jubet operas pariterque ipse devolat. Mons fractus cadit ab sese longe fragore qui concipi humana mente non possit eque efflatu incredibili spectant victores ruinam naturæ.*

The meaning of ver. 10 depends upon the signification of the יְאֹרִים. It is certainly the most natural that it should signify canals. The word is Egyptian ; *aur* in the language of the hieroglyphs signifies a river, and especially the Nile ; wherefore at the close of the Laterculus of Eratosthenes the name of the king, Φρονορῶ (Φονορῶ), is explained by ἤτοι Νεῖλος. If water-canals are intended, they may be either such as go in or come away. In the first case it may mean water let in like a cataract over the ruins of the blasted auriferous rock, the *corrugi* of Pliny : *Alius par labor ac vel majoris impendi : flumina ad lavandam hanc ruinam jugis montium obiter duxere a centesimo plerumque lapide ; corrugos vocant, a corrivatione credo ; mille et hic labores.* But בְּקַע is not a suitable word for such an extensive and powerful flooding with water for the purpose of washing the gold. It suits far better to understand the expression of galleries or ways cut horizontally in the rock to carry the water away. Thus von Veltheim explains it : " The miner makes ways through the hard rock into his section [in which the perpendicular shaft terminates], guides the water which is found in abundance at that depth through it [*i.e.* the water at the bottom of the pit that hinders the progress of the work], and is able [thus ver. 10*b* naturally is connected with what precedes] to judge of the ore and fragments that are at the bottom, and bring them to the light. This mode of mining by constantly forming one gallery under the other [so that a new gallery is made under the pit that is worked out by extending the shaft, and also freeing this from water by making another outlet below the previous one] is the oldest of all, of which anything certain is known in the history of mining, and the most natural in the days when they had no notion of hydraulics." This explanation is far more satisfactory than that of Herm. Sam. Reimarus, of the " Wolfenbütteler Fragmente " (in his edition of the *Neue Erkl. des B. Hiob*, by John Ad. Hoffmann, 1734, iv. S. 772) : " *He breaks open watercourses in the rocks.* What the miners call coming upon water, is when they break into a fissure from which strong streams of water gush forth. The miner not only knows how to turn such water to good account; but it is also a sign that there are rich veins of ore near at hand, as there is the most water by these courses and fissures. Hence follows : *and then his eye sees* *all kinds of precious things.*" But there is no ground for saying that water indicates rich veins of ore, and בקע is much more appropriate to describe the designed formation of courses to carry off the water than an accidental discovery of water in course of the work ; moreover, יארים is as appropriate to the former as it is inappropriate to the latter explanation, for it signifies elsewhere the arms of the Nile, into which the Nile is artificially divided; and therefore it may easily be transferred to the horizontal canals of the mine cut through the hard rock (or through the upper earth). Nevertheless, although the water plays an important part in mining operations, by giving rise to the greatest difficulties, as it frequently happens that a pit is deluged with water, and must be abandoned because no one can get down to it: it is improbable that ver. 10 as well as ver. 11 refers to this; we therefore prefer to understand יְאֹרִים as meaning the (horizontal) courses (galleries or drifts) in which the ore is dug,—a rendering which is all the more possible, since, on the one hand, in Coptic *jaro* (Sahidic *jero*) signifies the Nile of Egypt (*phiaro ente chêmi*); on the other, *ior* (*eioor*) signifies a ditch, διῶρυξ (comp. Isa. xxxiii. 21, יארים, LXX. διώρυχες), vid. Ges. *Thes.* Thus also ver. 10*b* is consistently connected with what precedes, since by cutting these *cuniculi* the courses of the ore (veins), and any precious stones that may also be embedded there, are laid bare.

Ver. 11*a*. Contrary to the correct indication of the accentuation, Hahn translates : he stops up the droppings of the watercourses ; מִבְּכִי has *Dechî*, and is therefore not to be connected with what follows as a genitive. But Reimarus' translation : from the drops he connects the streams, is inadmissible. " The trickling water," he observes, " is carefully caught in channels by the miners for use, and is thus brought together from several parts to the reservoir and the waterwheel. What Pliny calls *corrugus, corrivatio.*" On the contrary, Schlottm. remarks that חבש cannot signify such a connection, *i.e.* gathering together of watercourses; it occurs elsewhere only of uniting, *i.e.* binding up wounds. Nevertheless, although חבש cannot directly signify " to collect," the signification *coercere* (ch. xxxiv. 17), which is not far from this idea,—as is evident from the Arab. حَبْسٌ (حَبَسَ), a dam

or sluice for collecting water, and مَحْبِسُ الماءِ, a reservoir, cistern,—is easily transferable to water, in the sense of binding = catching up and accumulating. But it is contrary to the form of the expression that מבכי, with this use of חבש, should denote the *materia ex qua*, and that נְהָרוֹת should be referred to the miry ditches in which " the crushed ore is washed, for the purpose of separating the good from the worthless." On the contrary, from the form of the expression, it is to be translated: *a fletu* (not *e fletu*) *flumina obligat*, whether it be that *a fletu* is equivalent to *ne flent s. stillent* (Simeon Duran: שלא יזלו), or *obligat* equivalent to *cohibet* (Ralbag: מְהַזְּלָה). Thus von Veltheim explains the passage, since he here, as in ver. 10, understands the channels for carrying off the water. " The miner covers the bottom with mire, and fills up the crevices so exactly [*i.e.* he besmears it, where the channel is broken through, with some water-tight substance, *e.g.* clay], that it may entirely carry off the water that is caught by it out of the pit [in which the shaft terminates], and not let it fall through the fissures [crevices] to the company of miners below [to the vein that lies farther down] ; then the miner can descend still deeper [since the water runs outwards and does not soak through], and bring forth the ore that lies below the channel." This explanation overlooks the fact that יאֹרִים is used in ver. 10, whereas ver. 11 has נהרות. It is not probable that these are only interchangeable expressions for the channels that carry off the water.

יארים is an appropriate expression for it, but not נהרות, which as appropriately describes the conflux of water in the mine itself.

The meaning of ver. 11a is, that he (the miner) binds or stops the watercourses which his working out of the pit has interfered with and injured, so that they may not leak, *i.e.* that they may not in the least ooze through, whether by building up a wall or by collecting the water that streams forth in reservoirs (Arab. *mahbas*) or in the channels which carry it outwards,—all these modes of draining off the water may be included in ver. 11a, only the channel itself is not, with von Veltheim, to be understood by נהרות, but the concourse of the water which, in one way or the other, is rendered harmless to the pit-work, so that he (the miner), as ver. 11b says, can bring to light (לְאֹור = אֹור) whatever precious things the bowels of the earth conceals (תַּעֲלֻמָה, according to Kimchi and others, with euphonic *Mappik*, as according to the Masora כבכורה Isa. xxviii. 4, גֻשְׁמָה Ezek. xxii. 24, and also וגְלָה Zech. iv. 2, only לתפארת הקריאה ולא לבינוי, *i.e.* they have *Mappik* only for euphony, not as the expression of the *suff.*).

With the question in ver. 12 the description of mining attains the end designed : man can search after and find out silver, gold, and other metals and precious stones, by making the foundations of the earth accessible to him ; but wisdom, whence shall he obtain it, and which (וְאֵי־זֶה, according to another reading וְאֵיזֶה) is the place of understanding ? הַחָכְמָה has the *art.* to give prominence to its transcendency over the other attainable things. חכמה is the principal name, and בִּינָה interchanges with it, as תְּבוּנָה, Prov. viii. 1, and other synonyms in which the Chokma literature abounds elsewhere in Prov. i.–ix. בינה is properly the faculty of seeing through that which is distinguishable, consisting of the possession of the right criteria ; חכמה, however, is the perception, in general, of things in their true nature and their final causes.

13 *A mortal knoweth not its price,*
    And it is not found in the land of the living.
14 *The abyss saith : It is not in me,*
    And the sea saith : It is not with me.
15 *Pure gold cannot be given for it,*
    And silver cannot be weighed as its price ;
16 *And it is not outweighed with the fine gold of Ophir,*
    With the precious onyx and the sapphire.

It is self-evident that wisdom is found nowhere directly present and within a limited space, as at the bottom of the sea, and cannot be obtained by a direct exchange by means of earthly treasures. It is, moreover, not this self-evident fact that is denied here; but the meaning is, that even if a man should search in every direction through the land of the living, *i.e.* (as *e.g.* Ps. lii. 7) the world—if he should search through the תְּהוֹם, *i.e.* the subterranean waters that feed the visible waters (*vid.* Gen. xlix. 25)—if he should search through the sea, the largest bounded expanse of this water that wells up from beneath—yea, even if he would offer all riches and precious things to put himself in possession of the means and instruments for the acquirement of wisdom,—wisdom, *i.e.* the profoundest perception of the nature of things, would still be beyond him, and unattainable. עֶרְךְּ, ver. 13, an equivalent (from עָרַךְ, to range beside, to place at the side of), interchanges with מְחִיר (from מָחַר, cogn. מָהַר, מָכַר, *mercari*). סְגוֹר is זְהַב סָגוּר, 1 Kings vi. 20 and freq., which hardly signifies gold shut up = carefully preserved, rather : closed = compressed, unmixed; Targ. דְּהַב סָנִין, *aurum colatum* (*purgatum*). Ewald compares سَجَر, to seethe, heat ; therefore : heated, gained by smelting. On the other hand, כֶּתֶם from כָּתַם, كتم, *occulere*, seems originally to denote that which is precious, then precious gold in particular, LXX. χρυσίῳ Ωφείρ, *Cod.*

Vat. and *Cod. Sinaiticus,* Σωφίρ (Egyptized by prefixing the Egyptian *sa,* part, district, side, whence *e.g. sa-rēs,* the upper country, and *sa-hēt,* the lower country, therefore = *sa-ofir,* land of Ophir). שֹׁהַם is translated here by the LXX. ὄνυξ (elsewhere σαρδόνυξ or σάρδιος), of which Pliny, *h. n.* xxxvii. 6, 24, appealing to Sudines, says, *in gemma esse candorem unguis humani similitudinem;* wherefore Knobel, Rödiger, and others, compare the Arab. ساهم, which, however, does not signify pale, but lean, and parched by the heat, with which, in hot countries at least, not pallor, but, on the contrary, a dark brown-black colour, is identified (Fl.). مسهّم, striped (Mich.), would be more appropriate, since the onyx is marked through by white veins; but this is a *denom.* from *sahm,* a dart, prop. darted, and is therefore wide of the mark. On the etymology of סַפִּיר, *vid. Jesurun,* p. 61. Nevertheless both שהם and סַפִּיר are perhaps foreign names, as the name of the emerald (*vid. ib.* p. 108), which is Indian (Sanskr. *marakata,* or even *marakta*); and, on the other hand, it is called in hieroglyph (determined by the stone) *uot,* the green stone (in Coptic *p. auannēse,* the green colour) (Lauth).

The transcendent excellence of wisdom above the most precious earthly treasures, which the author of the introduction to the book of Proverbs briefly describes, ch. iii. 14 sq., is now drawn out in detail.

> 17   *Gold and glass are not equal to it,*
>   *Nor is it exchanged for jewels of gold.*
> 18   *Pearls and crystal are not to be mentioned,*
>   *And the acquisition of wisdom is beyond corals.*
> 19   *The topaz of Ethiopia is not equal to it,*
>   *It is not outweighed by pure fine gold.*

20 *Whence, then, cometh wisdom,*
    And which is the place of understanding?

Among the separate חפצים, Prov. iii. 15, which are here
detailed, apart from זהב, glass has the transparent name
זכוכית, or, as it is pointed in Codd., in old editions, and by
Kimchi, זכוכית with *Cholem* (in the dialects with ג instead of
כ). Symm. indeed translates crystal, and in fact the ancient
languages have common names for glass and crystal; but the
crystal is here called גָּבִישׁ, which signifies prop., like the Arab.
'gibs, ice; κρύσταλλος also signifies prop. ice, and this only in
Homer, then crystal, exactly as the cognate קֶרַח unites both
significations in itself. The reason of this homonymy lies
deeper than in the outward similarity,—the ancients really
thought the crystal was a product of the cold; Pliny, xxxvii.
2, 9, says: *non alibi certe reperitur quam ubi maxume hibernæ
nives rigent, glaciemque esse certum est, unde nomen Græci
dedere.* The Targ. translates נביש by בֵּירוּלִין, certainly in the
sense of the Arabico-Persic *bullûr* (*bulûr*), which signifies
crystal, or even glass, and moreover is the primary word for
βήρυλλος, although the identical Sanskrit word, according to
the laws of sound, *vaidurja* (Pali, *velurija*), is, according to
the lexicons, a name of the *lapis lazuli* (Persic, *lagurd*).
Of the two words רָאמוֹת and פְּנִינִים, the one appears to mean
pearls and the other corals; the ancient appellations of these
precious things which belong to the sea are also blended; the
Persic *mergân* (Sanskr. *mangara*) unites the signification
pearl and coral in itself. The root פן, فن, which has the

primary notion of pushing, especially of vegetation (whence فَنّ،

a branch, shoot, prop. motion; French, *jet*), and Lam. iv. 7,
where snow and milk, as figures of whiteness (purity), are
placed in contrast with פנינים as a figure of redness, favour
the signification corals for פנינים. The Coptic *b*e*nôni*, which

signifies *gemma,* favours (so far as it may be compared) corals rather than pearls. And the fact that ראמות, Ezek. xxvii. 16, appear as an Aramæan article of commerce in the market of Tyre, is more favourable to the signification pearls than corals; for the Babylonians sailed far into the Indian Ocean, and brought pearls from the fisheries of Bahrein, perhaps even from Ceylon, into the home markets (*vid.* Layard, *New Discoveries,* 536). The name is perhaps, from the Western Asiatic name of the pearl,[1] mutilated and Hebraized.[2]

The name of the פִּטְדָה of Ethiopia appears to be derived from τοπαζ by transposition; Pliny says of the topaz, xxxvii. 8, 32, among other passages: *Juba Topazum insulam in rubro mari a continenti stadiis CCC abesse dicit, nebulosam et ideo quæsitam sæpius navigantibus; ex ea causa nomen accepisse:*

---

[1] *Vid. Zeitschr. für d. Kunde des Morgenlandes,* iv. 40f. The recently attempted explanation of κοράλλιον from גּוֹרָל (to which κλῆρος the rather belongs), in the primary signification *lapillus* (Arab. *'garal*), is without support.

[2] Two reasons for פנינים = pearls (in favour of which Bochart compares the name of the pearl-oyster, πίννα) and ראמות = corals, which are maintained by Carey, are worthy of remark. (1.) That פנינים does not signify corals, he infers from Lam. iv. 7, for the redness of corals cannot be a mark of bodily beauty; "but when I find that there are some pearls of a slightly reddish tinge, then I can understand and appreciate the comparison." (2.) That ראמות signifies corals, is shown by the origin of the word, which properly signifies reêm- (wild oxen) horns, which is favoured by a mention of Pliny, *h. n.* xiii. 51 : (*Tradidere) juncos quoque lapideos perquam similes veris per litora, et in alto quasdam arbusculas colore bubuli cornus ramosas et cacuminibus rubentes.* Although Pliny there speaks of marine petrified plants of the Indian Ocean (not, at least in his sense, of corals), this hint of a possible derivation of ראמות is certainly surprising. But as to Lam. iv. 7, this passage is to be understood according to Cant. v. 10 (my friend is צח ואדום). The white and red are intended to be conceived of as mixed and overlapping one another, as our [Germ.] popular poetry speaks of cheeks which "shine with milk and purple;" and as in Homer, *Il.* iv. 141–146, the colour of the beautifully formed limbs of Menelaus is represented by the figure (which appears hideous to us): ὡς δ' ὅτε τίς τ' ἐλέφαντα γυνὴ Φοίνικι μιήνη (ebony stained with purple).

topazin enim Troglodytarum lingua significationem habere quæ-rendi. This topaz, however, which is said to be named after an island of the same name, the Isle of Serpents in Agathar-chides and Diodorus, is, according to Pliny, yellowish green, and therefore distinct from the otherwise so-called topaz. To make a candid confession, we grope about everywhere in the dark here, and the ancient versions are not able to help us out of our difficulty.[1] The poet lays everything under contribution to illustrate the thought, that the worth of wis-dom exceeds the worth of the most valuable earthly thing; beside which, in מֶשֶׁךְ חָכְמָה מִפְּנִינִים, "the acquisition or posses-sion (from מָשַׁךְ, مسك, to draw to one's self, to take hold of) of wisdom is above corals," there is an indication that, although not by the precious things of the earth, still in some way or other, wisdom can be possessed, so that consequently the question repeated at the end of the strophe will not remain unanswered. This is its meaning: now if wisdom is not to be found in any of the places named, and is not to be attained by any of the means mentioned, whence can man hope to attain it, and whither must he turn to find it? for its exist-ence is certain, and it is an indisputable need of man that he should partake of it.

> 21　*It is veiled from the eyes of all living,*
> 　　*And concealed from the fowls of heaven.*
> 22　*Destruction and death say:*
> 　　*With our ears we heard a report of it.—*
> 23　*Elohim understandeth the way to it,*

---

[1] The Targ. translates שֹׁהַם by בֵּירוּלִין, βήρυλλος; ספיר by שַׁבְזִיזָא (سبج‎, vid. Pott in the *Zeitschr. f. K. d. M.* iv. 275); פַּז by אוֹבְרִיזִין, ὄβρυζον; ראמות by סַנְדַּלְכִין, σανδαράχη, red gold-pigment (vid. Rödiger-Pott, as just quoted, S. 267); נביש again by בֵּירוּלִין in the sense of the Arabico-Persic *bullûr*, Kurd. *bellûr*, crystal; פנינים by מַרְגָּלִין, μαργαρῖται; פטדה by מַרְגְּלָא יְרָקָא (the green pearl); כתם by פְּטָלוֹן (perhaps פְּטָלוֹן, πέταλον, in the sense of *lamina auri*).

> *And He—He knoweth its place.*
> 24 *For He looketh to the ends of the earth,*
> *Under the whole heaven He seeth.*

No living created being (כָּל־חַי, as ch. xii. 10, xxx. 23) is able to answer the question; even the birds that fly aloft, that have keener and farther-seeing eyes than man, can give us no information concerning wisdom ; and the world at least proclaims its existence in a rich variety of its operations, but in the realm of Abaddon and of death below (comp. the combination שְׁאוֹל ואבדון, Prov. xv. 11, ᾅδου καὶ τοῦ θανάτου, Apoc. i. 18) it is known only by an indistinct hearsay, and from confused impressions. Therefore : no creature, whether in the realm of the living or the dead, can help us to get wisdom. There is but One who possesses a perfect knowledge concerning wisdom, namely Elohim, whose gaze extends to the ends of the earth, and who sees under the whole heaven, *i.e.* is everywhere present (תַּחַת, definition of place, not equivalent to אֲשֶׁר תַּחַת; comp. on ch. xxiv. 9*b*), who therefore, after the removal of everything earthly (sub-celestial), alone remains. And why should He with His knowledge, which embraces everything, not also know the way and place of wisdom? Wisdom is indeed the ideal, according to which He has created the world.

> 25 *When He appointed to the wind its weight,*
> *And weighed the water according to a measure,*
> 26 *When He appointed to the rain its law,*
> *And the course to the lightning of the thunder :*
> 27 *Then He saw it and declared it,*
> *Took it as a pattern and tested it also,*
> 28 *And said to man : Behold, the fear of the Lord is wisdom,*
> *And to depart from evil is understanding.*

It is impracticable to attach the *inf.* לַעֲשׂוֹת to ver. 24 as the purpose, because it is contrary to the meaning; but it is impossible, according to the syntax, to refer it to ver. 27 as the purpose placed in advance, or to take it in the sense of *perfecturus,* because in both instances it ought to have been יְתַכֵּן instead of תִּכֵּן, or at least וְתִכֵּן with the verb placed first (*vid.* ch. xxxvii. 15). But even the temporal use of לְ in לִפְנוֹת at the turn (of morning, of evening, *e.g.* Gen. xxiv. 63) cannot be compared, but לַעֲשׂוֹת signifies *perficiendo = quum perficeret* (as *e.g.* 2 Sam. xviii. 29, *mittendo = quum mitteret*), it is a gerundival *inf.* (Nägelsb. S. 197f, 2d edition); and because it is the past that is spoken of, the modal *inf.* can be continued in the *perf.,* Ges. § 132, rem. 2. The thought that God, when He created the world, appointed fixed laws of equable and salutary duration, he particularizes by examples: He appointed to the wind its weight, *i.e.* the measure of its force or feebleness; distributed the masses of water by measure; appointed to the rain its law, *i.e.* the conditions of its development and of its beginning; appointed the way, *i.e.* origin and course, to the lightning (חֲזִיז from חָזַז, حزّ, *secare*). When

He thus created the world, and regulated what was created by laws, then He perceived (רָאָהּ with *He . Mappic.* according to the testimony of the Masora) it, wisdom, viz. as the ideal of all things; then He declared it, *enarravit,* viz. by creating the world, which is the development and realization of its substance; then He gave it a place הֱכִינָהּ (for which Döderl. and Ewald unnecessarily read הֱבִינָהּ), viz. to create the world after its pattern, and to commit the arrangement of the world as a whole to its supreme protection and guidance; then He also searched it out or tested it, viz. its demiurgic powers, by setting them in motion to realize itself.

If we compare Prov. viii. 22–31 with this passage, we may say: the חכמה is the divine ideal-world, the divine imagination of all things before their creation, the complex unity of all the ideas, which are the essence of created things and the end of their development. "Wisdom," says one of the old theologians,[1] "is a divine imagination, in which the ideas of the angels and souls and all things were seen from eternity, not as already actual creatures, but as a man beholds himself in a mirror." It is not directly one with the Logos, but the Logos is the demiurg by which God has called the world into existence according to that ideal which was in the divine mind. Wisdom is the impersonal model, the Logos the personal master-builder according to that model. Nevertheless the notions, here or in the later cognate portion of Scripture, Prov. viii. 22–31, are not as yet so distinct as the New Testament revelation of God has first of all rendered possible. In those days, when God realized the substance of the חכמה, this eternal mirror of the world, in the creation of the world, He also gave man the law, corresponding to which he corresponds to His idea and participates in wisdom. Fearing the supreme Lord (אֲדֹנָי only here in the book of Job, one of the 134 ודאין, *i.e.* passages, where אדני is not merely to be read instead of יהוה, but is actually written[2]), and renouncing evil (סוּר מֵרָע, according to another less authorized mode of writing מֵרַע),—this is man's share of wisdom, this is his relative wisdom, by which he remains in connection with the absolute. This is true human φιλοσοφία, in contrast to all high-flown and profound speculations; comp. Prov. iii. 7, where, in like manner, "fear Jehovah" is placed side by side with "depart from evil," and Prov. xvi. 6, according to which it is rendered possible סור מרע, to escape the evil of sin and its punishment by fearing God. "The fear of God is the beginning of wisdom" (Prov. i. 7; comp. Ps. cxi. 10) is the *symbolum*, the motto and uppermost principle, of that Israelitish Chokma, whose greatest achievement is the book of Job. The whole

---

[1] *Vid.* Jul. Hamberger, *Lehre Jak. Böhme's*, S. 55.

[2] *Vid.* Buxtorf's *Tiberias*, p. 245 ; comp. Bär's *Psalterium*, p. 133.

of ch. xxviii. is a minute panegyric of this principle, the materials of which are taken from the far-distant past; and it is very characteristic, that, in the structure of the book, this twenty-eighth chapter is the clasp which unites the half of the δέσις with the half of the λύσις, and that the poet has inscribed upon this clasp that sentence, "The fear of God is the beginning of wisdom." But, moreover, Job's closing speech, which ends in this celebration of the praise of the הכמה, also occupies an important position, which must now be determined, in the structure of the whole.

After Job has refuted Bildad, and, continuing his description, has celebrated in such lofty strains the majesty of God, it can hardly be expected that the poet will allow Zophar to speak for the third time. Bildad is unable to advance anything new, and Zophar has already tried his utmost to terrify Job for the second time; besides, Job's speech furnishes no material for a reply (a motive which is generally overlooked), unless the controversy were designed to ramble on into mere personalities. Accordingly the poet allows Job to address the friends once more, but no longer in the extreme and excited tone of the previous dialogue, but, since the silence of the friends must produce a soothing impression on Job, tempering him to gentleness and forbearance, in a tone of confession conscious of victory, yet altogether devoid of haughty triumph,—a confession in which only one single word of reproach (ch. xxvii. 12b) escapes him. Ch. xxvii. xxviii. contain this confession—Job's final address to his friends.

Job once again most solemnly asserts his innocence before the friends; all attempts on the part of the friends to entice or to extort from him a confession which is against his conscience, have therefore been in vain: joyous and victorious he raises his head, invincible, even to death, in the conviction of that which is a fact of his consciousness that cannot be got rid of by denial. He is not an evil-doer; accordingly he must stand convicted as an evil-doer who treats him as such. For although he is not far from death, and is in sore vexation, he has not manifested the hopelessness and defection from God in which the evil-doer passes away. Job has indeed even expressed himself despondingly, and complained of God's wrath; but the true essence of his relation to God came to light in such words as ch. xvi. 19–21, xvii. 9, xix. 25–27. If the friends had not been blind to such brilliant aspirations of his life in God, how could they regard him as a godless man, and his affliction as the punishment of such an one! His affliction has, indeed, no connection with the terrible end of the evil-doer. Job here comes before the friends with the very doctrine they have so frequently advanced, but infatuated with the foolish notion that it is suited to his case. He here gives it back to them, to show them that it is not suited to him. He also does not deny, that in the rule the evil-doer meets a terrible end, although he has hitherto disputed the assertion of the friends, because of the exclusiveness with which it was maintained by them. His counter-assertion respecting the prosperity of the evil-doer, which from the beginning was not meant by him so exclusively as the friends meant theirs respecting the misfortune of the evil-doer, is here indirectly freed from the extreme appearance of exclusiveness by Job himself, and receives the necessary modification. Job does not deny, yea, he here brings it under the notice of the friends, that the sword, famine, and pestilence carry off the descendants of the evil-doer, and even himself; that his possessions at length fall into the hands of the righteous, and contain within themselves the germ of destruction from the very first; that God's curse pursues, and suddenly destroys, the godless rich man himself. Thus it comes to pass; for while silver and other precious things come from the depths of the earth, wisdom, whose worth far transcends all earthly treasures, is to be found with no created being, but is with God alone; and the fear of God, to avoid evil, is the share of wisdom to which man is directed according to God's primeval decree.

The object of the section, ch. xxviii., is primarily to confirm the assertion concerning the judgment that befalls the evil-doer, ch. xxvii. 13–23 ; the confirmation is, however, at the same time, according to the delicately laid plan of the poet, a glorious general confession, in which Job's dialogue with the friends comes to a close.   This panegyric of wisdom (similar to Paul's panegyric of charity, 1 Cor. xiii.) is the presentation of Job's predominant principle, and as such, is like a song of triumph, with which, without vain-glory, he closes the dialogue in the most appropriate manner.   If Job's life has such a basis, it is not possible that his affliction should be the punishment of an ungodly man.   And if the fear of God is the wisdom appointed to man, he also teaches himself that, though unable to see through the mystery of his affliction, he must still hold on to the fear of God, and teaches the friends that they must do the same, and not lay themselves open to the charge of injustice and uncharitableness towards him, the suffering one, in order to solve the mystery.   Job's conclusion, which is first intended to show that he who does not fear God is overtaken by the merited fate of a fool who rebels against God's moral government, shows at the same time that the afflictive lot of those who fear God must be judged of in an essentially different manner from that of the ungodly.

We may imagine what impression these last words of Job to the friends must have made upon them.   Since they were obliged to be silent, they will not have admitted that they are vanquished, although the drying up of their thoughts, and their involuntary silence, is an actual proof of it.   But does Job make them feel this oppressively?   Now that they are become so insignificant, does he read them a severe lecture? does he in general act towards them as vanquished? No indeed, but solemnly, and without vaunting himself over his accusers, he affirms his innocence; earnestly, but in a winning manner, he admonishes them, by tempering and modifying what was vehement and extreme in his previous replies. He humbly submits himself to the divine wisdom, by setting the fear of God, as man's true wisdom, before himself and the friends as their common aim. Thus he utters "the loftiest words, which must surprise the opponents as they exhibit him as the not merely mighty, but also wonderfully calm and modest conqueror, who here for the first time wears the crown of true victory, when, in outward victory conquering himself, he struggles on towards a more exalted clearness of perception."

Job's Monologue.—Chap. xxix.-xxxi.

FIRST PART.—CHAP. XXIX.

Schema : 10. 8. 8. 6. 6. 11.

[Then Job continued to take up his proverb, and said :]

2 *O that I had months like the times of yore,*
  Like the days when Eloah protected me,

3 *When He, when His lamp, shone above my head,*
  By His light I went about in the darkness ;

4 *As I was in the days of my vintage,*
  When the secret of Eloah was over my tent,

5 *When the Almighty was still with me,*
  My children round about me ;

6 *When my steps were bathed in cream,*
  And the rock beside me poured forth streams of oil.

Since the optative מִי־יִתֵּן (comp. on ch. xxiii. 3) is connected with the acc. of the object desired, ch. xiv. 4, xxxi. 31, or of that respecting which anything is desired, ch. xi. 5, it is in itself possible to explain: who gives (makes) me like the months of yore; but since, when מִי־יִתְּנֵנִי occurs elsewhere, Isa. xxvii. 4, Jer. ix. 1, the *suff.* is meant as the dative (= מִי־יִתֵּן לִי, ch. xxxi. 35), it is also here to be explained: who gives me (= O that one would give me, O that I had) like (*instar*) the months of yore, *i.e.* months like those of the past, and indeed those that lie far back in the past; for יַרְחֵי־קֶדֶם means more than עָבְרוּ (אֲשֶׁר) יְרָחִים. Job begins to describe the olden times, that he wishes back, with the virtu- ally genitive relative clause: "when Eloah protected me" (Ges. § 116, 3). It is impossible to take בְּהִלּוֹ as *Hiph.*: when He caused to shine (Targ. בְּאַנְהָרוּתֵיהּ); either בְּהַהֲלוֹ (Olsh.) or even בָּהֳלוֹ (Ew. in his *Comm.*) ought to be read then. On the other hand, הִלּוֹ can be justified as the form for *inf. Kal* of הָלַל (to shine, *vid.* ch. xxv. 5) with a weaken- ing of the *a* to *i* (Ew. § 255, *a*), and the *suff.* may, according to the syntax, be taken as an anticipatory statement of the object: when it, viz. His light, shone above my head; comp. Ex. ii. 6 (him, the boy), Isa. xvii. 6 (its, the fruit-tree's, branches), also xxix. 23 (he, his children); and Ew. § 309, *c*, also decides in its favour. Nevertheless it commends itself still more to refer the *suff.* of בהלו to אֱלוֹהַּ (comp. Isa. lx. 2, Ps. l. 2), and to take נֵרוֹ as a corrective, explanatory per- mutative: when He, His lamp, shone above my head, as we have translated. One is at any rate reminded of Isa. lx. in connection with ver. 3; for as בהלו corresponds to יזרח there, so לאורו corresponds to לְאוֹרֵךְ in the 3d ver. of the same: by His light I walked in darkness (חֹשֶׁךְ locative = בַּחֹשֶׁךְ), *i.e.* rejoicing in His light, which preserved me from its dangers (straying and falling).

In ver. 4 כַּאֲשֶׁר is not a particle of time, but of comparison, which was obliged here to stand in the place of the כְּ, which is used only as a preposition. And חָרְפִּי (to be written thus, not חָרְפִּי with an aspirated פ) may not be translated " (in the days) of my spring," as Symm. ἐν ἡμέραις νεότητός μου, Jer. *diebus adolescentiæ meæ*, and Targ. בְּיוֹמֵי חֲרִיפוּתִי, whether it be that חריפות here signifies the point, ἀκμή (from חרף, حرف، *acuere*), or the early time (spring time, from חרף, خرف، *carpere*). For in reference to agriculture חֹרֶף can certainly signify the early half of the year (on this, *vid. Genesis*, S. 270), inasmuch as sowing and ploughing time in Palestine and Syria is in November and December; wherefore خريف signifies the early rain or autumn rain; and in Talmudic, חָרֵף, premature (ripe too early), is the opposite of אָפֵל, late, but the derivatives of חרף only obtain this signification *connotative*, for, according to its proper signification, חֹרֶף (خريف with other forms) is the gathering time, *i.e.* the time of the fruit harvest (syn. אָסִיף), while the Hebr. אָבִיב (אֵב) corresponds to the spring in our sense. If Job meant his youth, he would have said בִּימֵי אָבִּי, or something similar; but as ver. 5*b* shows, he meant his manhood, and this he calls his autumn as the season of maturity, or rather of the abundance of fruits (Schult. : *ætatem virilem suis fructibus fœtum et exuberantum*),[1] which, according to Olympiodorus, also with ὅτε ἤμην ἐπιβρίθων ὁδούς (perhaps καρπούς) of the LXX., is what is intended. Then the blessed fellowship of Eloah (סוֹד, familiarity, confiding, unreserved intercourse, Ps. lv. 15, Prov. iii. 32, comp. Ps. xxv. 14) ruled over his tent; the Almighty

---

[1] The fresh vegetation, indeed, in hotter districts (*e.g.* in the valley of the Jordan and Euphrates) begins with the arrival of the autumnal rains, but the real spring (comp. Cant. ii. 11–13) only begins about the vernal equinox, and still later on the mountains. On the contrary, the late summer, קַיִץ, which passes over into the autumn, חֹרֶף, is the season for gathering the fruit. The produce of the fields, garden fruit, and grapes ripen before the commencement of the proper autumn; some (when the land can be irrigated) summer fruits, *e.g. Dhura* (maize) and melons, in like manner olives and dates, ripen in autumn. Therefore the translation, in the days of my autumn ("of my harvest"), is the only

was still with him (protecting and blessing him), His נְעָרִים were round about him. It certainly does not mean servants (Raschi: מְשָׁרְתִי), but children (as ch. i. 19, xxiv. 5); for one expects the mention of the blessing of children first of all (Ps. cxxvii. 3 sqq., cxxviii. 3). His steps (הֲלִיךְ, ἄπ λεγ.) bathed then בְּחֵמָה = בְּחֶמְאָה, ch. xx. 17 (as שָׁלָה = שְׁאֵלָה, 1 Sam. i. 17, and possibly נֵוֶה = וְאָוֶה), and the rocks poured forth, close by him, streams of oil (a figure which reminds one of Deut. xxxii. 13). A rich blessing surrounded him wherever he tarried or went, and flowed to him wonderfully beyond desire and comprehension.

> 7 *When I went forth to the gate of the city,*
> *Prepared my seat in the market,*
> 8 *Then the young men hid themselves as soon as they saw me,*
> *And the aged rose up, remained standing.*
> 9 *Princes refrained from speaking,*
> *And laid their hand on their mouth.*
> 10 *The voice of the nobles was hidden,*
> *And their tongue clave to their palate.*

When he left the bounds of his domain, and came into the city, he was everywhere received with the profoundest respect. From the facts of the case, it is inadmissible to translate *quum egrederer portam* after Gen. xxxiv. 24, comp. *infra*, ch. xxxi. 34, for the district where Job dwelt is to be

correct one. If חָרְפִּי were intended here in a sense not used elsewhere, it might signify, according to the Arabic with ح, "(in the days) of my prosperity," or "my power," or even with خ, "(in the days) of my youthful vigour;" for *charâfât* are rash words and deeds, *charfân* one who says or does anything rash from lightness, the feebleness of old age, etc. (according to Wetzst., very common words in Syria); חֹרֶף or חֶרֶף, therefore, the thoughtlessness of youth, جَهْل, *i.e.* the rash desire of doing something great, which חֵרֵף הַנְּפֶשׁ לָמוּת (Judg. v. 18). But it is most secure to go back to חרף, خَرَف, *carpere*, viz. *fructus*.

thought of as being without a gate. True, he did not dwell
with his family in tents, *i.e.* pavilions of hair, but in houses ;
he was not a nomad (a wandering herdsman), or what is the
same thing, a Beduin, otherwise his children would not have
been slain in a stone house, ch. i. 19. "The daughter of the
duck," says an Arabian proverb, "is a swimmer," and the son
of a Beduin never dwells in a stone house. He was, however, also, not a citizen, but a h*adari* (חֲצָרִי), *i.e.* a permanent
resident, a large landowner and husbandman. Thus therefore שַׁעַר (for which Ew. after the LXX. reads שַׁחַר : "when
I went up early in the morning to the city") is locative, for
שַׁעְרָה (comp. צֵא הַשָּׂדֶה, go out into the field, Gen. xxvii. 3) :
when he went forth to the gate above the city ; or even, since
it is natural to imagine the city as situated on an eminence :
up to the city (so that צֵאת includes in itself by implication
the notion of עֲלוֹת) ; not, however : to the gate near the city
(Stick., Hahn), since the gate of a city is not situated near
the city, but is part of the city itself. The gates of cities
and large houses in Western Asia are vaulted entrances,
with large recesses on either side, where people congregate
for business and negotiations.[1] The open space at the gate,
which here, as in Neh. viii. 1, 3, 16, is called רְחוֹב, *i.e.* the
open space within the gate and by the gate, was the forum
(ch. v. 4).

Ver. 8. When Job came hither to the meeting of the
tribunal, or the council of the elders of the city, within
which he had a seat and a voice, the young men hid themselves, conscious of his presence (which εἰρομένη λέξει, or, is
expressed paratactically instead of as a period), *i.e.* they
retired into the background, since they feared his look of
salutation ;[2] and old men (hoary heads) stood up, remained

---

[1] *Vid.* Layard, *New Discoveries*, p. 57.
[2] Comp. *jer. Schekalim* ii. 5 (in Pinner's *Compendium des Thalmud*,
S. 58) : "R. Jochanan was walking and leaning upon R. Chija bar-Abba,

standing (ἀσυνδέτως, as ch. xx. 19, xxviii. 4).   קוּם signifies
to stand up, עָמַד to advance towards any one and remain
standing (comp. vol. i. 357, note 1).   They rose in order not
to seat themselves until he was seated.   שָׂרִים are magnates
(*proceres*) of the city.   These עָצְרוּ בְמִלִּים, *cohibebant verba* (עצר
with *Beth* of the obj., as ch. iv. 2, xii. 15), and keeping a
respectful silence, they laid their hand on their mouth (comp.
xxi. 5).   All stepped back and desisted from speaking before
him : The speech of illustrious men (נְגִידִים from נגד, نَجَدَ, to
be visible, pleasant to the sight, comp. *supra*, p. 91) hid itself
(not daring to be heard), and the tongue of the same clave
(motionless) to their palate.   We do not translate : as to the
voice illustrious men hid themselves, for it is only the appearance produced by the attractional construction [Ges. § 148, 1]
that has led to the rendering of קוֹל־נגידים as an *acc.* of closer
definition (Schult., Hahn : *quod ad vocem eminentium, com-
primebantur*).   The verb is construed with the second member
of the genitival expression instead of with the first, as with
מספר, ch. xv. 20, xxi. 21, xxxviii. 21, and with ראֹשׁ, ch.
xxii. 12 ; a construction which occurs with קוֹל not merely in
such exclamatory sentences as Gen. iv. 10, Isa. lii. 8, but
also under other conditions, 1 Kings i. 41, comp. xiv. 6.
This may be best called an attraction of the predicate by the
second member of the compound subject, like the reverse instance, Isa. ii. 11 ; and it is sometimes found even where this
second member is not logically the more important.   Thus
Ew. transl. : " the voice of the nobles hides itself ; " whereas
Olsh., wrongly denying that the *partt.* in passages like Gen.
iv. 10, 1 Kings i. 41, are to be taken as predicative, wishes to

R. Eliezer perceived him and hid himself from him (וּמטמר לה מקמי).
Then said R. Jochanan : This Babylonian insulted him (R. Chija) by
two things ; first that he did not salute him, and then that he hid himself.   But R. Jakob bar-Idi answered him, it is the custom with them
for the less not to salute the greater,—a custom which confirms Job's
words : Young men saw me and hid themselves."

read נחבא, which is the more inadmissible, as even the choice
of the verb is determined by the attractional construction.

The strophe which follows tells how it came to pass that
those in authority among the citizens submitted to him, and
that on all sides the people were zealous to show him tokens
of respect.

11 *For an ear heard, and called me happy ;*
   And an eye saw, and bear witness to me :
12 *For I rescued the sufferer who cried for help,*
   And the orphan, and him that had no helper.
13 *The blessing of him that was ready to perish came upon me,*
   And I made the widow's heart rejoice.
14 *I put on justice, and it put me on ;*
   As a robe and turban was my integrity.

Thus imposing was the impression of his personal appearance wherever he appeared ; for (כִּי *explic.*) the fulness of
the blessing of the possession of power and of prosperity which
he enjoyed was so extraordinary, that one had only to hear of
it to call him happy, and that, especially if any one saw it
with his own eyes, he was obliged to bear laudatory testimony
to him. The *futt. consec.* affirm what was the inevitable consequence of hearing and seeing ; הֵעִיד, *seq. acc.*, is used like
הִזְכִּיר in the signification of laudatory recognition. The expression is not brachylogical for וַתָּעַד לִי (*vid.* on ch. xxxi. 18) ;
for from 1 Kings xxi. 10, 13, we perceive that העיד with the
acc. of the person signifies to make any one the subject of assertion, whether he be lower or higher in rank (comp. the New
Testament word, especially in Luke, μαρτυρεῖσθαι). It was,
however, not merely the outward manifestation of his unusual
prosperity which called forth such admiration, but his active
benevolence united with the abundant resources at his command. For where there was a sufferer who cried for help,
he relieved him, especially orphans and those who had no

helper. וְלֹא־עֹזֵר לוֹ is either a new third object, or a closer
definition of what precedes : the orphan and (in this state of
orphanhood) helpless one. The latter is more probable both
here and in the Salomonic primary passage, Ps. lxxii. 12 ; in
the other case וְאִשֶׁר אֵין־עֹזֵר לוֹ might be expected.

Ver. 13. The blessing (בִּרְכַּת with closely closed *penult.*) of
those who stood on the brink of destruction (אֹבֵד, *interiturus,*
as ch. xxxi. 19, Prov. xxxi. 6), and owed their rescue to him,
came upon him ; and the heart of the widow to whom he gave
assistance, compensating for the assistance of her lost husband,
he filled with gladness (הִרְנִין causative, as Ps. lxv. 9). For the
primary attribute, the fundamental character of his way of
thinking and acting, was צֶדֶק, a holding fast to the will of God,
which before everything else calls for sympathizing love
(root צדק, صدق, to be hard, firm, stiff, *e.g. rumh-un sadq-un,*
according to the Kamus : a hard, firm, straight spear), and
מִשְׁפָּט, judgment and decision in favour of right and equity
against wrong and injustice. Righteousness is here called
the garment which he put on (as Ps. cxxxii. 9, comp. Isa.
xi. 5, lix. 17), and right is the robe and turban with which
he adorns himself (comp. Isa. lxi. 10) ; as by Arabian poets
noble attributes are also called garments, which God puts on
any one, or which any one puts on himself (*albasa*).[1] Righteousness is compared to the לְבוֹשׁ (corresponding to the *thob,*
i.e. garment, *indusium,* of the nomads) which is worn on the
naked body, justice to the צָנִיף, a magnificent turban (corresponding to the *kefîje,* consisting of a thick cotton cloth, and
fastened with a cord made of camel's hair), and the magnificent
robe (corresponding to the second principal article of clothing,
the 'abâ). The LXX., Jer., Syr., and Arab. wrongly refer

---

[1] In Beidhâwi, if I remember rightly, this expression occurs once,
التدرّع بلباس التقوى, *i.e.* " clothing one's self in the armour of the
fear of God."

וַיִּלְבָּשֵׁנִי to מִשְׁפָּטִי of the second half of the verse, while, on the contrary, it is said of צֶדֶק, *per antanaclasin*, that Job put this on, and this in turn put Job on, *induit;* for וילבשני, as the usage of the language, as we have it, elsewhere shows, does not signify: it (righteousness) clothed me well (Umbr.), or: adorned me (Ew., Vaih.), also not: it dressed me out (Schlottm.), but only: it put me on as a garment, *i.e.* it made me so its own, that my whole appearance was the representation of itself, as in Judg. vi. 34 and twice in the Chronicles, of the Spirit of Jehovah it is said that He puts on any one, *induit*, when He makes any one the organ of His own manifestation.

15 *I was eyes to the blind,*
    And feet was I to the lame.
16 *I was a father to the needy,*
    And the cause of the unknown I found out,
17 *And broke the teeth of the wicked,*
    And I cast the spoil forth out of his teeth.

The less it is Job's purpose here to vindicate himself before the friends, the more forcible is the refutation which the accusations of the most hard-hearted uncharitableness raised against him by them, especially by Eliphaz, ch. xxii., find everywhere here. His charity relieved the bodily and spiritual wants of others—eyes to the blind (לַעִוֵּר with *Pathach*), feet to the lame. A father was he to the needy, which is expressed by a beautiful play of words, as if it were: the carer for the care-full ones; or what perhaps corresponds to the primary significations of אָב and אֶבְיוֹן:[1] the protector of

---

[1] There is an old Arabic defective verb, بَىٔ, which signifies "to seek an asylum for one's self," *e.g. anâ baj*, I come as one seeking protection, a suppliant, in the usual language synon. of تَدَخَّل, and thereby indicating its relationship to the Hebr. בּוֹא, perhaps the root of בַּיִת (בָּתִּים), the ת of which would then not be a radical letter, but, as according to Ges.

those needing (seeking) protection. The unknown he did not
regard as those who were nothing to him, but went unselfishly
and impartially into the ground of their cause. לֹא־יָדַעְתִּי is an
attributive clause, as ch. xviii. 21, Isa. lv. 5, xli. 3, and freq.,
with a personal obj. (*eorum*) *quos non noveram*, for the translation *causam quam nesciebam* (Jer.) gives a tame, almost
meaningless, thought.   With reference to the *suff.* in אֶחְקְרֵהוּ,
on the form *ehu* used seldom by *Waw consec.* (ch. xii. 4), and

Thes. in זָיִת, used only in the forming of the word, and the original
meaning would be " a refuge."   Traced to a secondary verb, אָבָה (properly to take up the fugitive, *qabila-l-bija*) springing from this primitive
verb, אַב would originally signify a guardian, protector; and from the
fact of this name denoting, according to the form פַּעֵל, properly in general
the protecting power, the ideal *femin.* in אָבוֹת (Arab. *abawât*) and the
Arabic dual *abawain* (properly both guardians), which embraces father
and mother, would be explained and justified.   Thus the rare phenomenon
that the same אבה signifies in Hebr. " to be willing," and in Arab. " to
refuse," would be solved.   The notion of taking up the fugitive would
have passed over in the Hebrew, taken according to its positive side, into
the notion of being willing, *i.e.* of receiving and accepting (קִבֵּל, *qabila*,
e.g. 1 Kings xx. 8, לֹא תֹאבֶה = *la taqbal*); in the Arabic, however,
taken according to its negative side, as refusing the fugitive to his pur-
suer, into that of not being willing; and the usage of the language favours
this : *abâhu 'aleihi*, he protected him against (علىٰ) the other (refused
him to the other); مَاٰبَىٰ = أَبَىٰ, protected, inaccessible to him who
longs for it; أُبِيَّة, the protection, *i.e.* the retention of the milk in the
udder.   Hence אַבְיוֹן, from the Hebrew signif. of the verb, signifies one
who desires anything, or a needy person, but originally (inasmuch as
אבה is connected with بَىٰ) one who needs protection; from the Arabic
signif. of أَبَىٰ, one who restrains himself because he is obliged, one to
whom what he wants is denied.   To the Arab. *ibja* (defence, being
hindered) corresponds in form the Hebr. אֵבֶה, according to which
אֳנִיּוֹת אֵבֶה, ch. ix. 26, may be understood of ships, which, with all sails
set and in all haste, seek the sheltering harbour before the approaching
storm.   We leave this suggestion for further research to sift and prove.
More on ch. xxxiv. 36.—WETZST.

by the *imper.* (ch. xl. 11 sq.), chiefly with a solemn calm tone
of speech, *vid.* Ew. § 250, *c.* Further : He spared not to
render wrong-doers harmless, and snatched from them what
they had taken from others. The cohortative form of the
fut. consec., וָאֲשַׁבְּרָה, has been discussed already on ch. i. 15,
xix. 20. The form מְתַלְּעוֹת is a transposition of מַלְתְּעוֹת, to
render it more convenient for pronunciation, for the Arab.
طلع, *efferre se,* whence a secondary form, تلع, although used
of the appearing of the teeth, furnishes no such appropriate
primary signification as the Arab. لذغ, *pungere, mordere,*
whence a secondary form, لثغ ; the Æthiopic *maltâht,* jaw-
bone (*maxilla*), also favours מלתעה as the primary form. He
shattered the grinders of the roguish, and by moral indignation against the robber he cast out of his teeth what he had
stolen.

> 18 *Then I thought : With my nest I shall expire,*
> *And like the phœnix, have a long life.*
> 19 *My root will be open for water,*
> *And the dew will lodge in my branches.*
> 20 *Mine honour will remain ever fresh to me,*
> *And my bow will become young in my hand.*

In itself, ver. 18*b* might be translated : "and like to the
sand I shall live many days" (Targ., Syr., Arab., Saad.,
Gecat., Luther, and, among moderns, Umbr., Stick., Vaih.,
Hahn, and others), so that the abundance of days is compared
to the multitude of the grains of sand. The calculation of
the immense total of grains of sand (atoms) in the world was,
as is known, a favourite problem of antiquity ; and in the
Old Testament Scriptures, the comprehensive knowledge of
Solomon is compared to " the sand upon the sea-shore,"
1 Kings v. 9,—how much more readily a long life reduced to
days! comp. Ovid, *Metam.* xiv. 136–138: *quot haberet corpora
pulvis, tot mihi natales contingere vana rogavi.* We would

willingly decide in favour of this rendering, which is admissible in itself, although a closer definition like הַיָּם is wanting by כְחוֹל, if an extensive Jewish tradition did not secure the signification of an immortal bird, or rather one rising ever anew from the dead. The testimony is as follows: (1) *b. Sanhedrin* 108*b*, according to which חוֹל is only another name for the bird אוּרְשִׁינָא,[1] of which the fable is there recorded, that when Noah fed the beasts in the ark, it sat quite still in its compartment, that it might not give more trouble to the patriarch, who had otherwise plenty to do, and that Noah wished it on this account the reward of immortality (יהא רעוא דלא תמות). (2) That this bird חוֹל is none other than the phœnix, is put beyond all doubt by the Midrashim (collected in the *Jalkut* on Job, § 517). There it is said that Eve gave all the beasts to eat of the fruit of the forbidden tree, and that only one bird, the חוֹל by name, avoided this death-food: "it lives a thousand years, at the expiration of which time fire springs up in its nest, and burns it up to about the size of an egg;" or even : that of itself it diminishes to that size, from which it then grows up again and continues to live (וחוזר ומתגדל איברים וחיה). (3) The Masora observes, that כחול occurs in two different

---

[1] The name is a puzzle, and does not accord with any of the mythical birds mentioned in the Zendavesta (*vid.* Windischmann, *Zoroastrische Studien*, 1863, S. 93). What Lewysohn, *Zoologie des Talmuds*, S. 353, brings forward from the Greek by way of explanation is untenable. The name of the bird, *Vâresha*, in an obscure passage of the Bundehesch in Windischmann, *ib.* S. 80, is similar in sound. Probably, however, אוּרְשִׁינָא is one and the same word as *Simurg*, which is composed of *si* (= *sin*) and *murg*, a bird (Pehlvi and Parsi *mru*). This *si* (*sin*) corresponds to the Vedic *çjena*, a falcon, and in the Zend form, *çaêna* (*çîna*), is the name of a miraculous bird ; so that consequently *Simurg* = *Sinmurg*, Parsi *Cinamru*, signifies the *Si-* or *Cina*-bird (comp. Kuhn, *Herabkunft des Feuers*, 1859, S. 125). In אוּרְשִׁינָא the two parts of the composition seem to be reversed, and אור to be corrupted from מור. Moreover, the *Simurg* is like the phœnix only in the length of its life ; another mythological bird, *Kuknus*, on the other hand (*vid.* the art. *Phönix* in Ersch u. Gruber), resembles it also in rising out of its own ashes.

significations (בתרי לישני), since in the present passage it does not, as elsewhere, signify sand. (4) Kimchi, in his *Lex.*, says: "in a correct Jerusalem MS. I found the observation : בשורק לנהרדעי ובחלם למערבאי, *i.e.* וְכַחוֹל according to the Nehardean (Babylonian) reading, וְבַחוֹל according to the western (Palestine) reading;" according to which, therefore, the Babylonian Masoretic school distinguished וכחול in the present passage from וכחול, Gen. xxii. 17, even in the pronunciation. A conclusion respecting the great antiquity of this lexical tradition may be drawn (5) from the LXX., which translates ὥσπερ στέλεχος φοίνικος, whence the Italic *sicut arbor palmæ*, Jerome *sicut palma*.

If we did not know from the testimonies quoted that חול is the name of the phœnix, one might suppose that the LXX. has explained וכחול according to the Arab. *nachl*, the palm, as Schultens does ; but by a comparison of those testimonies, it is more probable that the translation was ὥσπερ φοῖνιξ originally, and that ὥσπερ στέλεχος φοίνικος is an interpolation, for φοῖνιξ signifies both the immortal miraculous bird and the inexhaustibly youthful palm.[1] We have the reverse case in Tertullian, *de resurrectione carnis*, c. xiii., which explains the passage in Psalms, xcii. 13, δίκαιος ὡς φοῖνιξ ἀνθήσει, according to the translation *justus velut phœnix florebit*, of the *ales orientis* or *avis Arabiæ*, which symbolizes

---

[1] According to Ovid, *Metam.* xv. 396, the phœnix makes its nest in the palm, and according to Pliny, *h. n.* xiii..42, it has its name from the palm : *Phœnix putatur ex hujus palmæ argumento nomen accepisse, iterum mori ac renasci ex se ipsa ; vid.* A. Hahmann, *Die Dattelpalme, ihre Namen und ihre Verehrung in der alten Welt*, in the periodical *Bonplandia*, 1859, Nr. 15, 16. Masius, in his studies of nature, has very beautifully described on what ground " the intelligent Greek gave a like name to the fabulous immortal bird that rises again out of its own ashes, and the palm which ever renews its youth." Also comp. (Heimsdörfer's) *Christliche Kunstsymbolik*, S. 26, and Augusti, *Beiträge zur christl. Kunst-Geschichte und Liturgik*, Bd. i. S. 106–108, but especially Piper, *Mythologie der christl. Kunst* (1847), i. 446f.

man's immortality.[1] Both figures, that of the phœnix and that of the palm, are equally appropriate and pleasing in the mouth of Job ; but apart from the fact that the palm everywhere, where it otherwise occurs, is called תָּמָר, this would be the only passage where it occurs in the book of Job, which, in spite of its richness in figures taken from plants, nowhere mentions the palm,—a fact which is perhaps not accidental.[2] On the contrary, we must immediately welcome a reference to the Arabico-Egyptian myth of the phœnix, that can be proved, in a book which also otherwise thoroughly blends things Egyptian with Arabian, and the more so since (6) even the Egyptian language itself supports חֹל or חגל as a name of the phœnix ; for ΑΛΛΩΗ, ΑΛΛΟΗ is explained in the Coptico-Arabic glossaries by es-semendel (the Arab. name of the phœnix, or at least a phœnix-like bird, that, like the salamander, semendar, cannot be burned), and in Kircher by avis Indica, species Phœnicis.[3] חול is Hebraized from this Egyptian name of the

---

[1] Not without reference to Clemens Romanus, in his I. Ep. ad Corinth. c. xxv., according to which the phœnix is an Arabian bird, which lives five hundred years, then dies in a nest which it builds of incense, myrrh, and spices, and leaves behind it the larva of a young bird, which, when grown up, brings the nest with the bones of its father and places it upon the altar of the sun at the Egyptian Heliopolis. The source of this is Herodotus ii. 73 (who, however, has an egg of myrrh instead of a nest of myrrh) ; and Tacitus, Ann. vi. 28, gives a similar narrative. Lactantius gives a different version in his poem on the phœnix, according to which this, the only one of its race, "built its nest in a country that remained untouched by the deluge." The Jewish tragedy writer, Ezekiêlos, agrees more nearly with the statement of Arabia being the home of the phœnix. In his drama Ἐξαγωγή, a spy sent forward before the pilgrim band of Israel, he states that among other things the phœnix was also seen ; vid. my Gesch. der jüd. Poesie, S. 219.

[2] Without attempting thereby to explain the phenomenon observed above, we nevertheless regard it as worthy of remark, that in general the palm is not a common tree either in Syria or in Palestine. "At present there are not in all Syria five hundred palm-trees ; and even in olden times there was no quantity of palms, except in the valley of the Jordan, and on the sea-coast."—WETZST.

[3] Vid. G. Seyffarth, Die Phœnix-Periode, Deutsche Morgenländ. Zeitschr.

phœnix; the word signifies rotation (comp. Arab. haul, the year; haula, round about), and is a suitable designation of the bird that renews its youth periodically after many centuries of life : *quæ reparat seque ipsa reseminat ales* (Ovid), not merely beginning a new life, but also bringing in a new great year : *conversionem anni magni* (Pliny) ; in the hieroglyphic representations it has the circle of the sun as a crown. In the full enjoyment of the divine favour and blessing, and in the consciousness of having made a right use of his prosperity, Job hoped φοίνικος ἔτη βιοῦν (Lucian, *Hermot.* 53), to use a Greek expression, and to expire or die עִם־קִנִּי, as the first half of the verse, now brought into the right light, says. Looking to the form of the myth, according to which Ovid sings :

Quassa cum fulvâ substravit cinnama myrrhâ,
Se super imponit finitque in odoribus ævum,

it might be translated : together with my nest (Umbr., Hirz., Hlgst.) ; but with the wish that he may not see any of his dear ones die before himself, there is at the same time connected the wish, that none of them should survive him, which is in itself unnatural, and diametrically opposed to the character of an Arab, who in the presence of death cherishes the twofold wish, that he may continue to live in his children (a proverb says : *men chalaf el-weled el-fáli*h *ma mât*, he who leaves a noble child behind him is not dead), and that he may die in the midst of his family. Expressing this latter wish, עִם־קִנִּי signifies: with = in my nest, *i.e.* in the bosom of my family, not without reference to the phœnix, which, according to the form of the myth in Herodotus, Pliny, Clemens, and others, brings the remains of its father in a

iii. (1849) 63 ff., according to which *alloê* (Hierogl. *koli*) is the name of the false phœnix without head-feathers ; *bêne* or *bêni* (Hierogl. *bnno*) is the name of the true phœnix with head-feathers, and the name of the palm also. *Alloê*, which accords with חוֹל, is quite secured as a name of the phœnix.

nest or egg of myrrh to Heliopolis, into the sacred precincts of the temple of the sun, and thus pays him the last and highest tribute of respect. A different but similar version is given in Horapollo ii. 57, according to which the young bird came forth from the blood of its sire, σὺν τῷ πατρὶ πορεύεται εἰς τὴν Ἡλίου πόλιν τὴν ἐν Αἰγύπτῳ, ὃς καὶ παραγενόμενος ἐκεῖ ἅμα τῇ ἡλίου ἀνατολῇ τελευτᾷ. The father, therefore, in death receives the highest tribute of filial respect; and it is this to which the hope of being able to die with (in) his nest, expressed by Job, refers.

The following substantival clause, ver. 19*a*, is to be understood as future, like the similar clause, ver. 16*a*, as perfect: my root—so I hoped—will remain open (unclosed) towards the water, *i.e.* it will never be deficient of water in its vicinity, that it may plentifully supply the stem and branches with nourishment, and dew will lodge on my branches, *i.e.* will descend nightly, and remain upon them to nourish them. אֱלֵי (corresponding to the Arab. *ila*, originally *ilai*) occurs only in the book of Job, and here for the fourth and last time (comp. ch. iii. 22, v. 26, xv. 22). קָצִיר does not signify harvest here, as the ancient expositors render it, but, like ch. xiv. 9, xviii. 16, a branch, or the intertwined branches. The figure of the root and branch, the flow of vitality downwards and upwards, is the counterpart of ch. xviii. 16. In ver. 20 a substantival clause also comes first, as in vers. 19, 16 (for the established reading is חָדָשׁ, not חָדַשׁ), and a verbal clause follows: his honour—so he hoped—should continue fresh by him, *i.e.* should abide with him in undiminished value and splendour. It is his honour before God and men that is intended, not his soul (Hahn); כָּבוֹד, δόξα, certainly is an appellation of the נֶפֶשׁ (*Psychol.* S. 98), but חָדָשׁ is not appropriate to it as predicate. By the side of honour stands manliness, or the capability of self-defence, whose symbol is the bow: and my bow should become young again in my hand, *i.e.* gain ever new strength and elasticity. It is unnecessary to supply פֹּחַ (Hirz., Schlottm., and others). The verb חלף, خلف‎, signifies, as the Arab. shows, properly to turn the back, then to go forth, exchange ; the *Hiph.* to make progress, to cause something new to come into the place of the old, to grow young again. These hopes introduced with וָאֹמַר were themselves an element of his former happiness. Its description can therefore be continued in connection with the ואמר without any fresh indication.

21 *They hearkened to me and waited,*
    And remained silent at my decision.
22 *After my utterance they spake not again,*
    And my speech distilled upon them.
23 *And they waited for me as for the rain,*
    And they opened their mouth wide for the latter rain.
24 *I smiled to them in their hopelessness,*
    And the light of my countenance they cast not down.
25 *I chose the way for them, and sat as chief,*
    And dwelt as a king in the army,
    As one that comforteth the mourners.

Attentive, patient, and ready to be instructed, they hearkened to him (this is the force of שָׁמַע לְ), and waited, without interrupting, for what he should say. וַיִּחֵלּוּ, the pausal pronunciation with a reduplication of the last radical, as Judg. v. 7, חָדֵלּוּ (according to correct texts), Ges. § 20, 2, *c ;* the reading of Kimchi, וַיְחֵלּוּ, is the reading of Ben-Naphtali, the former the reading of Ben-Ascher (*vid.* Norzi). If he gave counsel, they waited in strictest silence : this is the meaning of יִדְּמוּ (*fut. Kal* of דָּמַם); לְמוֹ, poetic for לְ, refers the silence to its outward cause (*vid.* on Hab. iii. 16). After his words *non iterabant, i.e.* as Jerome explanatorily translates: *addere nihil audebant,* and his speech came down upon them relieving, rejoicing, and enlivening them. The figure indicated in תִּטֹּף is expanded in ver. 23 after Deut. xxxii. 2: they waited on his word, which penetrated deeply, even to the heart, as for rain, מָטָר, by which, as ver. 23b, the so-called (autumnal) early rain which moistens the seed is prominently thought of. They open their mouth for the late rain, מַלְקוֹשׁ (vid. on ch. xxiv. 6), i.e. they thirsted after his words, which were like the March or April rain, which helps to bring to maturity the corn that is soon to be reaped; this rain frequently fails, and is therefore the more longed for. פָּעַר פֶּה is to be understood according to Ps. cxix. 131, comp. lxxxi. 11; and one must consider, in connection with it, what raptures the beginning of the periodical rains produces everywhere, where, as e.g. in Jerusalem, the people have been obliged for some time to content themselves with cisterns that are almost dried to a marsh, and how the old and young dance for joy at their arrival!

In ver. 24a a thought as suited to the syntax as to the fact is gained if we translate: "I smiled to them—they believed it not," i.e. they considered such condescension as scarcely possible (Saad., Raschi, Rosenm., De Wette, Schlottm., and others); אֶשְׂחַק is then fut. hypotheticum, as ch. x. 16, xx. 24, xxii. 27 sq., Ew. § 357, b. But it does not succeed in putting ver. 24b in a consistent relation to this thought; for, with Aben-Ezra, to explain: they did not esteem my favour the less on that account, my respect suffered thereby no loss among them, is not possible in connection with the biblical idea of "the light of the countenance;" and with Schlottm. to explain: they let not the light of my countenance, i.e. token of my favour, fall away, i.e. be in vain, is contrary to the usage of the language, according to which הִפִּיל פָּנִים signifies: to cause the countenance to sink (gloomily, Gen. iv. 5), whether one's own, Jer. iii. 12, or that of another. Instead of פָּנַי we have a more pictorial and poetical expression here, אוֹר פָּנַי: light of my countenance, i.e. my cheerfulness (as Prov. xvi. 15). Moreover, the אישׁחק אליהם, therefore, furnishes the thought that he laughed, and did not allow anything to dispossess him of his easy and contented disposition. Thus, therefore, those to whom Job laughed are to be thought of as in a condition and mood which his cheerfulness might easily sadden, but still did not sadden; and this their condition is described by לֹא יַאֲמִינוּ (a various reading in Codd. and editions is וְלֹא), a phrase which occurred before (ch. xxiv. 22) in the signification of being without faith or hope, despairing (comp. הֶאֱמִין, to gain faith, Ps. cxvi. 10),—a clause which is not to be taken as attributive (Umbr., Vaih.: who had not confidence), but as a neutral or circumstantial subordinate clause (Ew. § 341, a). Therefore translate: I smiled to them, if they believed not, i.e. despaired; and however despondent their position appeared, the cheerfulness of my countenance they could not cause to pass away. However gloomy they were, they could not make me gloomy and off my guard. Thus also ver. 25a is now suitably attached to the preceding: I chose their way, i.e. I made the way plain, which they should take in order to get out of their hopeless and miserable state, and sat as chief, as a king who is surrounded by an armed host as a defence and as a guard of honour, attentive to the motion of his eye; not, however, as a sovereign ruler, but as one who condescended to the mourners, and comforted them (נִחַם Piel, properly to cause to breathe freely). This peaceful figure of a king brings to mind the warlike one, ch. xv. 24. כַּאֲשֶׁר is not a conj. here, but equivalent to כְּאִישׁ אֲשֶׁר, ut (quis) qui; consequently not: as one comforts, but: as he who comforts; LXX. correctly: ὃν τρόπον παθεινοὺς παρακαλῶν. The accentuation (כאשר Tarcha, אבלים Munach, ינחם Silluk) is erroneous; כאשר should be marked with Rebia mugrasch, and אבלים with Mercha-Zinnorith.

From the prosperous and happy past, absolutely passed, Job now turns to the present, which contrasts so harshly with it.

THE SECOND PART OF THE MONOLOGUE.—CHAP. XXX.

Schema: 10. 8. 9. 8. 8. 8. 8. 8.

1 *And now they who are younger than I have me in derision,*
  Those whose fathers I disdained
  To set with the dogs of my flock.
2 *Yea, the strength of their hands, what should it profit me?*
  They have lost vigour and strength.
3 *They are benumbed from want and hunger,*
  They who gnaw the steppe,
  The darkness of the wilderness and waste;
4 *They who pluck mallows in the thicket,*
  And the root of the broom is their bread.

With וְעַתָּה, which also elsewhere expresses the turning-
point from the premises to the conclusion, from accusation to
the threat of punishment, and such like, Job here begins to
bewail the sad turn which his former prosperity has taken.
The first line of the verse, which is marked off by *Mercha-
Mahpach,* is intentionally so disproportionately long, to form
a deep and long breathed beginning to the lamentation which
is now begun. Formerly, as he has related in the first part
of the monologue, an object of reverential fear to the respect-
able youth of the city (ch. xxix. 8), he is now an object of
derision (שָׂחַק עַל, to laugh at, distinct from שָׂחַק אֶל, ch. xxix. 24,
to laugh to, smile upon) to the young good-for-nothing vaga-
bonds of a miserable class of men. They are just the same
עֲנִיֵּי אֶרֶץ, whose sorrowful lot he reckons among the mysteries
of divine providence, so difficult of solution (ch. xxiv. 4*b*–8).
The less he belongs to the merciless ones, who take advantage of the calamities of the poor for their own selfish ends,
instead of relieving their distress as far as is in their power,

the more unjustifiable is the rude treatment which he now experiences from them, when they who meanly hated him before because he was rich, now rejoice at the destruction of his prosperity. Younger than he in days (לְיָמִים as ch. xxxii. 4, with לְ of closer definition, instead of which the simple *acc.* was inadmissible here, comp. on ch. xi. 9) laugh at him, sons of those fathers who were so useless and abandoned that he scorned (לְ מָאַס, comp. מִן מָאַס, 1 Sam. xv. 26) to entrust to them even a service so menial as that of the shepherd dogs. Schult., Rosenm., and Schlottm. take עִם שִׁית for עַל שִׁית, *præficere*, but that ought to be just simply עַל שִׁית; עִם שִׁית signifies to range beside, *i.e.* to place alike, to associate; moreover, the *oversight* of the shepherd dogs is no such menial post, while Job intends to say that he did not once consider them fit to render such a subordinate service as is that of the dogs which help the shepherds. And even the strength of their (these youths') hands (גַּם is referable to the *suff.* of יְדֵיהֶם: even; not: now entirely, completely, as Hahn translates), of what use should it be to him? (לָמָּה not *cur*, but *ad quid*, *quorsum*, as Gen. xxv. 32, xxvii. 46.) They are enervated, good-for-nothing fellows: כָּלַח is lost to them (עָלֵימוֹ trebly emphatic: it is placed in a prominent position, has a pathetic *suff.*, and is עַל for לְ, 1 Sam. ix. 3). The signif. *senectus*, which suits ch. v. 26, is here inapplicable, since it is not the aged that are spoken of, but the young; for that "old age is lost to them" would be a forced expression for the thought—which, moreover, does not accord with the connection—that they die off early. One does not here expect the idea of *senectus* or *senectus vegeta*, but *vigor*, as the Syriac ('*ushino*) and Arabic also translate it. May not כָּלַח perhaps be related to כֹּחַ, as שַׁלְאֲנָן to שַׁאֲנָן, the latter being a mixed form from שַׁאֲנָן and שָׁלֵו, the former from כֹּחַ and לֵחַ, fresh juicy vigour, or as we say: pith and marrow (*Saft and Kraft*)? At all events, if this is somewhat the idea of the word, it may be derived from

כָּלַח = כָּלָה (LXX. συντέλεια), or some other way (*vid.* on ch. v. 26) : it signifies full strength or maturity.[1]

With ver. 3*a* begins a new clause. It is גַּלְמוּד, not גַּלְמוּדִים, because the book of Job does not inflect this Hebræo-Arabic word, which is peculiar to it (besides only Isa. xlix. 21, גַּלְמוּדָה). It is also in Arab. more a substantive (stone, a mass) than an adj. (hard as stone, massive, *e.g. Hist. Tamerlani* in Schultens : الصخر الجلمود, the hardest rock) ; and, similar to the Greek χέρσος (*vid.* Passow), it denotes the condition or attribute of rigidity, *i.e.* sterility, ch. iii. 7 ; or stiff as death, ch. xv. 34 ; or, as here, extreme weakness and incapability of

---

[1] From the root كل (on its primary notion, *vid.* my review of Bernstein's edition of Kirsch's *Syr. Chrestomathie, Ergänzungsblatt der A.L.Z.* 1843, Nr. 16 and 17) other derivatives, as كلّا, كلب, كلت, كلث, كلد, كلز, كلج, etc., develop in general the significations to bring, take, or hold together, enclose, and the like ; but كلح in particular the signification to draw together, distort violently, viz. the muscles of the face in grinning and showing the teeth, or even sardonic laughing, and drawing the lips apart. The general signification of drawing together, شد, resolves itself, however, from that special reference to the muscles of the face, and is manifest in the IV. form كالح, to show one's self strict and firm (against any one) ; also more sensuously : to remain firm in one's place ; of the moon, which remains as though motionless in one of its twenty-eight halting-places. Hence دهر كالح, a hard season, زمان شديد and كلاح, كلاح (the latter as a kind of *n. propr.* invariably ending in *i*, and always without the article), a hard year, *i.e.* a year of failure of the crops, and of scarcity and want. If it is possible to apply this to כָּלַח without the hazardous comparison of قلحم, تحل, etc. [so *supra,* i. 103], the primary signification might perhaps be that of hardness, unbroken strength ; ch. v. 26, "Thou wilt go to the grave with unbroken strength," *i.e.* full of days indeed, but without having thyself experienced the infirmities and burdens of the *ætas decrepita,* as also a shock brought in " in its season " is at the highest point of ripeness ; xxx. 2 : " What (should) the strength of their hands profit me ? as for them, their vigour is departed."—FL.

working. The subj.: such are *they*, is wanting; it is ranged line upon line in the manner of a mere sketch, participles with the demonstrative article follow the elliptical substantival clause. The *part.* הָעֹרְקִים is explained by LXX., Targ., Saad. (فارين), and most of the old expositors, after עֲרַק, عرق, *fut.* يَعْرِق, *fugere, abire,* which, however, gives a tame and—since the desert is to be thought of as the proper habitation of these people, be they the Seir remnant of the displaced Horites, or the Hauran "races of the clefts"—even an inappropriate sense. On the contrary, عرق in Arab. (also *Pael* ʿarreq in Syriac) signifies to gnaw; and this Arabic signification of a word exclusively peculiar to the book of Job (here and ch. xxx. 17) is perfectly suitable. We do not, however, with Jerome, translate: *qui rodebant in solitudine* (which is doubly false), but *qui rodunt solitudinem,* they gnaw the sunburnt parched ground of the steppe, stretched out there more like beasts than men (what Gecatilia also means by his لازم, *adhærent*), and derive from it their scanty food. אֶמֶשׁ שׁוֹאָה וּמְשֹׁאָה is added as an explanatory, or rather further descriptive, permutative to צִיָּה. The same alliterative union of substantives of the same root occurs in ch. xxxviii. 27, Zeph. i. 15, and a similar one in Nah. ii. 11 (בּוּקָה וּמְבוּקָה), Ezek. vi. 14, xxxiii. 29 (שְׁמָה וּמְשַׁמָּה); on this expression of the superlative by heaping up similar words, comp. Ew. § 313, *c.* The verb שָׁאָה has the primary notion of wild confused din (*e.g.* Isa. xvii. 12 sq.), which does not pass over to the idea of desolation and destruction by means of the intermediate notion of ruins that come together with a crash, but by the transfer of what is confusing to the ear to confusing impressions and conditions of all kinds; the desert is accordingly called also תֹּהוּ, Deut. xxxii. 10, from תָּהָה = שָׁאָה (*vid. Genesis,* S. 93). The noun אֶמֶשׁ signifies elsewhere adverbially, in the past night, to grow night-like, and in general yesterday, according

to which it is translated: the yesterday of waste and desolation; or, retaining the adverbial form: waste and desolation
are of yesterday = long since. It is undeniable that מֵאֶתְמוּל
and אֶתְמוּל, Isa. xxx. 33, Mic. ii. 8, are used in the sense
pridem (not only to-day, but even yesterday); but our poet
uses תְּמוֹל, ch. viii. 9, in the opposite sense, *non pridem* (not
long since, but only of yesterday); and it is more natural to
ask whether אֶמֶשׁ then has not here the substantival signification from which it has become an adverb, in the signification
nightly or yesterday. Since it originally signifies yesterday
evening or night, then yesterday, it must have the primary
signification darkness, as the Arab. اَمْسِ is also traceable
to the primary notion of the sinking of the sun towards the
horizon; so that, consequently, although the usage of Arabic
does not allow this sense,[1] it can be translated (comp. צַלְמָוֶת,
Jer. ii. 6), "the evening darkness (gloominess) of the waste
and wilderness" (אֶמֶשׁ as *regens*, Ew. § 286, *a*). The Targ.

---

[1] اَمْسِ is manifestly connected with مَسَى, مَسِى, first by means of the
IV. form اَمْسَى; it has, however, like this, nothing to do with "darkness."

مَسَاء is, according to the original sources of information, properly the
whole afternoon until sunset; and this time is so called, because in
it the sun تَمَسُو or تَمَسِى, touches, *i.e.* sinks towards the horizon
(from the root مَسَ with the primary notion *stringere*, *terere*, *tergere*,
trahere, *prehendere*, *capere*). Just so they say تَدَلَّكَ الشَّمْسُ, properly
the sun rubs; تَضِيفَ, connects itself; تَشَفَّرَ, goes to the brink (شَفَرٌ,
شَفِير), all in the same signification. Used as a substantive, أَمْسِ
followed by the genitive is *la veille de* . . . , the evening before . . . ,
and then generally, the day before . . . , the opposite of غَدْ with the
same construction, *le lendemain de* —. It is absolutely impossible that it

also translates similarly, but takes אֱמֶשׁ as a special attribute : חֲשׁוּכָא הֵיךְ רוּמְשָׁא, "darkness like the late evening."
Olshausen's conjecture of אֶרֶץ makes it easier, but puts a
word that affirms nothing in the place of an expressive one.

Ver. 4 tells what the scanty nourishment is which the
chill, desolate, and gloomy desert, with its steppes and gorges,
furnishes them. מַלּוּחַ (also Talmudic, Syriac, and Arabic) is
the orach, and indeed the tall shrubby orach, the so-called
sea-purslain, the buds and young leaves of which are gathered
and eaten by the poor. That it is not merely a coast plant,
but grows also in the desert, is manifest from the narrative
b. *Kiduschin,* 66a: "King Jannai approached כוחלית in the
desert, and conquered sixty towns there [Ges. translates
wrongly, *captis LX talentis*]; and on his return with great
joy, he called all the orphans of Israel to him, and said: Our
fathers ate מלוחים in their time when they were engaged with
the building of the temple (according to Raschi: the second
temple; according to Aruch: the tabernacle in the wilder-

should refer to a far distant past. On the contrary, it is always used like
our "yesterday," in a general sense, for a comparatively near past, or
a past time thought of as near, as غَد is used of a comparatively near
future, or a future time thought of as near. Zamachschari in the *Kes-
schâf* on *Sur.* xvii. 25: It is a duty of children to take care of their aged
parents, "because they are so aged, and to-day (*el-jauma*) require those
who even yesterday (*bi-l-emsi*) were the most dependent on them of all
God's creatures." It never means absolutely *evening* or *night*. What
Gesenius, *Thes.,* cites as a proof for it from *Vita Timuri,* ii. 428—a supposed أَمْسِي, *vespertinus*—is falsely read and explained (as in general
Manger's translation of those verses abounds in mistakes) ;—both line 1
and line 9, أَمْسِي, IV. form of مَسَا, is rhetorically and poetically (as
" sister of كَان") of like signification with the general كَان or صَار. An
Arab would not be able to understand that אֱמֶשׁ שׁוֹאָה וּמְשֹׁאָה otherwise than : " on the eve of destruction and ruin," *i.e.* at the breaking in
of destruction and ruin which is just at hand or has actually followed
rapidly upon something else.—Fl.

ness) ; we will also eat מלוחים in remembrance of our fathers ! And מלוחים were served up on golden tables, and they ate." The LXX. translates, ἅλιμα (not: ἄλιμα) ; as in Athenæus, poor Pythagoreans are once called ἅλιμα τρώγοντες καὶ κακὰ τοιαῦτα συλλέγοντες.[1] The place where they seek for and find this kind of edible plant is indicated by עֲלֵי־שִׂיחַ. שִׂיחַ is a shrub in general, but certainly pre-eminently the شيح, that perennial, branchy, woody plant of uncultivated ground, about two-thirds of a yard high, and the same in diameter, which is one of the greatest blessings of Syria and of the steppe, since, with the exception of cow and camel's dung, it is often the only fuel of the peasants and nomads,—the principal, and often in a day's journey the only, vegetation of the steppe, in the shade of which, when everything else is parched, a scanty vegetation is still preserved.[2] The poor in search of the purslain surround this شيح (shîh), and as ver. 4b continues : the broom-root is their bread. Ges. understands לְחֻמָם according to Isa. xlvii. 14, where it is certainly the pausal form for לְחֻמָם ("there is not a coal to warm one's self"), and that because the broom-root is not eatable. But why should broom-root and not broom brushwood be mentioned as fuel? The root of the steppe that serves as fuel, together with the shîh, is called gizl (from גּוּל, to tear out), not retem, which is the broom (and is extraordinarily frequent in the Belka). The Arabs, however, not only call Genista monosperma so, but also Chamærops humilis, a degenerate kind of which produces a kind of arrow-root which the Indians in Florida use.[3]

---

[1] Huldrich Zwingli, in the Greek Aldine of 1518 (edited by Andrea of Asola), which he has annotated throughout in the margin, one of the choicest treasures of the Zurich town library, explains ἅλιμα by θαλάσσια, which was natural by the side of the preceding περικυκλοῦντες. We shall mention these marginal notes of Zwingli now and again.

[2] Thus Wetzstein in his *Reise in den beiden Trachonen und um das Haurangebirge*.

[3] The description of these eaters of the steppe plants corresponds exactly

לְחֻמָם in the signification *cibus eorum* is consequently not incomprehensible. LXX. (which throws vers. 4–6 into sad confusion) : οἳ καὶ ῥίζας ξύλων ἐμασσῶντο.[1] All the ancient versions translate similarly. One is here reminded of what Agatharchides says in Strabo concerning the Egyptio-Ethiopian eaters of the rush root and herb.[2]

to the reality, especially if that race, bodily so inferior, is contrasted with the agricultural peasant, and some allowance is made for the figure of speech مبالغة (*i.e.* a description in colours, strongly brought out), without which poetic diction would be flat and devoid of vividness in the eye of an Oriental. The peasant is large and strong, with a magnificent beard and an expressive countenance, while *e.g.* the Trachonites of the present day (*i.e.* the race of the *W'ar*, יְעַר), both men and women, are a small, unpleasant-looking, weakly race. It is certain that bodily perfection is a plant that only thrives in a comfortable house, and needs good nourishment, viz. bread, which the Trachonite of the present day very rarely obtains, although he levies heavy contributions on the harvest of the villagers. Therefore the roots of plants often serve as food. Two such plants, the *gahh* (נַח) and the *rubbe* halîle (רִבָּה חֲלִילָה), are described in my *Reisebericht*. A Beduin once told me that it should be properly called *rubh lêle* (רֻבַּח לַיְלָה), " the gain of a supper," inasmuch as it often takes the place of this, the chief meal of the day. To the genus *rubbe* belongs also the *holêwâ* (חֶלְיְוָא); in like manner they eat the bulbous plant, *qotên* (קְמֵין) ; of another, the *mesha'* (מִישְׁעַ), they eat leaves, stem, and root. I often saw the poor villagers (never Beduins) eat the broad thick fleshy leaves of a kind of thistle (the thistle is called شوك, *shôk*), the name of which is *'aqqub* (עַקּוּב) ; these leaves are a handbreadth and a half in length, and half a handbreadth in width. They gather them before the thorns on the innumerable points of the serrated leaves become strong and woody ; they boil them in salt and water, and serve them up with a little butter. Whole tribes of the people of the *Ruwala* live upon the small brown seed (resembling mustard-seed) of the *semh* (שְׂמַח). The seeds are boiled to a pulp.—WETZST.

[1] Zwingli observes here : Sigma only once. *Codd. Alex. and Sinait.* have the reading εμασωντο, which he prefers.

[2] *Vid.* Meyer, *Botanische Erläuterungen zu Strabons Geographie*, S. 108 ff.

5 *They are driven forth from society,*
   They cry after them as after a thief.
6 *In the most dismal valleys they must dwell,*
   In holes of the earth and in rocks.
7 *Among the bushes they croak,*
   Under nettles are they poured forth,
8 *Sons of fools, yea sons of base men :*
   They are driven forth out of the land !—

If, coming forth from their lurking-places, they allow
themselves to be seen in the villages of the plain or in the
towns, they are driven forth from among men, *e medio pellun-
tur* (to use a Ciceronian phrase). גֵּו (Syr. *gau*, Arab. *gaww,
guww*) is that which is internal, here the circle of social
life, the organized human community. This expression also
is Hebræo-Arabic ; for if one contrasts a house or district
with what is outside, he says in Arabic, جَوًّا وَبَرًّا, *guwwâ
wa-berrâ*, within and without, or الجوّانى والبرّانى, *el-guwwâni
wa'l-berrâni*, the inside and the outside. In ver. 5*b*, כַּגַּנָּב,
like the thief, is equivalent to, as after the thief, or since this
generic *Art.* is not usual with us [Germ. and Engl.] : after
a thief ; French, *on crie après eux comme après le voleur.* In
ver. 6*a*, לִשְׁכֹּן is, according to Ges. § 132, rem. 1 (comp. on
Hab. i. 17), equivalent to הָיוּ לִשְׁכֹּן, "they are to dwell" =
they must dwell ; it might also signify, according to the still
more frequent usage of the language, *habitaturi sunt ;* it here,
however, signifies *habitandum est eis*, as לִבְלוֹם, Ps. xxxii. 9,
obturanda sunt. Instead of בַּעֲרוּץ with *Shurek*, the reading
בַּעֲרוֹץ with *Cholem* (after the form סָגוֹר, Hos. xiii. 8) is also
found, but it is without support. עֲרוּץ is either a substantive
after the form גְּבוּל (Ges., as Kimchi), or the construct of
עָרוּץ = נֶעֱרָץ, feared = fearful, so that the connection of the
words, which we prefer, is a superlative one : *in horridissima*

vallium, in the most terrible valleys, as ch. xli. 22, *acutissimæ testarum* (Ew., according to § 313, *c*). The further description of the habitation of this race of men : in holes (בְּחֹרֵי = חֹרֵי) of the earth (עָפָר, earth with respect to its constituent parts) and rocks (LXX. τρῶγλαι πετρῶν), may seem to indicate the aborigines of the mountains of the district of Seir, who are called הַחֹרִים, τρωγλοδύται (*vid. Genesis*, S. 507); but why not, which is equally natural, חַוְרָן, Ezek. xlvii. 16, 18, the "district of caverns," the broad country about *Bosra*, with the two Trachônes (τράχωνες), of which the smaller western, the *Legâ*, is the ancient Trachonitis, and with Ituræa (the mountains of the Druses)? [1]

As ch. vi. 5 shows, there underlies ver. 7*a* a comparison of this people with the wild ass. The פֶּרֶא, *ferâ*, goes about in herds under the guidance of a so-called leader (*vid.* on ch. xxxix. 5), with which the poet in ch. xxiv. 5 compares the bands that go forth for forage ; here the point of comparison, according to ch. vi. 5, is their bitter want, which urges from them the cry of pain ; for יִנְהָקוּ, although not too strong, would nevertheless be an inadequate expression for their *sermo*

---

[1] Wetzstein also inclines to refer the description to the Ituræans, who, according to Apuleius, were *frugum pauperes*, and according to others, freebooters, and are perhaps distinguished from the *Arabes Trachonitæ* (if they were not these themselves), as the troglodytes are from the Arabs who dwell in tents (on the troglodytes in Eastern Hauran, *vid. Reisebericht*, S. 44, 126). " The troglodyte was very often able to go without nourishment and the necessaries of life. Their habitations are not unfrequently found where no cultivation of the land was possible, *e.g.* in *Safa*. They were therefore either rearers of cattle or marauders. The cattle-rearing troglodyte, because he cannot wander about from one pasture to another like the nomads who dwell in tents, often loses his herds by a failure of pasture, heavy falls of snow (which often produce great devastation, *e.g.* in Hauran), epidemics, etc. Losses may also arise from marauding attacks from the nomads. Still less is this marauding, which is at enmity with all the world, likely to make a race prosperous, which, like the troglodyte, being bound to a fixed habitation, cannot escape the revenge of those whom it has injured."—WETZST.

barbarus (Pineda), in favour of which Schlottmann calls to
mind Herodotus' (iv. 183) comparison of the language of
the Troglodyte Ethiopians with the screech of the night-owl
(τετρίγασι κατάπερ αἱ νυκτερίδες). Among bushes (especially
the bushes of the *shih*, which affords them some nourishment
and shade, and a green resting-place) one hears them, and
hears from their words, although he cannot understand them
more closely, discontent and lamentation over their desperate
condition: there, under nettles (חָרוּל, root חר, ﺣﺮ, as *urtica*
from *urere*), *i.e.* useless weeds of the desert, they are poured
forth, *i.e.* spread about in disorder. Thus most moderns
take סְפַח = שָׁפַךְ, ﺳﻔﺢ, comp. סָרוּחַ, *profusus*, Amos vi. 4, 7,
although one might also abide by the usual Hebrew meaning of the verb סְפַח (hardened from סְפָה), *adjungere, associare*
(*vid. Habak.* S. 88), and with Hahn explain: under nettles
they are united together, *i.e.* they huddle together. But
neither the *fut.* nor the *Pual* (instead of which one would
expect the *Niph.* or *Hithpa.*) is favourable to the latter interpretation; wherefore we decide in favour of the former, and
find sufficient support for a Hebr.-Arabic סְפַח in the signification *effundere* from a comparison of ch. xiv. 19 and the
present passage. Ver. 8, by dividing the hitherto latent subject, tells what sort of people they are: sons of fools, profane,
insane persons (*vid.* on Ps. xiv. 1); moreover, or of the like
kind (גַּם, not אַף), sons of the nameless, *ignobilium* or *in-
famium*, since בְּלִי־שֵׁם is here an adj. which stands in dependence, not *filii infamiæ* = *infames* (Hirz. and others), by which
the second בְנֵי is rendered unlike the first. The assertion
ver. 8*b* may be taken as an attributive clause: who are
driven forth . . . ; but the shortness of the line and the
prominence of the verb are in favour of the independence
of the clause like an exclamation in its abrupt and halting
form. נִכְאוּ is *Niph.* of נָכָא = נָכָה (נָכֵי), root נך, to hew, pierce,

strike.[1] On הָאָרֶץ, of arable land in opposition to the steppe, *vid.* on ch. xviii. 17.

9 *And now I am become their song,*
And a by-word to them.
10 *They avoid me, they flee far from me,*
And spare not my face with spitting.
11 *For my cord of life He hath loosed, and afflicted me,*
Therefore they let loose the bridle recklessly.
12 *The rabble presses upon my right hand,*
They thrust my feet away,
And cast up against me their destructive ways.

The men of whom Job complains in this strophe are none other than those in the preceding strophe, described from the side of their coarse and degenerate behaviour, as ch. xxiv. 4–8 described them from the side of the wrong which was practised against them. This rabble, constitutionally as well as morally degraded, when it comes upon Job's domain in its marauding expeditions, makes sport of the sufferer, whose former earnest admonitions, given from sympathizing anxiety for them, seemed to them as insults for which they revenge themselves. He is become their song of derision (נְגִינָתָם to be understood according to the dependent passage, Lam. iii. 14, and Ps. lxix. 13), and is לְמִלָּה to them, their θρύλλημα

---

[1] The root نك is developed in Hebr. נָכָה, הִכָּה, in Arab. نكا and نكى, first to the idea of outward injury by striking, hewing, etc.; but it is then also transferred to other modes of inflicting injury, and in نوك, to being injured in mind. The root shows itself in its most sensuous development in the reduplicated form نكنك, to strike one with repeated blows, fig. for: to press any one hard with claims. According to another phase, the obscene ناك *fut. i*, and the decent نكح, signify properly to pierce.—FL.

(LXX.), the subject of their foolish talk (מִלָּה = Arab. *mille*, not = *melle*, according to which Schultens inteprets it, *sum iis fastidio*). Avoiding him, and standing at a distance from him, they make their remarks upon him; and if they come up to him, it is only for the sake of showing him still deeper scorn : *a facie ejus non cohibent sputam*. The expositors who explain that, contrary to all decent bearing, they spit in his presence (Eichh., Justi, Hirz., Vaih., Hlgst.), or with Fie! spit out before him (Umbr., Hahn, Schlottm.), overlook the fact of its being מִפָּנַי, not לְפָנַי. The expression as it stands can only affirm that they do not spare his face with spitting (Jer. correctly : *conspuere non veruntur*), so that consequently he is become, as he has complained in ch. xvii. 6, a תֹפֶת, an object of spitting (comp. also the declaration of the servant of Jehovah, Isa. l. 6, which stands in close connection with this declaration of Job, according to previous explanations).

It now becomes a question, Who is the subj. in ver. 11*a*? The *Chethib* יִתְרוֹ demands an attempt to retain the previous subj. Accordingly, most moderns explain : *solvit unusquisque eorum funem suum, i.e. frenum suum, quo continebatur antea a me* (Rosenm., Umbr., Stick., Vaih., Hlgst., and others), but it is to be doubted whether יתר can mean *frenum*; it signifies a cord, the string of a bow, and of a harp. The reconciliation of the signification *redundantia*, ch. xxii. 20, and *funis*, is, in the idea of the root, to be stretched tight and long.[1] Hirz. therefore imagines the loosing of the cord

---

[1] The verb وَتَرَ shows its sensuous primary signification in يَتَر, وَتَّرَ, cord, bow-string, harp-string (Engl. *string*) : to stretch tight, to extend, so that the thing continues in one line. Hence then وَتَّرَ، وَتَر، separate, unequal, *singulus, impar, opp.* شَفَع, *bini, par*, just as *fard*, single, separate, unequal (*opp. zaug*, a pair, equal number), is derived from *farada*, properly, so to strain or stretch out, that the thing has no bends or folds; Greek ἐξαπλοῦν (as in the *Shepherd* of Hermas : ἐπάνω λεντίου ἐξηπλω-

round the body, which served them as a girdle, in order to strike Job with it. But whether one decides in favour of the *Chethib* יתרו or of the *Keri* יתרי, the persons who insult Job cannot in any case be intended. The isolated *sing.* form of the assertion, while the rabble is everywhere spoken of in the *plur.*, is against it; and also the כִּי, which introduces it, and after which Job here allows the reason to come in, why he is abandoned without any means of defence to such brutal misconduct. The subj. of ver. 11a is God. If יתרו is read, it may not be interpreted: He hath opened = taken off the covering of His string (= bow) (Ew., Hahn, and similarly even LXX., Jer.), for יתר does not signify the bow, but the string (Arab. *muwattar*, stretched, of a bow); and while פָּתַח, Ezek. xxi. 33 (usually שָׁלַף or הֵרִיק), can certainly be said of drawing a sword from its sheath, עֵרָה is the appropriate and usual word (*vid. Hab.* S. 164) for making bare the bow and shield. Used of the bow-string, פִּתַּח signifies to loose what is

μένον λίνου καρπάσινου), an original transitive signification still retained in low Arabic (*vid.* Bocthor under *Étendre* and *Déployer*). Then from وَتَّر spring the secondary roots تَتَّر and تَرَى, which proceed from the VIII. form (*ittatara*). The former (*tatara*) appears only in the adverb تَتْرًا and تَتْرَى, *sigillatim, alii post alios,* singly one after another, so that several persons or things form a row interrupted by intervals of space or time; the latter (*tara*) and its IV. form (*atra*) are equivalent to *wâtara*, to be active at intervals, with pauses between, as the Arabs explain: "We say أَتْرَى of a man when he so performs several acts which do not directly follow one another, that there is always a فَتْرَة, *intermissio,* between two acts." Hence also תְּרֵין, תַּרְתֵּין, תַּרְתִּין, duals of an assumed *sing.* תַּר, *singulus* (*um*), תַּרְתְּ *singula*, therefore prop. *duo singuli* (*a*), *duæ singulæ,* altogether parallel to the like meaning *thinâni* (*ithnâni*), *thinaini* (*ithnaini*), שְׁנַיִם; fem. *thintâni* (*ithnatâni*), *thintaini* (*ithnataini*), שְׁתַּיִם instead of שְׁנְתַּיִם, from an assumed *sing. thin-un* (*ithn-un*), *thint-un* strained, by sending the arrow swiftly forth from it, according to which, *e.g.* Elizabeth Smith translates: Because He hath let go His bow-string and afflicted me. One cannot, however, avoid feeling that וַיְעַנֵּנִי is not a right description of the effect of shooting with arrows, whereas an idea is easily gained from the *Keri* יִתְרִי, to which the description of the effect corresponds. It has been interpreted: He has loosed my rein or bridle, by means of which I hitherto bound them and held them in check; but יתר in the signification rein or bridle is, as already observed, not practicable. Better Capellus: *metaphora ducta est ab exarmato milite, cujus arcûs solvitur nervus sicque inermis redditur;* but it is more secure, and still more appropriate to the ויענני which follows, when it is interpreted according to ch. iv. 21: He has untied (loosened) my cord of life, *i.e.* the cord which stretched out and held up my tent (the body) (Targ. similarly: my chain and the threads of my cord, *i.e.* surely: my outward and inward stay of life), and

(*ithnat-un*), from ثِنًى, שֵׁנָה, like *bin* (*ibn*), *bint* (*ibnat*), בֵּן, בַּת (= בְּנֶת,

hence בַּתִּי) from בָּנָה, بِنًى.

The significations of *watara* which Freytag arranges under 1, 2, 3, 4, proceed from the transitive application of יָתַר, as the Italian *soperchiare*, *soverchiare*, from *supra*, to offend, insult; *oltraggiare*, *outrager*, from *ultra*; ὑβρίζειν from ὑπέρ. Similarly, تطاول عليه and استطال عليه (form VI. and X. from طال), to act haughtily towards any one, to make him feel one's superiority, properly to stretch one's self out over or against any one.

But in another direction the signif. to be stretched out goes into: overhanging, surpassing, projecting, to be superfluous, and to be left over, περιττὸν εἶναι, to exceed a number or bulk, *superare* (comp. Italian *soperchiare* as intrans.), περιεῖναι, ὑπερεῖναι; to prove, as result, gain, etc., περιεῖναι, etc. Similar is the development of the meaning of فَضْل and of طَائِل, gain, use, from طال, to be stretched out. In like manner, the German *reich, reichlich* [rich, abundant], comes from the root *reichen, recken* [to stretch, extend].—Fl.

bowed me down, *i.e.* deprived me of strength (comp. Ps.
cii. 24); or also: humbled me.   Even in this his feebleness
he is the butt of unbridled arrogance: and they let go the
bridle before me (not לְפָנַי, in my presence, but מִפָּנַי, before
me, before whom previously they had respect; מפני the same
as Lev. xix. 32), they cast or shake it off (שִׁלַּח as ch. xxxix. 3,
synon. of הִשְׁלִיךְ; comp. 1 Kings ix. 7 with 2 Chron. vii. 20).

Is it now possible that in this connection פִּרְחָח can denote
any else but the rabble of these good-for-nothing fellows?
Ewald nevertheless understands by it Job's sufferings, which
as a rank evil swarm rise up out of the ground to seize upon
him; Hahn follows Ew., and makes these sufferings the subj.,
as even in ver. 11*b*.   But if we consider how Ew. translates:
"they hung a bridle from my head;" and Hahn: "they have
cast a bit before my face," this might make us tired of all
taste for this allegorical mode of interpretation.   The stump
over which they must stumble is ver. 13*c*, where all climax
must be abandoned in order to make the words לֹא עֹזֵר לָמוֹ
intelligible in this allegorical connection.   No indeed; פִּרְחָח
(instead of which פַּרחח might be expected, as *supra*, ch. iii. 5,
כַּמרירי for כְּמרירי) is the offspring or rabble of those fathers
devoid of morals and honour, those צעירים of ver. 1, whose
laughing-stock Job is now, as the children of priests are
called in Talmudic פִּרְחֵי כְּהֻנָּה, and in Arabic فرخ denotes not
only the young of animals, but also a rascal or vagabond.
This young rabble rises עַל־יָמִין, on Job's right hand, which is
the place of an accuser (Ps. cix. 6), and generally one who
follows him up closely and oppresses him; and they press him
continually further and further, contending one foot's-breadth
after another with him: רַגְלַי שִׁלֵּחוּ, my feet thrust them forth,
protrudunt (שִׁלַּח the same as ch. xiv. 20).   By this pressing
from one place to another, a way is prepared for the description of their hostile conduct, which begins in ver. 12*c* under

the figure of a siege. The *fut. consec.* וַיִּסֹּלּוּ, ver. 12c, is not
meant retrospectively like וַיְעַנֵּנִי, but places present with present in the connection of cause and effect (comp. Ew. 343, a).
We must not be misled by the fact that וַיִּסֹלּוּ, ch. xix. 12
(which see), was said of the host of sufferings which come
against Job; here it is those young people who cast up the
ramparts of misfortune or burdensome suffering (אֵיד) against
Job, which they wish to make him feel. The tradition, supported by the LXX., that Job had his seat outside his
domain ἐπὶ τῆς κοπρίας, *i.e.* upon the *mezbele*, is excellently
suited to this and the following figures. Before each village
in Hauran there is a place where the households heap up the
sweepings of their stalls, and it gradually reaches a great
circumference, and a height which rises above the highest
buildings of the village.[1] Notwithstanding, everything is intelligible without this thoroughly Hauranitish conception of
the scene of the history. Bereft of the protection of his children and servants, become an object of disgust to his wife,
and an abhorrence to his brethren, forsaken by every attention of true affection, ch. xix. 13–19, Job lies out of doors;
and in this condition, shelterless and defenceless, he is aban-

---

[1] One ought to have a correct idea of a Hauranitish *mezbele*. The
dung which is heaped up there is not mixed with straw, because in warm,
dry countries no litter is required for the cattle, and comes mostly from
single-hoofed animals, since small cattle and oxen often pass the nights
on the pastures. It is brought in a dry state in baskets to the place
before the village, and is generally burnt once every month. Moreover,
they choose days on which the wind is favourable, *i.e.* does not cast the
smoke over the village. The ashes remain. The fertile volcanic ground
does not need manure, for it would make the seed in rainy years too luxuriant at the expense of the grain, and when rain fails, burn it up. If
a village has been inhabited for a century, the *mezbele* reaches a height
which far surpasses it. The winter rains make the ash-heaps into a
compact mass, and gradually change the *mezbele* into a firm mound of
earth, in the interior of which those remarkable granaries, *biâr el-ghalle*,
are laid out, in which the wheat can be completely preserved against
heat and mice, garnered up for years. The *mezbele* serves the inhabitants

doned to the hideous malignant joy of those gipsy hordes
which wander hither and thither.

> 13 *They tear down my path,*
> *They minister to my overthrow,*
> *They who themselves are helpless.*
> 14 *As through a wide breach they approach,*
> *Under the crash they roll onwards.*
> 15 *Terrors are turned against me,*
> *They pursue my nobility like the wind,*
> *And like a cloud my prosperity passed away.*—

They make all freedom of motion and any escape impossible
to him, by pulling down, *diruunt*, the way which he might go.
Thus is נָתְסוּ (cogn. form of נתץ, נתע, נתש) to be translated,
not: they tear open (*proscindunt*), which is contrary to the
primary signification and the usage of the language. They,
who have no helper, who themselves are so miserable and
despised, and yet so feelingless and overbearing, contribute to
his ruin. הוֹעִיל, to be useful, to do any good, to furnish anything effective (*e.g.* Isa. xlvii. 12), is here united with לְ of
the purpose; comp. לְ עָזַר, to help towards anything, Zech. i. 15.

of the district as a watch-tower, and on close oppressive evenings as a
place of assembly, because there is a current of air on the height. There
the children play about the whole day long ; there the forsaken one lies,
who, having been seized by some horrible malady, is not allowed to enter
the dwellings of men, by day asking alms of the passers-by, and at night
hiding himself among the ashes which the sun has warmed. There the
dogs of the village lie, perhaps gnawing at a decaying carcase that is
frequently thrown there. Many a village of Hauran has lost its original
name, and is called *umm el-mezâbil* from the greatness and number of
these mounds, which always indicate a primitive and extensive cultivation for the villages. And many a more modern village is built upon an
ancient *mezbele*, because there is then a stronger current of air, which
renders the position more healthy. The Arabic signification of the root
זבל seems to be similarly related to the Hebrew as that of the old Beduin
seken (שָׁבֶן), " ashes," to the Hebrew and Arabic משכן, " a dwelling."—
WETZST.

הַוָּה (for which the *Keri* substitutes the primary form הַוָּה), as was already said on ch. vi. 2, is prop. *hiatus,* and then *barathrum, pernicies,* like הַוָּה in the signification *cupiditas,* prop. *inhiatio.* The verb הָוָה, هوى, also signifies *delabi,* whence it may be extended (*vid.* on ch. xxxvii. 6) in like manner to the signification abyss (rapid downfall); but a suitable medium for the two significations, strong passion (Arab. *hawa*) and abyss (Arab. *hâwije, huwwe, mahwa*), is offered only by the signification of the root *flare* (whence *hawâ,* air). לֹא עֹזֵר לָמוֹ is a genuine Arabic description of these Idumæan or Hauranite pariahs. Schultens compares a passage of the *Hamâsa:* "We behold you ignoble, poor, *laisa lakum min sâir-in-nâsi nasirun, i.e.* without a helper among the rest of men." The interpretations of those who take לָמוֹ for לֹ, and this again for לִ (Eichh., Justi), condemn themselves. It might more readily be explained, with Stick.: without any one helping them, *i.e.* with their own strong hand; but the thought thus obtained is not only aimless and tame, but also halting and even untrue (*vid.* ch. xix. 13 sqq.).

Ver. 14. The figure of a siege, which is begun with ver. 12*c* and continued in ver. 13, leaves us in no doubt concerning פֶּרֶץ רָחָב and שֹׁאָה. The Targ. translates: like the force of the far-extending waves of the sea, not as though פֶּרֶץ could in itself signify a stream of water, but taking it as = פֶּרֶץ מַיִם, 2 Sam. v. 20 (synon. *diffusio aquarum*). Hitzig's translation :[1] "like a broad forest stream they come, like a rapid brook they roll on," gives unheard-of significations to the doubtful words. In ch. xvi. 14 we heard Job complain: He (Eloah) brake through me פֶּרֶץ עַל־פְּנֵי־פָרֶץ, breach upon breach,—by the divine decrees of sufferings, which are completed in this ill-treatment which he receives from good-for-nothing fellows, he is become as a wall with a wide-gaping breach, through

[1] *Vid. Deutsche Morgenländ. Zeitschr.* ix. (1855), S. 741, and *Proverbs,* S. 11.

which they rush in upon him (*instar rupturæ*, a concise mode of comparison instead of *tanquam per rupt.*), in order to get him entirely into their power as a plaything for their coarse passions. שֹׁאָה is the crash of the wall with the wide breaches, and תַּחַת שֹׁאָה signifies *sub fragore* in a local sense: through the wall which is broken through and crashes above the assailants. There is no ground in ver. 15a for dividing, with Umbreit, thus: He hath turned against me! Terrors drove away, etc., although this would not be impossible according to the syntax (comp. Gen. xlix. 22, בָּנוֹת צָעֲדָה). It is translated: terrors are turned against me; so that the predicate stands first in the most natural, but still indefinite, personal form, Ges. § 147, *a*, although בַּלָּהוֹת might also be taken as the accus. of the object after a passive, Ges. § 143, 1. The subj. of ver. 15b remains the same: they (these terrors) drive away my dignity like the wind; the construction is like ch. xxvii. 20, xiv. 19; on the matter, comp. ch. xviii. 11. Hirz. makes כָּרוּחַ the subj.: *quasi ventus aufert nobilitatem meam*, in which case the subj. would be not so much *ventus* as *similitudo venti*, as when one says in Arabic, '*gâani kazeidin*, there came to me one of Zeid's equals, for in the Semitic languages כְ has the manner of an indeclinable noun in the signification *instar*. But the reference to בלהות is more natural; and Hahn's objection, that calamity does not first, if it is there, drive away prosperity, but takes the place of that which is driven away, is sophisticated and inadequate, since the object of the driving away here is not Job's prosperity, but Job's נְדִיבָה, appearance and dignity, by which he hitherto commanded the respect of others (Targ. רַבָּנוּתִי). The storms of suffering which pass over him take this nobility away to the last fragment, and his salvation—or rather, since this word in the mouth of an extra-Israelitish hero has not the meaning it usually otherwise has, his prosperous condition (from وسع

amplum esse)—is as a cloud, so rapidly and without trace (ch. vii. 9; Isa. xliv. 22), passed away and vanished. Observe the music of the expression כְּעָב עָבְרָה, which cannot be reproduced in translation.

> 16 *And now my soul is poured out within me,*
>   *Days of suffering hold me fast.*
> 17 *The night rendeth my bones from me,*
>   *And my gnawers sleep not.*
> 18 *By great force my garment is distorted,*
>   *As the collar of my shirt it encompasseth me.*
> 19 *He hath cast me into the mire,*
>   *And I am in appearance as dust and ashes.*

With this third וְעַתָּה (vers. 1, 9) the elegiac lament over the harsh contrast between the present and the past begins for the third time. The dash after our translation of the second and fourth strophes will indicate that a division of the elegy ends there, after which it begins as it were anew. The soul is poured out within a man (עָלַי as ch. x. 1, *Psychol. S.* 152), when, "yielding itself without resistance to sadness, it is dejected to the very bottom, and all its organization flows together, and it is dissolved in the one condition of sorrow"—a figure which is not, however, come about by water being regarded as the symbol of the soul (thus Hitzig on Ps. xlii. 5), but rather by the intimate resemblance of the representation of a flood of tears (Lam. ii. 19): the life of the soul flows in the blood, and the anguish of the soul in tears and lamentations; and since the outward man is as it were dissolved in the gently flowing tears (Isa. xv. 3), his soul flows away as it were in itself, for the outward incident is but the manifestation and result of an inward action. יְמֵי־עֹנִי we have translated days of suffering, for עֳנִי, with its verb and the rest of its derivatives, is the proper word for suffering, and especially the passion of the Servant of Jehovah. Days of suffering

—Job complains—hold him fast ; אָחַז unites in itself, like הֶחֱזִיק, the significations *prehendere* and *prehensum tenere*. In ver. 17*a* we must not, with Arnh. and others, translate : by night it (affliction) pierces . . . , for עְנִי does not stand sufficiently in the foreground to be the subject of what follows ; it might sooner be rendered : by night it is pierced through (Targ., Rosenm., Hahn) ; but why is not לַיְלָה to be the subject, and נִקַּר consequently *Piel* (not *Niph.*)? The night has been personified already, ch. iii. 2; and in general, as Herder once said, Job is the brother of Ossian for personifications : Night (the restless night, ch. vii. 3 sq., in which every malady, or at least the painful feeling of it, increases) pierces his bones from him, *i.e.* roots out his limbs (synon. בַּדִּים, ch. xviii. 13) so inwardly and completely. The *lepra Arabica* (البرص, *el-baras*) terminates, like syphilis, with an eating away of the limbs, and the disease has its name جذام from حذم, *truncare, mutilare* : it feeds on the bones, and destroys the body in such a manner that single limbs are completely detached.

In ver. 17*b*, LXX. (νεῦρα), Parchon, Kimchi, and others translate עֹרְקַי according to the Targum. עָרְקִין (= גִּידִים), and the Arab. عروق, veins, after which Blumenf. : my veins are in constant motion. But עֹרְקַי in the sense of ch. xxx. 3 : my gnawers (Jer. *qui me comedunt*, Targ. דִּמְעַפָּן יָתִי, *qui me conculcant, conterunt*), is far more in accordance with the predicate and the parallelism, whether it be gnawing pains that are thought of—pains are unnatural to man, they come upon him against his will, he separates them from himself as wild beasts—or, which we prefer, those worms (רְמָּה, ch. vii. 5) which were formed in Job's ulcers (comp. Aruch, עַרְקָא, a leech, *plur.* עַרְקָתָא, worms, *e.g.* in the liver), and which in the extrabiblical tradition of Job's decease are such a standing feature, that the pilgrims to Job's monastery even now-a-days take away with them thence these supposedly petrified worms of Job.[1]

Ver. 18*a* would be closely and naturally connected with what precedes if לְבוּשִׁי could be understood of the skin and explained : By omnipotence (viz. divine, as ch. xxiii. 6, Ew. § 270*a*) the covering of my body is distorted, as even Raschi: מִשְׁתַּנֶּה גֶּלֶד אַחַר גֶּלֶד, it is changed, by one skin or crust being formed after another. But even Schultens rightly thinks it remarkable that לְבוּשׁ, ver. 18*a*, is not meant to signify the proper upper garment but the covering of the skin, but כֻּתָּנֶת, ver. 18*b*, the under garment in a proper sense. The astonishment is increased by the fact that הִתְחַפֵּשׂ signifies to disguise one's self, and thereby render one's self unrecognisable, which leads to the proper idea of לְבוּשׁ, to a clothing which looks like a disguise. It cannot be cited in favour of this unusual meaning that לְבוּשׁ is used in ch. xli. 5 of the scaly skin of the crocodile : an animal has no other לְבוּשׁ but its skin. Therefore, with Ew., Hirz., and Hlgst., we take לְבוּשׁ strictly : "by (divine) omnipotence my garment is distorted (becomes unlike itself), like the collar of my shirt it fits close to me." It is unnecessary to take כְּפִי as a compound *præp.* : according to

---

[1] In Mugir ed-dîn's large history of Jerusalem and Hebron (*kitâb el-ins el-gelîl*), in an article on Job, we read: God had so visited him in his body, that he got the disease that devours the limbs (*tegedhdhem*), and worms were produced (*dawwad*) in the wounds, while he lay on a dunghill (*mezbele*), and except his wife, who tended him, no one ventured to come too near him. In a beautiful Kurdic ballad "on the basket dealer" (*zembilfrosh*), which I have obtained from the Kurds in Salihîje, are these words : *Veki Gergis beshara beri | Jusuf veki abdan keri | bikesr' Ejub kurman deri | toh anin ser sultaneti | to men chalaski 'j zahmeti.*

> " When they divided Gergîs with a saw
> And sold Joseph like a slave,
> When worms fed themselves in Job's body,
> Then Thou didst guide them by a sure way :
> Thou wilt also deliver me from need."

More concerning these worms of Job in the description of the monastery of Job.—WETZST.

(comp. Zech. ii. 4, Mal. ii. 9 : " according as"), in the sense of
כְּמוֹ, as ch. xxxiii. 6, since פִּי כֻתֹּנֶת is, according to the nature of
the thing mentioned, a designation of the upper opening, by
means of which the shirt, otherwise only provided with arm-
holes (distinct from the Beduin shirt *thôb*, which has wide and
long sleeves), is put on.   Also, Ps. cxxxiii. 2, פִּי מִדּוֹתָיו signifies
not the lower edge, but the opening at the head (פִּי הָרֹאשׁ, Ex.
xxviii. 32) or the collar of the high priest's vestment (*vid.* the
passage cited).   Thus even LXX. ὥσπερ τὸ περιστόμιον
τοῦ χιτῶνός μου, and Jer.: *velut capitio tunicæ meæ*.   True,
Schlottm. observes against this rendering of ver. 18, that it is
unnatural according to substance, since on a wasted body it is
not the outer garment that assumes the appearance of a narrow
under one, but on the contrary the under garment assumes the
appearance of a wide outer one.   But this objection is not to
the point.   If the body is wasted away to a skeleton, there is
an end to the rich appearance and beautiful flow which the
outer garment gains by the full and rounded forms of the
limbs : it falls down straight and in perpendicular folds upon
the wasted body, and contributes in no small degree to make
him whom one formerly saw in all the fulness of health still
less recognisable than he otherwise is.   יְאַזְּרֵנִי, *cingit me*, is not
merely the falling together of the outer garment which was
formerly filled out by the members of the body, but its
appearance when the sick man wraps himself in it : then it
girds him, fits close to him like his shirt-collar, lying round
about the shrivelled figure like the other about a thin neck.
On the terrible wasting away which is combined with hyper-
trophical formations in elephantiasis, *vid.* ch. vii. 15, and
especially xix. 20.   The subject of ver. 19 is God, whom
ver. 18 also describes as efficient cause : He has cast me into,
or daubed[1] me with, mud, and I am become as (כְּ instead of
the *dat.*, Ew. § 221, *a*) dust and ashes.   This is also intended

---

[1] The reading wavers between הֹרָנִי and הֹרֵנִי, for the latter form of

pathologically: the skin of the sufferer with elephantiasis becomes first an intense red, then assumes a black colour; scales like fishes' scales are formed upon it, and the brittle, dark-coloured surface of the body is like a lump of earth.

20 *I cry to Thee for help, and Thou answerest not;*
   I stand there, and Thou lookest fixedly at me.
21 *Thou changest Thyself to a cruel being towards me,*
   With the strength of Thy hand Thou makest war upon me.
22 *Thou raisest me upon the stormy wind, Thou causest me*
    to drive along
   And vanish in the roaring of the storm.
23 *For I know: Thou wilt bring me back to death,*
   Into the house of assembly for all living.

If he cries for help, his cry remains unanswered; if he stands there looking up reverentially to God (perhaps עָמַד, with מִשַּׁוֵּעַ to be supplied, has the sense of desisting or restraining, as Gen. xxix. 35, xxx. 9), the troubling, fixed look of God, who looks fixedly and hostilely upon him, anything but ready to help (comp. ch. vii. 20, xvi. 9), meets his upturned eye. הִתְבֹּנֵן, to look consideringly upon anything, is elsewhere joined with עַד, עַל, אֶל, or even with the *acc.*; here, where a motionless fixed look is intended, with בְּ (= ڧ). It is impossible to draw the לֹא, ver. 20*a*, over to וַתִּתְבֹּנֵן (Jer., Saad., Umbr., Welte, and others), both on account of the *Waw consec.* (Ew. § 351*a*), and on account of the separation by the new antecedent עֲמַדְתִּי. On the reading of two Codd. ותתכנן ("Thou settest Thyself against me"), which Houbigant and Ew. prefer, Rosenm. has correctly pronounced judgment: *est potius pro mendo habenda.* Instead of consolingly answering his prayer, and instead of showing Himself willing to help, God, who was formerly so kind towards him, changes

writing is sometimes found even out of pause by conjunctive accents, *e.g.* 1 Sam. xxviii. 15, Ps. cxviii. 5.

towards him, His creature, into a cruel being, *sævum* (אַכְזָר in
the book of Job only here and ch. xli. 2, where it signifies
"foolhardy;" comp. לְאוֹיֵב in the dependent passage, Isa.
lxiii. 10), and makes war upon him (שָׂטַם as ch. xvi. 9) by
causing him to feel the strength of His omnipotent hand
(עֹצֶם יָד as Deut. viii. 17, synon. חֹזֶק).

It is not necessary in ver. 22a to forsake the accentuation,
and to translate: Thou raisest me up, Thou causest me go in
the wind (Ew., Hirz., and others); the accentuation of רוּחַ is
indeed not a disjunctive *Dechî*, but a conjunctive *Tarcha*, but
preceded by *Munach*, which, according to the rule, *Psalter*
ii. 500, § 5, here, where two conjunctives come together, has
a smaller conjunctive value. Therefore: *elevas me in ventum,
equitare facis me*, viz. *super ventum* (Dachselt), for one does
not only say הִרְכִּיב עַל, 1 Chron. xiii. 7, or לְ, Ps. lxvi. 12, but
also אֶל, 2 Sam. vi. 3; and accordingly תִּשָּׂאֵנִי אֶל־רוּחַ is also not
to be translated: Thou snatchest me into the wind or storm
(Hahn, Schlottm.), but: Thou raisest me up to the wind or
storm, as upon an animal for riding (Umbr., Olsh.). According to Oriental tradition, Solomon rode upon the east
wind, and in Arabic they say of one who hurries rapidly
by, *racab al-genáhai er-rîh*, he rides upon the wings of the
wind; in the present passage, the point of comparison is the
being absolutely passively hurried forth from the enjoyment
of a healthy and happy life to a dizzy height, whence a sudden
overthrow threatens him who is unwillingly removed (comp.
Ps. cii. 11, Thou hast lifted me up and hurled me forth).

The lot which threatens him from this painful suspense
Job expresses (ver. 22b) in the puzzling words: וּתְמֹגְגֵנִי תֻשִׁיָּה.
Thus the *Keri*, after which LXX. transl. (if it has not read
מִישׁוּעָה), καὶ ἀπέρριψάς με ἀπὸ σωτηρίας. The modern expositors who follow the *Keri*, by taking ותמגגני for ותמג לי
(according to Ges. § 121, 4), translate: Thou causest counsel
and understanding (Welte), happiness (Blumenf.), and the

like, to vanish from me; continuance, existence, duration would be better (*vid.* ch. vi. 13, and especially on ch. xxvi. 3). The thought is appropriate, but the expression is halting. Jerome, who translates *valide*, points to the correct thing, and Buxtorf (*Lex.* col. 2342 sq.) by interpreting the not less puzzling Targum translation *in fundamento* = *funditus* or *in essentia* = *essentialiter*, has, without intending it, hit upon the idea of the Hebr. *Keri*; תְּשִׁיָּה is intended as a closer defining, or adverbial, accusative: Thou causest me to vanish as to existence, *ita ut tota essentia pereat h.e. totaliter et omnino.* Perhaps this was really the meaning of the poet: most completely, most thoroughly, altogether, like the Arab. حَقًّا. But it is unfavourable to this *Keri*, that תושיה (from the verb יָשַׁי), as might be expected, is always written *plene* elsewhere; the correction of the תשוה is violent, and moreover this form, correctly read, gives a sense far more consistent with the figure, ver. 22*a*. Ges., Umbr., and Carey falsely read תְּשַׁוֶּה, *terres me;* this verb is unknown in Hebr., and even in Chaldee is only used in *Ithpeal*, אִשְׁתְּוִי (= Hebr. חָרַד); for a similar reason Böttcher's תִּשְׁוֶה (which is intended to mean : in despair) is also not to be used. Even Stuhlmann perceived that תשוה is equivalent to תְּשׁוּאָה; it is, with Ew. and Olsh., to be read תְּשֻׁאָה (not with Pareau and Hirz. תְּשַׁוֶּה without the *Dag.*), and this form signifies, as תשואה, ch. xxxvi. 29, from שׁוֹא = שָׁאָה, from which it is derived by change of consonants, the crash of thunder, or even the rumbling or roar as of a storm or a falling in (*procellæ sive ruinæ*). The meaning is hardly, that he who rides away upon the stormy wind melts and trickles down like drops of rain among the pealing of the thunder, when the thunder-storm, whose harbinger is the stormy wind, gathers; but that in the storm itself, which increases in fury to the howling of a tempest, he dissolves away. תְּשֻׁאָה for בִּתְשֻׁאָה, comp. Ps. cvii. 26 : their soul melted away (dissolved) בְּרָעָה. The compulsory journey in the air, therefore, passes into nothing or nearly nothing, as Job is well aware, ver. 23 : " for I know: (without כִּי, as ch. xix. 25, Ps. ix. 21) Thou wilt bring me back to death" (*acc.* of the goal, or locative without any sign). If תְּשִׁיבֵנִי is taken in its most natural signification *reduces*, death is represented as essentially one with the dust of death (comp. ch. i. 21 with Gen. iii. 19), or even with non-existence, out of which man is come into being; nevertheless הֵשִׁיב can also, by obliterating the notion of return, like *redigere*, have only the signification of the turn of destiny and change of condition that is effected. The assertion that שׁוּב always includes an " again," and retains it inexorably (*vid.* Köhler on Zech. xiii. 7, S. 239), is untenable. In post-biblical Hebrew, at least, it is certain that שׁוּב signifies not only "to become again," but also "to become," as عَادَ is used as synon. of جَاءَ, *devenir*.[1] With מָוֶת, the designation of the condition, is coupled the designation of the place : Hades (under the notion of which that of the grave is included) is the great involuntary rendezvous of all who live in this world.

24 *Doth one not, however, stretch out the hand in falling,*
     Doth he not raise a cry for help on that account in his ruin?
25 *Or have I not wept for him that was in trouble,*
     Hath not my soul grieved for the needy?—
26 *For I hoped for good, then evil came;*
     I waited for light, and darkness came.
27 *My bowels boiled without ceasing,*
     Days of misery met me.

Most of the ancient versions indulge themselves in strange fancies respecting ver. 24 to make a translatable text, or find their fancies in the text before them. The translation of the

---

[1] *Vid.* my *Anekdota der mittelalterlichen Scholastik unter Juden und Moslemen*, S. 347.

Targum follows the fancies of the Midrash, and places itself
beyond the range of criticism. The LXX. reads בי instead
of בעי, and finds in ver. 24 a longing for suicide, or death by
the hand of another. The Syriac likewise reads בי, although
it avoids this absurdity. Jerome makes an address of the
assertion, and, moreover, also moulds the text under the influence of the Midrash. Aq., Symm., and Theod. strive after a
better rendering than the LXX., but (to judge from the
fragments in the *Hexapla*) without success. Saadia and
Gecatilia wring a sense out of ver. 24*a*, but at the expense of
the syntax, and by dragging ver. 24*b* after it, contrary to the
tenor of the words. The old expositors also advance nothing
available. They mostly interpret it as though it were not
להן, but להם (a reading which has been forced into the Midrash texts and some Codd. instead of the reading of the text
that is handed down to us). Even Rosenm. thinks לָהֶן might,
like the Aram. לְהוֹן, be equivalent to לָהֶם; and Carey explains
the *enallage generis* from the perhaps existing secondary idea
of womanly fear, as 2 Sam. iv. 6, הֵנָּה instead of הֵמָּה is used
of the two assassins to describe them as cowards. But the
Hebr. לָהֶן is *fem.*; and often as the *enallage masc. pro fem.*
occurs, the *enallage fem. pro masc.* is unknown; הֵנָּה, 2 Sam.
iv. 6, is an adv. of place (*vid.*, moreover, Thenius *in loc.*).
It is just as absolutely inadmissible when the old expositors
combine שׁוּע with יָשַׁע (וְשֵׁע), or as *e.g.* Raschi with שִׁעֲשֵׁע, and
translate, "welfare" or "exhilaration" (refreshing). The
signif. "wealth" would be more readily admissible, so that
שׁוּע, as Aben-Ezra observes, would be the subst. to שׁוֹעַ, ch.
xxxiv. 19; but in ch. xxxvi. 19 (which see), שׁוּע (as שׁוֹעַ Isa.
xxii. 5) signifies a cry of distress (= שֶׁוַע), and an attempt
must be made here with this meaning before every other.

On the other hand comes the question whether בְעִי is not
perhaps to be referred to the verb בָּעָה, whether it be as
subst. after the form מְרִי (Ralbag after the Targ.) or as *part.*

pass. (Saad. غير انّه ليس المبتغى, "only that it is not desired"). The verb does not, indeed, occur elsewhere in the
book of Job, but is very consistent with its style, which so
abounds in Aramaisms, and is at the same time so coloured
with Arabic that we should almost say, its Hauranitish style.[1]
Thus taking בעי as one word, Ralbag transl.: prayer stretches
not forth the hand, which is intended to mean : is not able to
do anything, cannot cause the will of God to miscarry. This
meaning is only obtained by great violence ; but when Renan
(together with Böckel and Carey, after Rosenm.) translates:
Vaines prières! . . . *il étend sa main ; à quoi bon protester
contre ses coups?* the one may be measured with the other.
If בעי is to be derived from בעה, it must be translated either :
shall He, however, without prayer (*sine imploratione*), or :
shall He, however, unimplored (*non imploratus*), stretch out
His hand? The thought remains the same by both renderings of בעי, and suits as a vindication of the cry for help in
the context. But בָּעָה, in the specific signification *implorare,
deprecari,* is indeed the usage of the Targum, although strange
to the Hebr., which is here so rich in synonyms ; then, in the
former case, לֹא for בלא is harsh, and in the other, בעי as *part.
pass.* is too strong an Aramaism. We must therefore consider whether בְּעִי as עִי with the *præp.* בְּ gives a suitable
sense. Since שָׁלַח יָד בְּ, *e.g.* ch. xxviii. 9 and elsewhere, most
commonly means "to lay the hand on anything, stretch out
the hand to anything," it is most natural to take בעי in de-

---

[1] The verb بغا is still extensively used in Syria, and that in two forms:
بغا يبغى and بغا يبغا. In Damascus the *fut. i* is alone used ; whereas in Hauran and the steppe I have only found *fut. a.* Thus *e.g.* the
Hauranite poet *Kâsim el-Chinn* says : "The gracious God encompass thee
with His favour and whatever thy soul desires (*wa-l-nefsu ma tebghâ*), it
must obtain its desire" (*tanûlu munâhû,* in connection with which it is to
be observed that نال *fut. u* is used here in the signification *adipisci,*
comp. Fleischer on ch. xv. 29 [*supra* i. 270, note]).—WETZST.

pendence upon יִשְׁלַח יָדוֹ, and we really gain an impressive thought, if we translate: Only may He not stretch out His hand (to continue His work of destruction) to a heap of rubbish (which I am already become); but by this translation of ver. 24a, ver. 24b remains a glaring puzzle, insoluble in itself and in respect of the further course of the thought; for Schlottmann's interpretation, "Only one does not touch ruins, or the ruin of one is the salvation of another," which is itself puzzling, is no solution. The reproach against the friends which is said to lie in ver. 24a is contrary to the character of this monologue, which is turned away from his human opponents; then שׁוּעַ does not signify salvation, and there is no "one" and "another" to be found in the text. We must therefore, against our inclination, give up this dependent relation of בְעִי, so that בְעִי signifies either, upon a heap of rubbish, or, since this ought to be עַל־עִי: by the falling in; עִי (from עָוָה = 'iwj) can mean both: a falling in or overthrow (bouleversement) as an event, and ruins or rubbish as its result. Accordingly Hirz. translates: Only upon the ruins (more correctly at least: upon ruins) one will not stretch out his hand, and Ew.: Only— does not one stretch out one's hand by one's overthrow? But this "only" is awkward. Hahn is of opinion that אַךְ לֹא may be taken in the signification not once, and translates: may one not for once raise one's hand by one's downfall; but even this is lame, because then all connection with what precedes is wanting; besides, אַךְ לֹא does not signify ne quidem. The originally affirmative אַךְ has certainly for the most part a restrictive signification, which, as we observed on ch. xviii. 21, is blended with the affirmative in Hebr., but it is also, as more frequently אָכֵן, used adversatively, e.g. ch. xvi. 7, and in the combination אַךְ לֹא this adversative signification coincides with the restrictive, for this double particle signifies everywhere else: only not, however not, Gen. xx. 12, 1 Kings xi. 39, 2 Kings xii. 14, xiii. 6, xxiii. 9, 26. It would be more

natural to translate, as we have stated above : only may he
not, etc., but ver. 24*b* puts in its veto against this. If, as
Hirz., Ew., and Hahn also suppose, לֹא, ver. 24*a*, is equivalent
to הֲלֹא, so that the sentence is to be spoken with an interrogative accent, we must translate אַךְ as Jer. has done, by
verumtamen. He knows that he is being hurried forth to meet
death ; he knows it, and has also already made himself so
familiar with this thought, that the sooner he sees an end put
to this his sorrowful life the better—nevertheless does one not
stretch out one's hand when one is falling? This involuntary
reaction against destruction is the inevitable result of man's
instinct of self-preservation. It needs no proof that שלח יד
can signify "to stretch out one's hand for help ;" יִשְׁלַח is
used with a general subj. : one stretches out, as ch. xvii. 5,
xxi. 22. With this determination of the idea of ver. 24*a*,
24*b* is now also naturally connected with what precedes. It
is not, however, to be translated, as Ew. and Hirz. : if one is
in distress, is not a cry for help heard on account of it? If
אִם were intended hypothetically, a continuation of the power
of the interrogative לֹא from ver. 24*a* would be altogether
impossible. Hahn and Loch-Reischl rightly take אִם in the
sense of *an*. It introduces another turn of the question :
Does one, however, not stretch out one's hand to hasten the
fall, or in his downfall (raise) a cry for help, or a wail, on
that account? Döderlein's conjecture, לְחֵן for לְהֵן (praying
"for favour"), deserves respectful mention, but it is not
needed : לְהֵן signifies neutrally : in (under) such circumstances (comp. בָּהֶם, ch. xxii. 21, Isa. lxiv. 5), or is directly
equivalent to לָהֵן, which (Ruth i. 13) signifies *propterea*, and
even in biblical Chaldee, beside the Chaldee signif. *sed, nisi*,
retains this Hebrew signif. (Dan. ii. 6, 9, iv. 24). פִּיד, which
signifies dying and destruction (Talmud. in the peculiar
signif. : that which is hewn or pecked open), synon. of אֵיד,
has been already discussed on ch. xii. 5.

Ver. 25. The further progress of the thoughts seems to be well carried out only by our rendering of ver. 24. The manifestation of feeling—Job means to say—which he himself felt at the misfortune of others, will be still permitted to him in his own misfortune, the seeking of compassion from the sympathising: or have I not wept for the hard of day? *i.e.* him whose lot in life is hard (comp. قَسِى, *durus, miser*); did not my soul grieve for the needy? Here, also, לֹא from ver. 25*a* continues its effect (comp. ch. iii. 10, xxviii. 17); עָנַם is ἅπ. γεγρ., of like signification with אָגַם, whence אֲגַם Isa. xix. 10, אֲגָמָה (sadness) *b. Moëd katan* 14*b*, Arab. *agima*, to feel disgust. If the relation of ver. 25 to ver. 24 is confirmatory, ver. 26 and what follows refers directly to ver. 24: he who felt sympathy with the sufferings of others will nevertheless dare in his own affliction to stretch out his hand for help in the face of certain ruin, and pour forth his pain in lamentation; for his affliction is in reality inexpressibly great: he hoped for good (for the future from his prosperous condition, in which he rejoiced),[1] then came evil; and if I waited for light, deep darkness came. Ewald (§ 232, *h*) regards וַאֲיַחֵלָה as contracted from וָאֲיַחֵלָה, but this shortening of the vowel is a pure impossibility. The former signifies rather καὶ ἤλπιζον or ἐβουλόμην ἐλπίζειν, the latter καὶ ἤλπισα, and that cohortative *fut.* logically forms a hypothetical antecedent, exactly like ch. xix. 18, if I desire to rise (אָקוּמָה), they speak against me (*vid.* Ew. § 357, *b*). In feverish heat and anxiety his bowels were set boiling (רֻתַּח as ch. xli. 23, comp. Talmud. רַתְחָן, a hot-headed fellow), and rested not (from this boiling). The accentuation *Tarcha, Mercha,* and *Athnach* is here incorrect; instead of *Athnach, Rebia mugrasch* is required. Days of affliction came upon him (קִדְּמֻ as Ps. xviii. 6), viz.

---

[1] LXX. *Aldina:* ἐγὼ δὲ ἀπέχων ἀγαθοῖς, which Zwingli rightly corrects ἐπέχων (*Codd. Vat., Alex.,* and *Sinait.*).

as a hostile power cutting off the previous way of his prosperity.

28 *I wandered about in mourning without the sun;*
   I rose in the assembly, I gave free course to my complaint.
29 *I am become a brother of the jackals*
   And a companion of ostriches.
30 *My skin having become black, peels off from me,*
   And my bones are parched with dryness.
31 *My harp was turned to mourning,*
   And my pipe to tones of sorrow.

Several expositors (Umbr., Vaih., Hlgst.) understand קֹדֵר
of the dirty-black skin of the leper, but contrary to the usage
of the language, according to which, in similar utterances (Ps.
xxxv. 14, xxxviii. 7, xlii. 10, xliii. 2, comp. *supra*, ch. v. 11),
it rather denotes the dirty-black dress of mourners (comp. قَدَّرَ,
conspurcare vestem); to understand it of the dirty-black skin
as *quasi sordida veste* (Welte) is inadmissible, since this dis-
tortion of the skin which Job bewails in ver. 30 would hardly
be spoken of thus tautologically. קֹדֵר therefore means in the
black of the שַׂק, or mourning-linen, ch. xvi. 15, by which, however, also the interpretation of בְּלֹא חַמָּה, "without sunburn"
(Ew., Hirz.), which has gained ground since Raschi's day (לֹא
שְׁשׁוּפַתְנִי הַשֶּׁמֶשׁ), is disposed of; for "one can perhaps say of the
blackness of the skin that it does not proceed from the sun,
but not of the blackness of mourning attire" (Hahn). קדר
also refutes the reading בלא חֵמָה in LXX. *Complut.* (ἄνευ
θυμοῦ),[1] Syr., Jer. (*sine furore*), which ought to be understood
of the deposition of the gall-pigment on the skin, and therefore
of jaundice, which turns it (especially in tropical regions) not
merely yellow, but a dark-brown. Hahn and a few others

[1] Whereas *Codd. Alex., Vat.,* and *Sinait.,* ἄνευ φιμοῦ, which is correctly explained by κημοῦ in Zwingli's *Aldine,* but gives no sense.

render בלא חמה correctly in the sense of בחשך, "without the sun
having shone on him." Bereft of all his possessions, and finally
also of his children, he wanders about in mourning (הִלֵּךְ as ch.
xxiv. 10, Ps. xxxviii. 7), and even the sun had clothed itself
in black to him (which is what קָדַר הַשֶּׁמֶשׁ means, Joel ii. 10
and freq.); the celestial light, which otherwise brightened his
path, ch. xxix. 3, was become invisible. We must not forget
that Job here reviews the whole chain of afflictions which have
come upon him, so that by ver. 28a we have not to think
exclusively, and also not prominently, of the leprosy, since
הלכתי indeed represents him as still able to move about freely.
In ver. 28b the accentuation wavers between *Dechî, Munach,
Silluk,* according to which בְּקָהָל אֲשַׁוֵּעַ belong together, which
is favoured by the *Dagesh* in the *Beth,* and *Tarcha, Munach,
Silluk,* according to which (because *Munach,* according to
Psalter ii. 503, § 2, is a transformation of *Rebia mugrasch*)
קַמְתִּי בַּקָּהָל belong together. The latter mode of accentuation,
according to which בקהל must be written without the *Dag.*
instead of בַּקָּהָל (*vid.* Norzi), is the only correct one (because
Dechî cannot come in the last member of the sentence before
Silluk), and is also more pleasing as to matter: I rose (and
stood) in the assembly, crying for help, or more generally:
wailing. The assembly is not to be thought of as an assembly
of the people, or even tribunal (Ew.: "before the tribunal
seeking a judge, with lamentations"), but as the public; for
the thought that Job sought help against his unmerited sufferings before a human tribunal is absurd; and, moreover,
the thought that he cried for help before an assembly of the
people called together to take counsel and pronounce decisions
is equally absurd. Welte, however, who interprets: I was as
one who, before an assembled tribunal, etc., introduces a
quasi of which there is no trace in the text. בְּקָהָל must
therefore, without pressing it further, be taken in the sense
of *publice,* before all the world (Hirz.: comp. בקהל, ἐν

φανερῷ, Prov. xxvi. 26); אֲשַׁוֵּעַ, however, is a circumstantial clause declaring the purpose (Ew. § 337, *b*; comp. De Sacy, *Gramm. Arabe* ii. § 357), as is frequently the case after קוּם, ch. xvi. 8, Ps. lxxxviii. 11, cii. 14: *surrexi in publico ut lamentarer*, or *lamentaturus*, or *lamentando*. In this lament, extorted by the most intense pain, which he cannot hold back, however many may surround him, he is become a brother of those תַּנִּים, jackals (*canes aurei*), whose dolorous howling produces dejection and shuddering in all who hear it, and a companion of בְּנוֹת יַעֲנָה, whose shrill cry is varied by wailing tones of deep melancholy.[1] The point of comparison is not the insensibility of the hearers (*Sforno*), but the fellowship of wailing and howling together with the accompanying idea of the desert in which it is heard, which is connected with the idea itself (comp. Mic. i. 8).

Ver. 30. Now for the first time he speaks of his disfigurement by leprosy in particular: my skin (עוֹרִי, *masc.*, as it is also used in ch. xix. 26, only apparently as *fem.*) is become black (*nigruit*) from me, *i.e.* being become black, has peeled from me, and my bones (עַצְמִי, construed as *fem.* like ch. xix. 20, Ps. cii. 6) are consumed, or put in a glow (חָרָה, *Milel,*

---

[1] It is worth while to cite a passage from Shaw's *Travels in Barbary*, ii. 348 (transl.), here: "When the ostriches are running and fighting, they sometimes make a wild, hideous, hissing noise with their throats distended and beaks open ; at another time, if they meet with a slight opposition, they have a glucking or cackling voice like our domestic fowls : they seem to rejoice and laugh at the terror of their adversary. During the loneliness of the night however, as if their voice had a totally different tone, they often set up a dolorous, hideous moan, which at one time resembles the roar of the lion, and at another is more like the hoarser voice of other quadrupeds, especially the bull and cow. I have often heard them groan as if they were in the greatest agonies." In General Doumas' book on the *Horse of the Sahara*, I have read that the male ostrich (*delim*), when it is killed, especially if its young ones are near, sends forth a dolorous note, while the female (*remda*), on the other hand, does not utter a sound; and so, when the ostrich digs out its nest, one hears a languishing and dolorous tone all day long, and when it has laid its egg, its usual cry is again heard, only about three o'clock in the afternoon.

from חָרַר, as Ezek. xxiv. 11) by a parching heat. Thus, then,
his harp became mournful, and his pipe (וְעֻגָבִי with ‌ *raphatum*)
the cry of the weepers; the cheerful music (comp. ch. xxi. 12)
has been turned into gloomy weeping and sobbing (comp.
Lam. v. 15). Thus the second part of the monologue closes.
It is somewhat lengthened and tedious; it is Job's last sorrowful lament before the catastrophe. What a delicate touch of
the poet is it that he makes this lament, ver. 31, die away so
melodiously! One hears the prolonged vibration of its elegiac
strains. The festive and joyous music is hushed; the only
tones are tones of sadness and lament, *mesto, flebile.*

The Third Part of the Monologue.—Chap. XXXI.

Schema: 8. 9. 8. 6. 6. 10. 10. 4. 4. 5. 7. 6.

1 *I have made a covenant with mine eyes,*
   And how should I fix my gaze upon a maiden!
2 *What then would be the dispensation of Eloah from above,*
   And the inheritance of the Almighty from the heights—
3 *Doth not calamity overtake the wicked,*
   And misfortune the workers of evil?
4 *Doth He not see my ways*
   And count all my steps?

After Job has described and bewailed the harsh contrast
between the former days and the present, he gives us a
picture of his moral life and endeavour, in connection with
the character of which the explanation of his present affliction
as a divinely decreed punishment becomes impossible, and the
sudden overthrow of his prosperity into this abyss of suffering becomes to him, for the same reason, the most painful
mystery. Job is not an Israelite, he is without the pale of
the positive, Sinaitic revelation; his religion is the old patriarchal religion, which even in the present day is called *dîn
Ibrâhîm* (the religion of Abraham), or *dîn el-bedu* (the

religion of the steppe) as the religion of those Arabs who are
not Moslem, or at least influenced by the penetrating Islamism,
and is called by Mejânîshî *el-hanîfîje* (*vid. supra*, i. p. 216,
note) as the patriarchally orthodox religion.[1] As little as
this religion, even in the present day, is acquainted with the
specific Mohammedan commandments, so little knew Job of
the specifically Israelitish. On the contrary, his confession,
which he lays down in this third monologue, coincides remarkably with the ten commandments of piety (*el-felâh*)
peculiar to the *dîn Ibrâhîm*, although it differs in this respect,
that it does not give the prominence to submission to the
dispensations of God, that *teslîm* which, as the whole of this
didactic poem teaches by its issue, is the duty of the perfectly pious; also bravery in defence of holy property and
rights is wanting, which among the wandering tribes is
accounted as an essential part of the *hebbet er-rîh* (inspiration
of the Divine Being), *i.e.* active piety, and to which it is
similarly related, as to the binding notion of "honour" which
was coined by the western chivalry of the middle ages.

Job begins with the duty of chastity. Consistently with the
prologue, which the drama itself nowhere belies, he is living in
monogamy, as at the present day the orthodox Arabs, averse to
Islamism, are not addicted to Moslem polygamy. With the

[1] Also in the *Merg* district east of Damascus, which is peopled by
an ancient unmixed race, because the fever which prevails there kills
strangers, remnants of the *dîn Ibrâhîm* have been preserved despite the
penetrating Islamism. There the *mulaqqin* (Souffleur), who says the
creed into the grave as a farewell to the buried one, adds the following
words: "The *muslim* is my brother, the *muslima* my sister, Abraham is
my father (*abî*), his religion (*dînuh*) is mine, and his confession (*medh-
hebuh*) mine." It is indisputable that the words *muslim* (one who is submissive to God) and *islâm* (submission to God) have originally belonged
to the *dîn Ibrâhîm*. It is also remarkable that the Moslem salutation
selâm occurs only as a sign in war among the wandering tribes, and that
the guest parts from his host with the words: *dâimâ besât el-Chalîl, lâ
maqtû' walâ memnû'*, *i.e.* mayest thou always have Abraham's table, and
plenty of provisions and guests.—WETZST.

confession of having maintained this marriage (although, to
infer from the prologue, it was not an over-happy, deeply
sympathetic one) sacred, and restrained himself not only from
every adulterous act, but also from adulterous desires, his
confessions begin. Here, in the middle of the Old Testament, without the pale of the Old Testament νόμος, we meet
just that moral strictness and depth with which the Preacher
on the mount, Matt. v. 27 sq., opposes the spirit to the letter
of the seventh commandment. It is לְעֵינַי, not עִם־עֵינַי (comp.
ch. xl. 28), designedly ; כרת ברית עם or אֵת is the usual phrase
where two equals are concerned; on the contrary, כרת ברית לְ
where the superior—Jehovah, or a king, or conqueror—binds
himself to another under prescribed conditions, or the covenant is made not so much by a mutual advance as by the one
taking the initiative. In this latter case, the secondary notions
of a promise given (e.g. Isa. lv. 3), or even, as here, of a law
prescribed, are combined with כרת ברית : "as lord of my
senses I prescribed this law for my eyes" (Ew.). The eyes,
says a Talmudic proverb, are the procuresses of sin (סרסורי
נינהו דחטאה); "to close his eyes, that they may not feast on
evil," is, in Isa. xxxiii. 15, a clearly defined line in the picture
of him on whom the everlasting burnings can have no hold.
The exclamation, ver. 1b, is spoken with self-conscious indignation : Why should I . . . (comp. Joseph's exclamation,
Gen. xxxix. 9); Schultens correctly : *est indignatio repellens
vehementissime et negans tale quicquam committi par esse;* the
transition of the מה, لـ, to the expression of negation, which
is complete in Arabic, is here in its incipient state, Ew.
§ 325, b. הִתְבּוֹנֵן עַל is intended to express a fixed and inspect-
ing (comp. אֶל, 1 Kings iii. 21) gaze upon an object, combined
with a lascivious imagination (comp. Sir. ix. 5, παρθένον μὴ
καταμάνθανε, and ix. 8, ἀπόστρεψον ὀφθαλμὸν ἀπὸ γυναικὸς
εὐμόρφου καὶ μὴ καταμάνθανε κάλλος ἀλλότριον), a βλέπειν
which issues in ἐπιθυμῆσαι αὐτήν, Matt. v. 28. *Adulterium*

reale, and in fact two-sided, is first spoken of in the third strophe, here it is *adulterium mentale* and one-sided; the object named is not any maiden whatever, but any בְּתוּלָה, because virginity is ever to be revered, a most sacred thing, the holy purity of which Job acknowledges himself to have guarded against profanation from any lascivious gaze by keeping a strict watch over his eyes. The *Waw* of וּמָה is, as in ver. 14, copulative : and if I had done it, what punishment might I have looked for?

The question, ver. 2, is proposed in order that it may be answered in ver. 3 again in the form of a question : in consideration of the just punishment which the injurer of female innocence meets, Job disavows every unchaste look. On חֵלֶק and נַחֲלָה used of allotted, adjudged punishment, comp. ch. xx. 29, xxvii. 13 ; on נֵכֶר, which alternates with אֵיד (burden of suffering, misfortune), comp. Obad. ver. 12, where in its stead נֹכֶר occurs, as Arab. *nukr,* properly *id quod patienti paradoxum, insuetum, intolerabile videtur, omne ingratum* (Reiske). Conscious of the just punishment of the unchaste, and, as he adds in ver. 4, of the omniscience of the heavenly Judge, Job has made dominion over sin, even in its first beginnings and motions, his principle.

The הוּא, which gives prominence to the subject, means Him who punishes the unchaste. By Him who observes his walk on every side, and counts (יִסְפּוֹר, *plene,* according to Ew. § 138, *a,* on account of the pause, but *vid.* the similar form of writing, ch. xxxix. 2, xviii. 15) all his steps, Job has been kept back from sin, and to Him Job can appeal as a witness.

> 5 *If I had intercourse with falsehood,*
>   *And my foot hastened after deceit :*
> 6 *Let Him weigh me in the balances of justice,*
>   *And let Eloah know my innocence.*

> 7 *If my steps turned aside from the way,*
> *And my heart followed mine eyes,*
> *And any spot hath cleaved to my hands :*
> 8 *May I sow and another eat,*
> *And let my shoots be rooted out.*

We have translated שָׁוְא (on the form *vid.* on ch. xv. 31, and the idea on ch. xi. 11) falsehood, for it signifies desolateness and hollowness under a concealing mask, therefore the contradiction between what is without and within, lying and deceit, parall. מִרְמָה, deceit, delusion, imposition. The phrase הָלַךְ עִם־שָׁוְא is based on the personification of deceit, or on thinking of it in connection with the מְתֵי־שָׁוְא (ch. xi. 11). The form וַתַּחַשׁ cannot be derived from חוּשׁ, from which it ought to be וַתָּחַשׁ, like וַיֶּסַר Judg. iv. 18 and freq., וַיֶּשָׁר (*serravit*) 1 Chron. xx. 3, וַיַּעַט (*increpavit*) 1 Sam. xxv. 14. Many grammarians (Ges. § 72, rem. 9; Olsh. 257, *g*) explain the *Pathach* instead of *Kametz* as arising from the virtual doubling of the guttural (*Dagesh forte implicitum*), for which, however, no ground exists here; Ewald (§ 232, *b*) explains it by "the hastening of the tone towards the beginning," which explains nothing, since the retreat of the tone has not this effect anywhere else. We must content ourselves with the supposition that וַתַּחַשׁ is formed from a חָשָׁה having a similar meaning to חוּשׁ (חִישׁ), as also וַיַּעַט, 1 Sam. xv. 19, comp. xiv. 32, is from a עָטָה of similar signification with עִיט. The hypothetical antecedent, ver. 5, is followed by the conclusion, ver. 6: If he have done this, may God not spare him. He has, however, not done it; and if God puts him to an impartial trial, He will learn his תֻּמָּה, *integritas*, purity of character. The "balance of justice" is the balance of the final judgment, which the Arabs call ميزان الاعمال, "the balance of actions (works)." [1]

---

[1] The manual of ethics by Ghazzâli is entitled *mîzân el-aʿmâl* in the

Ver. 7 also begins hypothetically : if my steps (אֲשֻׁרִי from אַשֻּׁר, which is used alternately with אָשׁוּר without distinction, contrary to Ew. § 260, *b*) swerve (תִּטֶּה, the predicate to the *plur.* which follows, designating a thing, according to Ges. § 146, 3) from the way (*i.e.* the one right way), and my heart went after my eyes, *i.e.* if it followed the drawing of the lust of the eye, viz. to obtain by deceit or extortion the property of another, and if a spot (מֻאוּם, *macula,* as Dan. i. 4, = מוּם, ch. xi. 15; according to Ew., equivalent to מְחֻם, what is blackened and blackens, then a blemish, and according to Olsh., in מְאוּמָה . . . לֹא, like the French *ne . . . point*) clave to my hands : I will sow, and let another eat, and let my shoots be rooted out. The poet uses צֶאֱצָאִים elsewhere of offspring of the body or posterity, ch. v. 25, xxi. 8, xxvii. 14 ; here, however, as in Isaiah, with whom he has this word in common, ch. xxxiv. 2, xlii. 5, the produce of the ground is meant. Ver. 8*a* is, according to John iv. 37, a λόγος, proverb. In so far as he may have acted thus, Job calls down upon himself the curse of Deut. xxviii. 30 sq. : what he sows, let strangers reap and eat; and even when that which is sown does not fall into the hands of strangers, let it be uprooted.

9 *If my heart has been befooled about a woman,*
   And if I lay in wait at my neighbour's door :
10 *Let my wife grind unto another,*
   And let others bow down over her.
11 *For this is an infamous act,*
   And this is a crime [to be brought before] judges ;
12 *Yea, it is a fire that consumeth to the abyss,*
   And should root out all my increase.

As he has guarded himself against defiling virgin innocence

---

original, מאזני צדק in Bar-Chisdai's translation, *vid.* Gosche on Ghazzâli's life and works, S. 261 of the volume of the *Berliner Akademie d. Wissensch.* for 1858.

by lascivious glances, so is he also conscious of having made
no attempt to trespass upon the marriage relationship of his
neighbour (רֵעַ as in the Decalogue, Ex. xx. 17) : his heart
was not persuaded, or he did not allow his heart to be persuaded (נִפְתָּה like πείθεσθαι), i.e. misled, on account of a
woman (אִשָּׁה as אִשׁ אֵשֶׁת אִישׁ, in post-bibl. usage, of another's
wife), and he lay not in wait (according to the manner of
adulterous lovers described at ch. xxiv. 15, which see) at his
neighbour's door. We may here, with Wetzstein, compare the
like-minded confession in a poem of Muhâdi ibn-Muhammel :

ما نَبّ كلب الجار مِنا ولا عَوَى, i.e. "The neighbour's dog
never barked (נב, Beduin equivalent to נבח in the Syrian
towns and villages) on our account (because we had gone by
night with an evil design to his tent), and it never howled
(being beaten by us, to make it cease its barking lest it should
betray us)." In ver. 10 follows the punishment which he
wishes might overtake him in case he had acted thus : " may
my wife grind to another," i.e. may she become his " maid
behind the mill," Ex. xi. 5, comp. Isa. xlvii. 2, who must
allow herself to be used for everything; ἀλετρίς and a
common low woman (comp. Plutarch, non posse suav. viv.
c. 21, καὶ παχυσκελὴς ἀλετρὶς πρὸς μύλην κινουμένη) are
almost one and the same. On the other hand, the Targ.
(coeat cum alio), LXX. (euphemistically ἀρέσαι ἑτέρῳ, not,
as the Syr. Hexapl. shows, ἀλέσαι), and Jer. (scortum sit
alterius), and in like manner Saad., Gecat., understand תִּטְחַן
directly of carnal surrender ; and, in fact, according to the
traditional opinion, b. Sota 10a : אין טחינה אלא לשון עבירה, i.e.
" טחן everywhere in Scripture is intended of (carnal) trespass."
With reference to Judg. xvi. 21 and Lam. v. 13 (where מְחוֹן,

like طاحون, signifies the upper mill-stone, or in gen. the mill),
this is certainly incorrect; the parallel, as well as Deut.

xxviii. 30, favours this rendering of the word in the obscene sense of μύλλειν, *molere*, in this passage, which also is seen under the Arab. synon. of grinding, دهك (*trudere*); according to which it would have to be interpreted : let her grind to another, *i.e.* serve him as it were as a nether mill-stone. The verb טָחַן, used elsewhere (in Talmud.) of the man, would here be transferred to the woman, like as it is used of the mill itself as that which grinds. This rendering is therefore not refuted by its being תִּטְחַן and not תִּטָּחֵן. Moreover, the word thus understood is not unworthy of the poet, since he designedly makes Job seize the strongest expressions. Among moderns, תטחן is thus tropically explained by Ew., Umbr., Hahn, and a few others, but most expositors prefer the proper sense, in connection with which *molat* certainly, especially with respect to ver. 9*b*, is also equivalent to *fiat pellex*. It is hard to decide ; nevertheless the preponderance of reasons seems to us to be on the side of the traditional tropical rendering, by the side of which ver. 10*b* is not attached in progressive, but in synonymous parallelism : *et super ea incurvent se alii*, כָּרַע of the man, as in the phrase كرعت المرأة الى الرجل (*curvat se mulier ad virum*) of the acquiescence of the woman ; אֲחֵרִין is a poetical Aramaism, Ew. § 177, *a*. The sin of adultery, in case he had committed it, ought to be punished by another taking possession of his own wife, for that (הוּא a neutral *masc.*, *Keri* הִיא in accordance with the *fem.* of the following predicate, comp. Lev. xviii. 17) is an infamous act, and that (הִיא referring back to זִמָּה, *Keri* הוּא in accordance with the *masc.* of the following predicate) is a crime for the judges. On this wavering between הוּא and הִיא *vid.* Gesenius, *Handwörterbuch*, 1863, *s. v.* הוּא, S. 225. זִמָּה is the usual Thora-word for the shameless subtle encroachments of sensual desires (*vid.* Saalschütz, *Mosaisches Recht*, S. 791 f.), and עָוֹן פְּלִילִים (not עָוֹן), according to the usual view equivalent to *crimen et* *crimen quidem judicum* (however, on the form of connection intentionally avoided here, where the genitival relation might easily give an erroneous sense, *vid.* Ges. § 116, rem.), signifies a crime which falls within the province of the penal code, for which in ver. 28 it is less harshly עָוֺן פְּלִילִי: a judicial, *i.e.* criminal offence. פְּלִילִים is, moreover, not the *plur.* of פְּלִילִי (Kimchi), but of פָּלִיל, an arbitrator (root פָּל, *findere, dirimere*).

The confirmatory clause, ver. 12, is co-ordinate with the preceding: for it (this criminal, adulterous enterprise) is a fire, a fire consuming him who allows the sparks of sinful desire to rise up within him (Prov. vi. 27 sq.; Sir. ix. 8), which devours even to the bottom of the abyss, not resting before it has dragged him whom it has seized down with it into the deepest depth of ruin, and as it were melted him away, and which ought to root out all my produce (all the fruit of my labour).[1] The function of בְּ is questionable. Ew. (§ 217, *f*) explains it as local: in my whole revenue, *i.e.* throughout my whole domain. But it can also be *Beth objecti*, whether it be that the obj. is conceived as the means of the action (*vid.* on ch. xvi. 4, 5, 10, xx. 20), or that, "corresponding to the Greek genitive, it does not express an entire full coincidence, but an action about and upon the object" (Ew. § 217, S. 557). We take it as *Beth obj.* in the latter sense, after the analogy of the so-called pleonastic Arab. ب (*e.g.* *qaraa bi-suwari,* he has practised the act of reading upon the Suras of the Koran): and which ought to undertake the act of outrooting upon my whole produce.[2]

---

[1] It is something characteristically Semitic to express the notion of destruction by the figure of burning up with fire [*vid. supra,* i. 377, note], and it is so much used in the present day as a natural inalienable form of thought, that in curses and imprecations everything, without distinction of the object, is to be burned; *e.g. juhrik,* may (God) burn up, or *juhrak,* ought to burn, *biláduh,* his native country, *bedenuh,* his body, *'ênuh,* his eye, *shawáribuh,* his moustache (*i.e.* his honour), *nefesuh,* his breath, *'omruh,* his life, etc.—WETZST.

[2] On this pleonastic *Beth obj.* (*el-Bâ el-mezîde*) *vid.* Samachschari's

13 *If I despised the cause of my servant and my maid,*
   When they contended with me:
14 *What should I do, if God should rise up,*
   And if He should make search, what should I answer Him?
15 *Hath not He who formed me in the womb formed him also,*
   And hath not One fashioned us in the belly?

It might happen, as ver. 13 assumes, that his servant or
his maid (אָמָה, اَمَة, denotes a maid who is not necessarily a
slave, ʿabde, as ch. xix. 15, whereas שִׁפְחָה does not occur in
the book) contended with him, and in fact so that they on
their part began the dispute (for, as the Talmud correctly
points out, it is not בְּרִיבִי עִמָּם, but בְּרִיבָם עִמָּדִי), but he did not
then treat them as a despot; they were not accounted as *res*
but *personæ* by him, he allowed them to maintain their personal right in opposition to him.   Christopher Scultetus observes here: *Gentiles quidem non concedebant jus servo contra*
dominum, cui etiam vitæ necisque potestas in ipsum erat; sed
Iob amore justitiæ libere se demisit, ut vel per alios judices aut
arbitros litem talem curaret decidi vel sibi ipsi sit moderatus,
ut juste pronuntiaret.   If he were one who despised (אֶמְאַס,
not מָאַסְתִּי) his servants' cause: what should he do if God
arose and entered into judgment; and if He should appoint
an examination (thus Hahn correctly, for the conclusion
shows that פקד is here a synon. of בחן Ps. xvii. 3, and חקר Ps.
xliv. 22, نَقَدَ, V., VIII., *accurate inspicere*), what should he
answer?

Mufassal, ed. Broch, pp. 125, 132 (according to which it serves " to give
intensity and speciality "), and Beidhâwi's observation on *Sur.* ii. 191.
The most usual example for it is *alqa bi-jedeihi ila et-tahlike*, he has
plunged his hands, *i.e.* himself, into ruin.   The *Bâ el-megâz* (the metaphorical *Beth obj.*) is similar; it is used where the verb has not its most
natural signification but a metaphorical one, *e.g. ashada bidhikrihi*, he
has strengthened his memory: comp. De Sacy, *Chrestomathie Arabe*, i. 397.

Ver. 15. The same manner of birth, by the same divine
creative power and the same human agency, makes both
master and servant substantially brethren with equal claims :
Has not He who brought me forth in my mother's womb
(also) brought forth him (this my servant or my maid), and
has not One fashioned us in our mother's belly? אֶחָד, *unus*,
viz. God, is the subj., as Mal. ii. 10, אֶחָד (אָב) אֵל (for the
thought comp. Eph. vi. 9), as it is also translated by the
Targ., Jer., Saad., and Gecat.; whereas the LXX. (ἐν τῇ
αὐτῇ κοιλίᾳ), Syr., Symm. (as it appears from his translation
ἐν ὁμοίῳ τρόπῳ), construe אחד as the adj. to בְּרֶחֶם, which is
also the idea of the accentuation (*Rebia mugrasch, Mercha,
Silluk*). On the other hand, it has been observed (also
Norzi) that it ought to be הָאֶחָד according to this meaning;
but it was not absolutely necessary, *vid.* Ges. § 111, 2, *b.* אחד
also would not be unsuitable in this combination; it would, as
e.g. in חלום אחד, not affirm identity of number, but of character.
But אחד is far more significant, and as the final word of the
strophe more expressive, when referred to God. The form
וַיְכוֹנֶנּוּ is to be judged of just like וַתְּמוֹגְגֵנוּ, Isa. lxiv. 6 ; either
they are forms of an exceptionally transitive (as שׁוּב, Ps.
lxxxv. 5, and in שׁבות שׁוב) use of the *Kal* of these verbs (*vid.
e.g.* Parchon and Kimchi), or they are syncopated forms of
the *Pilel* for וַתְּמוֹגְגֵנוּ, וַיְכוֹנְנֵנוּ, syncopated on account of the same
letters coming together, especially in ויכננ נו (Ew. § 81, *a*, and
most others); but this coincidence is sought elsewhere (*e.g.*
Ps. l. 23, Prov. i. 28), and not avoided in this manner (*e.g.* Ps.
cxix. 73). Beside this syncope וַיְכוֹנְנֶנּוּ might also be expected,
while according to express testimony the first *Nun* is *raphatum* :
we therefore prefer to derive these forms from *Kal*, without
regarding them, with Olsh., as errors in writing. The *suff.*
is rightly taken by LXX., Targ., Abulwalid, and almost all
expositors,[1] not as singular (*ennu = êhu*), but as plural (*ennu*

---

[1] Also in the Jerusalem Talmud, where R. Johanan, eating nothing

= *ênu*); the Babylonian school pointed וַיְכוֹגְנוּ, like ממנו where it signifies *a nobis*, מִמֶּנּוּ (*Psalter* ii. 459, and further information in Pinsker's works, *Zur Geschichte des Karaismus*, and *Ueber das sogen. assyrische Punktationssystem*). Therefore: One, *i.e.* one and the same God, has fashioned us in the womb without our co-operation, in an equally animal way, which smites down all pride, in like absolute conditionedness.

16 *If I held back the poor from what they desired,*
   And caused the eyes of the widow to languish,
17 *And ate my morsel alone*
   Without letting the fatherless eat thereof:—
18 *No indeed, from my youth he grew up to me as to a father,*
   And from my mother's womb I guided her—

The whole strophe is the hypothetical antecedent of the imprecative conclusion, ver. 22 sq., which closes the following strophe. Since מָנַע דָּבָר מִמֶּנּוּ, *cohibere aliquid ab aliquo* (ch. xxii. 7), is said as much in accordance with the usage of the language as מָנְעוֹ מִדָּבָר, *cohibere aliquem ab aliquo* (Num. xxiv. 11, Eccl. ii. 10), in the sense of *denegare alicui aliquid*, there is no reason for taking מֵחֵפֶץ דַּלִּים together as a genitival clause (*a voto tenuium*), as the accentuation requires it. On חֵפֶץ, *vid.* on ch. xxi. 21; it signifies solicitude (what is ardently desired) and business, here the former: what is ever the interest and want of the poor (the reduced or those without means). From such like things he does not keep the poor back, *i.e.* does not refuse them; and the eyes of the widow

which he did not also share with his slave, refers to these words of Job. Comp. also the story from the Midrash in Guiseppe Levi's *Parabeln Legenden und Ged. aus Thalmud und Midrasch*, S. 141 (Germ. transl. 1863): The wife of R. Jose began a dispute with her maid. Her husband came up and asked the cause, and when he saw that his wife was in the wrong, told her so in the presence of the maid. The wife said in a rage: Thou sayest I am wrong in the presence of my maid? The Rabbi answered: I do as Job did.

he did not cause or allow to languish (כִּלָּה, to bring to an end, *i.e.* cause to languish, of the eyes, as Lev. xxvi. 16, 1 Sam. ii. 33); he let not their longing for assistance be consumed of itself, let not the fountain of their tears become dry without effect. If he had done the opposite, if he had eaten his bread (פַּת = פַּת לֶחֶם) alone, and not allowed the orphan to eat of it with him—but no, he had not acted thus; on the contrary (כִּי as Ps. cxxx. 4 and frequently), he (the parentless one) grew up to him (גְּדֵלַנִי = גָּדֵל לִי, Ges. § 121, 4, according to Ew. § 315, *b*, "by the interweaving of the dialects of the people into the ancient form of the declining language;" perhaps it is more correct to say it is by virtue of a poetic, forced, and rare brevity of expression) as to a father (= כְּמוֹ לְאָב), and from his mother's womb he guided her, the helpless and defenceless widow, like a faithful child leading its sick or aged mother. The hyperbolical expression מִבֶּטֶן אִמִּי dates this sympathizing and active charity back to the very beginning of Job's life. He means to say that it is in-born to him, and he has exercised it ever since he was first able to do so. The brevity of the form גְּדֵלַנִי, brief to incorrectness, might be removed by the pointing גִּדְּלַנִי (Olsh.): from my youth up he (the fatherless one) honoured me as a father; and גִּדְּלַנִי instead of כִּבְּדַנִי would be explained by the consideration, that a veneration is meant that attributed a dignity which exceeds his age to the נַעַר who was not yet old enough to be a father. But גִּדֵּל signifies "to cause to grow" in such a connection elsewhere (parall. רוֹמֵם, to raise), wherefore LXX. translates ἐξέτρεφον (גִּדַּלְתִּי); and גְּדֵלַנִי has similar examples of the construction of intransitives with the *acc.* instead of the *dat.* (especially Zech. vii. 5) in its favour: they became me great, *i.e.* became great in respect of me. Other ways of getting over the difficulty are hardly worth mentioning: the Syriac version reads כְּאֵב (pain) and אֲנָחוֹת; Raschi makes ver. 18*a*, the idea of benevolence, the subj., and ver. 18*b* (as מִדָּה, attribute) the obj.   The *suff.* of אֲנִחֶנָּה Schlottm. refers to the female orphan; but Job refers again to the orphan in the following strophe, and the reference to the widow, more natural here on account of the gender, has nothing against it.   The choice of the verb (comp. ch. xxxviii. 32) also corresponds to such a reference, since the *Hiph.* has an intensified *Kal*-signification here.[1]   From earliest youth, so far back as he can remember, he was wont to behave like a father to the orphan, and like a child to the widow.

19 *If I saw one perishing without clothing,*
   And that the needy had no covering ;
20 *If his loins blessed me not,*
   And he did not warm himself from the hide of my lambs ;
21 *If I have lifted up my hand over the orphan,*
   Because I saw my help in the gate :
22 *Let my shoulder fall out of its shoulder-blade,*
   And mine arm be broken from its bone ;
23 *For terror would come upon me, the destruction of God,*
   And before His majesty I should not be able to stand.

On אוֹבֵד comp. on ch. iv. 11, xxix. 13 ; he who is come down from his right place and is perishing (root בד, to sepa- rate, still perfectly visible through the Arab. *bâda, ba'ida,* to perish), or also he who is already perished, *periens* and *perdi- tus.*   The clause, ver. 19*b*, forms the second obj. to אִם אֶרְאֶה, which otherwise signifies *si video,* but here, in accordance

<hr />

[1] זכר and הזכיר, to remember ; זרע and הזריע, to sow, to cover with seed ; חרש and החריש, both in the signification *silere* and *fabricari* ; לעג and הלעיג, to mock, ch. xxi. 3 ; משל and המשיל, *dominari,* ch. xxv. 2 ; נטה and הטה, to extend, to bow ; קנה and הקנה (to obtain by purchase); קצר and הקציר, to reap, ch. xxiv. 6, are all similar.   In Arab. the *Kal nahaituhu* signifies I put him aside by going on one side (*nahw* or *nâhije*), the *Hiph. anhaituhu,* I put him aside by bringing him to the side (comp. יְנַחֵם, ch. xii. 23).

with the connection, signifies *si videbam*. The blessing of the thankful (ch. xxix. 13) is transferred from the person to the limbs in ver. 20*a*, which need and are benefited by the warmth imparted. אִם־לֹא here is not an expression of an affirmative asseveration, but a negative turn to the continuation of the hypothetical antecedents. The shaking, הֲנִיף, of the hand, ver. 21*a*, is intended, like Isa. xi. 15, xix. 16 (comp. the *Pilel*, ch. x. 32), Zech. ii. 13, as a preparation for a crushing stroke. Job refrained himself from such designs upon the defenceless orphan, even when he saw his help in the gate, *i.e.* before the tribunal (ch. xxix. 7), *i.e.* even when he had a certain prospect of powerful assistance there. If he has acted otherwise, his כָּתֵף, *i.e.* his upper arm together with the shoulder, must fall out from its שֶׁכֶם, *i.e.* the back which bears it together with the shoulder-blades, and his אֶזְרֹעַ, upper and lower arm, which is considered here according to its outward flesh, must be broken out of its קָנֶה, tube, *i.e.* the reed-like hollow bone which gives support to it, *i.e.* be broken asunder from its basis (Syr. *a radice sua*), this sinning arm, which did not compassionate the naked, and mercilessly threatened the defenceless and helpless. The ת *raphatum* which follows in both cases, and the express testimony of the Masora, show that מִשִּׁכְמָה and מִקָּנָה have no *Mappik*. The *He quiescens*, however, is in both instances softened from the *He mappic.* of the *suff.*, Ew. § 21, *f.* פַּחַד in ver. 23 is taken by most expositors as predicate : for terror is (was) to me evil as God, the righteous judge, decrees it. But אֵלַי is not favourable to this. It establishes the particular thing which he imprecates upon himself, and that consequently which, according to his own conviction and perception, ought justly to overtake him out of the general mass, viz. that terror ought to come upon him, a divinely decreed weight of afflic-tion. אֵיד אֵל is a permutative of פַּחַד = פַּחַד אֱלֹהִים, and אֵלֹי with *Dechî* equivalent to אֵלַי (יָבֹא) יִהְיֶה, comp. Jer. ii. 19 (where it is to be interpreted : and that thou lettest no fear before me

come over thee). Thus also ver. 23*b* is suitably connected
with the preceding : and I should not overcome His majesty,
i.e. I should succumb to it. The מִן corresponds to the *præ*
in *prævalerem;* שְׂאֵת (LXX. falsely, λῆμμα, judgment, decision = מַשָּׂא, Jer. *pondus*) is not intended otherwise than ch.
xiii. 11 (parall. פּחד as here).

> 24 *If I made gold my confidence,*
>   *And said to the fine gold : O my trust ;*
> 25 *If I rejoiced that my wealth was great,*
>   *And that my hand had gained much ;—*
> 26 *If I saw the sunlight when it shone,*
>   *And the moon walking in splendour,*
> 27 *And my heart was secretly enticed,*
>   *And I threw them a kiss by my hand :*
> 28 *This also would be a punishable crime,*
>   *For I should have played the hypocrite to God above.*

Not only from covetous extortion of another's goods was he
conscious of being clear, but also from an excessive delight in
earthly possessions. He has not made gold his כֶּסֶל, confidence
(*vid.* on כִּסְלָתֶךָ, ch. iv. 6) ; he has not said to כֶּתֶם, fine gold
(pure, ch. xxviii. 19, of Ophir, xxviii. 16), מִבְטַחִי (with *Dag.
forte implicitum* as ch. viii. 14, xviii. 14) : object (ground) of
my trust ! He has not rejoiced that his wealth is great (רַב,
adj.), and that his hand has attained כַּבִּיר, something great
(neutral *masc.* Ew. § 172, *b*). His joy was the fear of God,
which ennobles man, not earthly things, which are not worthy
to be accounted as man's highest good. He indeed avoided
πλεονεξία as εἰλωλολατρεία (Col. iii. 5), how much more
the heathenish deification of the stars ! אוֹר is here, as ch.
xxxvii. 21 and φάος in Homer, the sun as the great light of
the earth. יָרֵחַ is the moon as a wanderer (from ארח = רח),
i.e. night-wanderer (*noctivaga*), as the Arab. *târik* in a like
sense is the name of the morning-star. The two words

יְקַר הֹלֵי describe with exceeding beauty the solemn majestic wandering of the moon; יקר is *acc.* of closer definition, like תמים, Ps. xv. 2, and this "brilliantly rolling on" is the *acc.* of the predicate to אֶרְאֶה, corresponding to the כִּי יָהֵל, "that (or how) it shoots forth rays" (*Hiph.* of הָלַל, distinct from יֵהַל Isa. xiii. 20), or even : that it shot forth rays (*fut.* in signif. of an imperf. as Gen. xlviii. 17).

Ver. 27 proceeds with *futt. consec.* in order to express the effect which this imposing spectacle of the luminaries of the day and of the night might have produced on him, but has not. The *Kal* וַיִּפְתְּ is to be understood as in Deut. xi. 16 (comp. *ib.* iv. 19, נִדַּח) : it was enticed, gave way to the seducing influence. Kissing is called נָשַׁק as being a joining of lip to lip. Accordingly the kiss by hand can be described by נָשְׁקָה יָד לְפֶה; the kiss which the mouth gives the hand is to a certain extent also a kiss which the hand gives the mouth, since the hand joins itself to the mouth. Thus to kiss the hand in the direction of the object of veneration, or also to turn to it the kissed hand and at the same time the kiss which fastens on it (as compensation for the direct kiss, 1 Kings xix. 18, Hos. xiii. 2), is the proper gesture of the προσκύνησις and *adoratio* mentioned; comp. Pliny, *h. n.* xxviii. 2, 5 : *Inter adorandum dexteram ad osculum referimus et totum corpus circumagimus.* Tacitus, *Hist.* iii. 24, says that in Syria they salute the rising sun; and that this was done by kissing the hand (τὴν χεῖρα κύσαντες) in Western Asia as in Greece, is to be inferred from Lucian's Περὶ ὀρχήσεως, c. xvii.[1] In the passage before us Ew. finds an indication of the spread of the Zoroaster doctrine in the beginning of the seventh century B.C., at which period he is of opinion the book of Job was composed, but without any ground. The ancient Persian

[1] *Vid.* Freund's *Lat. Wörterbuch s. v. adorare*, and K. Fr. Hermann's *Gottesdienstliche Alterth. der Griechen*, c. xxi. 16, but especially *Excursus* 123 in Dougtæus' *Analecta.*

worship has no knowledge of the act of adoration by throwing a kiss; and the Avesta recognises in the sun and moon exalted genii, but created by Ahuramazda, and consequently not such as are to be worshipped as gods. On the other hand, star-worship is everywhere the oldest and also comparatively the purest form of heathenism. That the ancient Arabs, especially the Himjarites, adored the sun, שֶׁמֶשׁ, and the moon, שִׂין (סִין, whence סִינַי, the mountain dedicated to the moon), as divine, we know from the ancient testimonies,[1] and many inscriptions[2] which confirm and supplement them; and the general result of Chwolsohn's[3] researches is unimpeachable, that the so-called Sabians (صابيون with or without *Hamza* of the *Jê*), of whom a section bore the name of worshippers of the sun, *shemsîje*, were the remnant of the ancient heathenism of Western Asia, which lasted into the middle ages. This heathenism, which consisted, according to its basis, in the worship of the stars, was also spread over Syria, and its name, usually combined with צְבָא הַשָּׁמַיִם (Deut. iv. 19), perhaps is not wholly devoid of connection with the name of a district of Syria, אֲרַם צוֹבָה; certainly our poet found it already there, where he heard the tradition about Job, and in his hero presents to us a true adherent of the patriarchal religion, who had kept himself free from the influence of the worship of the stars, which was even in his time forcing its way among the tribes.

It is questionable whether ver. 28 is to be regarded as a conclusion, with Umbr. and others, or as a parenthesis, with Ew., Hahn, Schlottm., and others. We take it as a conclusion, against which there is no objection according to the syntax,

---

[1] *Vid.* the collection in Lud. Krehl's *Religion der vorislamischen Araber,* 1863.

[2] *Vid.* Osiander in the *Deutsche Morgenl. Zeitschr.* xvii. (1863) 795.

[3] In his great work, *Ueber die Ssabier und den Ssabismus,* 2 Bdd. Petersburg, 1856.

although strictly it is only a confirmation (*vid.* vers. 11, 23) of an implied imprecatory conclusion : therefore it is (would be) also a judicial misdeed, *i.e.* one to be severely punished, for I should have played the hypocrite to God above (לְאֵל מִמַּעַל, recalling the universal Arabic expression *allah ta'âla*, God, the Exalted One) by making gold and silver, the sun and moon my idols.   By פְּלִילִי both the sins belonging to the judgment-seat of God, as in ἔνοχος τῷ συνεδρίῳ, Matt. v. 22, are not referred to a human tribunal, but only described κατ᾽ ἄνθρωπον as punishable transgressions of the highest grade. כִּחֵשׁ לְ signifies to play the hypocrite to any one, whereas to disown any one is expressed by כחש בְּ.   His worship of God would have been hypocrisy, if he had disowned in secret the God whom he acknowledged openly and outwardly.

Now follow strophes to which the conclusion is wanting. The single imprecatory conclusion which yet follows (ver. 40), is not so worded that it might avail for all the preceding hypothetical antecedents.   There are therefore in these strophes no conclusions that correspond to the other clauses. The inward emotion of the confessor, which constantly increases in fervour the more he feels himself superior to his accusers in the exemplariness of his life hitherto, struggles against this rounding off of the periods.   A " yea then — !" is easily supplied in thought to these strophes which *per aposiopesin* are devoid of conclusions.

29 *If I rejoiced over the destruction of him who hated me,*
    And became excited when evil came upon him—
30 *Yet I did not allow my palate to sin*
    By calling down a curse upon his life.

The aposiopesis is here manifest, for ver. 29 is evidently equal to a solemn denial, to which ver. 30 is then attached as a simple negative.   He did not rejoice at the destruction

(פִּיד, Arab. فَيْد, *fêd*,[1] as ch. xii. 5, xxx. 24) of his enemy who
was full of hatred towards him (מְשַׂנְאִי, elsewhere also שֹׂנְאִי),
and was not excited with delight (הִתְעֹרֵר, to excite one's self,
a description of emotion, whether it be pleasure, or as ch.
xvii. 8, displeasure, as a not merely passive but moral incident)
if calamity came upon him, and he did not allow his palate
(חֵךְ as the instrument of speech, like ch. vi. 30) to sin by
asking God that he might die as a curse. Love towards an
enemy is enjoined by the Thora, Ex. xxiii. 4, but it is more
or less with a national limitation, Lev. xix. 18, because the
Thora is the law of a people shut out from the rest of the
world, and in a state of war against it (according to which
Matt. v. 43 is to be understood); the books of the Chokma,
however (comp. Prov. xxiv. 17, xxv. 21), remove every limit
from the love of enemies, and recognise no difference, but
enjoin love towards man as man. With ver. 30 this strophe
closes. Among modern expositors, only Arnh. takes in ver.
31 as belonging to it : " Would not the people of my tent
then have said : Would that we had of his flesh ?! we have
not had enough of it," *i.e.* we would eat him up both skin
and hair. Of course it does not mean after the manner of
cannibals, but figuratively, as ch. xix. 22 ; but in a figurative
sense " to eat any one's flesh" in Semitic is equivalent to
lacerare, vellicare, obtrectare (*vid.* on ch. xix. 22, and comp.
also *Sur.* xlix. 12 of the Koran, and Schultens' *Erpenius*,
pp. 592 sq.), which is not suitable here, as in general this
drawing of ver. 31 to ver. 29 sq. is in every respect, and

---

[1] Gesenius derives the noun פִּיד from the verb פִּיד, but the Arabic,
which is the test here, has not only the verb *fâda* as *med. u* and as *med. i*
in the signification to die, but also in connection with *el-feid* (*fêd*) the
substantival form *el-fîd* (= *el-môt*), which (= *fiwd*, comp. p. 26, *note*) is
referable to *fâda*, *med. u.* Thus *Neshwân*, who in his *Lexicon* (vol. ii.
fol. 119) even only knows *fâda, med. u*, in the signif. to die (comp. *infra*
on ch. xxxix. 18, *note*).

especially that of the syntax, inadmissible.   It is the duty of
beneficence, which Job acknowledges having practised, in
ver. 31 sq.

31 *If the people of my tent were not obliged to say :*
    Where would there be one who has not been satisfied with
        his flesh ? !—
32 *The stranger did not lodge out of doors,*
    I opened my door towards the street.

Instead of אָמְרוּ, it might also be יֹאמְרוּ (*dicebant*) ; the *perf.*,
however, better denotes not merely what happens in a general
way, but what must come to pass.   The "people of the tent"
are all who belong to it, like the Arab. *ahl* (tent, metonym.
dwellers in the tent), here pre-eminently the servants, but
without the expression in itself excluding wife, children, and
relations.   The optative מִי־יִתֵּן, so often spoken of already, is
here, as in ver. 35, ch. xiv. 4, xxix. 2, followed by the *acc.
objecti*, for נִשְׂבָּע is *part.* with the long accented *ā* (*quis ex-
hibebit* or *exhibeat non saturatum*), and מִבְּשָׂרוֹ is not meant of
the flesh of the person (as even the LXX. in bad taste
renders : that his maids would have willingly eaten him, their
kind master, up from love to him), but of the flesh of the cattle
of the host.   Our translation follows the accentuation, which,
however, perhaps proceeds from an interpretation like that of
Arnheim given above.   His constant and ready hospitality is
connected with the mention of his abundant care and provision for his own household.   It is unnecessary to take אֹרַח,
with the ancient versions, for אֹרֵחַ, or so to read it ; לָאֹרַח signifies towards the street, where travellers are to be expected,
comp. *Pirke aboth* i. 5 : "May thy house be open into the
broad place (לִרְוָחָה), and may the poor be thy guests."   The
Arabs pride themselves on the exercise of hospitality.   "To
open a guest-chamber" is the same as to establish one's own
household in Arabic.   Stories of judgments by which the

want of hospitality has been visited, form an important element of the popular traditions of the Arabs.[1]

33　*If I have hidden my wickedness like Adam,*
　　Concealing my guilt in my bosom,
34　*Because I feared the great multitude*
　　And the contempt of families affrighted me,
　　So that I acted secretly, went not out of the door.—

Most expositors translate כְּאָדָם : after the manner of men; but appropriate as this meaning of the expression is in Ps. lxxxii. 7, in accordance with the antithesis and the parallelism (which see), it would be as tame here, and altogether expressionless in the parallel passage Hos. vi. 7[2]—the passage which comes mainly under consideration here—since the force of the prophetic utterance: "they have כאדם transgressed the covenant," consists in this, "that Israel is accused of a trans-

---

[1] In the spring of 1860—relates Wetzstein—as I came out of the forest of *Gôlan*, I saw the water of *Râm* lying before us, that beautiful round crater in which a brook that runs both summer and winter forms a clear but fishless lake, the outflow of which underground is recognised as the fountain of the Jordan, which breaks forth below in the valley out of the crater *Tell el-Kadi;* and I remarked to my companion, the physician *Regeb*, the unusual form of the crater, when my Beduins, full of astonishment, turned upon me with the question, "What have you Franks heard of the origin of this lake?" On being asked what they knew about it, they related how that many centuries ago a flourishing village once stood here, the fields of which were the plain lying between the water and the village of *Megdel Shems*. One evening a poor traveller came while the men were sitting together in the open place in the middle of the village, and begged for a supper and a resting-place for the night, which they refused him. When he assured them that he had eaten nothing since the day before, an old woman amidst general laughter reached out a *gelle* (a cake of dried cow-dung, which is used for fuel), and drove him out of the village. Thereupon the man went to the village of *Nimra* (still standing, south of the lake), where he related his misfortune, and was taken in by them. The next morning, when the inhabitants of Nimra woke, they found a lake where the neighbouring village had stood.

[2] Pusey also (*The Minor Prophets with Commentary*, P. i. 1861) improves "like men" by translating "like Adam."

gression which is only to be compared to that of the first man created: here, as there, a like transgression of the expressed will of God" (von Hofmann, *Schriftbeweis*, i. 412f.); as also, according to Rom. v. 14, Israel's transgression is that fact in the historical development of redemption which stands by the side of Adam's transgression. And the mention of Adam in Hosea cannot surprise one, since he also shows himself in other respects to be familiar with the contents of Genesis, and to refer back to it (*vid. Genesis*, S. 11–13). Still much less surprising is such a reference to primeval history in a book that belongs to the literature of the Chokma (*vid.* Introduction, § 2). The descent of the human race from a single pair, and the fall of those first created, are, moreover, elements in all the ancient traditions; and it is questionable whether the designation of men by *beni Adama* (children of Adam), among the Moslems, first sprang from the contact of Judaism and Christianity, or whether it was not rather an old Arabic expression. Therefore we translate with Targ., Schult., Bouillier, Rosenm., Hitz., Kurtz, and von Hofm.: if I have hidden (disowned) like Adam my transgression. The point of comparison is only the sinner's dread of the light, which became prominent as the prototype for every succeeding age in Adam's hiding himself. The לְטְמוֹן which follows is meant not so much as indicating the aim, as gerundive (*abscondendo*); on this use of the *inf. constr.* with לְ, *vid.* Ew. § 280, *d.* חֹב, bosom, is ἀπ. γεγρ.; Ges. connects it with the Arab. *habba*, to love; it is, however, to be derived from the חב, *occulere*, whence *chabibe*, that which is deep within, a deep valley (comp. חָבָּא, *chabaa*, with their derivatives); in Aramaic it is the common word for the Hebr. חֵיק.

Ver. 34*a*. With כִּי follows the motive which Job might have had for hiding himself with his sin: he has been neither an open sinner, nor from fear of men and a feeling of honour a secret sinner. He cherished within him no secret accursed thing, and had no need for playing the hypocrite, because he dreaded (עָרַץ only here with the *acc.* of the obj. feared) the great multitude of the people (רַבָּה not adv. but adj.; הָמוֹן with *Mercha-Zinnorith*, consequently *fem.*, as עַם sometimes, Ew. § 174, *b*), and consequently the moral judgment of the people; and because he feared the stigma of the families, and therefore the loss of honour in the higher circles of society, so that as a consequence he should have kept himself quiet and retired, without going out of the door. One might think of that abhorrence of voluptuousness, with which, 'in the consciousness of its condemnatory nature, a man shuts himself up in deep darkness; but according to ver. 33 it is in general deeds that are intended, which Job would have ground for studiously concealing, because if they had become known he would have appeared a person to be scouted and despised: he could frankly and freely meet any person's gaze, and had no occasion to fear the judgment of men, because he feared sin. He did nothing which he should have cause for carefully keeping from the light of publicity. And yet his affliction is to be accounted as the punishment of hidden sin! as proof that he has committed punishable sin, which, however, he will not confess!

35 *O that I had one who would hear me!*
   Behold my signature—the Almighty will answer me—
   And the writing which my opponent hath written!
36 *Truly I will carry it upon my shoulder,*
   I will wind it about me as a crown.
37 *The number of my steps I will recount to Him,*
   As a prince will I draw near to Him.

The wish that he might find a ready willing hearer is put forth in a general way, but, as is clear in itself, and as it becomes manifest from what follows, refers to Him who, because it treats of a contradiction between the outward

appearance and the true but veiled fact, as searcher of the
heart, is the only competent judge. It may not be translated: *et libellum* (the indictment, or even: the reply to Job's
self-defence) *scribat meus adversarius* (Dachselt, Rosenm.,
Welte)—the accentuation seems to proceed from this rendering, but it ought to be סֵפֶר וְכָתַב; if כָּתַב governed by יַעֲנֵנִי were
intended to be equivalent to יִכְתֹּב, and referred to God, the
longing would be, as it runs, an unworthy and foolish one—
nor: (O that I had one who would hear me . . .) and had
the indictment, which my adversary has written (Ew., Hirz.,
Schlottm.)—for וספר is too much separated from מִי יִתֵּן by
what intervenes—in addition to which comes the consideration that the wish, as it is expressed, cannot be referred to
God, but only to the human opponent, whose accusations
Job has no occasion to wish to hear, since he has already
heard amply sufficient even in detail. Therefore הֵן (instead
of הֶן with a conjunctive accent, as otherwise with *Makkeph*)
will point not merely to תָּוִי, but also to *liber quem scripsit
adversarius meus* as now lying before them, and the parenthetical שַׁדַּי יַעֲנֵנִי will express a desire for the divine decision
in the cause now formally prepared for trial, ripe for discussion. By תָּוִי, my sign, *i.e.* my signature (comp. Ezek. ix. 4,
and Arab. *tiwa*, a branded sign in the form of a cross), Job
intends the last word to his defence which he has just spoken,
ch. xxxi.; it is related to all his former confessions as a confirmatory mark set below them; it is his ultimatum, as it were,
the letter and seal to all that he has hitherto said about his
innocence in opposition to the friends and God. Moreover,
he also has the indictment of the triumvirate which has come
forward as his opponent in his hands. Their so frequently
repeated verbal accusations are fixed as if written; both—their
accusation and his defence—lie before him, as it were, in the
documentary form of legal writings. Thus, then, he wishes
an observant impartial hearer for this his defence; or more

exactly: he wishes that the Almighty may answer, *i.e.* decide.
Hahn interprets just as much according to the syntax, but
understanding by תוי the witness which Job carries in his
breast, and by ספר וגו' the testimony to his innocence written
by God in his own consciousness; which is inadmissible, because, as we have often remarked already, אישׁ ריבי (comp. ch.
xvi. 21) cannot be God himself.

In ver. 36 Job now says how he will appear before Him
with this indictment of his opponent, if God will only condescend to speak the decisive word. He will wear it upon
his shoulder as a mark of his dignity (comp. Isa. xxii. 22,
ix. 5), and wind it about him as a magnificent crown of
diadems intertwined and heaped up one above another (Apoc.
xix. 12, comp. Köhler on Zech. vi. 11)—confident of his
victory at the outset; for he will give Him, the heart-searcher,
an account of all his steps, and in the exalted consciousness
of his innocence, he will approach Him as a prince (קֶרֶב intensive of *Kal*). How totally different from Adam, who was
obliged to be drawn out of his hiding-place, and tremblingly,
because conscious of guilt, underwent the examination of the
omniscient God! Job is not conscious of cowardly and slyly
hidden sins; no secret accursed thing is cherished in the
inmost recesses of his heart and home.

> 38 *If my field cry out against me,*
> *And all together its furrows weep;*
> 39 *If I have devoured its strength without payment,*
> *And caused the soul of its possessor to expire:*
> 40 *May thistles spring up instead of wheat,*
> *And darnel instead of barley.*

The field which he tills has no reason to cry out on account
of violent treatment, nor its furrows to weep over wrong done
to them by their lord.[1] אֲדָמָה, according to its radical signifi-

---

[1] In a similar figure a Rabbinic proverb says (with reference to Mal.

cation, is the covering of earth which fits close upon the body of the earth as its skin, and is drawn flat over it, and therefore especially the arable land ; תֶּלֶם (Arab. *telem*, not however directly referable to an Arab. root, but as also other words used in agriculture, probably borrowed from the North Semitic, first of all the Aramaic or Nabataic), according to the explanation of the Turkish Kamus, the " ditch-like crack which the iron of the ploughman tears in the field," not the ridge thrown up between every two furrows (*vid.* on Ps. lxv. 11). He has not unlawfully used (which would be the reason of the crying and weeping) the usufruct of the field (בֹּחַ meton., as Gen. iv. 12, of the produce, proportioned to its capability of production) without having paid its value, by causing the life to expire from the rightful owner, whether slowly or all at once (Jer. xv. 9). The wish in ver. 40 is still stronger than in vers. 8, 12 : there the loss and rooting out of the produce of the field is desired, here the change of the nature of the land itself ; the curse shall and must come upon it, if its present possessor has been guilty of the sin of unmerciful covetousness, which Eliphaz lays to his charge in ch. xxii. 6–9.

According to the view of the Capuchin Bolducius (1637), this last strophe, vers. 38–40, stood originally after ver. 8, according to Kennicott and Eichhorn after ver. 25, according to Stuhlmann after ver. 34. The modern expositors retain it in its present position. Hirzel maintains the counter arguments : (1) that none of the texts preserved to us favour the change of position ; (2) that it lay in the plan of the poet not to allow the speeches of Job to be rounded off, as would be the case by vers. 35–37 being the concluding strophe, but to break off suddenly without a rhetorical conclusion. If now we imagine the speeches of Elihu as removed, God interrupts

ii. 13), that the altar of God weeps over him who separates himself from the wife of his youth.

Job, and he must cease without having come to an end with what he had to say. But these counter arguments are an insufficient defence: for (1) there is a number of admitted misplacements in the Old Testament which exceed the Masora (*e.g.* 1 Sam. xiii. 1, Jer. xxvii. 1), and also the LXX. (*e.g.* 1 Sam. xvii. 12, באנשים, LXX. ἐν ἀνδράσιν, instead of בשנים); (2) Job's speech would gain a rhetorical conclusion by vers. 38–40, if, as Hirzel in contradiction of himself supposes, vers. 35–37 ought to be considered as a parenthesis, and ver. 40 as a grammatical conclusion to the hypothetical clauses from ver. 24 onwards. But if this strange view is abandoned, it must be supposed that with ver. 38 Job intends to begin the assertion of his innocence anew, and is interrupted in this course of thought now begun, by Jehovah. But it is improbable that one has to imagine this in the mind of such a careful poet. Also the first word of Jehovah, " Who is this that darkeneth counsel with words without knowledge? " ch. xxxviii. 2, is much more appropriate to follow directly on ch. xxxi. 37 than ch. xxxi. 40 ; for a new course of thought, which Jehovah's appearing interrupts, begins with ver. 35; and the rash utterance, ver. 37, is really a " darkening of the divine decree." For by declaring he will give an account to God, his judge, concerning each of his steps, and approach Him like a prince, Job does not merely express the injustice of the accusations raised by his human opponents, but he casts a reflection of injustice upon the divine decree itself, inasmuch as it appears to him to be a *de facto* accusation of God.

Nevertheless, whether Elihu's speeches are to be put aside as not forming an original portion of the book, or not, the impression that vers. 38–40 follow as stragglers, and that vers. 35–37 would form a more appropriate close, and a more appropriate connection for the remonstrance that follows, whether it be Jehovah's or Elihu's, remains. For the assertion in vers. 38–40 cannot in itself be considered to be a justifiable boldness; but in vers. 35–37 the whole condition of Job's inner nature is once more mirrored forth : his longing after God, by which Satan's prediction is destroyed ; and his over-stepping the bounds of humility, on account of which his affliction, so far as it is of a tentative character, cannot end before it is also become a refining fire to him.   Therefore we cannot refrain from the supposition that it is with vers. 38–40 just as with Isa. xxxviii. 21 sq.   The LXX. also found these two verses in this position ; they belong, however, after Isa. xxxviii. 6, as is clear in itself, and as is evident from 2 Kings xx. 7 sq.   There they are accidentally omitted, and are now added at the close of the narration as a supplement.   If the change of position, which is there an oversight, is considered as too hazardous here, vers. 35–37 must be put in the special and close relation to the preceding strophe indicated by us in the exposition, and vers. 38–40 must be regarded as a final round-ing off (not as the beginning of a fresh course of thought) ; for instead of the previous aposiopeses, this concluding strophe dies away, and with it the whole confession, in a particularly vigorous, imprecative conclusion.

Let us once more take a review of the contents of the three sharply-defined monologues.   After Job, in ch. xxvii. xxviii., has closed the controversy with the friends, in the first part of this trilogy, ch. xxix., he wishes himself back in the months of the past, and describes the prosperity, the activity, for the good of his fellow-men, and the respect in which he at that time rejoiced, when God was with him.   It is to be observed here, how, among all the good things of the past which he longs to have back, Job gives the pre-eminence to the fellow-ship and blessing of God as the highest good, the spring and fountain of every other.   Five times at the beginning of ch. xxix. in diversified expressions he describes the former days as a time when God was with him.   Look still further from the beginning of the monologue to its close, to the likewise very expressive כאשר אבלים ינחם. The activity which won every heart to Job, and toward which he now looks back so long-ingly, consisted of works of that charity which weeps with them that weep, and rejoices not in injustice, ch. xxix. 12–17. The righteousness of life with which Job was enamoured, and which manifested itself in him, was therefore charity arising from faith (*Liebe aus Glauben*). He knew and felt himself to be in fellowship with God; and from the fulness of this state of being apprehended of God, he practised charity. He, however, is blessed who knows himself to be in favour with God, and in return loves his fellow-men, especially the poor and needy, with the love with which he himself is loved of God. Therefore does Job wish himself back in that past, for now God has withdrawn from him; and the prosperity, the power, and the important position which were to him the means for the exercise of his charity, are taken from him.

This contrast of the past and present is described in ch. xxx., which begins with ועתה. Men who have become completely animalized, rough hordes driven into the moun-tains, with whom he sympathized, but without being able to help them as he had wished, on account of their degeneracy, —these mock at him by their words and acts. Now scorn and persecution for the sake of God is the greatest honour of which a man can be accounted worthy; but, apart from the consideration that this idea could not yet attain its rightful expression in connection with the present, temporal character of the Old Testament, it was not further from any one than from him who in the midst of his sufferings for God's sake regards himself, as Job does now, as rejected of God. That scorn and his painful and loathsome disease are to him a decree of divine wrath; God has, according to his idea, changed to a tyrant; He will not hear his cry for help. Accordingly, Job can say that his welfare as a cloud is passed away. He is conscious of having had pity on those who needed help, and

yet he himself finds no pity now, when he implores pity
like one who, seated upon a heap of rubbish, involuntarily
stretches forth his hand for deliverance. In this gloomy
picture of the present there is not even a single gleam of
light; for the mysterious darkness of his affliction has not
been in the slightest degree lighted up for Job by the treatment the friends have adopted. Also he is as little able as the
friends to think of suffering and sin as unconnected, for which
very reason his affliction appears to him as the effect of divine
wrath; and the sting of his affliction is, that he cannot consider this wrath just. From the demand made by his faith,
which here and there breaks through his conflict, that God
cannot allow him to die the death of a sinner without testifying to his innocence, Job nowhere attains the conscious conclusion that the motive of his affliction is love, and not wrath.

In the third part of the speech (ch. xxxi.), which begins
with the words, " I had made a covenant," etc., without everywhere going into the detail of the visible conjunction of the
thought, Job asserts his earnest struggle after sanctification,
by delivering himself up to just divine punishment in case
his conduct had been the opposite. The poet allows us to
gain a clear insight into that state of his hero's heart, and
also of his house, which was well-pleasing to God. Not
merely outward adultery, even the adulterous look; not
merely the unjust acquisition of property and goods, but
even the confidence of the heart in such things; not merely
the share in an open adoration of idols, but even the side-
glance of the heart after them, is accounted by him as condemnatory. He has not merely guarded himself from using
sinful curses against his enemies, but he has also not rejoiced
when misfortune overtook them. As to his servants, even
when he has had a dispute with any of them, he has not forgotten that master and servant, without distinction of birth,
are creatures of one God. Towards orphans, from early

youth onwards, he has practised such tender love as if he were their father; towards widows, as if he were their son. With the hungry he has shared his bread, with the naked his clothes; his subordinates had no reason to complain of niggardly sustenance; his house always stood open hospitably to the stranger; and, as the two final strophes affirm: he has not hedged in any secret sin, anxious only not to appear as a sinner openly, and has not drawn forth wailings and tears from the ground which he cultivated by avarice and oppressive injustice. Who does not here recognise a righteousness of life and endeavour, the final aim of which is purity of heart, and which, in its relation to man, flows forth in that love which is the fulfilling of the law? The righteousness of which Job (ch. xxix. 14) says, he has put it on like a garment, and it has put him on, is essentially the same as that which the New Testament Preacher on the mount enjoins. As the work of an Israelitish poet, ch. xxxi. is a most important evidence in favour of the assertion, that a life well-pleasing to God is not, even in the Old Testament, absolutely limited to the Israelitish nation, and that it enjoins a love which includes man as man within itself, and knows of no distinction.

If, now, Job can lay down the triumphant testimony of such a genuine righteousness of life concerning himself, in opposition to men's misconstruction, the contrast of his past and present becomes for the first time mysterious; but we are also standing upon the extreme boundary where the knot that has been tied must be untied. The injustice done to Job in the accusations which the friends bring against him must be laid bare by the appearance of accusation on the part of God, which his affliction casts upon him, being destroyed. With the highest confidence in a triumphant issue, even before the trial of his cause, Job longs, in the concluding words, vers. 35-37, for the judicial decision of God. As

a prince he will go before the Judge, and bind his indictment
like a costly diadem upon his brow. For he is certain that
he has not merited his affliction, that neither human nor
divine accusation can do anything against him, and that he
will remain conqueror—as over men, so over God Himself.

Thus has the poet, in this threefold monologue of Job,
prepared the way for the *catastrophe*, the unravelment of the
knot of the drama. But will God enter into a controversy
respecting His cause with Job?   This is contrary to the
honour of God; and that Job desires it, is contrary to the lowliness which becomes him towards God. On this very account
God will not at once acknowledge Job as His servant: Job
will require first of all to be freed from the sinful presumption
concerning God with which he has handled the problem of
his sufferings. But he has proved himself to be a servant of
God, in spite of the folly into which he has fallen; the design
of Satan to tear him away from God is completely frustrated.
Thus, therefore, after he has purified himself from his sin
into which, both in word and thought, he has allowed himself
to be drawn by the conflict of temptation, Job must be proved
to be the servant of God in opposition to the friends.

But before God Himself appears in order to bring about
the unravelment, there follow still four speeches, ch. xxxii.–
xxxvii., of a speaker, for whose appearance the former part
of the drama has in no way prepared us. It is also remarkable that they are marked off from the book of Job, as far as
we have hitherto read, by the formula תַּמּוּ דִּבְרֵי אִיּוֹב, *are ended
the words of Job*. Carey is of the opinion that these three
words may possibly be Job's own closing *dixi*. According to
Hahn, the poet means to imply by them that Job has now
said all that he intended to say, so that it would now have
been the friends' turn to speak. These views involve a perplexity like that of those who think that Ps. lxxii. 20 must be
regarded as a constituent part of the Psalm. As in that posi-

tion the words, " The prayers of David the son of Jesse are finished," are as a memorial-stone between the original collection and its later extensions, so this תמו דברי איוב, which is transferred by the LXX. (καὶ ἐπαύσατο ᾽Ιὼβ ῥήμασιν) to the historical introduction of the Elihu section, seems to be an important hint in reference to the origin of the book of Job in its present form.   Since Job has come to an end with his speeches, and is silent at the four speeches of a new speaker, although they strongly enough provoke him to reply; according to the idea of the poet, Elihu's appearance is to be regarded as belonging to the catastrophe itself.   And since a hasty glance at the speeches of Jehovah shows that they do not say anything concerning the motive and object of Job's affliction, these speeches of Elihu, in so far as they seem to be an integral part of the whole, as they cast light upon this dark point, will therefore prove in the midst of the action of the drama, what we know already from the prologue, that Job's affliction has not the wrath of God as its motive power, nor the punishment of Job as ungodly for its object.   If the four speeches really furnish this, it is still not absolutely decisive in favour of their forming originally a part of the book.   For it would be even possible that a second poet might have added a part, in harmony with its idea, to the work of the first.   What we expect, moreover, is the mark of the same high poetic genius which we have hitherto regarded with amazement. But since we are now passing on to the exposition of these speeches, it must be with the assumption that they have a like origin with the whole, and that they also really belong to this whole with which they are embodied, in the place where they now stand.   We shall only be able to form a conclusive judgment concerning the character of their form, the solution of their problem, and the manner of their composition, after the exposition is completed, by then taking a comprehensive and critical review of the impressions produced, and our observations.

FOURTH PART.—THE UNRAVELMENT.

CHAP. XXXII.–XLII.

THE SPEECHES OF ELIHU WHICH PREPARE THE WAY FOR THE UNRAVELMENT.—CHAP. XXXII.–XXXVII.

Historical Introduction to the Section.—Chap. xxxii. 1–6a.

A short introduction in historical prose, which introduces the speaker and justifies his appearance, opens the section. It is not, like the prologue and epilogue, accented as prose; but, like the introductions to the speeches and the clause, ch. xxxi. 40 *extra,* is taken up in the network of the poetical mode of accentuation, because a change of the mode of accentuation in the middle of the book, and especially in a piece of such small compass, appeared awkward. The opposition of the three has exhausted itself, so that in that respect Job seems to have come forth out of the controversy as conqueror.

Vers. 1–3. *So these three men ceased to answer Job, because he was righteous in his own eyes. And the wrath of Elihu, the son of Barachel the Buzite, of the family of Ram, was kindled: against Job was his wrath kindled, because he justified himself at the expense of God. And against his three friends was his wrath kindled, because they found no answer, and condemned Job.*

The name of the speaker is אֱלִיהוּא (with *Mahpach*), son of בָּרַכְאֵל (with *Munach*) the בּוּזִי (with *Zarka*). The name *Elihu* signifies " my God is He," and occurs also as an Israelitish name, although it is not specifically Israelitish, like *Elijah* (my God is Jehovah). *Bárach'el* (for which the mode of writing בַּרַכְאֵל with *Dag. implic.* is also found) signifies " may

God bless!" (Olsh. § 277, S. 618); for proper names, as the Arabian grammarians observe, can be formed both into the form of assertory clauses (*ichbâr*), and also into the form of modal (*inshâ*); the name בְּרַכְאֵל is in this respect distinguished from the specifically Israelitish name בֶּרֶכְיָה (Jehovah blesseth). The accompanying national name defines the scene; for on the one side בּוּז and עוּץ, according to Gen. xxii. 21, are the sons of Nahor, Abraham's brother, who removed with him (though not at the same time) from Ur Casdim to Haran, therefore by family Aramæans; on the other side, בּוּז, Jer. xxv. 23, appears as an Arab race, belonging to the קְצוּצֵי פֵאָה (comp. Jer. ix. 25, xlix. 32), *i.e.* to the Arabs proper, who cut the hair of their heads short all round (περιτρόχαλα, Herodotus iii. 8), because wearing it long was accounted as disgraceful (*vid.* Tebrîzi on the *Hamâsa*, p. ٢٥٩, 1. 10 sqq.). Within the Buzite race, Elihu sprang from the family of רָם. Since רם is the name of the family, not the race, it cannot be equivalent to אֲרָם (like רַמִּים, 2 Chron. xxii. 5, = ארמים), and it is therefore useless to derive the Aramaic colouring of Elihu's speeches from design on the part of the poet. But by making him a Buzite, he certainly appears to make him an Aramæan Arab, as Aristeas in Euseb. *præp.* ix. 25 calls him Ἐλιοῦν τὸν Βαραχιὴλ τὸν Ζωβίτην (from ארם צובה). It is remarkable that Elihu's origin is given so exactly, while the three are described only according to their country, without any statement of father or family. It would indeed be possible, as Lightfoot and Rosenm. suppose, for the poet to conceal his own name in that of Elihu, or to make allusion to it; but an instance of this later custom of Oriental poets is found nowhere else in Old Testament literature.

The three friends are silenced, because all their attempts to move Job to a penitent confession that his affliction is the punishment of his sins, have rebounded against this fact, that he was righteous in his own eyes, *i.e.* that he imagined himself righteous; and because they now (שָׁבַת of persons, in distinction from חדל, has the secondary notion of involuntariness) know of nothing more to say. Then Elihu's indignation breaks forth in two directions. First, concerning Job, that he justified himself מֵאֱלֹהִים, *i.e.* not *a Deo* (so that He would be obliged to account him righteous, as ch. iv. 17), but *præ Deo.* Elihu rightly does not find it censurable in Job, that as a more commonly self-righteous man he in general does not consider himself a sinner, which the three insinuate of him (ch. xv. 14, xxv. 4), but that, declaring himself to be righteous, he brings upon God the appearance of injustice, or, as Jehovah also says further on, ch. xl. 8, that he condemns God in order that he may be able to maintain his own righteousness. Secondly, concerning the three, that they have found no answer by which they might have been able to disarm Job in his maintenance of his own righteousness at the expense of the divine justice, and that in consequence of this they have condemned Job. Hahn translates: so that they should have represented Job as guilty; but that they have not succeeded in stamping the servant of God as a רשע, would wrongly excite Elihu's displeasure. And Ewald translates: and that they had nevertheless condemned him (§ 345, *a*);. but even this was not the real main defect of their opposition. The *fut. consec.* describes the condemnation as the result of their inability to hit upon the right answer; it was a miserable expedient to which they had recourse. According to the Jewish view, וַיַּרְשִׁיעוּ אֶת־אִיּוֹב is one of the eighteen תקוני סופרים (*correctiones scribarum*), since it should be וירשיעו את־האלהים. But it is not the friends who have been guilty of this sin of הַרְשִׁיעַ against God, but Job, ch. xl. 8, to whom Elihu opposes the sentence אל לא־ירשיע, ch. xxxiv. 12. Our judgment of another such *tiqqûn*, ch. vii. 20, was more favourable. That Elihu, notwithstanding the inward conviction to the contrary by which he is followed during the course of the controversial dialogue, now speaks for the first time, is explained by what follows.

Vers. 4–6. *And Elihu had waited for Job with words, for they were older than he in days. And Elihu saw that there was no answer in the mouth of the three men, then his wrath was kindled. And Elihu the son of Barachel the Buzite began, and said.*

He had waited (*perf.* in the sense of the *plusquamperf.*, Ew. § 135, *a*) for Job with words (בִּדְבָרִים as elsewhere בְּמִלִּים, בְּמִלִּין), *i.e.* until Job should have spoken his last word in the controversial dialogue. Thus he considered it becoming on his part, for they (הֵמָּה, *illi*, whereas אֵלֶּה according to the usage of the language is *hi*) were older (*seniores*) than he in days (לְיָמִים as ver. 6, less harsh here, instead of the *acc.* of closer definition, ch. xv. 10, comp. xi. 9). As it now became manifest that the friends made no reply to Job's last speeches for want of the right solution of problem, and therefore also Job had nothing further to say, he believes that he may venture, without any seeming want of courtesy, to give utterance to his long-restrained indignation; and Elihu (with *Mahpach*) the son of Barach'el (*Mercha*) the Buzite (with *Rebia parvum*) began and spoke (וַיֹּאמַר not with *Silluk*, but *Mercha mahpach.*, and in fact with *Mercha* on the accented penult., as ch. iii. 2, and further).

Elihu's First Speech.—Chap. xxxii. 6*b*–xxxiii.

Schema: 5. 6. 10. 6. 10. | 6. 8. 10. 13. 8. 6. 10. 10.

Ch. xxxii. 6*b* I am young in days, and ye are hoary,
    Therefore I stood back and was afraid
    To show you my knowledge.
   7 I thought: Let age speak,
    And the multitude of years teach wisdom.

It becomes manifest even here that the Elihu section has in part a peculiar usage of the language. זָחַל in the signification of زحل, cogn. with ذَحَل, וְחַל, to frighten back;[1] and דֵּעַ for דַּעַת (here and vers. 10, 17, ch. xxxvi. 3, xxxvii. 16) occurs nowhere else in the Old Testament; עַל־כֵּן (comp. לָכֵן, ch. xlii. 3) is used only by Elihu within the book of Job. יָמִים, days = fulness of days, is equivalent to advanced age, old age with its rich experience. רֹב with its plural genitive is followed (as כֹּל usually is) by the predicate in the *plur.*; it is the attraction already described by מספר, ch. xv. 10, xxi. 21, Ges. § 148, 1.

8 *Still the spirit, it is in mortal man,*
   And the breath of the Almighty, that giveth them under-
       standing.
9 *Not the great in years are wise,*
   And the aged do not understand what is right.
10 *Therefore I say : O hearken to me,*
   I will declare my knowledge, even I.

The originally affirmative and then (like אוּלָם) adversative אָכֵן also does not occur elsewhere in the book of Job. In contradiction to biblical psychology, Rosenm. and others take ver. 8 as antithetical: Certainly there is spirit in man, but . . .

---

[1] The lexicographers explain the Arab. زحل by *zâla* (זוּל), to stand away from, back, to retreat, or *tanahha*, to step aside ; *Piel, Hiph.*, to push any one aside, place anything back ; *Hithpa.*, to keep one's self on one side ; adj. זָחֵל, זָחִיל, זָחוּל, etc., standing back. Thus the town of *Zahla* in the plain of the Lebanon takes its name from the fact that it does not stand out in the plain, but is built close at the foot of the mountain in a corner, and consequently retreats. And *zuhale* (according to the *Kamus*) is an animal that creeps backwards into its hole, *e.g.* the scorpion ; and hence, improperly, a man who, as we say with a similar figure, never comes out of his hole, always keeps in his hole, *i.e.* never leaves his dwelling, as *zuhal* in general signifies a man who retires or keeps far from active life ; in connection with which also the planet Saturn is called *Zuhal*, the retreating one, on account of its great distance

The two halves of the verse are, on the contrary, a synonymous ("the spirit, it is in man, viz. that is and acts") or progressive parallelism (thus according to the accents: "the spirit, even that which is in man, and . . ."). It is the Spirit of God to which man owes his life as a living being, according to ch. xxxiii. 4; the spirit of man is the principle of life creatively wrought, and indeed breathed into him, by the Spirit of God; so that with regard to the author it can be just as much God's רוּחַ or נְשָׁמָה, ch. xxxiv. 14, as in respect of the possessor: man's- רוח or נשמה. All man's life, his thinking as well as his bodily life, is effected by this inwrought principle of life which he bears within him, and all true understanding, without being confined to any special age of life, comes solely from this divinely originated and divinely living spirit, so far as he acts according to his divine origin and basis of life. רַבִּים are here (as the opposite of צעירים, Gen. xxv. 23) *grandes* = *grandævi* (LXX. πολυχρόνιοι). לֹא governs both members of the verse, as ch. iii. 10, xxviii. 17, xxx. 24 sq. Understanding or ability to form a judgment is not limited to old age, but only by our allowing the πνεῦμα to rule in us in its connection with the divine. Elihu begs a favourable hearing for that of which he is conscious. דֵּעַ, and the Hebr.-Aramaic חָוָה, which likewise belong to his favourite words, recur here.

from the rest. Slippery (of ground) is זַחֲלוּל, because it draws the foot backwards (*muzhil*) by its smoothness, and thus causes the walker to fall. A further formation is זחלק, to be slippery, and to slip in a slippery place; beside which, זלק, a word of similar meaning, is no longer used in Syria. According to this Arabic primary notion of زَحَل, it appears זחלי ארץ, Mic. vii. 17, is intended to describe the serpents not as creeping upon the earth, but as creeping into the earth (comp. the name of the serpent, *achbi' at el-ard*, those that hide themselves in the earth); but in Talmud. and Aram. זחל used of animals has the general signification to creep, and of water, to glide (flow gently down). The primary notion, to *glide* (to slip, creep, flow gently, *labi*), is combined both in the derivatives of the root זח and in those of the root זל with the notion of a departing and retreating motion.—WETZST. and FL.

11 *Behold, I waited upon your words,*
   Hearkened to your perceptions,
   While ye searched out replies.
12 *And I attended closely to you,*
   Yet behold: there was no one who refuted Job,
   Who answered his sentences, from you.
13 *Lest ye should say : " We found wisdom,*
   God is able to smite him, not man !"
14 *Now he hath not arranged his words against me,*
   And with your sentences I will not reply to him.

He has waited for their words, viz. that they might give
utterance to such words as should tend to refute and silence
Job. In what follows, עַד still more emphatically than לְ
refers this aim to that to which Elihu had paid great attention : I hearkened to your understandings, *i.e.* explanations
of the matter, that, or whether, they came forth, (I hearkened)
to see if you searched or found out words, *i.e.* appropriate
words. Such abbreviated forms as אָזִין = אַאֲזִין (comp. מְזִין =
מִיזִין for מַאֲזִין, Prov. xvii. 4, Ges. § 68, rem. 1, if it does not
signify *nutriens*, from זוּן) we shall frequently meet with in
this Elihu section. In ver. 12, 12*a* evidently is related as an
antecedent to what follows : and I paid attention to you
(עֲדֵיכֶם contrary to the analogy of the cognate *præp.* instead of
עֲדֵיכֶם, moreover for אֲלֵיכֶם, with the accompanying notion :
intently, or, according to Aben-Duran : thoroughly, without
allowing a word to escape me), and behold, intently as I paid
attention : no one came forward to refute Job ; there was no
one from or among you who answered (met successfully) his
assertions. Every unbiassed reader will have an impression
of the remarkable expressions and constructions here, similar
to that which one has in passing from the book of the Kings
to the characteristic sections of the Chronicles. The three,
Elihu goes on to say, shall not indeed think that in Job a

wisdom has opposed them—a false wisdom, indeed—which only God and not any man can drive out of the field (נָדַף, ندف, *discutere*, *dispellere*, as the wind drives away chaff or dry leaves); while he has not, however (וְלֹא followed directly by a *v. fin.* forming a subordinate clause, as ch. xlii. 3, Ps. xliv. 18, and freq., Ew. § 341, *a*), arrayed (עָרַךְ in a military sense, ch. xxxiii. 5; or forensic, xxiii. 4; or even as ch. xxxvii. 19, in the general sense of *proponere*) words against him (Elihu), *i.e.* utterances before which he would be compelled to confess himself affected and overcome. He will not then also answer him with such opinions as those so frequently repeated by them, *i.e.* he will take a totally different course from theirs in order to refute him.

> 15 *They are amazed, they answer no more,*
> *Words have fled from them.*
> 16 *And I waited, for they spake not,*
> *For they stand still, they answer no more.*
> 17 *Therefore I also will answer for my part,*
> *I will declare my knowledge, even I.*

In order to give a more rapid movement and an emotional force to the speech, the figure asyndeton is introduced in ver. 15, as perhaps in Jer. xv. 7, Ew. § 349, *a*. Most expositors render הֶעְתִּיקוּ passively, according to the sense: they have removed from them, *i.e.* are removed from them; but why may העתיק not signify, like Gen. xii. 8, xxvi. 22, to move away, viz. the tent = to wander on (Schlottm.)? The figure: words are moved away (as it were according to an encampment broken up) from them, *i.e.* as we say: they have left them, is quite in accordance with the figurative style of this section. It is unnecessary to take וְהוֹחַלְתִּי, ver. 16*a*, with Ew. (§ 342, *c*) and Hirz. as *perf. consec.* and interrogative: and should I wait, because they speak no more? Certainly the interrog. part. sometimes disappears after the *Waw* of consequence, *e.g.* Ezek. xviii. 13, 24 (and will he live?); but by what would והוחלתי be distinguished as *perf. consec.* here? Hahn's interpretation: I have waited, until they do not speak, for they stand . . ., also does not commend itself; the poet would have expressed this by עד לא ידברו, while the two כי, especially with the poet's predilection for repetition, appear to be co-ordinate. Elihu means to say that he has waited a long time, surprised that the three did not speak further, and that they stand still without speaking again. Therefore he thinks the time is come for him also to answer Job. אֶעֱנֶה cannot be *fut. Kal,* since where the 1 *fut. Kal* and *Hiph.* cannot be distinguished by the vowel within the word (as in the *Ayin Waw* and double *Ayin* verbs), the former has an inalienable *Segol;* it is therefore 1 *fut. Hiph.,* but not as in Eccl. v. 19 in the signification to employ labour upon anything (LXX. περισπᾶν), but in an intensive *Kal* signification (as הִזְעִיק for זָעַק, ch. xxxv. 9, comp. on ch. xxxi. 18): to answer, to give any one an answer when called upon. Ewald's supposedly proverbial: I also plough my field! (§ 192, *c*, Anm. 2) does unnecessary violence to the usage of the language, which is unacquainted with this הֶעֱנָה, to plough. It is perfectly consistent with Elihu's diction, that חֶלְקִי beside אֲנִי as permutative signifies, "I, my part," although it might also be an *acc.* of closer definition (as *pro parte mea,* for my part), or even—which is, however, less probable—*acc.* of the obj. (my part). Elihu speaks more in the scholastic tone of controversy than the three.

18 *For I am full of words,*
   The spirit of my inner nature constraineth me.
19 *Behold, my interior is like wine which is not opened,*
   Like new bottles it is ready to burst.
20 *I will speak, that I may gain air,*
   I will open my lips and reply.

21 *No, indeed, I will accept no man's person,*
And I will flatter no man.
22 *For I understand not how to flatter;*
My Maker would easily snatch me away.

The young speaker continues still further his declaration, promising so much. He has a rich store of מִלִּים, words, *i.e.* for replying. מִלֵּתִי defective for מִלֵּאתִי, like יָצָתִי for יָצָאתִי, ch. i. 21; whereas מָלוּ, Ezek. xxviii. 6, is not only written defectively, but is also conjugated after the manner of a *Lamed He* verb, Ges. §§ 23, 3, 74, rem. 4, 75, 21, *c*. The spirit of his inner nature constrains him, since, on account of its intensity and the fulness of this interior, it struggles to break through as through a space that is too narrow for it. בֶּטֶן, as ch. xv. 2, 35, not from the curved appearance of the belly, but from the interior of the body with its organs, which serve the spirit life as the strings of a harp; comp. Arab. *batn*, the middle or interior; *bâtin*, inwardly (opposite of *zâhir*, outwardly). His interior is like wine לֹא יִפָּתֵחַ, which, or (as an adverbial dependent clause) when it is not opened, *i.e.* is kept closed, so that the accumulated gas has no vent, LXX. δεδεμένος (bound up), Jer. *absque spiraculo;* it will burst like new bottles. יִבָּקֵעַ is not a relative clause referring distributively to each single one of these bottles (Hirz. and others), and not an adverbial subordinate clause (Hahn: when it will explode), but predicate to בְּטֶנִי: his interior is near bursting like new bottles (אֹבוֹת *masc.* like נֹאדוֹת, Josh. ix. 13), *i.e.* not such as are themselves new (ἀσκοὶ καινοί, Matt. ix. 17, for these do not burst so easily), but like bottles of new wine, which has to undergo the action of fermentation, LXX. ὥσπερ φυσητήρ (*Cod. Sinait.*[1] φυσητής) χαλκέως, *i.e.* חֲרָשִׁים (whence it is evident that a bottle and also a pair of bellows were called אוֹב). Since he will now yield to his irresistible impulse, in order that he may obtain air or free space, *i.e.*

disburdening and ease (וְיִרְוַח לִי), he intends to accept no man's person, *i.e.* to show partiality to no one (*vid.* on ch. xiii. 8), and he will flatter no one. כִּנָּה signifies in all three dialects to call any one by an honourable name, to give a surname, here with אֶל, to speak fine words to any one, to flatter him. This Elihu is determined he will not do; for לֹא יָדַעְתִּי אֲכַנֶּה, I know not how to flatter (French, *je ne sais point flatter*), for כַּנּוֹת or לְכַנּוֹת; comp. the similar constructions, ch. xxiii. 3 (as Esth. viii. 6), x. 16, 1 Sam. ii. 3, Isa. xlii. 21, lii. 1, Ges. 142, 3, *c;* also in Arabic similar verbs, as "to be able" and "to prepare one's self," are thus connected with the *fut.* without a particle between (*e.g. anshaa jef'alu,* he began to act). Without partiality he will speak, flattery is not his forte. If by flattery he should deny the truth, his Maker would quickly carry him off. כִּמְעַט followed by subjunct. *fut.:* for a little (with disjunctive accent, because equivalent to *haud multum abest quin*), *i.e.* very soon indeed, or easily would or might . . . ; יִשָּׂאֵנִי (as ch. xxvii. 21) seems designedly to harmonize with עֹשֵׂנִי.

Ch. xxxiii. 1 *But nevertheless, O Job, hear my speeches,*
   And hearken to all my words.
  2 *Behold now, I have opened my mouth,*
   My tongue speaketh in my palate.
  3 *Sincere as my heart are my utterances,*
   And knowledge that is pure my lips declare.

The issue of the impartial discussion which Elihu designs to effect, is subject to this one condition, that Job listens to it, and observes not merely this or that, but the whole of its connected contents; and in this sense וְאוּלָם, which is used just as in ch. i. 11, xi. 5, xii. 7, xiii. 4, xiv. 18, xvii. 10, in the signification *verumtamen,* stands at the head of this new turn in his speech. Elihu addresses Job, as none of the previous speakers have done, by name. With הִנֵּה־נָא (as ch. xiii. 18),

he directs Job's observation to that which he is about to say :
he has already opened his mouth, his tongue is already in
motion,—circumstantial statements, which solemnly inaugu-
rate what follows with a consciousness of its importance.
Job has felt the absence of אִמְרֵי־יֹשֶׁר, ch. vi. 25, in the speeches
of the three; but Elihu can at the outset ensure his word
being "the sincerity of his heart," *i.e.* altogether heartily
well meant : and—thus it would be to be translated according
to the accentuation—the knowledge of my lips, they (my lips)
utter purely. But "the knowledge of the lips" is a notion
that seems strange with this translation, and בָּרוּר is hardly
intended thus adverbially. דַּעַת, contrary to the accentuation,
is either taken as the accusative of the obj., and בָּרוּר as the
acc. of the predicate (*masc.* as Prov. ii. 10, xiv. 6) : knowledge
my lips utter pure; or interpreted, if one is not willing to
depart from the accentuation, with Seb. Schmid : *scientiam
labiorum meorum quod attinet* (the knowledge proceeding from
my lips), *puram loquentur sc. labia mea.* The notions of
purity and choice coincide in ברור (comp. Arab. *ibtarra*, to
separate one's self ; *asfa*, to prove one's self pure, and to
select). The *perff.*, vers. 2 sq., describe what is begun, and
so, as relatively past, extending into the present.

4 *The Spirit of God hath made me,*
   And the breath of the Almighty hath given me life.
5 *If thou canst, answer me,*
   Prepare in my presence, take thy stand!
6 *Behold, I am like thyself, of God,*
   Formed out of clay am I also.
7 *Behold, my terror shall not affright thee,*
   And my pressure shall not be heavy upon thee.

He has both in common with Job : the spirituality as well
as the earthliness of man's nature; but by virtue of the
former he does not, indeed, feel himself exalted above Job's

person, but above the present standpoint taken up by Job ;
and in consideration of this, Job need not fear any unequal
contest, nor as before God, ch. ix. 34, xiii. 21, in order that
he may be able to defend himself against Him, make it a
stipulation that His majesty may not terrify him.   It is man's
twofold origin which Elihu, vers. 4, 6, gives utterance to in
harmony with Gen. ii. 7 : the mode of man's origin, which is
exalted above that of all other earthly beings that have life ;
for the life of the animal is only the individualizing of the
breath of the Divine Spirit already existing in matter.   The
spirit of man, on the contrary (for which the language has
reserved the name נְשָׁמָה), is an inspiration directly coming
forth from God the personal being, transferred into the bodily
frame, and therefore forming a person.[1]   In the exalted consciousness of having been originated by the Spirit of God,
and being endowed with life from the inbreathed breath of
the Almighty, Elihu stands invincible before Job : if thou
canst, refute me (הֲשִׁיב with *acc.* of the person, as ch. xxxiii. 32) ;
array thyself (עֶרְכָה for עָרְכָה, according to Ges. 63, rem. 1)
before me (here with the additional thought of מִלְחָמָה, as
ch. xxiii. 4, in a forensic sense with מִשְׁפָּט), place thyself in
position, or take thy post (*imper. Hithpa.* with the *ah* less
frequent by longer forms, Ew. § 228, *a*).

On the other side, he also, like Job, belongs to God, *i.e.* is
dependent and conditioned.   הֶן־אֲנִי is to be written with *Segol*
(not *Ssere*) ; לָאֵל is intended like לֹו, ch. xii. 16 ; and כְּפִיךָ signifies properly, according to thine utterance, *i.e.* standard, in
accordance with, *i.e.* like thee, and is used even in the Pentateuch (*e.g.* Ex. xvi. 21) in this sense *pro ratione ;* כְּפִי, ch.
xxx. 18, we took differently.   He, Elihu, is also nipped from
the clay, *i.e.* taken from the earth, as when the potter nips off

---

[1] God took a small piece of His own life—says the tradition among the
Karens, a scattered tribe of Eastern India—blew into the nostrils of His
son and daughter, and they became living beings, and were really human.

a piece of his clay (comp. Aram. קְרָץ, a piece, Arab. *qurs*, a bread-cake, or a dung-cake, *vid. supra*, vol. i. p. 377, from *qarasa*, to pinch off, take off, cogn. *qarada*, to gnaw off, cut off, ii. p. 40). Thus, therefore, no terribleness in his appearing will disconcert Job, and his pressure will not be a burden upon him. By a comparison of ch. xiii. 21*a*, it might seem that אַכְפִּי is equivalent to כַּפִּי (LXX. ἡ χείρ μου), but כְּבֵד is everywhere connected only with יָד, never with כַּף; and the ἀπ. γεγρ. is explained according to Prov. xvi. 26, where אָכַף signifies to oppress, drive (Jer. *compulit*), and from the dialects differently, for in Syr. *ecaf* signifies to be anxious about anything (*ecaf li*, it causes me anxiety, *curæ mihi est*), and in Arab. *accafa*, to saddle, *ucáf*, Talmud. אוּכָף, a saddle, so that consequently the Targ. translation of אַכְפִּי by טוּנִי, my burden, and the Syr. by אוכפני, my pressing forward (Arabic version *iqbáli*, my touch), are supported, since אֶכֶף signifies pressure, heavy weight, load, and burden ; according to which it is also translated by Saad. (my constraint), Gecat. (my might). It is therefore not an opponent who is not on an equality with him by nature, with whom Job has to do. If he is not able to answer him, he will have to be considered as beaten.

> 8 *Verily thou hast said in mine ears,*
>   *And I heard the sound of thy words :*
> 9 " *I am pure, without transgression ;*
>   " *Spotless am I, and I have no guilt.*
> 10 " *Behold, He findeth malicious things against me,*
>   " *He regardeth me as His enemy ;*
> 11 " *He putteth my feet in the stocks,*
>   " *He observeth all my paths.*"
> 12 *Behold, therein thou art not right, I will answer thee,*
>   *For Eloah is too exalted for man.*

With אַךְ אָמַרְתָּ Elihu establishes the undeniable fact,

whether it be that אַף is intended as restrictive (only thou hast
said, it is not otherwise than that thou . . .), or as we have
translated, according to its primary meaning, affirmative
(forsooth, it is undeniable).   To say anything בְּאָזְנֵי of another
is in Hebrew equivalent to not saying it secretly, and so as
to be liable to misconstruction, but aloud and distinctly.   In
ver. 9, Elihu falls back on Job's own utterances, as ch. ix. 21,
תַּם אָנִי; xvi. 17, תְּפִלָּתִי זַכָּה; xii. 4, where he calls himself
צַדִּיק תָּמִים, comp. x. 7, xiii. 18, 23, xxiii. 10 sqq., xxvii. 5 sq.,
ch. xxix. xxxi.   The expression חַף, *tersus*, did not occur in
the mouth of Job; Geiger connects חף with the Arab. hanîf
(*vid.* on ch. xiii. 16); it is, however, the adj. of the Semitic
verb חַף, حَفَّ, to rub off, scrape off; Arab. to make smooth by
scraping off the hair; Targ., Talm., Syr., to make smooth by
washing and rubbing (after which Targ. שֵׁזִיג, *lotus*).[1]   אָנֹכִי
has here, as an exception, retained its accentuation of the
final syllable in pause.   In ver. 10 Elihu also makes use of a
word that does not occur in Job's mouth, viz. תְּנוּאוֹת, which,
according to Num. xiv. 34, signifies "alienation," from נוּא
(הֵנִיא), to hinder, restrain, turn aside, *abalienare*, Num. xxxii. 7;
and according to the Arab. نَاءَ (to rise heavily),[2] III. to lean
one's self upon, to oppose any one; it might also signify directly,
"hostile risings;" but according to the Hebr. it signifies
grounds and occasions for hostile aversion.   Moreover, Elihu
here recapitulates what Job has in reality often in meaning

---

[1] *Vid.* Nöldecke in *Benfey's Zeitschrift*, 1863, S. 383.

[2] Nevertheless Zamachschari does not derive ناوى, to treat with
enmity, from نو, but from نوى, so that *nâwa fulânan* signifies "to have
evil designs against any one, to meditate evil against one."   The phrases
iluh 'alêji nijât, he has evil intentions (wicked designs) against me, *nijetuh
zerîje aleik*, he has evil intentions against thee, and similar, are very
common.—WETZST.

said, *e.g.* ch. x. 13–17; and ver. 10*b* are his own words, ch. xiii. 24, ותחשבני לאויב לך; xix. 11, ויחשבני לו כצריו; xxx. 21, תהפך לאכזר לי. In like manner, ver. 11 is a *verbatim* quotation from ch. xiii. 27; יָשֵׂם is a poetic contracted *fut.* for יָשִׂים. It is a principal trait of Job's speeches which Elihu here makes prominent: his maintenance of his own righteousness at the expense of the divine justice. In ver. 12 he first of all refutes this צָדֵק נַפְשׁוֹ מֵאֱלֹהִים in general. The verb צָדֵק does not here signify to be righteous, but to be in the right (as ch. xi. 2, xiii. 18)—the prevailing signification in Arabic (*sadaqa*, to speak the truth, be truthful). זֹאת (with *Munach*, not *Dechî*) is *acc. adv.*: herein, in this case, comp. on ch. xix. 26. רָבָה מִן is like Deut. xiv. 24 (of the length of the way exceeding any one's strength), but used, as nowhere else, of God's superhuman greatness; the Arabic version has the preposition عَنْ in this instance for מִן. God is too exalted to enter into a defence of Himself against such vainglorying interwoven with accusations against Him. And for this reason Elihu will enter the lists for God.

13 *Why hast thou contended against Him,*
   That He answereth not concerning all His doings?
14 *Yet no—in one way God speaketh,*
   And in two, only one perceiveth it not.
15 *In the dream, in a vision of the night,*
   When deep sleep falleth upon men,
   In slumberings upon the bed:
16 *Then He openeth the ear of men,*
   And sealeth admonition for them,
17 *That He may withdraw man from mischief,*
   And hide pride from man;
18 *That He may keep back his soul from the pit,*
   And his life from the overthrow of the sword.

Knowing himself to be righteous, and still considering himself treated as an enemy by God, Job has frequently inquired of God, Why then does He treat him thus with enmity, ch. vii. 20, and why has He brought him into being to be the mark of His attack? ch. x. 18. He has longed for God's answer to these questions; and because God has veiled Himself in silence, he has fallen into complaint against Him, as a ruler who governs according to His own sovereign arbitrary will. This is what Elihu has before his mind in ver. 13. רִיב (elsewhere in the book of Job with עִם or the *acc.* of the person with whom one contends) is here, as Jer. xii. 1 and freq., joined with אֶל and conjugated as a contracted *Hiph.* (רִיבוֹתָ instead of רַבְתָּ, Ges. § 73, 1); and עָנָה with the *acc.* signifies here: to answer anything (comp. ch. xxxii. 12, xl. 2, and especially ix. 3); the *suff.* does not refer back to אֱנוֹשׁ of the preceding strophe (Hirz., Hahn), but to God. דְּבָרָיו are the things, *i.e.* facts and circumstances of His rule; all those things which are mysterious in it He answers not, *i.e.* He answers concerning nothing in this respect (comp. כֹּל לֹא, ch. xxxiv. 27), He gives no kind of account of them (Schnurr., Ges., and others). כִּי, ver. 14*a*, in the sense of *imo*, is attached to this negative thought, which has become a ground of contention for Job: yet no, God does really speak with men, although not as Job desires when challenged and in His own defence. Many expositors take בְּאַחַת and בִּשְׁתַּיִם after LXX., Syr., and Jer., in the signification *semel, secundo* (thus also Hahn, Schlottm.); but *semel* is אַחַת, whereas באחת is nowhere equivalent to בְּפַעַם אחת, for in Num. x. 4 it signifies with one, viz. trumpet; Prov. xxviii. 18, on one, viz. of the many ways; Jer. x. 8, in one, *i.e.* in like folly (not: altogether, at once, which כְּאֶחָד, Syr. *bachdo*, signifies); then further on it is not twice, but two different modes or means of divine attestation, viz. dreams and sicknesses, that are spoken of; wherefore it is rightly translated by the Targ.

una loquela, by Pagn. *uno modo,* by Vatabl., Merc., *una via.*
The form of the declaration: by one—by two, is that of the
so-called number-proverbs, like ch. v. 19. In diverse ways
or by different means God speaks to mortal man—he does
not believe it, it is *his own* fault if he does perceive it. לֹא
יְשׁוּרֶנָּה, which is correctly denoted as a separate clause by
Rebia mugrasch, is neither with Schlottm. to be regarded as a
circumstantial clause (without one's . . .), nor with Vatablus
and Hahn as a conditional clause (if one does not attend to
it), nor with Montanus and Piscator as a relative clause (to
him who does not observe it), but with Tremellius as a co-
ordinate second predicative clause without a particle (one
might expect אַךְ): he (mortal man) or one observes it not
(שׁוּר with neut. *suff.* exactly like ch. xxxv. 13).

Vers. 15 sqq. Elihu now describes the first mode in which
God speaks to man: He Himself comes forward as a witness
in man's sleep, He makes use of dreams or dream-like visions,
which come upon one suddenly within the realm of nocturnal
thought (*vid. Psychol.* S. 282 sq.), as a medium of revelation
—a usual form of divine revelation, especially in the heathen
world, to which positive revelation is wanting. The reading
בְּחֶזְיוֹן (Codd., LXX., Syr., Symm., Jer.), as also the accentuation of the בחלום with *Mehupach Legarme,* proceeds from the
correct assumption, that vision of the night and dream are
not coincident notions; moreover, the detailing ver. 15, is
formed according to ch. iv. 13. In this condition of deep or
half sleep, *revelat aurem hominum,* a phrase used of the preparation of the ear for the purpose of hearing by the removal
of hindrances, and, in general, of confidential communication,
therefore: He opens the ear of men, and seals their admonition, *i.e.* the admonition that is wholesome and necessary for
them. Elihu uses חָתַם בְּ here and ch. xxxvii. 7 as חָתַם בְּעַד
is used in ch. ix. 7: to seal anything (to seal up), comp. حتم,
σφραγίζειν, in the sense of infallible attestation and confirma-

tion (John vi. 27), especially (with ـب) of divine revelation or inspiration, distinct in meaning from خَتَم, σφραγίζειν, in the proper sense. Elihu means that by such dreams and visions, as rare overpowering facts not to be forgotten, God puts the seal upon the warning directed to them which, sent forth in any other way, would make no such impression. Most ancient versions (also Luther) translate as though it were יְחִתֵּם (LXX. ἐξεφόβησεν αὐτούς). מֹסֵר is a secondary form to מוּסָר, ch. xxxvi. 10, which occurs only here. Next comes the fuller statement of the object of the admonition or warning delivered in such an impressive manner. According to the text before us, it is to be explained: in order that man may remove (put from himself) mischief from himself (Ges. § 133, 3); but this inconvenient change of subject is avoided, if we supply a מ to the second, and read אדם ממעשׂה, as LXX. ἀποστρέψαι ἄνθρωπον ἀπὸ ἀδικίας αὐτοῦ (which does not necessarily pre-suppose the reading ממעשׂיהו), Targ. ab opere malo; Jer. not so good : ab his quæ fecit. מֲעֲשֶׂה signifies facinus, an evil deed, as 1 Sam. xx. 19, and פֹּעַל, ch. xxxvi. 9, evil-doing. The infin. constr. now passes into the v. fin., which would be very liable to misconstruction with different subjects: and in order that He (God) may conceal arrogance from man, i.e. altogether remove from him, unaccustom him to, render him weary of, the sin of pride (גֵּוָה from גֵּוָה = גֵּאָה, as ch. xxii. 29, according to Ges., Ew., Olsh., for גֵּאֲוָה = גֵּאֲוָה). Here everything in thought and expression is peculiar. Also חַיָּה, ver. 18b (as vers. 22, 28), for חַיִּים (ver. 30) does not occur elsewhere in the book of Job, and the phrase עָבַר בַּשֶּׁלַח here and ch. xxxvi. 12 (comp. עָבַר בַּשַּׁחַת, ver. 28) nowhere else in the Old Testament. שֶׁלַח (Arab. siláh, a weapon of offence, opp. metá´, a weapon of defence) is the engine for shooting, from שָׁלַח, emittere, to shoot; and עבר בשלח is equivalent to נפל בעד השלח, Joel ii. 8, to pass away by (precipitate one's self into) the weapon for shooting. To deliver man from sin, viz. sins of carnal

security and imaginary self-importance, and at the same time
from an early death, whether natural or violent, this is the disciplinary design which God has in view in connection with this
first mode of speaking to him; but there is also a second mode.

19   *He is chastened also with pain upon his bed,*
     And with the unceasing conflict of his limbs;
20   *And his life causeth him to loathe bread,*
     And his soul dainty meat.
21   *His flesh consumeth away to uncomeliness,*
     And his deranged limbs are scarcely to be seen.
22   *Then his soul draweth near to the grave,*
     And his life to the destroyers.

Another and severer lesson which God teaches man is by
painful sickness: he is chastened with pain (בְּ of the means)
on his bed, he and the vigorous number of his limbs, *i.e.* he
with this hitherto vigorous (Raschi), or : while the multitude
of his limbs is still vigorous (Ew.).   Thus is the *Keri* וְרֹב to
be understood, for the interpretation : and the multitude of
his limbs with unceasing pain (Arnh. after Aben-Ezra), is
unnatural.   But the *Chethib* is far more commendable : and
with a constant tumult of his limbs (Hirz. and others).   Ver.
19*b* might also be taken as a substantival clause : and the
tumult of his limbs is unceasing (Umbr., Welte); but that
taking over of בְּ from במכאוב is simpler and more pleasing.   רִיב
(opposite of שָׁלוֹם, *e.g.* Ps. xxxviii. 4) is an excellent description
of disease which consists in a disturbance of the equilibrium of
the powers, in the dissolution of their harmony, in the excitement of one against another (*Psychol.* S. 287).   אֵיתָן for אֵיתָן
belongs to the many defective forms of writing of this section.
In ver. 20 we again meet a Hebræo-Arabic *hapaxlegomenon*,
זִהֵם from זָהַם.   In Arab. *zahuma* signifies to stink, like the
Aram. זְהַם (whence זוּהֲם, dirt and stench), *zahama* to thrust
back, restrain, after which Abu Suleiman Daûd Alfâsi, in his

Arabic *Lexicon* of the Hebrew, interprets: "his soul thrusts back (תזהם נפסה) food and every means of life,"[1] beside which the *suff.* of וְזִהֲמַתּוּ is taken as an anticipation of the following object (*vid.* on ch. xxix. 3): his life feels disgust at it, at bread, and his soul at dainty meat. The *Piel* has then only the intensive signification of *Kal* (synon. תִּעֵב, Ps. cvii. 18), according to which it is translated by Hahn with many before him. But if the poet had wished to be so understood, he would have made use of a less ambiguous arrangement of the words, וזהמתו לחם חיתו. We take זְהֵם with Ew. § 122, *b*, as causative of *Kal*, in which signification the *Piel*, it is true, occurs but rarely, yet it does sometimes, instead of *Hiph.*; but without translating, with Hirz., חיה by hunger and נפש by appetite, which gives a confused thought. Schlottm. appropriately remarks: "It is very clearly expressed, as the proper vital power, the proper ψυχή, when it is inwardly consumed by disease, gives one a loathing for that which it otherwise likes as being a necessary condition of its own existence." Thus it is: health produces an appetite, sickness causes nausea; the soul that is in an uninjured normal state longs for food, that which is severely weakened by sickness turns the desire for dainties into loathing and aversion.

Ver. 21*a*. The contracted future form יִכָל, again, like יֵשֶׁם, ver. 11*a*, is poetic instead of the full form: his flesh vanishes מֵרֹאִי, from sight, *i.e.* so that it is seen no longer; or from comeliness, *i.e.* so that it becomes unsightly; the latter (comp. 1 Sam. xvi. 12 with Isa. liii. 2, ולא־מראה) might be preferred. In ver. 21*b* the *Keri* corrects the text to וְשֻׁפּוּ, *et contrita sunt*, whereas the *Chethib* is to be read וּשְׁפִי, *et contritio*. The verb שָׁפָה, which has been explained by Saadia from the Talmudic,[2] signifies *conterere, comminuere*; Abulwalîd (in Ges.

---

[1] *Vid.* Pinsker's *Likkute Kadmoniot*, p. קמג.

[2] He refers to *b. Aboda zara* 42*a*: If a heathen have broken an idol to pieces (שָׁפָה) to derive advantage from the pieces, both the (shattered)

Thes.) interprets it here by *suhifet wa-baradet*, they are consumed and wasted away, and explains it by כְּתִתוּ. The radical
notion is that of scraping, scratching, rubbing away (not to
be interchanged with سفا, ספה, which, starting from the radical
notion of sweeping away, vanishing, comes to have that of
wasting away; cognate, however, with the above ساكف,
whence *suháf*, consumption, prop. a rasure of the plumpness
of the body). According to the *Keri*, ver. 21*b* runs: and his
bones (limbs) are shattered (fallen away), they are not seen,
i.e. in their wasting away and shrivelling up they have lost
their former pleasing form. Others, taking the bones in their
strict sense, and שפה in the signification to scrape away = lay
bare, take לא ראו as a relative clause, as Jer. has done : *ossa
quæ tecta fuerant nudabuntur* (rather *nudata sunt*), but this
ought with a change of mood to be וַיְשֻׁפּוּ . . . לֹא רֻאוּ. To the
former interpretation corresponds the unexceptionable *Chethib:*
and the falling away of his limbs are not seen, *i.e.* (*per
attractionem*) his wasting limbs are diminished until they are
become invisible. רֻאוּ is one of the four Old Testament words
(Gen. xliii. 26, Ezra viii. 18, Lev. xxiii. 17) which have a
Dagesh in the *Aleph;* in all four the *Aleph* stands between
two vowels, and the dageshing (probably the remains of a
custom in the system of pointing which has become the prevailing one, which, with these few exceptions, has been suffered to fall away) is intended to indicate that the *Aleph* is
here to be carefully pronounced as a guttural (to use an
Arabic expression, as *Hamza*), therefore in this passage *ru-'ú.*[1]
Thus, then, the soul (the bearer of the life of the body) of the

idol and the fragments (שִׁפּוּיִין) are permitted (since both are deprived of
their heathenish character).

[1] *Vid.* Luzzatto's *Grammatica della Lingua Ebraica* (1853), § 54.
Ewald's (§ 21) view, that in these instances the pointed *Aleph* is to be
read as *j* (therefore *ruju*), is unfounded ; moreover, the point over the
Aleph is certainly only improperly called *Dagesh*, it might at least just as
suitably be called *Mappik*.

sick man, at last succumbing to this process of decay, comes near to the pit, and his life to the מְמִתִים, destroying angels (comp. Ps. lxxviii. 49, 2 Sam. xxiv. 16), *i.e.* the angels who are commissioned by God to slay the man, if he does not anticipate the decree of death by penitence. To understand the powers of death in general, with Rosenm., or the pains of death, with Schlottm. and others, does not commend itself, because the Elihu section has a strong angelological colouring in common with the book of Job. The following strophe, indeed, in contrast to the ממיתים, speaks of an angel that effects deliverance from death.

> 23 *If there is an angel as mediator for him,*
>   *One of a thousand,*
>   *To declare to man what is for his profit:*
> 24 *He is gracious to him, and saith:*
>   *Deliver him, that he go not down to the pit—*
>   *I have found a ransom.*

The former case, vers. 15–18, was the easier; there a strengthening of the testimony of man's conscience by a divine warning, given under remarkable circumstances, suffices. This second case, which the LXX. correctly distinguishes from the former (it translates ver. 19, πάλιν δὲ ἤλεγξεν αὐτὸν ἐν μαλακίᾳ ἐπὶ κοίτης), is the more difficult: it treats not merely of a warning against sin and its wages of death, but of a deliverance from the death itself, to which the man is almost abandoned in consequence of sin. This deliverance, as Elihu says, requires a mediator. This course of thought does not admit of our understanding the מַלְאָךְ of a human messenger of God, such as Job has before him in Elihu (Schult., Schnurr., Boullier, Eichh., Rosenm., Welte), an "interpreter of the divine will, such as one finds one man among a thousand to be, a God-commissioned speaker, in one word: a prophet" (von Hofmann in *Schriftbew.* i. 336f.). The

מלאך appears not merely as a declarer of the conditions of the deliverance, but as a mediator of this deliverance itself. And if the מְמִתִים, ver. 22b, are angels by whom the man is threatened with the execution of death, the מלאך who comes forward here for him who is upon the brink of the abyss cannot be a man. We must therefore understand מלאך not as in ch. i. 14, but as in ch. iv. 18 ; and the more surely so, since we are within the extra-Israelitish circle of a patriarchal history. In the extra-Israelitish world a far more developed doctrine of angels and demons is everywhere found than in Israel, which is to be understood not only subjectively, but also objectively; and within the patriarchal history after Gen. xvi., that מלאך יהוה (אלהים) appears, who is instrumental in effecting the progress of the history of redemption, and has so much the appearance of the God of revelation, that He even calls himself God, and is called God. He it is whom Jacob means, when (Gen. xlviii. 15 sq.), blessing Joseph, he distinguishes God the Invisible, God the Shepherd, i.e. Leader and Ruler, and "the Angel who delivered (הַגֹּאֵל) me from all evil;" it is the Angel who, according to Ps. xxxiv. 8, encampeth round about them that fear God, and delivereth them ; "the Angel of the presence" whom Isaiah in the *Thephilla*, ch. lxiii. 7 sqq., places beside Jehovah and His Holy Spirit as a third *hypostasis*. Taking up this perception, Elihu demands for the deliverance of man from the death which he has incurred by his sins, a superhuman angelic mediator. The "Angel of Jehovah" of primeval history is the oldest prefigurement in the history of redemption of the future incarnation, without which the Old Testament history would be a confused *quodlibet* of premises and radii, without a conclusion and a centre; and the angelic form is accordingly the oldest form which gives the hope of a deliverer, and to which it recurs, in conformity to the law of the circular connection between the beginning and end, in Mal. iii. 1.

The strophe begins without any indication of connection
with the preceding: one would expect וְאִם or אָז אִם, as we felt
the absence of אַף in ver. 14, and לְכֵן in ch. xxxii. 17. We might
take מַלְאָךְ מֵלִיץ together as substantive and *epitheton;* the accentuation, however, which marks both מלאך and מליץ with
Rebia magnum (in which case, according to Bär's *Psalterium,*
p. xiv., the second distinctive has somewhat less value than
the first), takes מלאך as subj., and מליץ as predicate : If there
is then for him (עליו, *pro eo,* Ew. § 217, *i*) an angel as מליץ,
i.e. mediator; for מליץ signifies elsewhere an interpreter, Gen.
xlii. 23; a negotiator, 2 Chron. xxxii. 31; a God-commissioned
speaker, *i.e.* prophet, Isa. xliii. 27 ;—everywhere (if it is not
used as in ch. xvi. 20, *in malam parte*) the shades of the
notion of this word are summarized under the general notion
of *internuncius,* and therefore of mediator (as the Jewish
name of the mediating angel מטטרון, probably equivalent to
mediator, not μετάθρονος, which is no usable Greek word).
The Targ. translates by פרקליטא, παράκλητος (*opp.* קטיגור,
κατήγορος, κατήγωρ). Therefore : if an angel undertakes the
mediatorial office for the man, and indeed one of a thousand,
i.e. not any one whatever of the thousands of the angels
(Deut. xxxiii. 2, Ps. lxviii. 18, Dan. vii. 10, comp. Tobit
xii. 15, εἷς ἐκ τῶν ἑπτά), but one who soars above the thousands, and has not his equal among them (as Eccl. vii. 28).
Hirz. and Hahn altogether falsely combine : one of the thousands, whose business it is to announce . . . The accentuation is correct, and that forced mode of connection is without
reason or occasion. It is the function of the מלאך itself as
מליץ, which the clause which expresses the purpose affirms :
if an angel appears for the good of the man as a mediator, to
declare to him יָשְׁרוֹ, his uprightness, *i.e.* the right, straight
way (comp. Prov. xiv. 2), in one word : the way of salvation,
which he has to take to get free of sin and death, viz. the
way of repentance and of faith (trust in God) : God takes

pity on the man . . . Here the conclusion begins; Rosenm.
and others erroneously continue the antecedent here, so that
what follows is the intercession of the angel; the angel, however, is just as a mediator who brings about the favour of
God, and therefore not the חֹנֵן himself. He renders pardon
possible, and brings the man into the state for receiving it.

Therefore: then God pardons, and says to His angel: Deliver him from the descent to the pit, I have found a ransom.
Instead of פְּדָעֵהוּ, it would be admissible to read פְּרָעֵהוּ, let him
free (from פרע, فرغ), if the angel to whom the command is
given were the angel of death. פָּדַע is a cognate form, perhaps dialectic, with פָּדָה, root פד (as יפה, יפע, وفع ,وفى, from
the common root וף, יף).[1] The verb מָצָא (מְטָא) signifies to
come at, ch. xi. 7, to attain something, and has its first signification here, starting from which it signifies the finding on
the part of the seeker, and then when weakened finding
without seeking. One is here reminded of Heb. ix. 12,
αἰωνίαν λύτρωσιν εὑράμενος. כֹּפֶר (on this word, vid. *Hebräer-
brief*, S. 385, 740), according to its primary notion, is not a
covering = making good, more readily a covering = cancel-
ling (from כָּפַר, Talmud. to wipe out, away), but, as the usual
combination with עַל shows, a covering of sin and guilt before
wrath, punishment, or execution on account of guilt, and in
this sense λύτρον, a means of getting free, ransom-money.
The connection is satisfied if the repentance of the chastened
one (thus *e.g.* also von Hofm.) is understood by this ransom,
or better, his affliction, inasmuch as it has brought him to repentance. But wherefore should the mediatorship of the angel
be excluded from the notion of the כֹּפֶר? Just this mediatorship is meant, inasmuch as it puts to right him who by his

---

[1] Wetzstein is inclined to regard פדע as a metathesis of דפע, دفع:
thrust (tear, hold) him back from the grave. A proper name, *fed ân*,
which often occurs among the Beduins, is of uncertain signification;
perhaps it would serve as an explanation of פדעהו.

sins had worked death, *i.e.* places him in a condition in which
no further hindrance stands in the way of the divine pardon.
If we connect the mediating angel, like the angel of Jehovah
of the primeval history, with God Himself, as then the logos
of this mediating angel to man can be God's own logos communicated by him, and he therefore as מליץ, God's speaker
(if we consider Elihu's disclosure in the light of the New
Testament), can be the divine Logos himself, we shall here
readily recognise a presage of the mystery which is unveiled
in the New Testament: "God was in Christ, and recon-
ciled the world unto Himself." A presage of this mystery,
flashing through the darkness, we have already read in ch.
xvii. 3 (comp. ch. xvi. 21; and, on the other hand, in order
to see how this anticipation is kindled by the thought of the
opposite, ch. ix. 33). The presage which meets us here is
like another in Ps. cvii.—a psalm which has many points of
coincidence with the book of Job—where in ver. 20 we find,
" He sent His word, and healed them." [1] At any rate, Elihu
expresses it as a postulate, that the deliverance of man can
only be effected by a superhuman being, as it is in reality
accomplished by the man who is at the same time God, and
from all eternity the Lord of the angels of light.

The following strophe now describes the results of the
favour wrought out for man by the מלאך מליץ.

25 *His flesh swelleth with the freshness of youth,*
   He returneth to the days of his youth.
26 *If he prayeth to Eloah, He showeth him favour,*
   So that he seeth His face with joy,
   And thus He recompenseth to man his uprightness.

---

[1] In his introduction, p. 76, Schlottmann says: " The conceptions of
Wisdom and of the Revealing Angel were already united in that of the
Eternal Word in the ante-Christian, Jewish theology. Therein the fact
of the divine revelation in Christ found the forms in which it could
accommodate itself to the understanding, and stimulate succeeding ages

27 *He singeth to men and saith:*
  " *I had sinned and perverted what was straight,*
  " *And it was not recompensed to me.*
28 " *He hath delivered my soul from going down into the pit,*
  " *And my life rejoiceth in the light.*"

Misled by the change of the *perf.* and *fut.* in ver. 25, Jer. translates 25*a*: *consumta est caro ejus a suppliciis;* Targ.: His flesh had been weakened (אִתְחַלִּישׁ), or made thin (אִתְקְלִישׁ), more than the flesh of a child; Raschi: it had become burst (French אישקושא, in connection with which only פֹּשׁ appears to have been in his mind, in the sense of springing up, *prendre son escousse*) from the shaking (of disease). All these interpretations are worthless; נֹעַר, peculiar to the Elihu section in the book of Job (here and ch. xxxvi. 14), does not signify shaking, but is equivalent to נְעוּרִים (ch. xiii. 26, xxxi. 18); and רֻטֲפַשׁ is in the *perf.* only because the passive quadriliteral would not so easily accommodate itself to inflexion (by which all those asserted significations, which suit only the *perf.* sense, fall to the ground). The *Chateph* instead of the simple *Shevâ* is only in order to give greater importance to the passive *u*. But as to the origin of the quadriliteral (on the four modes of the origin of roots of more than three radicals, *vid. Jesurun,* pp. 160–166), there is no reason for regarding it as a mixed form derived from two different verbs: it is formed just like פַּרְשֵׁז (from פָּרַשׁ, by Arabizing = פָּרַשׂ) with a sibilant termination from רָטֹף = רָטֹב, and therefore signifies to be (to have been made) over moist or juicy. However, there is yet another almost more commendable explanation possible. In Arab. طرفش signifies to further thought and penetration." Thus it is: between the Chokma of the canonical books and the post-biblical development of the philosophy of religion (dogmatism) which culminates in Philo, there is an historical connection, and, indeed, one that has to do with the development of redemption. *Vid. Luth. Zeitschrift,* 1863, S. 219 ff.

to recover, prop. to grow green, become fresh (perhaps from
t*arufa*, as in the signification to blink, from t*arafa*). From
this Arab. *tarfasha*, or even from a Hebr. טְרַפֵּשׁ,[1] *pinguefacere*
(which may with Fürst be regarded as springing from טָפַשׁ,
to be fleshy, like כִּרְבֵּל, (כִּרְסֵם), רְטַפַּשׁ might have sprung by
transposition. In a remarkable manner one and the same
idea is attained by all these ways: whether we regard רטפשׁ
as a mixed form from רטב and טפשׁ, or as an extended root-
form from one or other of these verbs, it is always according
to the idea: a superabundance of fresh healthfulness. The
מִן of מִנַּעַר is chiefly regarded as comparative: more than
youth, *i.e.* leaving this behind, or exceeding it, Ew. § 221, *a*;
but ver. 25*b*, according to which he who was hitherto sick
unto death actually renews his youth, makes it more natural
to take the מִן as causal: it swells from youth or youthfulness.
In this description of the renovation which the man experiences, it is everywhere assumed that he has taken the
right way announced to him by the mediating angel. Accordingly, ver. 26*a* is not intended of prayer that is heard,
which resulted in pardon, but of prayer that may be heard
continually, which results from the pardon: if he prays to
Eloah (*fut. hypotheticum* as ch. xxii. 27, *vid.* on xxix. 24),

He receives him favourably (רָצָה, رِضَى, with ב, بِ, to have
pleasure in any one, with the acc. *eum gratum vel acceptum
habere*), and he (whose state of favour is now established
anew) sees God's countenance (which has been hitherto veiled

---

[1] The Talmud. טרפשׁא דליבא (*Chullin*, 49*b*) signifies, according to the
customary rendering, the pericardium, and טרפשׁא דכבדא (*ib.* 46*a*) the
diaphragm, or rather the little net (*omentum minus*). Originally, however, the former signified the cushion of fat under the pericardium on
which the heart rests, especially in the crossing of the furrows; the latter
the accumulation of fat on the porta (πύλη) and between the laminæ of
the little net. For טרפשׁ is correctly explained by שׁומן, fat. It has
nothing to do with τράπεζα (an old name for a part of the liver), with
which Ges. after Buxtorf connects it.

from him, ch. xxxiv. 29) with rejoicing (as Ps. xxxiii. 3 and freq.), and He (God) recompenses to the man his upright- ness (in his prolonged course of life), or prop., since it is not וַיְשַׁלֵּם, but וַיָּשֶׁב, He restores on His part his relation in accord- ance with the order of redemption, for that is the idea of צְדָקָה; the word has either a legal or a so-to-speak evangeli- cal meaning, in which latter, used of God (as so frequently in Isaiah II.), it describes His rule in accordance with His counsel and order of redemption; the primary notion is strict observance of a given rule.

In ver. 27*a* the favoured one is again the subj. This change of person, without any indication of the same, belongs to the peculiarities of the Hebrew, and, in general, of the Oriental style, described in the *Geschichte der jüd. Poesie*, S. 189 [*History of Jewish Poetry*]; the reference of וַיַּרְא, as *Hiph.*, to God, which is preferred by most expositors, is con- sequently unnecessary. Moreover, the interpretation: He causes his (the favoured one's) countenance to behold joy (Umbr., Ew.), is improbable as regards the phrase (נראה) ראה פְּנֵי ה׳, and also syntactically lame; and the interpretation: He causes (him, the favoured one) to behold His (the divine) countenance with joy (Hirz., Hahn, Schlottm., and others), halts in like manner, since this would be expressed by וַיַּרְאֵהוּ (וַיַּרְאֶנּוּ). By the reference to psalmody which follows in ver. 27 (comp. ch. xxxvi. 24), it becomes natural that we should understand ver. 26*b* according to such passages in the Psalms as xcv. 2, lxvii. 2, xvii. 15. יָשֹׁר is a poetically con- tracted *fut.* after the manner of a jussive, for יָשׁוּר; and per- haps it is a dialectic form, for the *Kal* שׁוּר = שִׁיר occurs only besides in 1 Sam. xviii. 6 as *Chethîb*. With עַל (comp. Prov. xxv. 20) it signifies to address a song to any one, to sing to him. Now follows the psalm of the favoured one in outline; ver. 28 also belongs to it, where the *Keri* (Targ. Jer.), without any evident reason whatever, gets rid of the 1 *pers.* (LXX.,

Syr.). I had sinned—he says, as he looks back ashamed and thankful—and perverted what was straight (comp. the confession of the penitent, Ps. cvi. 6), וְלֹא שָׁוָה לִי, *et non æquale factum s. non æquatum est mihi*,[1] *i.e.* it has not been recompensed to me according to my deserts, favour instead of right is come upon me. שָׁוָה (سوى) is intended neutrally, not so that God would be the subj. (LXX. καὶ οὐκ ἄξια ἤτασέ με ὧν ἥμαρτον). Now follows, ver. 28, the positive expression of the favour experienced. The phrase עָבַר בַּשַּׁחַת, after the analogy of עָבַר בַּשֶּׁלַח above, and also חַיָּה for חַיִּים, are characteristic of the Elihu section. Beautiful is the close of this psalm *in nuce:* "and my life refreshes itself (רָאָה בְּ as ch. xx. 17 and freq.) in the light," viz. in the light of the divine countenance, which has again risen upon me, *i.e.* in the gracious presence of God, which I am again become fully conscious of.

> 29 *Behold, God doeth all*
> *Twice, thrice with man,*
> 30 *To bring back his soul from the pit,*
> *That it may become light in the light of life.*
> 31 *Listen, O Job, hearken to me;*
> *Be silent and let me speak on.*
> 32 *Yet if thou hast words, answer me;*
> *Speak, for I desire thy justification.*
> 33 *If not, hearken thou to me;*
> *Be silent and I will teach thee wisdom.*

After having described two prominent modes of divine in-

---

[1] In Arabic سوى (*sawa*) is the most general expression for "to be worth, to cost," usually with the *acc.* of price, but also with *li*, *e.g.* in the proverb *hal ka'ke mâ tiswe li-hal da'ke*, this (wretched) bite of bread (of subsistence) is not worth this (excessive) pressure after it. Accordingly וְלֹא שָׁוָה לִי would signify: it (what I suffered) came not equal to me (did not balance me), which at any rate is equivalent to "it did not cost my life" (Wetzst.), but would be indistinctly expressed.

terposition for the moral restoration and welfare of man, he adds, vers. 29 sq., that God undertakes (observe the want of parallelism in the distich, ver. 29) everything with a man twice or thrice (asyndeton, as *e.g.* Isa. xvii. 6, in the sense of *bis terve*) in order to bring back his soul from the pit (שַׁחַת, here for the fifth time in this speech, without being anywhere inter-changed with שְׁאוֹל or another synonym, which is remarkable), that it, having hitherto been encompassed by the darkness of death, may be, or become, light (לְאוֹר, *inf. Niph.*, syncopated from לְהֵאוֹר, Ew. § 244, *b*) in the light of life (as it were bask in the new and restored light of life)—it does not always happen, for these are experiences of no ordinary kind, which interrupt the daily course of life; and it is not even repeated again and again constantly, for if it is without effect the first time, it is repeated a second or third time, but it has an end if the man trifles constantly with the disciplinary work of grace which designs his good. Finally, Elihu calls upon Job quietly to ponder this, that he may proceed; neverthe-less, if he has words, *i.e.* if he thinks he is able to advance any appropriate objections, he is continually to answer him (הֵשִׁיב with *acc.* of the person, as ver. 5), for he (Elihu) would willingly justify him, *i.e.* he would gladly be in the position to be able to acknowledge Job to be right, and to have the accusation dispensed with. Hirz. and others render falsely: I wish thy justification, *i.e.* thou shouldst justify thyself; in this case נַפְשֶׁךְ ought to be supplied, which is unnecessary: חָפֵץ, without a change of subject, has the *inf. constr.* here without לְ, as it has the *inf. absol.* in ch. xiii. 3, and צַדֵּק signi-fies to vindicate (as ch. xxxii. 2), or acknowledge to be in the right (as the *Piel* of צָדַק, ver. 12), both of which are blended here. The LXX., which translates θέλω γὰρ δικαιωθῆναί σε, has probably read צְדָקֶךָ (Ps. xxxv. 27). If it is not so (אִם־אַיִן as Gen. xxx. 1), viz. that he does not intend to defend himself with reference to his expostulation with God on account of the affliction decreed for him, he shall on his part (אַתָּה) listen, shall be silent and be further taught wisdom.

Quasi hac ratione Heliu sanctum Iob convicerit! exclaims Beda, after a complete exposition of this speech. He regards Elihu as the type of the false wisdom of the heathen, which fails to recognise and persecutes the servant of God: *Sunt alii extra ecclesiam, qui Christo ejusque ecclesiæ similiter adversantur, quorum imaginem prætulit Balaam ille ariolus, qui et Elieu sicut patrum traditio habet* (Balaam and Elihu, one person—a worthless conceit repeated in the Talmud and Midrash), *qui contra ipsum sanctum Iob multa improbe et injuriose locutus est, in tantum ut etiam displiceret in una ejus et indisciplinata loquacitas.*[1] Gregory the Great, in his *Moralia,* expresses himself no less unfavourably at the conclusion of this speech:[2] *Magna Eliu ac valde fortia protulit, sed hoc unusquisque arrogans habere proprium solet, quod dum vera ac mystica loquitur subito per tumorem cordis quædam inania et superba permiscet.* He also regards Elihu as an emblem of confident arrogance, yet not as a type of a heathen philosopher, but of a believing yet vain and arrogant teacher. This tone in judging of Elihu, first started by Jerome, has spread somewhat extensively in the Western Church. In the age of the Reformation, *e.g.,* Victorin Strigel takes this side: Elihu is regarded by him as *exemplum ambitiosi oratoris qui plenus sit ostentatione et audacia inusitata sine mente.* Also in the Greek Eastern Church such views are not wanting. Elihu says much that is good, and excels the friends in this, that he does not condemn Job; Olympiodorus adds, πλὴν οὐκ ἐνόησε τοῦ δικαίου τὴν διάνοιαν, but he has not understood the true idea of the servant of God![3]

---

[1] *Bedæ Opp. ed. Basil.* iii. col. 602 sq. 786. The commentary also bears the false name of Jerome [Hieronymus], and as a writing attributed to him is contained in *tom.* v. *Opp. ed. Vallarsi.*

[2] *Opp. ed. Paris,* i. col. 777.

[3] *Catena in Job. Londin.* p. 484, where it is further said, Ὅθεν λογιζό-

In modern times, Herder entertains the same judgment. Elihu's speech, in comparison with the short, majestic, solemn language of the Creator, he calls "the weak rambling speech of a boy." "Elihu, a young prophet"—he says further on in his *Geist der Ebr. Poesie,* where he expounds the book of Job as a composition—"arrogant, bold, alone wise, draws fine pictures without end or aim; hence no one answers him, and he stands there merely as a shadow."[1] Among the latest expositors, Umbreit (Edition 2, 1832) consider's Elihu's appearance as "an uncalled-for stumbling in of a conceited young philosopher into the conflict that is already properly ended; the silent contempt with which one allows him to speak is the merited reward of a babbler." In later years Umbreit gave up this depreciation of Elihu.[2] Nevertheless Hahn, in his *Comm. zu Iob* (1850), has sought anew to prove that Elihu's speeches are meant indeed to furnish a solution, but do not really do so: on the contrary, the poet intentionally represents the character of Elihu as that "of a most conceited and arrogant young man, boastful and officious in his undeniable knowingness." The unfavourable judgments have been carried still further, inasmuch as an attempt has even been made to regard Elihu as a disguise for Satan in the organism of the drama;[3] but it may be more suitable to break off this unpleasant subject than to continue it.

In fact this dogmatic criticism of Elihu's character and speeches produces a painful impression. For, granted that it might be otherwise, and the poet really had designed to bring forward in these speeches of Elihu respecting God's

---

μεθα καὶ τὸν θεὸν μήτε ἐπαινέσαι τὸν Ελιοὺς, ἐπειδὴ μὴ νενόηκε τοῦ Ἰὼβ τοὺς λόγους, μήτε μὴν καταδικάσαι, ἐπειδὴ μὴ ἀσεβείας αὐτὸν κατέκρινε.

[1] Edition 1805, S. 101, 142.

[2] *Vid.* Riehm, *Blätter der Erinnerung an F. W. C. Umbreit* (1862), S. 58.

[3] Thus the writer of a treatise in the 3d vol. of Bernstein's *Analekten,* entitled: *Der Satan als Irrgeist und Engel des Lichts.*

own appearing an incontrovertible apology for His holy
love, as a love which is at work even in such dispensations
of affliction as that of Job: what offence against the deep
earnestness of this portion of Holy Scripture would there be
in this degradation of Elihu to an absurd character, in that
depreciation of him to a babbler promising much and per-
forming little!   But that the poet is really in earnest in
everything he puts into Elihu's mouth, is at once shown by
the description, ch. xxxiii. 13–30, which forms the kernel of
the contents of the first speech.   This description of the
manifold ways of the divine communication to man, upon a
contrite attention to which his rescue from destruction depends,
belongs to the most comprehensive passages of the Old Testament; and I know instances of the powerful effect which it
can produce in arousing from the sleep of security and
awakening penitence.   If one, further, casts a glance at the
historical introduction of Elihu, ch. xxxii. 1–5, the poet
there gives no indication that he intends in Elihu to bring
the odd character of a young poltroon before us.   The
motive and aim of his coming forward, as they are there given,
are fully authorized.   If one considers, further, that the poet
makes Job keep silence at the speeches of Elihu, it may also
be inferred therefrom that he believes he has put answers
into Elihu's mouth by which he must feel himself most
deeply smitten; such truths as ch. xxxii. 13–30, drawn
from the depths of moral experience, could not have been
put forth if Job's silence were intended to be the punishment
of contempt.

These counter-considerations also really affect another possible and milder apprehension of the young speaker, inasmuch
as, with von Hofmann, the gravitating point of the book of Job
is transferred to the fact of the Theophany as the only satisfactory practical solution of the mystery of affliction: it is
solved by God Himself coming down and acknowledging Job

as His servant. Elihu—thus one can say from this point of view—is not one of Job's friends, whose duty it was to comfort him; but the moral judgment of man's perception of God is made known by this teacher, but without any other effect than that Job is silent. There is one duty towards Job which he has not violated, for he has not to fulfil the duty of friendship: The only art of correct theorizing is to put an opponent to silence, and to have spoken to the wind is the one punishment appropriate to it. This milder rendering also does not satisfy; for, in the idea of the poet, Elihu's speeches are not only a thus negative, but the positive preparation for Jehovah's appearing. In the idea of the poet, Job is silent because he does not know how to answer Elihu, and therefore feels himself overcome.[1] And, in fact, what answer should he give to this first speech? Elihu wishes to dispute Job's self-justification, which places God's justice in the shade, but not indeed in the friends' judging, condemnatory manner: he wishes to dispute Job's notion that his affliction proceeds from a hostile purpose on the part of God, and sets himself here, as there, a perfectly correct task, which he seeks to accomplish by directing Job to regard his affliction, not indeed as a punishment from the angry God, but as a chastisement of the God who desires his highest good, as disciplinary affliction which is intended to secure him against hurtful temptation to sin, especially to pride, by salutary humiliation, and will have a glorious issue, as soon as it has in itself accomplished that at which it aims.

It is true one must listen very closely to discover the difference between the tone which Elihu takes and the tone in

---

[1] The preparation is negative only so far as Elihu causes Job to be silent and to cease to murmur; but Jehovah draws from him a confession of penitence on account of his murmuring. This positive relation of the appearing of Jehovah to that for which Elihu negatively prepares the way, is rightly emphasized by Schlottm., Räbiger (*De l. Iobi sententia primaria*, 1860, 4), and others, as favourable to the authenticity.

which Eliphaz began his first speech. But there is a difference notwithstanding: both designate Job's affliction as a chastisement (מוסר), which will end gloriously, if he receives it without murmuring; but Eliphaz at once demands of him humiliation under the mighty hand of God; Elihu, on the contrary, makes this humiliation lighter to him, by setting over against his longing for God to answer him, the pleasing teaching that his affliction in itself is already the speech of God to him,—a speech designed to educate him, and to bring about his spiritual well-being. What objection could Job, who has hitherto maintained his own righteousness in opposition to affliction as a hostile decree, now raise, when it is represented to him as a wholesome medicine reached forth to him by the holy God of love? What objection could Job now raise, without, in common, offensive self-righteousness, falling into contradiction with his own confession that he is a sinful man, ch. xiv. 4, comp. xiii. 26? Therefore Elihu has not spoken to the wind, and it cannot have been the design of the poet to represent the feebleness of theory and rhetoric in contrast with the convincing power which there is in the fact of Jehovah's appearing.

But would it be possible, that from the earliest times one could form such a condemnatory, depreciating judgment concerning Elihu's speeches, if it had not been a matter of certainty with them? If of two such enlightened men as Augustine and Jerome, the former can say of Elihu: *ut primas partes modestiæ habuit, ita et sapientiæ*, while the latter, and after his example Bede, can consider him as a type of a heathen philosophy hostile to the faith, or of a selfishly perverted spirit of prophecy: they must surely have two sides which make it possible to form directly opposite opinions concerning them. Thus is it also in reality. On the one side, they express great, earnest, humiliating truths, which even the holiest man in his affliction must suffer himself to be told, especially if he has fallen into such vain-glorying and such murmuring against God as Job did; on the other side, they do not give such sharply-defined expression to that which is intended characteristically to distinguish them from the speeches of the friends, viz. that they regard Job not as רשע, and his affliction not as just retribution, but as a wholesome means of discipline, that all misunderstanding would be excluded, as all the expositors who acknowledge themselves unable to perceive an essential difference between Elihu's standpoint and the original standpoint of the friends, show. But the most surprising thing is, that the peculiar, true aim of Job's affliction, viz. his being proved as God's servant, is by no means thoroughly clear in them. From the prologue we know that Job's affliction is designed to show that there is a piety which also retains its hold on God amid the loss of all earthly goods, and even in the face of death in the midst of the darkest night of affliction; that it is designed to justify God's choice before Satan, and bring the latter to ruin; that it is a part of the conflict with the serpent, whose head cannot be crushed without its sting being felt in the heel of the conqueror; in fine, expressed in New Testament language, that it falls under the point of view of the cross ($\sigma\tau\alpha\nu\rho\acute{o}\varsigma$), which has its ground not so much in the sinfulness of the sufferer, as in the share which is assigned to him in the conflict of good with evil that exists in the world. It cannot be supposed that the poet would, in the speeches of Elihu, set another design in opposition to the design of Job's affliction expressed in the prologue; on the contrary, he started from the assumption that the one design does not exclude the other, and in connection with the imperfectness of the righteousness even of the holiest man, the one is easily added to the other; but it was not in his power to give expression to both grounds of explanation of Job's affliction side by side, and thus to make this intermediate section " the beating heart"[1] of the whole. The aspect of the affliction as a chastisement so greatly preponderates, that the other, viz. as a trial or proving, is as it were swallowed up by it. One of the old writers[2] says, "Elihu proves that it can indeed be that a man may fear and honour God from the heart, and consequently be in favour with God, and still be heavily visited by God, either for a trial of faith, hope, and patience, or for the revelation and improvement of the sinful blemishes which now and then are also hidden from the pious." According to this, both aspects are found united in Elihu's speeches; but in this first speech, at least, we cannot find it.

There is another poet, whose *charisma* does not come up to that of the older poet, who in this speech pursues the well-authorized purpose not only of moderating what is extreme in Job's speeches, but also of bringing out what is true in the speeches of the friends.[3] While the book of Job, apart from these speeches, presents in the Old Testament way the great truth which Paul, Rom. viii. 1, expresses in the words, οὐδέν κατάκριμα τοῖς ἐν Χριστῷ Ἰησοῦ, this other poet has given expression at the same time, in the connection of the drama, to the great truth, 1 Cor. xi. 32, κρινόμενοι ὑπὸ τοῦ κυρίου παιδευόμεθα, ἵνα μὴ σὺν τῷ κόσμῳ κατακριθῶμεν. That it is another poet, is already manifest from his inferior, or if it is preferred, different, poetic gift. True, A. B. Davidson has again recently asserted, that by supporting it by such observations, the critical question is made " a question of subjective taste." But if these speeches and the other parts of the book are said to have been written by *one* poet, there is an end to all critical judgment in such questions generally. One cannot

---

[1] *Vid.* Hengstenberg, *Lecture on the Book of Job.*

[2] Jacob Hoffmann (of St Gallen), *Gedult Iobs*, Basel, 1663 (a rare little book which I became acquainted with in the town library of St Gallen).

[3] On this subject see my Art. *Hiob* in Herzog's *Real-Encyklopädie*, vi. 116–119, and comp. Kahnis, *Dogmatik*, i. 306–309, and my *Für und wider Kahnis* (1863), S. 19–21.

avoid the impression of the distance between them; and if it be suppressed for a time, it will nevertheless make itself constantly felt. But do the prophecies of Malachi stand lower in the scale of the historical development of revelation, because the Salomonic glory of prophetic speech which we admire in Isaiah is wanting in them? Just as little do we depreciate the spiritual glory of these speeches, when we find the outward glory of the rest of the book wanting in them. They occupy a position of the highest worth in the historical development of revelation and redemption. They are a perfecting part of the canonical Scriptures. In their origin, also, they are not much later;[1] indeed, I venture to assert that they are by a cotemporary member even of the Chokma-fellowship from which the book of Job has its rise. For they stand in like intimate relation with the rest of the book to the two Ezrahite Psalms, lxxxviii., lxxxix.; they have, as to their doctrinal contents, the fundamental features of the Israelitish Chokma in common; they speak another and still similar Aramaizing and Arabizing language (*hebraicum arabicumque sermonem et interdum syrum,* as Jerome expresses it in his *Præf. in l. Iobi*); in fact, we shall further on meet with linguistic signs that the poet who wrote this addition has lived together with the poet of the book of Job in one spot beyond the Holy Land, and speaks a Hebrew bearing traces of a like dialectic influence.

[1] Seinecke (*Der Grundgedanke des B. Hiob*, 1863) places it, with Ewald, 100–200 years later; and, moreover, asserts that the book of Job has no foundation whatever in oral tradition—Job is the Israel of the exile, Uz is Judæa, etc.

Elihu's Second Speech.—Chap. xxxiv.

Schema: 6. 10. 5. 8. 12. 6. 10. 9. 13.

[Then began Elihu and said:]

2 *Hear, ye wise men, my words,*
　And ye experienced ones, give ear to me!

3 *For the ear trieth words,*
　As the palate tasteth by eating.

4 *Let us find out what is right,*
　Let us explore among ourselves what is good.

After his first speech Elihu has made a brief pause; now since Job is silent, he begins anew. ויען ויאמר, LXX. correctly, here as in all other instances where the phrase occurs: ὑπολαβὼν λέγει, taking up the word he said. The wise and the knowing (Arab. *ʿulamâ*), whose attention he bespeaks, are not Job and the three (Umbr., Hahn), who are indeed a party, and as such a subject for the arbitrative appearance of Elihu; also not every one capable of forming a judgment (Hirz.); but those in the circle of spectators and listeners which, as is assumed, has assembled round the disputants (Schlottm.). In ver. 3 Elihu does not expressly mean his own ear, but that of the persons addressed: he establishes his summons to prove what he says by the general thought brought over from ch. xii. 11, and as there (comp. ch. v. 7, xi. 12), clothed in the form of the emblematic proverb,—that as there is a bodily, so there is also a mental organ of sense which tries its perceptions. לֶאֱכֹל is not intended as expressing a purpose (*ad vescendum*), but as gerundive (*vescendo*). The phrase בָּחַר מִשְׁפָּט, occurring only here, signifies neither to institute a search for the purpose of decision (Schult. and others), since בחר does not signify to decide upon anything, nor to investigate a cause (Hahn), which would be נבחנה, but to test and choose what is right, δοκιμάζειν καὶ τὸ καλὸν κατέχειν, 1 Thess. v. 21, after which the parallel runs: *cognoscamus inter nos* (*i.e.* in common) *quid bonum.*

> 5 *For Job hath said: " I am guiltless,*
> " *And God hath put aside my right.*
> 6 " *Shall I lie in spite of my right,*
> " *Incurable is mine arrow without transgression."*
> 7 *Where is there a man like Job,*
> *Who drinketh scorning like water,*
> 8 *And keepeth company with the workers of iniquity,*
> *And walketh with wicked men,*
> 9 *So that he saith: " A man hath no profit*
> " *From entering into fellowship with God"? !*

That in relation to God, thinking of Him as a punishing judge, he is righteous or in the right, *i.e.* guiltless (צָדַקְתִּי with *Pathach* in pause, according to Ew. § 93, *c*, from צָדֵק = צָדַק, but perhaps, comp. Prov. xxiv. 30, Ps. cii. 26, because the *Athnach* is taken only as of the value of *Zakeph*), Job has said *verbatim* in ch. xiii. 18, and according to meaning, ch. xxiii. 10, xxvii. 7, and throughout; that He puts aside his right (the right of the guiltless, and therefore not of one coming under punishment): ch. xxvii. 2. That in spite of his right (עַל, to be interpreted, according to Schultens' example, just like ch. x. 7, xvi. 17), *i.e.* although right is on his side, yet he must be accounted a liar, since his own testimony is belied by the wrathful form of his affliction, that therefore the appearance of wrong remains inalienably attached to him, we find in idea in ch. ix. 20 and freq. Elihu makes Job call his affliction חִצִּי, *i.e.* an arrow sticking in him, viz. the arrow of the wrath of God (on the objective *suff.* comp. on ch. xxiii. 2), after ch. vi. 4, xvi. 9, xix. 11; and that this his arrow, *i.e.* the pain which it causes him, is incurably bad, desperately malignant without (בְּלִי as ch. viii. 11) פֶּשַׁע, *i.e.* sins existing as the ground of it, from which he would be

obliged to suppose they had thrust him out of the condition
of favour, is Job's constant complaint (*vid. e.g.* ch. xiii. 23 sq.).
Another utterance of Job closely connected with it has so
roused Elihu's indignation, that he prefaces it with the exclamation of astonishment : Who is a man like Job, *i.e.* where
in all the world (מִי as 2 Sam. vii. 23) has this Job his equal,
who . . . The attributive clause refers to Job ; "to drink
scorn (here : blasphemy) like water," is, according to ch.
xv. 16, equivalent to to give one's self up to mockery with
delight, and to find satisfaction in it.   אָרַח לְחֶבְרָה, to go over
to any one's side, looks like a poeticized prose expression.
לָלֶכֶת is a continuation of the אָרַח, according to Ew. § 351, *c*,
but not directly in the sense " and he goes," but, as in the
similar examples, Jer. xvii. 10, xliv. 19, 2 Chron. vii. 17, and
freq., in the sense of : " he is in the act of going ;" comp. on
ch. xxxvi. 20 and Hab. i. 17.   The utterance runs : a man
does not profit, viz. himself (on the use of סָכַן of persons as
well as of things, *vid.* on ch. xxii. 2), by his having joyous
and familiar intercourse (בִּרְצֹתוֹ, as little equivalent to בְּרוּץ as
in Ps. l. 18) with God.   Job has nowhere expressly said this,
but certainly the declaration in ch. ix. 22, in connection with
the repeated complaints concerning the anomalous distribution
of human destinies (*vid.* especially ch. xxi. 7 sqq., xxiv. 1 sqq.),
are the premises for such a conclusion.   That Elihu, in vers.
7 sq., is more harsh against Job than the friends ever were
(comp. *e.g.* the well-measured reproach of Eliphaz, ch. xv. 4),
and that he puts words into Job's mouth which occur nowhere
verbatim in his speeches, is worked up by the Latin fathers
(Jer., Philippus Presbyter, Beda,[1] Gregory) in favour of their

---

[1] Philippus Presbyter was a disciple of Jerome.   His *Comm. in Iobum*
is extant in many forms, partly epitomized, partly interpolated (on this
subject, *vid. Hieronymi Opp. ed. Vallarsi,* iii. 895 sqq.).   The commentary
of Beda, dedicated to a certain Nectarius (Vecterius), is fundamentally
that of this Philippus.

unfavourable judgment of Elihu; the Greek fathers, however, are deprived of all opportunity of understanding him
by the translation of the LXX. (in which μυκτηρισμόν
signifies the scorn of others which Job must swallow down,
comp. Prov. xxvi. 6), which here perverts everything.

10 *Therefore, men of understanding, hearken to me!*
    Far be it from God to do evil,
    And the Almighty to act wrongfully.
11 *No indeed, man's work He recompenseth to him,*
    And according to man's walk He causeth it to be with him.

"Men of heart," according to *Psychol.* S. 249, comp. 254,
is equivalent to νοήμονες or νοηροί (LXX. συνετοὶ καρδίας).
The clause which Elihu makes prominent in the following
reply is the very axiom which the three defend, perfectly true
in itself, but falsely applied by them: evil, wrong, are incon-
ceivable on the part of God; instead of וּלְשַׁדַּי it is only וְשַׁדַּי
in the second member of the verse, with the omission of the
præp.—a frequent form of ellipsis, particularly in Isaiah (ch.
xv. 8, xxviii. 6, xlviii. 14, lxi. 7, comp. Ezek. xxv. 15). Far
removed from acting wickedly and wrongfully, on the contrary He practises recompense exactly apportioned to man's
deeds, and ever according to the walk of each one (אֹרַח like
דֶּרֶךְ or דַּרְכֵי, *e.g.* Jer. xxxii. 19, in an ethical sense) He causes
it to overtake him, *i.e.* to happen to him (הַמְצִיא only here
and ch. xxxvii. 13). The general assertion brought forward
against Job is now proved.

12 *Yea verily God acteth not wickedly,*
    And the Almighty perverteth not the right.
13 *Who hath given the earth in charge to Him?*
    And who hath disposed the whole globe?
14 *If He only set His heart upon Himself,*
    If He took back His breath and His inspiration to Himself:

15 *All flesh would expire together,*
And man would return to dust.

With אַף אָמְנָם (Yea verily, as ch. xix. 4, "and really")
the counter-assertion of ver. 11 is repeated, but negatively
expressed (comp. ch. viii. 3). הִרְשִׁיעַ signifies sometimes to
act as רָשָׁע, and at others to be set forth and condemned as a
רֹשַׁע; here, as the connection requires, it is the former. Ver.
13 begins the proof. Ewald's interpretation: who searcheth,
and Hahn's: who careth for the earth beside Him, are
hazardous and unnecessary. פָּקַד with עַל of the person and
the *acc.* of the thing signifies: to enjoin anything as a duty
on any one, to entrust anything to any one, ch. xxxvi. 23,
Num. iv. 27, 2 Chron. xxxvi. 23; therefore: who has made
the earth, *i.e.* the care of it, a duty to Him? אַרְצָה (*Milel*) is
not to be refined into the meaning "to the earth" (as here
by Schultens and a few others, Isa. viii. 23 by Luzzatto: he
hath smitten down, better: dishonoured, to the earth with a
light stroke), but is poetically equivalent to אֶרֶץ, as לַיְלָה (comp.
modern Greek ἡ νύχθα) is in prose equivalent to לֵיל. Ver.
13*b* is by no means, with Ew. and Hahn, to be translated:
who observes (considers) the whole globe, שִׂים as ver. 23, ch.
iv. 20, xxiv. 12—the expression would be too contracted to
affirm that no one but God bestowed providential attention
upon the earth; and if we have understood ver. 13*a* correctly,
the thought is also inappropriate. A more appropriate thought
is gained, if עָלָיו is supplied from ver. 13*a*: who has enjoined
upon Him the whole circle of the earth (Saad., Gecat., Hirz.,
Schlottm.); but this continued force of the עליו into the second
independent question is improbable in connection with the repetition of מִי. Therefore: who has appointed, *i.e.* established
(שָׂם as ch. xxxviii. 5, Isa. xliv. 7),—a still somewhat more
suitable thought, going logically further, since the one giving
the charge ought to be the lord of him who receives the com-

mission, and therefore the Creator of the world. This is just God alone, by whose רוּחַ and נְשָׁמָה the animal world as well as the world of men (vid. xxxii. 8, xxxiii. 4) has its life, ver. 14: if He should direct His heart, i.e. His attention (שִׂים לֵב אֶל as ch. ii. 3), to Himself (emphatic: Himself alone), draw in (אָסַף as Ps. civ. 29; comp. for the matter Eccl. xii. 7, Psychol. S. 406) to Himself His inspiration and breath (which emanated from Him or was effected by Him), all flesh would sink together, i.e. die off at once (this, as it appears, has reference to the taking back of the animal life, רוח), and man would return (this has reference to the taking back of the human spirit, נשמה) to dust (עַל instead of אֶל, perhaps with reference to the usual use of the עַל־עָפָר, ch. xvii. 16, xx. 11, xxi. 26).

Only a few modern expositors refer אֵלָיו, as Targ. Jer. and Syr., to man instead of reflexively to God; the majority rightly decide in favour of the idea which even Grotius perceived: *si sibi ipsi tantum bonus esse (sui unius curam habere) vellet.* אִם followed by the *fut.* signifies either *si velit* (LXX. εἰ βούλοιτο), as here, or as more frequently, *si vellet*, Ps. l. 12, cxxxix. 8, Obad. ver. 4, Isa. x. 22, Amos ix. 2-4. It is worthy of remark that, according to Norzi's statement, the Babylonian texts presented יָשִׁיב, ver. 14a, as *Chethîb*, יָשִׂים as *Kerî* (like our Palestine text, Dan. xi. 18), which a MS. of De Rossi, with a Persian translation, confirms; the reading gives a fine idea: that God's heart is turned towards the world, and is unclosed; its ethical condition of life would then be like its physical ground of life, that God's spirit dwells in it; the drawing back of the heart, and the taking back to Himself of the spirit, would be equivalent to the exclusion of the world from God's love and life. However, יָשִׂים implies the same; for a reference of God's thinking and willing to Himself, with the exclusion of the world, would be just a removal of His love. Elihu's proof is this: God does

not act wrongly, for the government of the world is not a
duty imposed upon Him from without, out a relation entered
into freely by Him : the world is not the property of another,
but of His free creative appointment; and how unselfishly,
how devoid of self-seeking He governs it, is clear from the
fact, that by the impartation of His living creative breath He
sustains every living thing, and does not, as He easily might,
allow them to fall away into nothingness.   There is therefore
a divine love which has called the world into being and keeps
it in being; and this love, as the perfect opposite of sovereign
caprice, is a pledge for the absolute righteousness of the
divine rule.

16   *And oh understand now, hear this;*
    Hearken to the sound of my words.
17   *Would one who hateth right also be able to subdue?*
    Or wilt thou condemn the All-just?
18   *Is it becoming to say to a king: Worthless One!?*
    Thou evil-doer! to princes?
19   *To Him who accepteth not the person of rulers,*
    And regardeth not the noble before the poor:
    For they are all the work of His hands.
20   *In a moment they die, and at midnight*
    The people are overthrown and perish,
    And they put aside the mighty—not by the hand of man.

This strophe contains several grammatical rarities.   At
first sight it appears that ver. 16*a* ought to be translated:
" and if there is understanding (viz. to thee = if thou hast),
then hear this."   But בִּינָה is accented as *Milel* and with
Mercha, and can therefore not be a substantive (Hirz., Hahn,
and others); for the retreat of the accent would be absolutely
incomprehensible, and instead of a conjunctive, a distinctive,
viz. *Dechî*, ought to be expected.   Several of the old expositors, therefore, interpret with Nolde: *quod quum ita sit,*

intellige; but this elliptical וְאִם, well as it might also be used for ch. xxi. 4, is unsupportable; the *Makkeph* between the two words is also against it, which rather arises from the assumption that בִּינָה is the *imperat.*, and אִם as an exception, like Gen. xxiii. 13, is an optative particle joined to the *imper.* instead of to the *fut.*: "and if thou shouldst observe" (= וְאִם־תָּבִין). To translate ver. 17a with Schultens: *num iram osor judicii frenabit,* is impracticable on account of the order of the words, and gives a thought that is inappropriate here. אַף is a particle, and the *fut.* is *potentialis:* is it also possible that an enemy of right should govern? (חָבַשׁ, *imperio coercere,* as עָצַר 1 Sam. ix. 17, אָסַר Ps. cv. 22); right and government are indeed mutually conditioned, without right everything would fall into anarchy and confusion. In ver. 17b this is applied to the Ruler of the world: or (וְאִם, *an,* as ch. viii. 3, xxi. 4, xl. 9) wilt thou condemn the mighty just One, *i.e.* the All-just? As Elihu calls God שַׂגִּיא כֹחַ, ch. xxxvii. 23, as the Almighty, and as the Omniscient One, תְּמִים דֵּעִים, ch. xxxvii. 16, so here as the All-just One, צַדִּיק כַּבִּיר. The two adjectives are put side by side ἀσυνδέτως, as is frequently the case in Arabic, and form one compound idea, Ew. § 270, *d.*

Ver. 18a. The interrogative הַ is joined to the *inf.*, not, however, as ch. xl. 2 (*num litigare cum Deo castigator, scil. vult*), with the *inf. absol.*, but with the *inf. constr.*; the form אֲמֹר for אֱמֹר occurs also in Prov. xxv. 7, and is also otherwise not rare, especially in combination with particles, *e.g.* בֶּאֱכֹל, Num. xxvi. 10, Olsh. § 160, *b.*[1] It is unnecessary to suppose that the *inf. constr.*, which sometimes, although rarely, does occur (Ges. § 131, rem. 2), is used here instead of the *inf. absol.*; it is thus, as after טוֹב, *e.g.* Judg. ix. 2 (הֲמְשֹׁל), Prov. xxv. 7, Ps. cxxxiii. 1, and Ps. xl. 6 after אֵין, used as *n.*

---

[1] Ezek. xxv. 8 is also to be read אֲמֹר according to the Masora and old editions (as אֲבֹד Deut. vii. 20, אֲכֹל xii. 23, אֲחֹז 1 Kings vi. 6), for distinction from the imperatives, which have *Chateph-Segol.*

actionis, since הֲ in a pregnant sense is equivalent to *num licet* (הֲטוֹב), if one does not prefer, with Olsh., to suppose an aposiopesis: "(dare one be so bold as) to say to a king: Thou worthless one! Thou evil-doer! to princes?" The reading הָאֹמֵר is an unnecessary lightening of the difficulty. It were a *crimen læsæ,* if one reproached a king with being unjust, and therefore thereby denied him the most essential requisite of a ruler; and now even Him (Merc. correctly supplies *tanto minus ei*) who does not give the preference to the person (נָשָׂא פְנֵי as ch. xiii. 8, xxxii. 21) of princes, and does not (with preference) regard (on נִכַּר *vid.* on ch. xxi. 29, also here *Piel,* and according to the statement of the Masora, *Milel,* for an acknowledged reason which can be maintained even in remarkable instances, like Deut. x. 5 in וַיִּהְיוּ, Ezek. xxxii. 26 in מֵחַלְלֵי, whereas 1 Sam. xxiii. 7 is *Milra*) the rich before (לִפְנֵי in the sense of *præ*) the poor! therefore the King of kings, who makes no partial distinction, because the king and the beggar are the work of His hands: they stand equally near to Him as being His creatures, and He is exalted above both alike as their Creator, this order and partiality are excluded;—what a *nota bene* against the doctrine of the *decretum absolutum,* which makes the love of the Creator a partial love, and turns this love, which in its very nature is perfect love, into caprice! In ver. 20 Elihu appeals to human history in favour of this impartiality of the Ruler of the world. It may there appear as though God with partiality suffered rulers and peoples in authority in the world to do as they please; but suddenly they die away, and in fact in the middle of the night (here *Mercha-mahpach*), the individuals of a great people (thus must עָם be understood in accordance with the prominently-placed plur. predicate, Ges. § 146, 1) tremble and perish; and they remove (וְיָסִירוּ instead of the passive, as ch. iv. 20 and frequently) the mighty—לֹא־בְיָד. It is not the hand of man which does this, but an invisible higher power (which, if it is called יד, only bears this name *per anthropomorphismum*) ; comp. Dan. ii. 34, לָא בִידַיִן ; Dan. viii. 25, בְּאֶפֶס יָד ; and also ch. xx. 26, like the New Testament use of οὐ χειροποίητος. The subj. of ver. 20*a* are the previously mentioned princes. The division according to the accents may be received with hesitation, since the symmetry of the stichs, which it restores, is not unfrequently wanting in the Elihu section. Ver. 20*c* refers back to the possessors of power, and in the interval, ver. 20*b* describes the fate of those who belong to the people which has become subservient to their lust of conquest, for עָם cannot signify "in crowds" (Ew., Hahn); it is therefore, and especially when mentioned as here between princes and rulers, the people, and in fact, in distinction from גוי, the people together forming a state.

> 21 *For His eyes are upon the ways of each one,*
> *And He seeth all his steps.*
> 22 *There is no darkness nor shadow of death*
> *Wherein the workers of iniquity might hide themselves.*
> 23 *For He needeth not long to regard a man*
> *That he may enter into judgment with God.*

As the preceding strophe showed that God's creative order excludes all partiality, so this strophe shows that His omniscience qualifies Him to be an impartial judge. He sees everything, nothing can escape His gaze; He sees through man without being obliged to wait for the result of a judicial investigation. שִׂים with עַל does not here signify: to lay upon (Saad., Gecat.), but as ch. xxxvii. 15, and as with אֶל (ver. 14) or בְּ (ch. xxiii. 6): to direct one's attention (supply לִבּוֹ, ch. i. 8) towards anything; the *fut.* has here a modal signification; עוֹד is used as *e.g.* Gen. xlvi. 29: again and again, continuously; and in the clause expressive of purpose it is אֶל־אֵל (instead of אֵלָיו, a very favourite combination used throughout the whole book, ch. v. 8, viii. 5, xiii. 3, and so on) from the human standpoint: He, the all-seeing One, needs not to observe him long that he should enter into judgment with God—He knows him thoroughly before any investigation takes place, which is not said without allusion to Job's vehement longing to be able to appear before God's tribunal.

24 *He breaketh the mighty in pieces without investigation*
   And setteth others in their place.
25 *Thus He seeth through their works,*
   And causeth their overthrow by night, thus they are crushed.
26 *He smiteth them after the manner of evil-doers*
   In the sight of the public.
27 *For for such purpose are they fallen away from Him*
   And have not considered any of His ways,
28 *To cause the cry of the poor to come up to Him,*
   And that He should hear the cry of the needy.

He makes short work (לֹא־חֵקֶר for בְּלֹא, as ch. xii. 24, xxxviii. 26: without research, viz. into their conduct, which is at once manifest to Him; not: in an incomprehensible manner, which is unsuitable, and still less: *innumerabiles*, as Jer., Syr.) with the mighty (כַּבִּירִים, Arab. *kibár, kubará*), and in consequence of this (*fut. consec.*) sets up (*constituit*) others, *i.e.* better and worthier rulers (comp. אַחֵר, ch. viii. 19, Isa. lxv. 15), in their stead. The following לָכֵן is not equivalent to לְכֵן אֲשֶׁר, for which no satisfactory instance exists; on the contrary, לכן here, as more frequently, introduces not the real consequence (ch. xx. 2), but a logical inference, something that directly follows in and with what precedes (corresponding to the Greek ἄρα, just so, consequently), comp. ch. xlii. 3, Isa. xxvi. 14, lxi. 7, Jer. ii. 33, v. 2, Zech. xi. 7 (*vid.* Köhler *in loc.*). Thus, then, as He hereby proves, He is thoroughly acquainted with their actions (מַעְבָּד, nowhere besides in the book of Job, an Aramaizing expression for מעשה). This abiding fact of divine omniscience, inferred from the previously-mentioned facts, then serves again in its turn, in ver. 25*b*, as the source of facts by which it is verified. לַיְלָה is by no means an obj. The expositions: *et inducit noctem* (Jer.), He walks in the night in which He has veiled Himself (Umbr.), *convertit eos in noctem* (Syr., Arab.), and such like, all read in the two words what they do not imply. It is either to be translated: He throws them by night (לילה as ch. xxvii. 20) upon the heaps (הָפַךְ as Prov. xii. 7), or, since the verb has no objective *suff.*: He maketh a reformation or overthrow during the night, *i.e.* creates during the night a new order of things, and they who stood at the head of the former affairs are crushed by the catastrophe.

Ver. 26. The following תַּחַת רְשָׁעִים cannot signify: on the place of the evil-doers, *i.e.* in the place where evil-doers are punished (Hirz., Hahn, and others), for תַּחַת (תַּחְתַּי) only has this signification with the *suff.* (*vid.* on Hab. iii. 16); but not otherwise than: in the evil-doers' stead, taking them and treating them as such, as Jer. has correctly translated: *quasi impios* (comp. Isa. x. 4, Jerome, *cum interfectis*). The place first mentioned afterwards is not exactly the usual place of judgment, but any place whatever where all can see it. There He smites those who hitherto held positions of eminence, as of unimpeachable honour, like the common criminal; סָפַק, صفق, *complodere*, and then *ictu resonante percutere*, as the likewise cognate سفع signifies first to box the ear (as سفق = صفق), then so to strike that it smacks. As little as לְכֵן, ver. 25*a*, was = לָכֵן אֲשֶׁר, just so little is אֲשֶׁר עַל־כֵּן, ver. 27*a*, = עַל־כֵּן אֲשֶׁר (*vid.* on the other hand what is said on Gen. xviii. 5 concerning כִּי־עַל־כֵּן). Elihu wishes to say that they endure such a destiny of punishment, because they therefore, *i.e.* in order to suffer such, have turned aside from following after God, and have not thought on all His ways, *i.e.* guidings, by which He manifested Himself to them: they have thus sought to cause the cry of the poor to come (Jer. well renders:

ut pervenire facerent ad eum) before Him (עָלָיו, perhaps with the idea of urging forward = לְפָנָיו or בְּאָזְנָיו), and that He may hear the cry of the lowly (construction exactly like ch. xxxiii. 17), *i.e.* have sought to bring forth His avenging justice by injustice that cries aloud to heaven.

29 *If He, however, maketh peace, who will then condemn?*
  And if He hideth His countenance—who then can behold Him?—
  Both concerning numbers and individuals together:
30 *That godless men reign not,*
  That they be not nets to the people.
31 *For one, indeed, saith to God,*
  " *I have been proud, I will not do evil;*
32 " *What I see not, show Thou me;*
  " *If I have done wrong, I will do it no more" !?—*

If God makes peace (יַשְׁקִט as Ps. xciv. 13, comp. Isa. xiv. 7, שָׁקְטָה כל־הארץ, viz. after the overthrow of the tyrant) in connection with such crying oppression of the poor, who will then condemn Him without the rather recognising therein His comprehensive justice? The conjecture יַרְעֵשׁ[1] is not required either here or 1 Sam. xiv. 47 (where הרשיע signifies to punish the guilty); יַרְשִׁעַ is also not to be translated *turbabit* (Rosenm.), since רָשַׁע (رسع, رسخ) according to its primitive notion does not signify "to be restless, to rage," but " to be relaxed, hollow" (opposite of צדק, صدق, to be hard, firm, tight). Further: If God hides His countenance, *i.e.* is angry and punishes, who can then behold Him, *i.e.* make Him, the veiled One, visible and claim back the favour withdrawn? The *Waw* of וּמִי, if one marks off the periods of the paratactic expression, is in both cases the *Waw* of conclusion after hypothetical antecedents, and ver. 29*b* refers to Job's impetuous challenging of God. Thus exalted above human controversy

1 *Vid.* Grätz in Frankel's *Monatsschrift*, 1861. i.

and defiance, God rules both over the mass and over individuals alike. יַחַד gives intensity to the equality thus correlatively
(*et — et*) expressed (Targ., Syr.) ; to refer it to אדם as gene-
ralizing (LXX., Jer. *et super omnes homines*), is forbidden by
the antithesis of peoples and individuals.　To the thought,
that God giveth rest (from oppressors) and hides His countenance (from the oppressors and in general those who act
wrongly), two co-ordinate negative final clauses are attached:
in order that godless men may not rule (מִמְּלֹךְ, as *e.g.* 2 Kings
xxiii. 33, *Keri*), in order that they may no longer be (מ = מִהְיוֹת,
under the influence of the notion of putting aside contained
in the preceding final clause, therefore like Isa. vii. 8 מֵעָם,
xxv. 2 מֵעִיר, Jer. xlviii. 2 מִגּוֹי, and the like) snares of the
people, *i.e.* those whose evil example and bad government
become the ruin of the community.

In ver. 31*a* the view of those who by some jugglery con
cerning the laws of the vowel sounds explain הֶאָמַר as *imper.*
Niph. (= הֵאָמֵר), be it in the sense of לְהֵאָמֵר, *dicendum est*
(Rosenm., Schlottm., and others, after Raschi), or even in
the unheard-of reflexive signification: express thyself (Stick.,
Hahn), is to be rejected.　The syncopated form of the *infin.*
בְּהֵרֹג, Ezek. xxvi. 15, does not serve as a palliation of this
adventurous imperative.　It is, on the contrary, אָמַר with
הֲ *interrog.*, as Ezek. xxviii. 9 הֶאָמֹר, and probably also הֶאָמוּר
Mic. ii. 7 (*vid.* Hitz.).　A direct exhortation to Job to penitence would also not be in place here, although what Elihu
says is levelled against Job.　The כִּי is confirmatory.　Thus
God acts with that class of unscrupulous men who abuse their
power for the destruction of their subjects: for he (one of
them) says (or : has said, from the standpoint of the execution
of punishment) to God, etc.　Ew. differently : "for one says
thus to God even : I expiate what I do not commit," by
understanding the speech quoted of a defiance which reproach-
fully demands an explanation.　It is, however, manifestly

a compendious model confession. And since Elihu with כִּי establishes the execution of punishment from this, that it never entered the mind of the אָדָם חָנֵף thus to humble himself before God, so נִשֵׂאתִי here cannot signify: I have repented (put up with and had to bear what I have deserved); on the contrary, the confession begins with the avowal: I have exalted myself (נָשָׂא, *se efferre*, in Hos. xiii. 1, Ps. lxxxix. 10), which is then followed by the vow: I will not (in the future) do evil (חָבַל synon. עָוָה, as Neh. i. 7, and probably also *supra*, ch. xxiv. 9), and the entreaty, ver. 32: beside that which I behold (elliptical object-clause, Ew. § 333, *b*), *i.e.* what lies beyond my vision (= נִסְתָּרוֹת or עֲלָמִים, Ps, xix. 13, xc. 8, unacknowledged sins), teach me; and the present vow has reference to acknowledged sins and sins that have still to be acknowledged: if I have done wrong, I will do it no more. Thus speaking—Elihu means—those high ones might have anticipated the punishment of the All-just God, for favour instead of wrath cannot be extorted, it is only reached by the way of lowly penitence.

33 *Shall He recompense it as thou wilt?   For thou hast found*
   fault,
   So that thou hast to determine, not I,
   And what thou knowest speak out!
34 *Men of understanding will say to me,*
   And a wise man who listeneth to me:
35 *" Job speaketh without knowledge,*
   " And his words are without intelligence."
36 *O would that Job were proved to the extreme*
   On account of his answers after the manner of evil men;
37 *For he addeth transgression to his sin,*
   Among us he clappeth
   And multiplieth his speeches against God.

The question put to Job, whether then from him or accord-

ing to his idea (עָם in מֵעִמְּךָ as ch. xxiii. 10, xxvii. 11, which
see) shall God recompense it (viz., as this "it" is to be understood according to ver. 32*b* : man's evil-doing and actions in
general), Elihu proves from this, that Job has despised
(shown himself discontented with it) the divine mode of
recompense, so that therefore (this second כִּי signifies also
nam, but is, because extending further on account of the
first, according to the sense equivalent to *ita ut*) he has to
choose (seek out) another mode of recompense, not Elihu (who
is perfectly satisfied with the mode with which history furnishes us); which is then followed by the challenge (דַּבֵּר not
infin., but as ch. xxxii. 33) : what (more corresponding to just
retribution) thou knowest, speak out then ! Elihu on his part
knows that he does not stand alone against Job, the censurer
of the divine government of the world, but that men of heart
(understanding) and (every) wise man who listens to him will
coincide with him in the opinion that Job's talk is devoid of
knowledge and intelligence (on the form of writing הַשְׂכִּיל as
Jer. iii. 15, *vid.* Ges. § 53, rem. 2).

In ver. 36 sq. we will for the present leave the meaning of
אבי undecided ; יְבָחֵן is certainly intended as optative : let Job
be tried to the extreme or last, *i.e.* let his trial by affliction
continue until the matter is decided (comp. Hab. i. 4), on
account of the opposition among men of iniquity, *i.e.* after the
manner of such (on this *Beth* of association comp. בְּקֻדְשִׁים, ch.
xxxvi. 14), for to חַטָּאת, by which the purpose of his affliction
is to be cleared up, he adds פֶּשַׁע, viz. the wickedness of blas-
phemous speeches : among us (therefore without fear) he
claps (vīz. his hands scornfully together, יִסְפּוֹק only here thus
absolute instead of יִשְׂפֹּק כַּפָּיו, ch. xxvii. 23, comp. בשׂפק ch.
xxxvi. 18 with ספקו xx. 22[1]) and multiplies (יֶרֶב, *fut. apoc.*
Hiph. as ch. x. 17, and instead of the full fut., as יָשֹׁר, ch.

_____

[1] The mode of writing with ס instead of שׂ is limited in the book of
Job, according to the Masora, to ch. xxxiv. 26, 37.

xxxiii. 27) his speeches against God, *i.e.* exceeds himself in speeches which irreverently dictate to and challenge God.

But we now ask, what does that אָבִי, ver. 36*a*, signify? According to the accentuation with *Rebia*, it appears to be intended to signify *pater mi* (Jer.), according to which Saad. (*jâ rabbî*) and Gecat. (*munshiî*, my Creator) translate it. This would be the only passage where an Old Testament saint calls God אבי; elsewhere God is called the Father of Israel, and Israel as a people, or the individual comprehending himself with the nation, calls Him אבינו. Nevertheless this *pater mi* for Elihu would not be inappropriate, for what the writer of the Epistle to the Hebrews, ch. xii. 7, says to believers on the ground of Prov. iii. 11: εἰς παιδείαν ὑπομένετε, ye suffer for the purpose of paternal discipline, is Elihu's fundamental thought; he also calls God in ch. xxxii. 22, xxxvi. 3, with a like reference to himself, עֹשֵׂנִי and פֹעֲלִי—this ejaculatory " my Father!" especially in conjunction with the following wish, remains none the less objectionable, and only in the absence of a more agreeable interpretation should we, with Hirz., decide in its favour. It would be disproportionately repulsive if ver. 36 sq. still belonged to the assenting language of another, and Elihu represented himself as addressed by אבי (Wolfson, Maur.). Thus, therefore, אבי must be taken somehow or other interjectionally. It is untenable to compare it with אֲבוֹי, Prov. xxiii. 29, for אוי ואבוי (Arab. *âh wa-âwâh*) is " ah! and alas !" The Aramaic בייא בייא, *væ væ* (Buxtorf, col. 294), compared by Ges. to בִּי, signifies just the same. The Targ. translates צְבֵינָא, I wish; after which Kimchi, among moderns, Umbr., Schlottm., Carey, and others derive אָבִי from אָבָה, a wish (after the form חָזֶה, קָצֶה), but the participial substantival-form badly suits this signification, which is at once improbable according to the usage of the language so far as we at present know it. This interpretation also does not well suit the בִּי, which is to be explained at the same time. Ewald,

§ 358, *a*, regards אֲבִי as the fuller form of בִּי, and thinks אבי is dialectic = לְבִי = לְוִי = לִי, but this is an etymological leger-demain. The two Schultens (died 1750 and 1793) were on the right track when they traced back אבי to בוא, but their interpretation: *rem eo adducam ut* (אבי = אביא, as it is cer-tainly not unfrequently written, *e.g.* 1 Kings xxi. 29, with the assumption of a root בי cognate with בא), is artificial and without support in the usage of the language and in the syntax. Körber and Simonis opened up the right way, but with inadequate means for following it out, by referring (*vid.* Ges. *Thes. s.v.* בִּי) to the formula of a wish and of respect, *bawwâk allah*, which, however, also is *bajjâk*. The Kamus interprets *bajjâk*, though waveringly, by *bawwâk*, the meaning of which (may he give thee a resting-place) is more trans-parent. In an annotated Codex of Zamachschari *hajjâk allah wa-bajjâk* is explained: God preserve thy life and grant thee to come to a place of rest, *bawwaaka* (therefore بَوَّأ = بَوَى)

menzilan. That אֲבִי (as also בִּי) is connected with this *bajjâk* since the latter is the *Piel*-form of an old verb *bajja* (*vid. supra,* p. 125), which with the forms بَاء (whence بِيئَة, a sheltering house) and بَوَأ (بَوَى) has one root similar in signification with בוא, the following contributions of Wetzstein will show.

In elucidation of the present passage he observes: The expressions *abî, tebî, jebî; nebî, tebû, jebû*, are so frequent in Damascus, that they very soon struck me, and on my first inquiry I always received the same answer, that they are a mutilation of أبْغِي, *abghi,* I desire, etc. [*vid. supra,* p. 165], until one day a fugitive came into the consulate, and with these words, *abî wâlidêk*, seized me in that part of the body where the Arabs wear the girdle (*zunnâr*), a symbolic action by which one seeks some one's protection. Since the word here could not be equivalent to *abghi* ("I desire" thy parents), I turned to the person best acquainted with the idiom of the country, the scribe *Abderrahmân el-Midâni,* whose father had been a wandering minstrel in the camps for twenty years; and he explained to me that *abghi* only signifies "I desire;" on the contrary, *abî,* "I implore importunately, I pray for God's sake," and the latter belongs to a defective verb, بِيٌ, from which, except the forms mentioned, only the part. *anâ bâj,* "I come as a suppliant," and its plur. *nahn bâjin,* is used. The poet *Musa Rârâ* from Krêje in the south of Hauran, who lived with me six months in Damascus in order to instruct me in the dialect of his district, assured me that among the Beduins also the *perf.* forms *bît, bînâ* (I have, we have entreated), and the *fut.* forms *tabîn* (thou, woman . . .), *jaben* (they, the women . . .), and *taben* (ye women . . .), are used. In the year 1858, in the course of a journey in his native country, I came to *Dîmâs,* whither they had brought two strange Beduins who had been robbed of their horses in that desert (Sahra *Dîmâs*), and one of them had at the same time received a mortal gunshot-wound. As I came to these men, who were totally forsaken, the wounded man began to express his importunate desire for a surgeon with the words *jâ shêch nebî 'arabak,* "Sir, we claim the protection of thy Arabs," *i.e.* we adjure thee by thy family. Naturally *abî* occurs most frequently. It generally has its obj. in the *acc.,* often also with the *præpos.* على, exactly like دخل (to enter, to flee anywhere and hide), which is its correct synonym and usual substitute in common life. It is often used without an obj., and, indeed, very variously. With women it is chiefly the introduction to a question prompted by curiosity, as: *abî* (ah, tell me), have you really betrothed your daughter? Or the word is accompanied by a gesture by the five fingers of the right hand, with the tips united, being stretched out towards the hasty or impatient listener, as if one wished to show some costly object, when *abî* signifies as much as: I pray thee wait till I have shown thee this precious thing, *i.e.* allow me to make one more remark to thee in reference to the matter. Moreover, בִּי (probably not corrupted from אָבִי, but a derived *nomen concretum* in the sense of *dachîl* or *mustagîr*, one seeking protection, protégé, after the form אִי, צִי, from בוא = בוה) still exists unaltered in Hauran and in the steppe. The Beduin introduces an important request with the words *anâ bî ahlak*, I am a protégé of thy family, or *anâ bî 'irdak*, I trust to thine honour, etc.; while in Damascus they say, *anâ dachîl ahlak, harîmak, aulâdak,* etc. The Beduin women make use of this *bî* in a weakened signification, in order to beg a piece of soap or sugar, and *anâ bî lihjetak,* I pray by thy beard, etc., is often heard.

If now we combine that אָבִי of Elihu with *abghi* (from بَغَى, Hebr. בָּעָה, Aram. בְּעָא, *fut.* יִבְעֶי, as בִּי with בְּעִי) or with *abî* = אַבָּא, from the verb *bajja* = בוא (בִי),[1] it always remains a remarkable instance in favour of the Arabic colouring of the Elihu section similar to the rest of the book,—a colouring, so to speak, dialectically Hauranitish; while, on the other hand, even by this second speech, one cannot avoid the impression of a great distance between it and the rest of the book: the language has a lofty tone, without its special harshness, as there, being the necessary consequence of a carefully concentrated fulness of thought; moreover, here in general the usual

---

[1] We cannot in any case, with Wetzst., explain the אָבִי אָבִי, 2 Kings ii. 12, xiii. 14, according to the above, so that the king of Israel adjured the dying prophet by the national army and army of the faithful not to forsake him, as an Arab is now and then adjured in most urgent and straitened circumstances " by the army of Islam ;" *vid.* on the other hand, 2 Kings vi. 21, comp. v. 13, viii. 9 (בְּנִי). Here rather, if an Arabian parallel be needed, the usual death wail, *bi-abî anta* (thou wast dear as a father to me), *e.g.* in Kosegarten, *Chrestom.* p. 140, 3, is to be compared. אָבִי, 1 Sam. xxiv. 12, might more readily, with Ew. § 101, *c*, be brought in here and regarded as belonging to the North Palestine peculiarities of the book of Kings; but by a comparison of the passages cited, this is also improbable.

regularity of the strophe-lines no longer prevails, and also the usual symmetrical balance of thought in them.

If we confine our attention to the real substance of the speech, apart from the emotional and rough accessories, Elihu casts back the reproach of injustice which Job has raised, first as being contradictory to the being of God, ch. xxxiv. 10 sq. ; then he seeks to refute it as contradicting God's government, and this he does (1) apagogically from the unselfish love with which God's protecting care preserves the breath of every living thing, while He who has created all things might bring back all created things to the former non-existence, ch. xxxiv. 12–15; (2) by induction from the impartial judgment which He exercises over princes and peoples, and from which it is inferred that the Ruler of the world is also all-just, ch. xxxiv. 16–20. From this Elihu proves that God can exercise justice, and from that, that He is omniscient, and sees into man's inmost nature without any judicial investigation, ch. xxxiv. 21–28; inaccessible to human accusation and human defiance, He rules over peoples and individuals, even over kings, and nothing turns His just punishment aside, but lowly penitence blended with the prayer for the disclosure of unperceived sin, ch. xxxiv. 29–32. For in His retributive rule God does not follow the discontented demands of men arrogant and yet devoid of counsel, ch. xxxiv. 33. It is worthy of recognition, that Elihu does not here coincide with what has been already said (especially ch. xii. 15 sqq.), without applying it to another purpose; and that his theodicy differs essentially from that proclaimed by the friends. It is not derived from mere appearance, but lays hold of the very principles. It does not attempt the explanation of the many apparent contradictions to retributive justice which outward events manifest, as agreeing with it; it does not solve the question by mere empiricism, but from the idea of the Godhead and its relation to the world, and by such inner necessity guarantees to the mysteries still remaining to human shortsightedness, their future solution.

Elihu's Third Speech.—Chap. xxxv.

Schema : 6. 8. 10. 6.

[Then began Elihu, and said :]

2 *Dost thou consider this to be right,*
  Sayest thou : my righteousness exceedeth God's,
3 *That thou sayest, what advantage is it to thee,*
  What doth it profit me more than my sin?
4 *I will answer thee words,*
  And thy companions with thee.

The neutral זאֹת, ver. 2*a*, refers prospectively to כִּי־תֹאמַר, ver. 3*a* : this that thou sayest. חָשַׁב with *acc.* of the obj. and לְ of the predicate, as ch. xxxiii. 10, comp. xiii. 24, and freq. The second interrogative clause, ver. 2*b*, is co-ordinate with the first, and the collective thought of this ponderous construction, vers. 2, 3, is this : Considerest thou this to be right, and thinkest thou on this account to be able to put thy righteousness above the divine, that, as thou maintainest, no righteousness on the side of God corresponds to this thy righteousness, because God makes no distinction between righteousness and the sin of man, and allows the former to go unrewarded ? צִדְקִי (for which Olsh. wishes to read צָדַקְתִּי, as ch. ix. 27 אמרתי for אָמְרִי) forms with מֵאֵל a substantival clause : *justitia mea est præ Deo (præ divina)* ; מִן comparative as ch. xxxii. 2, comp. on the matter xxxiv. 5, not equivalent to ἀπό as ch. iv. 17. כי־תאמר is first followed by the *oratio obliqua* : what it (viz. צדקך) advantageth thee, then by the *or. directa* (on this change *vid.* Ew. § 338, *a*) : what profit have I (viz. בצדקי), *præ peccato meo* ; this מִן is also comparative ; the constantly ambiguous combination would be allowable from the fact that, according to the usage of the language, " to

obtain profit from anything " is expressed by הוֹעִיל בְּ, not by
הוֹעִיל מִן. Moreover, *præ peccato meo* is equivalent to *plus
quam inde quod pecco*, comp. Ps. xviii. 24 מֵעֲוֹנִי, Hos. iv. 8
אֶל־עֲוֹנָם. We have already on ch. xxxiv. 9 observed that Job
has not directly said (he cites it, ch. xxi. 15, as the saying of
the ungodly) what Elihu in ver. 3 puts into his mouth, but
as an inference it certainly is implied in such utterances as
ch. ix. 22. Elihu's polemic against Job and his companions
(רֵעֶיךָ are not the three, as LXX. and Jer. translate, but the
אַנְשֵׁי אָוֶן, to whom Job is likened by such words as ch. xxxiv.
8, 36) is therefore not unauthorized; especially since he
assails the conclusion together with its premises. In the
second strophe the vindication of the conclusion is now
refuted.

5 *Look towards heaven and see,*
  And behold the ethereal heights : they are high above thee.
6 *If thou sinnest, what dost thou effect with Him?*
  And if thy transgressions are many, what doest thou to Him?
7 *If thou art righteous, what dost thou give Him,*
  Or what doth He take from thy hand?
8 *To man like thee thy godlessness availeth,*
  And to thee, a son of man, thy righteousness.

Towards heaven he is to direct his gaze, to obtain from the
height of heaven a notion of the exaltation of God who dwells
above the heavens. The combination הִבִּיט וְרָאָה is like Ps.
lxxx. 15 and freq. שְׁחָקִים (שַׁחַק), سحق, to rub in pieces, make
thin, therefore the opposite of עָבִים) are the thin transparent
strata of the atmosphere above the hanging clouds. מִן after
גָּבַהּ denotes the height that is on the opposite side to the
beholder. From the exaltation of God it is then further
inferred that it is impossible to exercise any human influence
upon Him, by which He might suffer. The pointing wavers
here between תִּפְעַל (the common *fut.* form) and תִּפְעָל (as a con-

traction of תִּפְעָל after the form אֶזְעָם, Num. xxiii. 8). Human wrong or right doing neither diminishes nor increases His blessedness; injury or advantage is only on the side of man, from whom it proceeds. Others, whom his conduct affects, are not included in ver. 8: righteous or ungodly doing, Elihu means to say, as such and with its consequences, belongs solely to the doer himself, the man "like thee" (לְאִישׁ with *Munach*, כָּמוֹךָ with *Munach*), the son of man, *i.e.* man, capable of evil as of good, and who always, after deciding in favour of the latter or the former, determines his fortune or misfortune, in distinction from God, who ever remains unchangeably the same in His perfect righteousness. What Elihu here says we have already heard from Eliphaz, ch. xxii. 2 sq., and Job even expresses himself similarly in ch. vii. 20; but to Elihu's mind it all becomes for Job new and powerful motives to quiet submission, for what objection should Job raise in justification of his complaints concerning his affliction against such sentiments as these, that goodness bears its reward and evil its punishment in itself, and that God's reward of goodness is not a work of indebtedness, nor His punishment of evil a work of necessity? Before such truth he must really hold his peace.

9 *By reason of the multitude of oppressions they raise a cry,*
   They call for help by reason of the arm of the great,
10 *But none saith: Where is Eloah my Creator,*
   Who giveth songs of praise in the night,
11 *Who teacheth us by the beasts of the earth,*
   And maketh us wise by the fowls of heaven?
12 *Then they cry, yet He answereth not,*
   Because of the pride of evil men.
13 *Vanity alone God heareth not,*
   And the Almighty observeth it not.

In ver. 9*a* the accentuation of מֵרֹב with *Dechi*, according

to which Dachselt interprets : *præ multitudine* (*oppressionum*)
oppressi clamabunt, is erroneous; it is to be written מֵרֹב, as
everywhere else, and this (according to Codd. and the editions
of Jablonski, Majus, Michaelis, and others) is to be accented
with *Munach,* which is followed by עֲשׁוּקִים with a vicarious
Munach : præ multitudine oppressionum (עֲשׁוּקִים like Eccl.
iv. 1*a,* and probably also Amos iii. 9) *edunt clamorem* (*Hiph.*
in the intensive *Kal* signification, as *e.g.* הִזְנָה, to commit forni-
cation, Hos. iv. 10, and freq., comp. p. 185, note).   On זְרוֹעַ,
ver. 9*b, vid.* vol. i. 432 ; רַבִּים are the great or lords (Arab.
arbâb).   The *plur.* with a general subj. is followed by the
sing. in ver. 10*a :* and no ône says (exactly as in הֵאָמֵר, ch.
xxxiv. 31).   Elihu weakens the doubt expressed by Job in
ch. xxiv. 12, that God allows injustice to prevail, and oppressed innocence remains without vindication.   The failure
of the latter arises from the fact of the sufferers complaining,
but not seeking earnestly the only true helper, God their
maker (עֹשִׂים, intensive *plur.,* as Isa. xxii. 11, liv. 5, Ps.
cxlix. 2), who gives (to which may be compared a passage
of the Edda : " Wuodan gives songs to the Scalds") songs
(זְמִרוֹת, from the onomatopoetic זמר) in the night, *i.e.* who in
the night of sorrow puts songs of praise concerning the dawn-
ing light of help into the mouth of the sufferers.   The singing
of the glory of the nightly heavens (Stick., Hahn) is to be as
little thought of as the music of the spheres ; the night is, as
ch. xxxiv. 20, 25, the time of unexpectedly sudden change.

In ver. 11 most expositors (last of all Schlottm.) take the
two מִן as comparative.   Elihu would then, since he feels the
absence of the asking after this God on the part of the sufferers, mean the conscious relation in which He has placed
us to Himself, and in accordance with which the sufferer
should not merely instinctively complain, but humbly bow
himself and earnestly offer up prayer.   But according to ch.
xii. 7 (comp. Prov. vi. 6, וחכם), it is to be translated : who

teaches (מַלְּפֵנוּ = מְאַלְּפֵנוּ, comp. 2 Sam. xxii. 40, *Psalter* i. 160)
us from the beasts of the earth (so that from them as a means
of instruction teaching comes to us), and makes us wise from
the birds of heaven. The *fut.* interchanging with the *part.*
better accords with this translation, according to which ver.
11 is a continuation of the assertion of a divine instruction,
by means of the animal creation; the thought also suits the
connection better, for of the many things that may be learned
from the animal creation, prayer here comes under consideration,—the lions roar, Ps. civ. 21; the thirsty cattle cry to
God, Joel i. 20; the ravens call upon God, Ps. cxlvii. 9.
If we now determine the collective thought of vers. 10 sq.,
that affliction does not drive most men to God the almighty
Helper, who will be humbly entreated for help: it is more
natural to take שָׁם (*vid.* on ch. xxiii. 7) in the sense of then
(τότε), than, with reference to the scene of oppression, in the
sense of there (LXX., Jer.: *ibi*). The division of the verse
is correct, and H. B. Starcke has correctly interpreted: *Tunc
clamabunt (sed non respondebit) propter superbiam (insolen-
tiam) malorum.* מִפְּנֵי is not to be connected with יַעֲנֶה in the
sense of *non exaudiet et servabit*, by which *constr. prægnans*
one would expect מֶן, Ps. xxii. 22, instead of מפני, nor in the
sense of *non exaudiet propter* (Hirz., Schlottm.), for the arrogant רָעִים are not those who complain unheard: but, as the
connection shows, those from whom the occasion of complaint
proceeds. Therefore: not allowing themselves to be driven
to God by oppression, they cry then, without, however, being
heard of God, by reason of the arrogance of evil men which
they have to endure. Ver. 13 gives the reason of their obtain-
ing no answer: Only emptiness (*i.e.* mere motion of the lips
without the true spirit of prayer) God heareth not, and the
Almighty observeth it not. Hahn wrongly denies אַךְ the
significations *certo* and *verumtamen;* but we prefer the restrictive signification (sheer emptiness or hollowness) which

proceeds from the affirmative primary signification[1] here, to the adversative (nevertheless emptiness), since the adversative thought, *verumtamen non exaudit*, has found its expression already in וְלֹא יַעֲנֶה.

14 *Although thou sayest, thou seest Him not:*
  The cause lieth before Him, and thou mayest wait for Him.
15 *Now, then, if His wrath hath not yet punished,*
  Should He not be well acquainted with sullenness?
16 *While Job openeth his mouth without reason,*
  Without knowledge multiplieth words.

The address is not directed to Job exclusively, for it here treats first of the acts of injustice which prevail among men and remain apparently unpunished; but to Job, however, also, so far as he has, ch. xxiii. 8–10, comp. xix. 7, xxx. 20, thus complained concerning his prayer being unanswered. אַף כִּי signifies elsewhere *quanto minus*, ch. iv. 19, or also *quanto magis*, Prov. xv. 11, but nowhere *quanto minus si* (Hirz., Hlgst.) or *quanto magis si* (Hahn), also not Ezek. xv. 5, where it signifies *etiamne quum*. As it can, however, naturally signify *etiam quum*, it can also signify *etiamsi*, *etsi*, as here and Neh. ix. 18. This *quamvis dicas* (*opineris*) is followed by the *oratio obliqua*, as ch. xxxv. 3a. The relation of the matter—says the conclusion, ver. 14b—is other than thou thinkest: the matter to be decided lies before Him, is therefore well known to Him, and thou mightest only wait for Him (חוֹלֵל instead of יָחֵל or הוֹחִיל only here, comp. Ps. xxxvii. 7, וְהִתְחוֹלֵל לוֹ); the decision, though it pass by, will not fail. In vers. 15 sq., ver. 15 is taken by most modern commentators as antecedent to ver. 16, in which case, apart from the distortions introduced, two interpretations are possible: (1) However now, because His (God's) wrath does not visit . . . Job opens his mouth; (2) However now, because

---

[1] *Vid.* Hupfeld in the *Zeitschr. für Kunde des Morgenl.* ii. 441 f.

He (God) does not visit his (Job's) wrath (comp. on this reference of the אַפּוֹ to Job, ch. xviii. 4, xxxvi. 13, 18) . . . Job
opens, etc.   That a clause with a confirmatory כִּי is made to
precede its principal clause is not without example, Gen.
iii. 14, 17; but in connection with this arrangement the verb
is accustomed always, in the principal clause or in the conclusion, to stand prominent (so that consequently we should
expect וִיפְצֶה אִיוֹב), although in Arabic this position of the
words, וְאִיוֹב יִפְצֶה, and in fact فَأَيُّوبُ instead of وَأَيُّوبُ (in connection with a difference of the subj. in the antecedent and
in the conclusion, vid. De Sacy, Gramm. Arabe, § 1201, 2),
is regular.   Therefore for a long time I thought that ver. 15
was to be taken interrogatively: And now (וְעַתָּה as logical
inference and conclusion, which is here its most probable
function, Ew. § 353, b) should His wrath not punish (פָּקַד as
absolute as ch. xxxi. 14), and should He not take notice, etc.,
כִּי interrogative as 1 Sam. xxiv. 20, xxviii. 13, 1 Kings xi. 22,
as הֲכִי (is it so that, or: should it be so that), ch. vi. 22, and
freq., in connection with which, what is said on Gen. xxi. 7
concerning the modal use of the *præt.* might be compared
on the two *prætt.*   But by this rendering the connection of
ver. 16 with what precedes is awkward.   Ewald has given
the correct rendering (apart from the misunderstanding of
פֶּשׁ): Therefore, because His wrath has not yet punished, He
does not know much about foolishness!   Ver. 15*b* requires
to be taken as the conclusion to ver. 15*a*, yet not as an exclamation, but as an interrogative.   The interrogative use of
וְלֹא is not unusual, 2 Sam. xix. 44, Ezek. xvi. 43, 47, 56,
xxxii. 27; and just as here, this interrogative וְלֹא is found
after a hypothetical antecedent clause, 1 Sam. xx. 9, Ex.
viii. 22.

In connection with this interrogative rendering of ver. 15,
it still remains questionable whether it refers to Job's sin, or
sin which prevails among men.   The theme of this third

speech of Elihu requires the latter reference, although perhaps not without a side-glance at Job's own arrogant behaviour. The translation shows how suitably ver. 16 is connected with what precedes: ver. 16 is a circumstantial clause, or, if one is not willing to take it as a subordinate clause, but prefers to take it as standing on a level with ver. 15, an adversative clause attached with *Waw*, as is frequently the case: but (nevertheless) Job . . . ; פְּצָה פֶּה of opening the mouth in derision, as Lam. ii. 16, iii. 46 ; הֶבֶל is the *acc.* of closer definition to it (= בְּהֶבֶל), and the הִכְבִּיר, which occurs only here and ch. xxxvi. 31, signifies without distinction *magnificare* and *multiplicare:* Job multiplies high emotional words. As this יַכְבִּיר is, so to speak, Hebræo-Arabic (Arab. *akbara*), so is ver. 15 full of Arabisms: (1) The combination אֵין פָּקַד, which has not its like in the Hebrew language (whether it be originally intended as relative or not: *non est quod visitaverit*, Ew. § 321, *b*), corresponds to the popular Arabic use of ليس for لا, Ges. *Thes.* i. 82, *b*; probably אַיִן has the value of an intensive negation (Carey: not at all). (2) The combination יָדַע בְּ, to know about anything, to take knowledge of anything (differently ch. xii. 9, but comp. ch. xxiv. 12 on the idea), is like the Arab. construction of the verb ʻ*alima* with *bi* (concerning) or *bianna* (because that) of the obj.; מְאֹד (on this *vid.* on Ps. xxxi. 12) belongs not to בפשׁ (which is indeed possible), but, according to Ps. cxxxix. .14, to ידע. (3) פֶּשׁ is especially to be explained from the Arabic. The signification a multitude (Jewish expositors, after פּוּשׁ, *Niph. se diffundere*, Nah. iii. 18) is not suitable; the signification evil (LXX., Jer., and others: פֶּשׁ = פֶּשַׁע) presents a forcibly mutilated word, and moreover one devoid of significance in this connection; whereas the

Arab. فَشّ (but not in its derivatives, *fashsh*, empty-headed; *fâshûsh*, empty-headedness, imbecility, with its metaphorical sense) indicates a development of signification which leads to the desired end, especially in the Syro-Arabic usage most natural here. The verb فَشَّ (פָּשַׁשׁ, cogn. فَشَرَ, فَرَشَ, to extend, *expandere*) is used originally of water (*fashsh el-mâ*): to overflow its dam, to overflow its banks, whence a valley by the lake of *el-Higâne*, into which the waters of the lake flow after the winter rains, is called *el-mefeshsh;* then of a leathern bottle: to run out (t*arf mefshûsh,* an emptied bottle), of a tumour (*waram*): to disperse, disappear, and tropically of anger (*el-chulq*): to break forth, vent itself on anything, hence the phrase: dost thou make me a *mefeshshe* (an object for the venting) of thine anger? From this فَشّ (distinct from فَاش med. *Waw,* to swim on the surface, trop. to be above, not to allow one's self to be kept down, and med. *Je,* comp. פּוּשׁ, Hab. i. 8, Jer. l. 11, Mal. iii. 20, signifies to be proud) is פָּשׁ, formed after the forms מֵם, מַד, בַּד, a synon. of זָדוֹן, or even of עֶבְרָה in the signification of excessive haughtiness, pride that bursts forth violently.[1]

Thus, even at the close of this third speech of Elihu, the Arabic, and in fact Syro-Arabic colouring, common to this

---

[1] The signification *expandere* also underlies the noun *fishshe,* the lungs (in Egypt.); the signification *discutere* (especially *carminare,* to card wool), which the Talmud. פִּשְׁפֵּשׁ also has, is only a shade of the same signification; the origin of the trop. signification *fatuum esse* is clear from *'gaus fashûsh,* empty nuts. The rice from the Palestine valley of *Hûle,* it is somewhere said, is worse than the Egyptian, because (what is a fault in the East) in cooking *tufeshfish, i.e.* it bursts, breaks in pieces (comp. on the other hand: if the seed for sowing sinks to the bottom when put into water, it is good; if it swims on the surface, *jefûsh,* it is bad). The *Piel* of this *fashsha* signifies to cause the water to overflow, trop. *fashshasha qalbahu,* he gave air to his heart, *i.e.* he revealed a secret which burdened him. A proverb says: the market (with its life and changing scenes) is a *feshshâsh* of cares, *i.e.* consoles a troubled heart. In the *Hiph.* one says in like manner proverbially, *el-bukâ jufishsh,* weeping removes the anguish of the soul.—WETZST.

section with the rest of the book, is confirmed; while, on the other hand, we miss the bold, original figures which up to ch. xxxi. followed like waves one upon another, and we perceive a deficiency of skill, as now and then between Koheleth and Solomon. The chief thought of the speech we have also heard already from the three friends and Job himself. That the piety of the pious profits himself without involving God in any obligation to him, Eliphaz has already said, ch. xxii. 2 sq.; and that prayer that is heard in time of need and the unanswered cry of the godly and the ungodly are distinct, Job said, ch. xxvii. 9 sq. Elihu, however, deprives these thoughts of their hitherto erroneous application. If piety gives nothing to God which He ought to reward, Job dare not regard his affliction, mysterious as it is to him, as unjust; and if the godly do not directly experience the avenging wrath of God on the haughtiness of their oppressors, the question, whether then their prayer for help is of the right kind, is more natural than the complaint of a want of justice in God's government of the world. Job is silent also after this speech. It does not contain the right consolation; it contains, however, censure which he ought humbly to receive. It touches his heart. But whether it touches the heart of the idea of the book, is another question.

Elihu's Fourth Speech.—Chap. xxxvi. xxxvii.

Schema: 6. 7. 6. 6. 6. 7. 6. 8. 8. 8. | 11. 11. 8. 6. 8. 11.

[Then Elihu continued and said :]

2 *Suffer me a little, and I will inform thee,*
   For there is something still to be said for Eloah.

3 *I will fetch my knowledge from afar,*
   And to my Creator will I ascribe right.

4 *For truly my words are not lies,*
   One perfect in knowledge stands before thee.

Elihu's preceding three speeches were introduced by וַיַּעַן;
this fourth, in honour of the number three, is introduced only
as a continuation of the others. Job is to wait yet a little
while, for he still has (= לִי עוֹד), or: there still are, words in
favour of Eloah; *i.e.* what may be said in vindication of God
against Job's complaints and accusations is not yet exhausted.
This appears to be the only instance of the Aramaic כַּתַּר being
taken up as Hebr.; whereas חַוָּה, *nunciare* (Arab. وحى, I. IV.),
is a poetic Aramaism occurring even in Ps. xix. 3 (comp. on
the construction ch. xxxii. 6); and זְעֵיר (a diminutive form,
after the manner of the Arab. *zuʻair*) belongs in Isa. xxviii.
10, 13 to the popular language (of Jerusalem), but is here
used poetically. The verb נָשָׂא, ver. 3*a*, is not to be understood according to נשׂא משׁל, but according to 1 Kings x. 11;
and לְמֵרָחוֹק signifies, as also ch. xxxix. 29, Isa. xxxvii. 26, *e
longinquo*, viz. out of the wide realm of history and nature.
The expression נָתַן צֶדֶק follows the analogy of (עז) נתן כבוד.
דֵּעָה, ver. 4*b*, interchanges with the דֵּע which belongs exclusively to Elihu, since Elihu styles himself תְּמִים דֵּעוֹת, as ch.
xxxvii. 16 God תְּמִים דֵּעִים (comp. 1 Sam. ii. 3, אֵל דֵּעוֹת). תמים
in this combination with דעות cannot be intended of purity
of character; but as Elihu there attributes absolute perfection
of knowledge in every direction to God, so here, in reference
to the theodicy which he opposes to Job, he claims faultless-
ness and clearness of perception.

5 *Behold, God is mighty, and yet doth not act scornfully,*
  Mighty in power of understanding.
6 *He preserveth not the life of the ungodly,*
  And to the afflicted He giveth right.
7 *He withdraweth not His eyes from the righteous,*
  But with kings on the throne
  He establisheth them for ever, and they are exalted.

The obj. that must be mentally supplied to וְלֹא יִמְאָס is, as

in ch. xlii. 6, to be derived from the connection. The idea of
the verb is, as in ch. viii. 20 : He is exalted, without however
looking down disdainfully (*non despicit*) from His height, or
more definitely : without setting Himself above the justice
due to even the meanest of His creatures—great in power of
heart (comp. ch. xxxiv. 33 אַנְשֵׁי לֵבָב, Arab. *ûlû-l-elbâb*), *i.e.*
understanding (νοῦς, πνεῦμα), to see through right and wrong
everywhere and altogether. Vers. 6, 7 describe how His rule
among men evinces this not merely outward but spiritual
superiority coupled with condescension to the lowly. The
notion of the object, וְאֶת־מְלָכִים לַכִּסֵּא (as Isa. ix. 11 the subject),
becomes the more distinctly prominent by virtue of the *fut.
consec.* which follows like a conclusion, and takes it up again.
Ewald thinks this explanation contrary to the accents and the
structure of the sentence itself ; but it is perfectly consistent
with the former, and indisputably syntactic (Ges. § 129, 2, *b*,
and Ew. himself, § 344, *b*). Ps. ix. 5, comp. cxxxii. 12, Isa.
xlvii. 1, shows how לַכִּסֵּא is intended (He causes them to sit
upon the throne). Ch. v. 11, 1 Sam. ii. 8, Ps. cxiii. 7 sq. are
parallel passages.

8 *And if they are bound with chains,*
    Holden in cords of affliction :
9 *Then He declareth to them their doing*
    And their transgressions, that they have been vainglorious ;
10 *Then He openeth their ear to warning,*
    And commandeth them to turn from iniquity.

The subj. is in no case the רְשָׁעִים (Hahn), but the צַדִּיקִים, or
those who are as susceptible to discipline as it is needful to
them, just as in Ps. cvii., which in general presents many
instances for an extensive comparison with the speeches of
Elihu. The chains, ver. 8*a*, are meant literally, and the
bands, ver. 8*b*, figuratively ; the Psalmist couples both in
אֲסִירֵי עֳנִי וּבַרְזֶל, cvii. 10. The conclusion begins with ver. 9,

and is repeated in another application, ver. 10. פֹּעַל in the sense of *maleficium*, as Arab. فَعَل, recalls מַעֲשֶׂה, *facinus*, ch. xxxiii. 17. כִּי, ver. 9*b*, is, as in ver. 10*b*, an objective *quod*. It is not translated, however, *quod invaluerint* (Rosenm.), which is opposed to the most natural sense of the *Hithpa.*, but according to ch. xv. 25 : *quod sese extulerint.* מוּסָר, παιδεία, *disciplina*, interchanges here with the more rare מֹסָר used in ch. xxxiii. 16 ; there we have already also met with the phrase גָּלָה אֹזֶן, to uncover the ear, *i.e.* to open. אָמַר כִּי corresponds to the Arab. *amara an (bi-an)*, to command that. The fundamental thought of Elihu here once again comes unmistakeably to view : the sufferings of the righteous are well-meant chastisements, which are to wean them from the sins into which through carnal security they have fallen—a warning from God to penitence, designed to work their good.

> 11 *If they hear and yield,*
> *They pass their days in prosperity*
> *And their years in pleasure.*
> 12 *And if they hear not,*
> *They pass away by the bow*
> *And expire in lack of knowledge.*

Since a declaration of the divine will has preceded in ver. 10*b*, it is more natural to take וְיַעֲבֹדוּ in the sense of *obsequi*, to do the will of another (as 1 Kings xii. 7, comp. מַעֲבָד from עָבַד in the generalized sense of *facere*), than, with Umbr., in the sense of *colere scil. Deum* (as Isa. xix. 23, Arab. *'abid*, one who reveres God, a godly person). Instead of יְבַלּוּ, Isa. lxv. 22 (on which the Masora observes לִית, *i.e.* "nowhere else") and ch. xxi. 13 *Chethîb*, it is here without dispute יְכַלּוּ (Targ. יְשַׁלְּמוּן, *peragent*, as Ezek. xliii. 27). נְעִימִים is, as Ps. xvi. 6, a neutral masc.: *amœna.* On עָבַר בִּשֶׁלַח, to precipitate one's self into the weapon, *i.e.* to incur peremptory

punishment, comp. ch. xxxiii. 18.   On בבלי דעת comp. xxxv.
16, iv. 21.   Impenitence changes affliction, which is intended
to be a means of rescue, into total destruction; yet there are
some who will not be warned and affrighted by it.

> 13 *Yet the hypocrites in heart cherish wrath,*
> *They cry not when He hath chained them.*
> 14 *Thus their soul dieth in the vigour of youth,*
> *And their life is like that of the unclean.*
> 15 *Yet He delivereth the sufferer by his affliction,*
> *And openeth their ear by oppression.*

He who is angry with God in his affliction, and does not
humbly pray to Him, shows thereby that he is a חָנֵף, one
estranged from God (on the idea of the root, *vid.* i. 216),
and not a צדיק.   This connection renders it natural to understand not the divine wrath by אַף: θησαυρίζουσιν ὀργήν
(Rosenm. after Rom. ii. 5), or: they heap up wrath upon
themselves (Wolfson, who supplies עֲלֵיהֶם), but the impatience, discontent, and murmuring of man himself: they
cherish or harbour wrath, viz. בְּלִבָּם (comp. ch. xxii. 22, where
שׂים בלב signifies to take to heart, but at the same time to
preserve in the heart).   Used thus absolutely, שִׂים signifies
elsewhere in the book, to give attention to, ch. iv. 20, xxiv.
12, xxxiv. 23, or (as وضع) to lay down a pledge; here it
signifies *reponunt s. recondunt* (with an implied *in ipsis*), as
also شام *fut. i*, to conceal with the idea of sinking into
(*immittentem*), *e.g.* the sword in the sheath.   With תָּמֹת, for
וְתָמֹת (Isa. l. 2) or וַתָּמָת, the punishment which issues forth
undistinguished from this frustration of the divine purpose
of grace follows ἀσυνδέτως, as *e.g.* Hos. vii. 16.   חַיָּה interchanges with נפשׁ, as ch. xxxiii. 22, 28; נֹעַר (likewise a
favourite word with Elihu) is intended just as ch. xxxiii. 25,
and in the Ps. lxxxviii. ver. 16, which resembles both the Elihu
section and the rest of the book.   The *Beth* of בַּקְּדֵשִׁים has

the sense of *æque ac* (Targ. הֵין), as ch. xxxiv. 36, comp. תַּחַת, ch. xxxiv. 26. Jer. translates *inter effeminatos;* for קְדֵשִׁים (heathenish, equivalent to קְדוֹשִׁים, as כְּמָרִים, heathenish, equivalent to כֹּהֲנִים) are the consecrated men, who yielded themselves up, like the women in honour of the deity, to passive, prematurely-enervating incontinence (*vid.* Keil on Deut. xxiii. 18), a heathenish abomination prevailing now and again even in Israel (1 Kings xiv. 24, xv. 12, xxii. 47), which was connected with the worship of Astarte and Baal that was transferred from Syria, and to which allusion is here made, in accordance with the scene of the book. For the sufferer, on the other hand, who suffers not merely of necessity, but willingly, this his suffering is a means of rescue and moral purification. Observe the play upon the words יְחַלֵּץ and בְּלַחַץ. The *Beth* in both instances is, in accordance with Elihu's fundamental thought, the *Beth instrum.*

16 *And He even bringeth thee out of the jaws of distress*
   To a broad place, whose ground hath no straitness,
   And the adorning of thy table shall be full of fatness.
17 *Yet thou art become full of the judging of the evil-doer :*
   Judging and judgment lay hold on one another !
18 *For let not anger indeed entice thee to scorning,*
   And let not the greatness of the ransom mislead thee.

With ver. 16*a* Elihu passes over to the application to Job of what he said in the preceding strophe. Since it is usual to place אַף (like גַּם and אַךְ) at the beginning of the sentence, although not belonging to the member of the sentence which immediately follows, וְאַף הֲסִיתְךָ for וְהֵסִית אַף אֹתְךָ cannot be remarkable. The *præt.* הֲסִיתְךָ is not promissory, but Elihu says with what design God has decreed the present suffering for Job. הֵסִית מִן is like 2 Chron. xviii. 31: out of distress (צָר for צַר by *Rebia magnum*), which has him in its jaws, and threatens to swallow him, God brings him away to great

prosperity; a thought which Elihu expresses in the imagery
of the Psalms of a broad place and a bountiful table (comp.
e.g. Ps. iv. 2, xxiii. 5). רַחַב is locative, and לֹא־מוּצָק תַּחְתֶּיהָ
is either a relative clause: whose beneath (ground) is not
straitened, no-straitness (in which case מוּצָק would not be
constr. from the n. hophal. מוּצָק, Isa. viii. 23, but absol. after
the form מֻחְנַק, ch. vii. 15, Ew. § 160, c, Anm. 4), Saad.
لا ضيق فى موضعها (cujus in loco non angustiæ); or it is virtually
an adj.: without (לֹא = בְּלֹא, as ch. xxxiv. 24, comp. on ch.
xii. 24) straitness of what is beneath them, eorum quæ sub se
habet (comp. on ch. xxviii. 5). רַחַב is fem., like רְחוֹב, Dan.
ix. 25. A special clause takes the place of the locative, ver.
16c : and the settling or spreading, i.e. the provision (from
נוּחַ, to come down gradually, to seat one's self) of thy table
shall be full of fatness. מָלֵא (whether it be adj. or verb) is
treated by attraction, according to the gender of the governed
noun; and it is unnecessary, with Rosenm. and others, to
derive נַחַת from נָחַת (Aram. for יָרַד).

In ver 17, דִּין is intended of Job's negative judgment concerning God and His dealings (comp. Ps. lxxvi. 9, where it
signifies a judicial decision, and Prov. xxii. 10, where it signifies a wrangling refusal of a fair decision). Ver. 17a is not
a conditional clause (Hahn), in which case the præt. hypothet.
would have a prominent position, but an adversative predicative clause: but (nevertheless) thou art full of the judging of
the evil-doer (evil judging); after which, just as ἀσυνδέτως as
ver. 14a, the sad issue in which this judging after the manner
of evil-doers results is expressed: such judging and judgment
border closely upon one another. Röd., Dietr., and Schlottm.
have wrongly reproduced this idea, discerned by Ges., when
they translate: judgment and sentence (guilt and punishment) shall seize thee. יִתְמֹכוּ, prehendunt scil. se (Ebr.: put
forth the hand), is used like the Aram. סְמַךְ, to draw nearer,
fasten together (Rabb. סָמוּךְ, near at hand), Arab. tamâsaka

(from مسك = סמך, as *e.g.* *hanash* = נָחָשׁ). In ver. 18 we leave the signification thick milk or cream (חֵמָה = חֶמְאָה, as ch. xxix. 6) to those who persuade themselves that cream can be metaphorically equivalent to superfluity (Ew., Hirz., Vaih., Hlgst). Renan's translation: *N'espère pas détourner la colère de Dieu par une amende,* we also leave as a simple puzzle to its discoverer, who, with this one exception, is destitute of thoughts proper to the book of Job. In general, the thought, "do not imagine by riches, by a great ransom, to be able to satisfy the claims of God," is altogether out of place here. Moreover, חֵמָה, which, as *e.g.* דְּאָגָה, Prov. xii. 25 (Ew. § 174, *g*), is construed as *masc.*, cannot be understood of God's wrath, since the poet by הֵסִית will not at one time have ascribed to God a well-meant incitation, at another an enticement *in malam partem.* That which allures is Job's own חֵמָה, and that not the excitement of his affliction (Hahn), but of his passion; comp. אַף, ver. 13. שֶׂפֶק is, however, to be explained according to ch. xxxiv. 37, comp. xxvii. 23 (clapping of hands = derision); and כֹּפֶר signifies reconciliation or expiation, as ch. xxxiii. 24. Elihu admonishes Job not to allow himself to be drawn by the heat of passion into derision, or to deride; nor to be allured from the right way by the ransom which is required of him as the price of restoration to happiness, viz. humble submission to the divine chastisement, as though this ransom were exceeding great. The connection is clear: an adverse verdict (דִּין) and condemnation (מִשְׁפָּט) are closely connected; for (כִּי) hastiness of temper, let it not (פֶּן) lead thee astray . . . thou wouldst not escape the judgment of God!

19 *Shall thy crying place thee beyond distress,*
   And all the efforts of strength?
20 *Long not for the night to come,*
   Which shall remove people from their place!

21 *Take heed, incline not to evil;*
For this thou hast desired more than affliction.

Those expositors who found in ver. 18*b* the warning, that
Job should not imagine that he would be able to redeem
himself from judgment by a large ransom, go on to explain:
will He esteem thy riches? (Farisol, Rosenm., Umbr.,
Carey, Ebr., and others); or: will thy riches suffice? (Hirz.,
Schlottm.); or some other way (Ew.). But apart from the
want of connection of this insinuation, which is otherwise
not mentioned in the book, and apart from the violence
which must be done to הֲיַעֲרֹךְ to accommodate it to it, שׁוּעַ,
although it might, as the abstract of שׁוֹעַ, ch. xxxiv. 19, signify wealth (comp. اسع, *amplitudo*), is, however, according to
the usage of the language (*vid.* ch. xxx. 24), so far as we
can trace it, a secondary form of שֶׁוַע (שַׁוְעָה), a cry for help;
and ch. xxxv. 9 sq., ver. 13, and other passages, also point
to this signification. What follows is still less appropriate
to this thought of ransom; Hirz. translates: Oh, not God
and all the treasures of wealth! But בְּצָר is nowhere equivalent to בֶּצֶר, ch. xxii. 24; but צָר, ver. 16, signifies distress;
and the expression לֹא בְצָר, in a condition devoid of distress,
is like לֹא בחכמה, ch. iv. 21, and לֹא בְיַד, ch. xxxiv. 20.
Finally, אַמִּיץ כֹּחַ signifies mighty in physical strength, ch.
ix. 4, 19, and מַאֲמַצֵּי־כֹחַ strong proofs of strength, not "treasures of wealth." Stick. correctly interprets: "Will thy
wild raging cry, then, and all thine exertions, as a warrior
puts them forth in the tumult of battle to work his way out,
put thee where there is an open space?" but the figure of a
warrior is, with Hahn, to be rejected; עָרַךְ is only a nice
word for שִׁית, שִׂים, to place, set up, ch. xxxvii. 19.

Ver. 20. Elihu calls upon Job to consider the uselessness
of his vehement contending with God, and then warns him

against his dreadful provocation of divine judgment: *ne anheles* (ch. vii. 2) *noctem illam* (with the emphatic *art.*) *sublaturam populos loco suo.* לַעֲלוֹת is equivalent to *futuram* (הַהֹוֶה or הָעֲתִידָה) *ut tollat* = *sublaturam* (*vid.* on ch. v. 11, לָשׂוּם, *collocaturus;* xxx. 6, לִשְׁבּוֹ, *habitandum est*), syncopated from לְהַעֲלוֹת, in the sense of Ps. cii. 25; and תַּחְתָּם signifies, as ch. xl. 12 (comp. on Hab. iii. 16), nothing but that just where they are, firmly fixed without the possibility of escape, they are deprived of being. If whole peoples are overtaken by such a fate, how much less shall the individual be able to escape it! And yet Job presses forward on to the tribunal of the terrible Judge, instead of humbling himself under His mighty hand. Oh that in time he would shrink back from this absolute wickedness (אָוֶן), for he has given it the preference before עֳנִי, quiet, resigned endurance. בָּחַר עַל signifies, 2 Sam. xix. 39, to choose to lay anything on any one; here as בחר בְּ, elsewhere to extend one's choice to something, to make something an object of choice; perhaps also under the influence of the phrase הִתְעַנֵּג עַל, and similar phrases. The construction is remarkable, since one would sooner have expected זֶה בָחַרְתָּ עַל־עֳנִי, *hanc elegisti præ toleratione.*

22 *Behold, God acteth loftily in His strength;*
   Who is a teacher like unto Him?
23 *Who hath appointed Him His way,*
   And who dare say: Thou doest iniquity!?
24 *Remember that thou magnify His doing,*
   Which men have sung.
25 *All men delight in it,*
   Mortal man looketh upon it from afar.

Most modern expositors, after the LXX. δυνάστης, give מוֹרֶה the signification lord, by comparing the Arab. *mar-un* (*imru-un*), Syr. *mor* (with the art. *moro*) or *more* (with the art. *morjo*), Chald. מָרֵא, Talmud. מַר (comp. Philo, ii. 522, *ed.*

Mangey: οὕτως, viz. μάριν, φασὶ τὸν κύριον ὀνομάζεσθαι παρὰ Σύροις), with it; but Rosenm., Arnh., Löwenthal, Wolfson, and Schlottm., after the Targ., Syr., and Jer., rightly abide by the signification : teacher.   For (1) מוֹרֶה (from הוֹרָה, Ps. xxv. 8, 12, xxxii. 8) has no etymological connection with מר (of מְרָא, مَرَّ, *opimum*, *robustum esse*); (2) it is, moreover,

peculiar to Elihu to represent God as a teacher both by dreams and dispensations of affliction, ch. xxxiii. 14 sqq., xxxiv. 32, and by His creatures, xxxv. 11; and (3) the designation of God as an incomparable teacher is also not inappropriate here, after His rule is described in ver. 22*a* as transcendently exalted, which on that very account commands to human research a reverence which esteems itself lightly.   Ver. 23*a* is not to be translated : who overlooketh Him in His way? (פָּקַד with עַל of the personal and *acc.* of the neutral obj.), which is without support in the language; but : who has prescribed to Him (פקד על as ch. xxxiv. 13) His way? *i.e.* as Rosenm. correctly interprets : *quis ei praescripsit quae agere deberet*, He is no mandatory, is responsible to no one, and under obligation to no one, and who should dare to say (*quis dixerit;* on the *perf.* comp. on ch. xxxv. 15) : Thou doest evil?—man shall be a docile learner, not a self-satisfied, conceited censurer of the absolute One, whose rule is not to be judged according to the laws of another, but according to His own laws.   Thus, then, shall Job remember (*memento* = *cura ut*) to extol (תַשְׂגִּיא, ch. xii. 23) God's doings, which have been sung (comp. *e.g.* Ps. civ. 33) by אֲנָשִׁים, men of the right order (ch. xxxvii. 24) ; Jer. *de quo cecinerunt viri.*   שֹׁרֵר nowhere has the signification *intueri* (Rosenm., Umbr.) ; on the other hand, Elihu is fond of direct (ch. xxxiii. 27, xxxv. 10) and indirect allusions to the Psalms.   All men—he continues, with reference to God's פֹּעַל, working—behold it, viz., as בוֹ implies, with pleasure and astonishment; mortals gaze upon it (reverentially) from afar,—the same thought as that which has already (ch. xxvi. 14) found the grandest expression in Job's mouth.

26 *Behold, God is exalted—we know Him not entirely;*
   The number of His years, it is unsearchable.
27 *For He draweth down the drops of water,*
   They distil as rain in connection with its mist,
28 *Which the clouds do drop,*
   Distil upon the multitude of men.
29 *Who can altogether understand the spreadings of the clouds,*
   The crash of His tabernacle?

The *Waw* of the quasi-conclusion in ver. 26*b* corresponds to the *Waw* of the train of thought in ver. 26*a* (Ges. § 145, 2). מִסְפַּר שָׁנָיו is, as the subject-notion, conceived as a nominative (*vid.* on ch. iv. 6, vol. i. 91, note 1), not as in similar quasi-antecedent clauses, *e.g.* ch. xxiii. 12, as an *acc.* of relation. שְׁנִיא here and ch. xxxvii. 23 occurs otherwise only in Old Testament Chaldee. In what follows Elihu describes the wondrous origin of rain. "If Job had only come," says a Midrash (*Jalkut,* § 518), "to explain to us the matter of the race of the deluge (*vid.* especially ch. xxii. 15–18), it had been sufficient; and if Elihu had only come to explain to us the matter of the origin of rain (מעשה ירידת גשמים), it had been enough." In Gesenius' *Handwörterbuch,* ver. 27 is translated: when He has drawn up the drops of water to Himself, then, etc. But it is יִגְרַע, not גֵּרַע; and גָּרַע neither in Hebr. nor in Arab. signifies *attrahere in sublime* (Rosenm.), but only *attrahere* (root גר) and *detrahere;* the latter signification is the prevailing one in Hebr. (ch. xv. 8, xxxvi. 7). With כִּי the transcendent exaltation of the Being who survives all changes of creation is shown by an example: He draws away (draws off, as it were) the water-drops, viz. from the waters that are confined above on the circle of the sky, which

pass over us as mist and cloud (*vid. Genesis*, S. 107) ; and
these water-drops distil down (רָקַק, to ooze, distil, here not in
a transitive but an intransitive signification, since the water-
drops are the rain itself) as rain, לְאֵדוֹ, with its mist, *i.e.* since
a mist produced by it (Gen. ii. 6) fills the expanse (רְקִיעַ), the
downfall of which is just this rain, which, as ver. 28 says,
the clouds (called שְׁחָקִים on account of its thin strata of air,
in distinction from the next mist-circle) cause to flow gently
down upon the multitude of men, *i.e.* far and wide over the
mass of men who inhabit the district visited by the rain ;
both verbs are used transitively here, both נָזַל as Isa. xlv. 8,
and רָעַף, as evidently Prov. iii. 20. אַף אִם, ver. 29*a*, com-
mences an intensive question : moreover, could one understand = could one completely understand ; which certainly,
according to the sense, is equivalent to : how much less (אַף כִּי).
אִם is, however, the interrogative *an*, and אַף אִם corresponds
to הַאַף in the first member of the double question, ch.
xxxiv. 17, xl. 8 sq. מִפְרְשֵׂי are not the burstings, from פָּרַשׂ =
פָּרַם, *frangere, findere*, but spreadings, as Ezek. xxvii. 7 shows,
from פָּרַשׂ, *expandere*, Ps. cv. 39, comp. *supra* on ch. xxvi. 9.
It is the growth of the storm-clouds, which collect often from
a beginning "small as a man's hand" (1 Kings xviii. 44), that
is intended ; majestic omnipotence conceals itself behind these
as in a סֻכָּה (Ps. xviii. 12) woven out of thick branches ; and
the rolling thunder is here called the crash (תְּשֻׁאוֹת, as ch.
xxxix. 7, is formed from שׁוֹא, to rumble, whence also שׁוֹאָה, if
it is not after the form גּוֹלָה, migration, exile, from שׁאה, *vid.*
on ch. xxx. 3) of this pavilion of clouds in which the Thun-
derer works.

> 30 *Behold, He spreadeth His light over Himself,*
> *And the roots of the sea He covereth.*
> 31 *For thereby He judgeth peoples,*
> *He giveth food in abundance.*

32 *Both hands He covereth over with light,*
  And directeth it as one who hitteth the mark.
33 *His noise announceth Him,*
  The cattle even that He is approaching.

A few expositors (Hirz., Hahn, Schlottm.) understand the
celestial ocean, or the sea of the upper waters, by יָם, ver. 30*b*;
but it is more than questionable (*vid.* on ch. ix. 8) whether
ים is used anywhere in this sense. Others as (Umbr., Ew.)
the masses of water drawn up to the sky out of the depths of
the sea, on which a Persian passage cited by Stick. (who,
however, regards the *Waw* of וְשֹׁרֶשׁ as *Waw adæquationis*) from
Schebisteri may be compared: " an exhalation rises up out of
the sea, and comes down at God's command upon the deserts."
In both cases כִּפָּה would be equivalent to כסה עָלָיו, *obtegit se,*
which in and of itself is possible. But he who has once witnessed a storm in the neighbourhood of the sea, will decide
in favour of one of the three following explanations: (1.)
He covereth the uprooted ground of the sea (comp. Ps. xviii.
15 sq.) with the subsiding waves (Blumenf.) ; but then ver.
30*a* would require to be understood of the light of the brighten-
ing sky following the darkness of the storm, which is improbable in respect of ver. 32*a*. (2.) While the sky is brilliantly
lighted up by the lightning, the abysses of the ocean are
veiled in a so much deeper darkness; the observation is correct,
but not less so another, that the lightning by a thunder-storm,
especially when occurring at night, descends into the depths
of the sea like snares that are cast down (פַּחִים, Ps. xi. 6), and
the water is momentarily changed as it were into a sea of
flame; accordingly it may be explained, (3.) Behold, He
spreadeth over Himself His light (viz. the light which inces-
santly illumines the world), and the roots of the sea, *i.e.* the
sea down to its depths, He covers with it, since He makes it
light through and through (Stuhlm., Wolfs.). Thus, as it

appears, Jerome also interprets : *Et (si voluerit) fulgurare lumine suo desuper, cardines quoque maris operiet.*[1]

This, that He makes the light of the lightning His manifestation (פָּרַשׂ עָלָיו), and that He covers the earth down to the roots of the sea beneath with this light, is established in ver. 31 from the design, partly judicial, partly beneficial, which exists in connection with it. בָּם refers as neuter (like בָּהֶם, ch. xxii. 21) to the phenomena of the storm; מַכְבִּיר (with the adverbial לְ like לְרֹב, ch. xxvi. 3), what makes great = a making great, abundance (only here), is *n. hiphil.* after the form מַשְׁחִית, *perdens* = *perditio.* In ver. 32 God is represented under a military figure as a slinger of lightnings : He covers light over both hands, *i.e.* arms both completely with light (comp. סִכְּסֵךְ and شَلّ, *totum se operire armis*), and directs it (עָלֶיהָ referring to אוֹר as *fem.* like Jer. xiii. 16, and sometimes in the Talmud). But what is the meaning of בְּמַפְגִּיעַ? Hahn takes מפגיע as *n. hiphil.* like מכביר : an object of attack; but what then becomes of the original *Hiphil* signification? It ought to be בְּמִפְגָּע (ch. vii. 20), as Olsh. wishes to read it. Ew., Hirz., and others, after the example of Theod. (LXX.), Syr., Jer., translate : against the adversary ; מפגיע signifies indeed the opposite in Isa. lix. 16 : *intercessor* (properly, one who assails with prayers) ; however, it would be possible for this word, just as פגע *c. acc.* (which signifies usually a hostile meeting, Ex. v. 3 and freq., but sometimes also a friendly, Isa. xlvii. 3, lxiv. 4), to be an ἐναντιόσημον. We prefer to abide by the usage of the language as we have it, according

---

[1] The Targ. translates אוֹר, vers. 30, 32, by מִטְרָא, *pluvia*, according to the erroneous opinion of R. Jochanan : כל אורה שנאמר באליהוא אינו אלא בירידת גשמים. Aben-Ezra and Kimchi explain even עֲלֵי־אוֹר, Isa. xviii. 4, according to this passage. The LXX. translates ver. 30*a* : ἰδοὺ ἐκτενεῖ ἐπ᾽ αὐτὸν ἠδώ (*Cod. Alex.* επ αυτον το τοξον ; *Cod. Sinait.* επ αυτην ηωδη with the corrections ηδω and τοξον), probably according to the reading אידו for אורו. But what connection have ηδώ and rainbow ?

to which הִפְגִּיעַ signifies *facere ut quid incurset s. petat,* Isa.
liii. 6 ; מַפְגִּיעַ therefore is one who hits, in opposition to one who
misses the mark. The *Beth* is the *Beth essentiæ* (*vid.* on ch.
xxiii. 13), used here like Ex. vi. 3, Ps. lv. 19, Isa. xl. 10.
With both hands He seizes the substance of the lightning, fills
them with it so that they are completely covered by it, and
gives it the command (appoints it its goal), a sure aimer!

Ver. 33*a.* Targ., Syr., Symm., Theod. (from which ver.
32 sq. is supplied in the LXX.[1]), Jer., Luther, and others
destroy the idea, since they translate רֵעוֹ = רֵעֵהוּ, "his friend
(companion)." Among moderns, only Umbr. and Schlottm.
adopt this signification; Böttch. and Welte, after the example
of Cocceius, Tingstad, and others, attempt it with the signification "thought = determination;" but most expositors, from
Ew. to Hahn, decide in favour of the rendering as simple as
it is consistent with the usage of the language and the connection: His noise (רֵעוֹ as Ex. xxxii. 17) gives tidings concerning Him (announces Him). In ver. 33*b* Theod. (LXX.),
Syr., and Jer. point מקנה like our text, but translate *possessio,*
with which we can do nothing. It seems that in the three
attempts of the Targ. to translate ver. 33, the translators had
קִנְאָה and קִנָּא before their mind, according to which Hahn
translates: the arousing of anger (announces) the comer,
which assumes מִקְנֶה instead of מִקְנֵה; and Schlottm.: fierce
wrath (goes forth) over evil (according to Symm. ζῆλον περὶ
ἀδικίας), which assumes the reading עוֹלָה (עֹלָה), ἀδικία, adopted
also by Syr., Theod. (LXX.). Schultens even renders similarly: *rubedinem flammantem nasi contra elatum,* and Tingstad: *zelum iræ in iniquitatem.* But it is not probable that the
language was acquainted with a subst. מִקְנֶה, exciting, although
in Ezek. viii. 3 הַמַּקְנֶה is equivalent to הַמַּקְנִיא, so that one might

---

[1] *Vid.* Bickel, *De indole ac ratione versionis Alex. in interpretando l.
Iobi,* p. 50. *Cod. Sinait.* has, like *Cod. Vat.:* αναγγελει περι αυτου φιλον
(corr. φιλοσ) αυτου κσ κτησισ και περι αδικιασ.

more readily be tempted (*vid.* Hitz. *in loc.*) to read מַקְנֶה אַף,
" one who excites anger against evil," if one is not willing to
decide with Berg, and recently Bleek, in favour of (מַקְנֶה) מְקַנֵּא
אַף בְּעַוְלָה, *excandescens* (*zelans*) *irâ contra iniquitatem.* But
does the text as it stands really not give an appropriate idea?
Aben-Ezra and Duran have understood it of the foreboding
of an approaching thunder-storm which is manifested by
cattle, מִקְנֶה. Accordingly Ew. translates : His thunder announces Him, the cattle even, that He is approaching ; and
peculiarly new (understanding יַגִּיד not of a foreboding but of
a thankful lowing) is Ebrard's rendering : also the cattle at
fresh sprouting grass. But such a change of the position of
אַף is without precedent. Hirz. and Ges. : His rumble (rumble
of thunder) announces Him to the herds, Him, and indeed as
Him who rises up (approaches). But this new interpunction
destroys the division of the verse and the syntax. Better
Rosenm. like Duran : *pecus non tantum pluviam proximam,
sed et antequam nubes in sublime adscenderint adscensuras
præsagit,* according to Virgil, *Georg.* i. 374 sq.:

> *illum* (*imbrem*) *surgentem vallibus imis
> Aeriæ fugere grues.*

But עָלָיו refers to God, and therefore עַל־עוֹלֶה also, viz. Him who
leads forth the storm-clouds (Jer. x. 13, li. 16, Ps. cxxxv. 7),
and Himself rising up in them ; or, what עָלָה frequently signifies, coming on as to battle. It is to be interpreted : His
thunder-clap announces Him (who is about to reveal Himself
as a merciful judge), the cattle even (announce) Him at His
first rising up, since at the approach of a storm they herd
together affrighted and seek shelter. The speakers are
Arabian, and the scene is laid in the country : Elihu also
refers to the animal world in ch. xxxv. 11 ; this feature of
the picture, therefore, cannot be surprising.

Ch. xxxvii. 1 *Yea, at this my heart trembleth*
   And tottereth from its place.
   2 *Hear, O hear the roar of His voice,*
   And the murmur that goeth out of His mouth.
   3 *He sendeth it forth under the whole heaven,*
   And His lightning unto the ends of the earth.
   4 *After it roareth the voice of the thunder,*
   He thundereth with the voice of His majesty,
   And spareth not the lightnings, when His voice is heard.
   5 *God thundereth with His voice marvellously,*
   Doing great things, incomprehensible to us.

Louis Bridel is perhaps right when he inserts after ch. xxxvi. the observation: *L'éclair brille, la tonnerre gronde.* לְזֹאת does not refer to the phenomenon of the storm which is represented in the mind, but to that which is now to be perceived by the senses. The combination שָׁמְעוּ שָׁמוֹעַ can signify both hear constantly, Isa. vi. 9, and hear attentively, ch. xiii. 17; here it is the latter. רֹגֶז of thunder corresponds to the verbs رحز and رجس, which can be similarly used. The repetition of קוֹל five times calls to mind the seven קוֹלוֹת (ἑπτὰ βρονταί) in Ps. xxix. The parallel is הֶגֶה, ver. 2*b*, a murmuring, as elsewhere of the roar of the lion and the cooing of the dove. The *suff.* of יְשָׁרֵהוּ refers to the thunder which rolls through the immeasurable breadth under heaven; it is not *perf. Piel* of יִשֵּׁר (Schlottm.), for " to give definite direction" (2 Chron. xxxii. 30) is not appropriate to thunder, but *fut. Kal* of שָׁרָה, to free, to unbind (Ew., Hirz., and most others). What ver. 3*a* says of thunder, ver. 3*b* says of light, *i.e.* the lightning: God sends it forth to the edges, πτέρυγες, *i.e.* ends, of the earth. אַחֲרָיו, ver. 4*a*, naturally refers to the lightning, which is followed by the roar of the thunder; and יְעַקְּבֵם to the flashes, which, when once its rumble is heard, God does not restrain (עַקֵּב = עִקֵּב of the Targ., and Arab. ʿaqqaba, to leave behind, postpone), but causes to flash forth in quick

succession.   Ewald's translation : should He not find (prop.
non investigaverit) them (the men that are to be punished),
gives a thought that has no support in this connection.   In
ver. 5a נִפְלָאוֹת, *mirabilia*, is equivalent to *mirabiliter*, as Dan.
viii. 24, comp. Ps. lxv. 6, cxxxix. 14.   וְלֹא נֵדָע is intended to
say that God's mighty acts, with respect to the connection
between cause and effect and the employment of means,
transcend our comprehension.

> 6 *For He saith to the snow : Fall towards the earth,*
>   *And to the rain-shower*
>   *And the showers of His mighty rain.*
> 7 *He putteth a seal on the hand of every man,*
>   *That all men may come to a knowledge of His creative work.*
> 8 *The wild beast creepeth into a hiding-place,*
>   *And in its resting-place it remaineth.*
> 9 *Out of the remote part cometh the whirlwind,*
>   *And cold from the cloud-sweepers.*
> 10 *From the breath of God cometh ice,*
>   *And the breadth of the waters is straitened.*

Like אֲבִי, ch. xxxiv. 36, and פֶּשׁ, ch. xxxv. 15, הֱוֵא, ver. 6a
(is falsely translated " be earthwards " by LXX., Targ., and
Syr.), also belongs to the most striking Arabisms of the Elihu
section: it signifies *delabere* (Jer. *ut descendat*), a signification
which the Arab. هَوَى does not gain from the radical signification placed first in Gesenius-Dietrich's *Handwörterbuch*, to
breathe, blow, but from the radical signification, to gape,
yawn, by means of the development of the meaning which
also decides in favour of the primary notion of the Hebr. הַוָּה,
according to which, what was said on ch. vi. 2, xxx. 13 is to
be corrected.[1]   The ל of לְשֶׁלֶג influences ver. 6*bc* also.   The

---

[1] هَوَى is originally χαίνειν, to gape, yawn, *hiare*, *e.g. hawat et-ta'natu,*
the stab gapes (imperf. *tahwî,* inf. *huwîjun*), " when it opens its mouth "

Hebr. name for rain, גֶּשֶׁם (cogn. with Chald. נִשׁם, Arab. *gism*, a body), denotes the rain collectively. The expression ver. 6*b* is exceeded in ver. 6*c*, where מְטְרוֹת does not signify rain-drops (Ew.), but, like the Arab. *amtâr*, rain-showers. The wonders of nature during the rough season (סְתָיו, חֹרֶף, Cant. ii. 11, comp. p. 119), between the autumnal and vernal equinoxes, are meant ; the rains after the autumnal equinox (the early rain), which begin the season, and the rains before the vernal equinox (the late rain, Zech. x. 1), which close it, with the falls of snow between, which frequently produce great desolation, especially the proper winter with its frosty winds and heavy showers, when the business of the husbandmen as of the nomads is brought to a stand-still, and every one retreats to his house or seeks a sheltering corner (*vid.* p. 23, note). This is the meaning of ver. 7 : He sealeth up (בְּ חָתַם as

—the Turkish Kamus adds, to complete the picture : like a tulip. Thence next *hâwijatun*, χαίνουσα, χαῖνον, *i.e.* χάσμα = *hûwatun, uhwîjatun, huwâatun, mahwâtun*, a cleft, yawning deep, chasm, abyss, βάραθρον, *vorago* ; *hawîjatun* and *hauhâtun* (a reduplicated form), especially a very deep pit or well. But these same words, *hâwijatun, hûwatun, uhwîjatun, mahwâtun*, also signify, like the usual هُوَّة, the χάσμα between heaven and earth, *i.e.* the wide, empty space, the same as '*gauwun*. The wider significations, or rather applications and references of *hawâ :* air set in motion, a current of air, wind, weather, are all secondary, and related to that primary signification as *samâ*, rain-clouds, rain, grass produced by the rain, to the prim. signification height, heaven, *vid.* Mehren, *Rhetorik d. Araber*, S. 107, Z. 14 ff. This *hawâ*, however, also signifies in general : a broad, empty space, and by transferring the notion of "empty" to mind and heart, as the reduplicated forms *hûhatun* and *hauhâtun :* devoid of understanding and devoid of courage, *e.g. Koran* xiv. 44 : *wa-af'i-datuhum hawâun*, where Beidhâwî first explains *hawâ* directly by *chalâ*, emptiness, empty space, *i.e.*, as he adds, *châlijetun 'an el-fahm*, as one says of one without mind and courage *qalbuhu hawâun*. Thence also *hauwun*, emptiness, a hole, *i.e.* in a wall or roof, a dormar-window (*kauwe, kûwe*), but also with the genit. of a person or thing : their hole, *i.e.* the space left empty by them, the side not taken up by them, *e.g. qa'ada fi hauwihi*, he set himself beside him. From the signification to be empty then comes, (1) *hawat el-mar'atu, i.e. vacua fuit mulier = orba liberis*, as χήρα,

ch. xxxiii. 16) the hand of all men that they cannot, viz. on
account of the cold out of doors, be opened for work, that all
people of His work (*i.e.* thanking Him for their origin as His
handiwork, ch. xxxiv. 19) may come to the perception (of
Him who doeth all things). The expression is remarkable,
and by the insertion of a מ may be as easily cleared up as ch.
xxxiii. 17 : לָדַעַת כָּל־אֲנָשִׁים מַעֲשֵׂהוּ, in order that each and every
one may acknowledge His work; after which even Jer.
translates: *ut noverint singuli opera sua.* The conjecture
אנשים עֹשֵׂהוּ (Schultens junior, Reiske, Hirz.) is inferior to the
former (Olsh.) by its awkward *synecdoche num.* The *fut.
consec.* in ver. 8 continues the description of what happens in
consequence of the cold rainy season; the expression calls to
mind Ps. civ. 22, as ch. xxxiv. 14 sq. does Ps. civ. 29. The
winter is also the time of the stormy and raw winds. In
ver. 9*a* Elihu means the storms which come across from the
great wide desert, ch. i. 19, therefore the south (Isa. xxi. 1,

vidua, properly empty, French *vide;* (2) *hawâ er-ragulu, i.e. vacuus,
inanis factus est vir = exanimatus* (comp. فرغ, he became empty, euphe-
mistic for he died).

From this variously applied primary signification is developed the
generally known and usual هوى, loose and free, without being held or
holding to anything one's self, to pass away, fly, swing, etc., *libere ferri,
labi*, in general in every direction, as the wind, or what is driven hither
and thither by the wind, especially however from above downwards, *labi,
delabi, cadere, deorsum ruere.* From this point, like many similar, the
word first passes into the signification of sound (as certainly also שָׁאָה,
שָׁעָ): as anything falling has a dull noise, and so on, δουπεῖν, *rumorem,
fragorem edere (fragor* from *frangi)*, hence *hawat udhnuhu hawîjan* of a
singing in the ears.

Finally, the mental هوى (perf. *hawija*, imperf. *jahwâ* with the acc.),
animo ad or *in aliquid ferri*, is attached to the notion of passing and
falling through space (though by no means to *hiare*, or the supposed
meaning "to breathe, blow"). It is used both emotionally of desire,
lust, appetites, passions, and strong love, and intellectually of free opinions
or assertions springing from mere self-willed preference, caprices of the
understanding.—FL.

Zech. ix. 14), or rather (*vid.* p. 77, note) south-east winds
(Hos. xiii. 15), increasing in violence to storms. הַחֶדֶר (properly
the surrounded, enclosed space, never the storehouse,—so that
Ps. cxxxv. 7 should be compared,—but *adytum*, *penetrale*, as
Arab. *chidr*, *e.g.* in *Vita Timuri* ii. 904 : after the removal of
the superincumbent earth, they drew away *sitr chidrihâ*, the
curtain of its innermost part, *i.e.* uncovered its lowest depth)
is here the innermost part of the south (south-east),—comp.
ch. ix. 9 חדרי תימן, and xxiii. 9 יעטף ימין (so far as יעטף there
signifies *si operiat se*),—especially of the great desert lying to
the south (south-east), according to which אֶרֶץ חַדְרָךְ, Zech.
ix. 1, is translated by the Targ. ארעא דרומא. In opposition to
the south-east wind, מְזָרִים, ver. 9*b*, seems to mean the north
winds ; in and of itself, however, the word signifies the
scattering or driving, as also in the Koran the winds are
called the scatterers, *dhârijât*, *Sur.* li. 1.[1] In מזרים, Reiske,
without any ground for it, traces the Arab. *mirzam* (a name
of two stars, from which north wind, rain, and cold are derived); the Targ. also has one of the constellations in view :
מִכַּוַּת מְזָרִים (from the window, *i.e.* the window of the vault of
heaven, of the *mezarim*) ; Aq., Theod. ἀπὸ μαζούρ (= מזרות,
ch. xxxviii. 32) ; LXX. ἀπὸ δὲ τῶν ἀκρωτηρίων, we know not
wherefore. Concerning מִנִּשְׁמַת־אֵל (with causal מִן) with reference to the wind, *vid.* on ch. iv. 15. יִתֵּן, it gives, *i.e.* comes
to light, is used as in Gen. xxxviii. 28, Prov. xiii. 10. The
idea of מוּצָק (not *fusum* from יָצַק, but *coarctatum* from צוּק)
cannot be doubtful in connection with the antithesis of רֹחַב,
comp. ch. xxxvi. 16, the idea is like ch. xxxviii. 30 (comp.
Mutenebbi : "the flood is bound by bands of ice") ; the בְּ of
בְּמוּצָק is, as ch. xxxvi. 32, the *Beth essentiæ*, used far more
extensively in Hebr. than in Arab. as an exponent of the

---

[1] This *dhârijât* is also differently explained ; but the first explanation
in Beidhâwi (ii. 183, Fleischer's edition) is, " the winds which scatter
(blow away) the dust and other things."

predicate: the breadth of the water is (becomes) straitened (forcibly drawn together).

> 11 *Also He loadeth the clouds with water,*
> *He spreadeth far and wide the cloud of His light,*
> 12 *And these turn themselves round about,*
> *Directed by Him, that they execute*
> *All that He hath commanded them*
> *Over the wide earth.*
> 13 *Whether for a scourge, or for the good of His earth,*
> *Or for mercy, He causeth it to discharge itself.*

With אַף extending the description, Elihu, in the presence of the storm that is in the sky, continually returns to this one marvel of nature. The old versions connect בְּרִי partly with בַּר, *electus* (LXX., Syr., Theod.) or *frumentum* (Symm., Jer.), partly with בְּרָה = בָּרַר in the signification *puritas, serenitas* (Targ.); but בְּרִי is, as Schultens has already perceived, the Hebr.-Arabic רִי, رِيّ, *rîj-un* (from רוה = *riwj*), abundant irrigation, with בְּ; and יַטְרִיחַ does not signify, according to the Arab. *atraha,* "to hurl down," so that what is spoken of would be the bursting of the clouds (Stick.),[1] but, according to טָרַח, a burden (comp. Arab. *taraha ala,* to load), "to burden;" with fluidity (Ew., Hirz., Hahn, Schlottm.), better: fulness of water, He burdens the clouds (comp. *rawij-un* as a designation of cloud as the place of rain). עֲנַן אוֹרוֹ, His cloud of light, is that that is charged with lightning, and הֵפִיץ has here its Hebr.-Arab. radical signification *effundere, diffundere,* with a preponderance of the idea not of scattering, but of spreading out wide (Arab. *faid,* abundance). וְהוּא, ver. 12a, refers to the cloud pregnant with lightning; this turns

---

[1] This "*atraha*" is, moreover, a pure invention of our ordinary Arabic lexicons instead of *ittaraha* (VIII. form): (1) to throw one's self, (2) to throw anything from one's self, with an *acc.* of the thing.—FL.

round about (מְסִבּוֹת, adv. as מֵסַב, round about, 1 Kings vi. 29) seeking a place, where it shall unburden itself by virtue of His (God's) direction or disposing (תַחְבּוּלֹת, a word belonging to the book of Proverbs; LXX., *Cod. Vat.* and *Alex.*, untranslated: εν θεεβουλαθωθ, *Cod. Sinait.* still more monstrous), in order that they (the clouds full of lightning) may accomplish everything that He commands them over the surface of the earth; אָרְצָה as ch. xxxiv. 13, and the combination תֵבֵל אָרְצָה as Prov. viii. 31, comp. אֶרֶץ וְתֵבֵל, Ps. xc. 2. The reference of the pronominal *suff.* to men is as inadmissible here as in ver. 4c. In ver. 13 two אִם have certainly, as. ch. xxxiv. 29, two וְ, the correlative signification *sive . . . sive* (Arab. *in . . . wa-in*), and a third, as appears, a conditional, but which? According to Ew., Hirz., Hahn, Schlottm., and others, the middle one : if it (the rod) belongs to His land, *i.e.* if it has deserved it. But even the possessive *suff.* of לְאַרְצוֹ shows that the לְ is to be taken as *dat. commodi:* be it for a rod, be it for the good of His land; which is then followed by a conditional verbal clause : in case He mercifully causes it (the storm) to come, *i.e.* causes this His land to be overtaken by it (הִמְצִיא here with the *acc.*, the thing coming, whereas in ch. xxxiv. 11 of the thing to be overtaken). The accentuation, indeed, appears to assume a threefold *sive :* [whether He causeth it to discharge itself upon] man for punishment, man for mercy, or His earth for good with reference to man. Then Elihu would think of the uninhabited steppe in connection with אִם לְאַרְצוֹ. Since a conditional אִם by the side of two correlatives is hazardous, we decide finally with the LXX., Targ., and all the old versions, in favour of the same rendering of the threefold אִם, especially since it corresponds to the circumstances of the case.

14 *Hearken unto this, O Job;*
   Stand still and consider the wonderful works of God!

15 *Dost thou know when God designeth*
   To cause the light of His clouds to shine?
16 *Dost thou understand the balancings of the clouds,*
   The wondrous things of Him who is perfect in knowledge?

Job is to stand still, instead of dictating to God, in order
to draw from His wondrous acts in nature a conclusion with
reference to his mystery of suffering. In ver. 15*a* בְּ יָדַע does
not, as ch. xxxv. 15 (Ew. § 217, S. 557), belong together,
but בְּ is the temporal *Beth*. שׂוּם is equivalent to שִׂים לְבוֹ (*vid.*
on ch. xxxiv. 23); עֲלֵיהֶם does not refer to נִפְלָאוֹת (Hirz.) or
the phenomena of the storm (Ew.), but is intended as neuter
(as בָּם ch. xxxvi. 31, בָּהֶם xxii. 21), and finds in ver. 15*b* its
distinctive development: "the light of His clouds" is their
effulgent splendour. Without further support, יָדַע עַל is to
have knowledge concerning anything, ver. 16*a;* מִפְלְשֵׂי is also
ἀπ. γεγρ. It is unnecessary to consider it as wrongly written
from מִפְרָשֵׂי, ch. xxxvi. 29, or as from it by change of letter (as
אַלְמָנוֹת = אַרְמָנוֹת, Isa. xiii. 22). The verb פִּלֵּס signifies to make
level, prepare (viz. a way, also weakened: to take a certain
way, Prov. v. 6), once: to weigh, Ps. lviii. 3, as *denom.* from
פֶּלֶס, a balance (and indeed a steelyard, *statera*), which is
thus mentioned as the means of adjustment. מִפְלְשֵׂי accordingly signifies either, as synon. of מִשְׁקְלֵי (thus the Midrash,
vid. Jalkut, § 522), weights (the relations of weight), or even
equipoised balancings (Aben-Ezra, Kimchi, and others), Lat.
quomodo librentur nubes in aëre.[1] מִפְלָאוֹת is also a word that
does not occur elsewhere; in like manner דֵּעַ belongs exclu-

---

[1] The word is therefore a metaphor taken from the balance, and it may
be observed that the Syro-Arabic, on account of the most extensive application of the balance, is unusually rich in such metaphors. Moreover, the
Arabic has no corresponding noun : the *teflis* (a balance) brought forward
by Ges. in his *Thes.* and *Handwörterbuch* from Schindler's *Pentaglotton,*
is a word devoid of all evidence from original sources and from the
modern usage of the language, in this signification.

sively to Elihu. God is called תְּמִים דֵּעִים (comp. ch. xxxvi. 4)
as the Omniscient One, whose knowledge is absolute as to
its depth as well as its circumference.

> 17 *Thou whose garments become hot,*
> *When the land is sultry from the south:*
> 18 *Dost thou with Him spread out the sky,*
> *The strong, as it were molten, mirror?*
> 19 *Let us know what we shall say to Him!—*
> *We can arrange nothing by reason of darkness.*
> 20 *Shall it be told Him that I speak,*
> *Or shall one wish to be destroyed?*

Most expositors connect ver. 17*a* with ver. 16: (Dost
thou know) how it comes to pass that . . . ; but אֲשֶׁר after
ידע signifies *quod*, Ex. xi. 7, not *quomodo*, as it sometimes
occurs in a comparing antecedent clause, instead of כַּאֲשֶׁר,
Ex. xiv. 13, Jer. xxxiii. 22. We therefore translate: thou
whose . . .,—connecting this, however, not with ver. 16 (*vid.
e.g.* Carey), but as Bolduc. and Ew., with ver. 18 (where הֲ
before תַּרְקִיעַ is then the less missed): thou who, when the
land (the part of the earth where thou art) keeps rest, *i.e.* in
sultriness, when oppressive heat comes (on this *Hiph. vid.*
Ges. § 53, 2) from the south (*i.e.* by means of the currents
of air which come thence, without דָּרוֹם signifying directly
the south wind),—thou who, when this happens, canst endure
so little, that on the contrary the heat from without becomes
perceptible to thee through thy clothes: dost thou now and
then with Him keep the sky spread out, which for firmness is
like a molten mirror? Elsewhere the hemispheric firmament, which spans the earth with its sub-celestial waters, is
likened to a clear sapphire Ex. xxiv. 10, a covering Ps. civ. 2,
a gauze Isa. xl. 22; the comparison with a metallic mirror
(מוּצָק here not from צוּק, ver. 10, ch. xxxvi. 16, but from יָצַק)
is therefore to be understood according to Petavius: *Cœlum*

aëreum στερέωμα *dicitur non a naturæ propria conditione, sed ab effectu, quod perinde aquas separet, ac si murus esset solidissimus.* Also in תרקיע lies the notion both of firmness and thinness; the primary notion (root רק) is to beat, make thick, *stipare* (رقع, to stop up in the sense of *resarcire, e.g.* to mend stockings), to make thick by pressure. The ל joined with תרקיע is *nota acc.;* we must not comp. ch. viii. 8, xxi. 22, as well as ch. v. 2, xix. 3.

Therefore: As God is the only Creator (ch. ix. 8), so He is the all-provident Preserver of the world—make us know (הוֹדִיעֵנוּ, according to the text of the Babylonians, *Keri* of הוֹדִיעֵנִי) what we shall say to Him, viz. in order to show that we can cope with Him! We cannot arrange, viz. anything whatever (to be explained according to עֲרֹךְ מִלִּין, ch. xxxii. 14, comp. "to place," ch. xxxvi. 19), by reason of darkness, viz. the darkness of our understanding, σκότος τῆς διανοίας; מִפְּנֵי is much the same as ch. xxiii. 17, but different from ch. xvii. 12, and חֹשֶׁךְ different from both passages, viz. as it is often used in the New Testament, of intellectual darkness (comp. Eccl. ii. 14, Isa. lx. 2). The meaning of ver. 20 cannot now be mistaken, if, with Hirz., Hahn, and Schlottm., we call to mind ch. xxxvi. 10 in connection with אָמַר כִּי: can I, a short-sighted man, enshrouded in darkness, wish that what I have arrogantly said concerning and against Him may be told to God, or should one earnestly desire (אָמַר, a modal *perf.*, as ch. xxxv. 15*b*) that (*an jusserit s. dixerit quis ut*) he may be swallowed up, *i.e.* destroyed (comp. לְבַלְּעוֹ, ch. ii. 3)? He would, by challenging a recognition of his unbecoming arguing about God, desire a tribunal that would be destructive to himself.

> 21 *Although one seeth not now the sunlight*
> *That is bright in the ethereal heights :*
> *A wind passeth by and cleareth them up.*

22 *Gold is brought from the north,—*
   Above Eloah is terrible majesty.
23 *The Almighty, whom we cannot find out,*
   The excellent in strength,
   And right and justice He perverteth not.
24 *Therefore men regard Him with reverence,*
   He hath no regard for all the wise of heart.

He who censures God's actions, and murmurs against God, injures himself—how, on the contrary, would a patiently submissive waiting on Him be rewarded! This is the connection of thought, by which this final strophe is attached to what precedes. If we have drawn the correct conclusion from ch. xxxvii. 1, that Elihu's description of a storm is accompanied by a storm which was coming over the sky, וְעַתָּה, with which the speech, as ch. xxxv. 15, draws towards the close, is not to be understood as purely conclusive, but temporal: And at present one does not see the light (אוֹר of the sun, as ch. xxxi. 26) which is bright in the ethereal heights (בָּהִיר again a Hebr.-Arab. word, comp. *bâhir*, outshining, surpassing, especially of the moon, when it dazzles with its brightness); yet it only requires a breath of wind to pass over it, and it clears it, *i.e.* brings the ethereal sky with the sunlight to view. Elihu hereby means to say that the God who is hidden only for a time, respecting whom one runs the risk of being in perplexity, can suddenly unveil Himself, to our surprise and confusion, and that therefore it becomes us to bow humbly and quietly to His present mysterious visitation. With respect to the removal of the clouds from the beclouded sun, to which ver. 21 refers, זָהָב, ver. 22*a*, seems to signify the gold of the sun; *esh-shemsu bi-tibrin*, the sun is gold, says Abulola. Oriental and Classic literature furnishes a large number of instances in support of this calling the sunshine gold; and it should not perplex us here, where we have

an Arabizing Hebrew poet before us, that not a single
passage can be brought forward from the Old Testament
literature. But מִצָּפוֹן is against this figurative rendering of
the זהב (LXX. νέφη χρυσαυγοῦντα). In Ezek. i. 4 there
is good reason for the storm-clouds, which unfold from
their midst the glory of the heavenly Judge, who rideth
upon the cherubim, coming from the north; but wherefore
should Elihu represent the sun's golden light as breaking
through from the north? On the other hand, in the conception of the ancients, the north is the proper region for
gold: there griffins (γρυπές) guard the gold-pits of the
Arimaspian mountains (Herod. iii. 116); there, from the
narrow pass of the Caucasus along the Gordyæan mountains, gold is dug by barbarous races (Pliny, h. n. vi. 11),
and among the Scythians it is brought to light by the ants
(ib. xxxiii. 4). Egypt could indeed provide itself with gold
from Ethiopia, and the Phœnicians brought the gold of
Ophir, already mentioned in the book of Job, from India;
but the north was regarded as the fabulously most productive
chief mine of gold; to speak more definitely: Northern Asia,
with the Altai mountains.[1] Thus therefore ch. xxviii. 1, 6
is to be compared here.

What Job describes so grandly and minutely in ch. xxviii.,
viz. that man lays bare the hidden treasures of the earth's
interior, but that the wisdom of God still transcends him, is
here expressed no less grandly and compendiously: From
the north cometh gold, which man wrests from the darkness
of the gloomy unknown region of the north (צָפוֹן, ζόφος, from
צפן, cogn. טמן, טמר,[2] vid. p. 53, note, comp. p. 11, note); upon

---

[1] Vid. the art. Gold, S. 91, 101, in Ersch and Gruber. The Indian
traditions concerning Uttaraguru (the "High Mountain"), and concerning the northern seat of the god of wealth Kuvêra, have no connection
here; on their origin comp. Lassen, Indische Alterthumskunde, i. 848.

[2] The verb צָפָה, obducere, does not belong here, but to צפח, and signifies properly to flatten (as רקע, to make thin and thick by striking),

Eloah, on the contrary, is terrible majesty (not genitival: terror of majesty, Ew. § 293, *c*), *i.e.* it covers Him like a garment (Ps. civ. 1), making Him inaccessible (הוֹד, glory as resounding praise, *vid.* on ch. xxxix. 20, like כבוד as imposing dignity). The beclouded sun, ver. 21 said, has lost none of the intensity of its light, although man has to wait for the removing of the clouds to behold it again. So, when God's doings are mysterious to us, we have to wait, without murmuring, for His solution of the mystery. While from the north comes gold—ver. 22 continues—which is obtained by laying bare the interior of the northern mountains, God, on the other hand, is surrounded by inaccessibly terrible glory: the Almighty—thus ver. 23 completes the thought towards which ver. 22 tends—we cannot reach, the Great in power, *i.e.* the nature of the Absolute One remains beyond us, the counsel of the Almighty impenetrable; still we can at all times be certain of this, that what He does is right and good: " Right and the fulness of justice (וְרֹב־ according to the Masora, not וְרָב־) He perverteth not." The expression is remarkable: עָנָה מִשְׁפָּט is, like the Talmudic עָנָה דִין, equivalent elsewhere to הִטָּה מִשׁפּט; and that He does not pervert רֹב־צְדָקָה, affirms that justice in its whole compass is not perverted by Him; His acts are therefore perfectly and in every way consistent with it: רֹב־צְדָקָה is the *abstract.* to צַדִּיק כַּבִּיר, ch. xxxiv. 17, therefore *summa justitia.* One may feel tempted to draw שַׂגִּיא כֹחַ to וּמִשְׁפָּט, and to read וְרָב according to Prov. xiv. 29 instead of וְרֹב, but the expression gained by so doing is still more difficult than the combination וּמִשְׁפָּט . . . לֹא יְעַנֶּה; not merely difficult, however, but putting a false point in place of a correct one, is the reading לֹא יַעֲנֶה (LXX., Syr., Jer.),

comp. صفح, to strike on something flat (whence *el-musâfaha*, the salutation by striking the hand), and صفع, to strike with the flat hand on anything, therefore *diducendo obducere.*

according to which Hirz. translates: He answers not, *i.e.*
gives no account to man. The accentuation rightly divides
ver. 23 into two halves, the second of which begins with
וּמִשְׁפָּט—a significant *Waw*, on which J. H. Michaelis observes:
*Placide invicem in Deo conspirant infinita ejus potentia et
justitia quæ in hominibus sæpe disjuncta sunt.*

Elihu closes with the practical inference: Therefore men,
viz. of the right sort, of sound heart, uncorrupted and unaffected, fear Him (יְרָאוּהוּ *verentur eum*, not יִרְאוּהוּ *veremini
eum*); He does not see (regard) the wise of heart, *i.e.* those
who imagine themselves such and are proud of their לֵב, their
understanding. The *qui sibi videntur* (Jer.) does not lie in
לב (comp. Isa. v. 21), but in the antithesis. Stick. and others
render falsely: Whom the aggregate of the over-wise beholds
not, which would be יִרְאֶנּוּ. God is the subj. as in ch. xxviii. 24,
xxxiv. 21, comp. xli. 26. The assonance of יראוהו and יראה,
which also occurs frequently elsewhere (*e.g.* ch. vi. 21), we
have sought to reproduce in the translation.

In this last speech also Elihu's chief aim (ch. xxxvi. 2–4)
is to defend God against Job's charge of injustice. He shows
how omnipotence, love, and justice are all found in God.
When judging of God's omnipotence, we are to beware of
censuring Him who is absolutely exalted above us and our
comprehension; when judging of God's love, we are to beware
of interpreting His afflictive dispensations, which are designed
for our well-being, as the persecution of an enemy; when
judging of His justice, we are to beware of maintaining our
own righteousness at the cost of the Divine, and of thus
avoiding the penitent humbling of one's self under His well-
meant chastisement. The twofold peculiarity of Elihu's
speeches comes out in this fourth as prominently as in the
first: (1) They demand of Job penitential submission, not by
accusing him of coarse common sins as the three have done,
but because even the best of men suffer for hidden moral

defects, which must be perceived by them in order not to perish on account of them. Elihu here does for Job just what in Bunyan (*Pilgrim's Progress*) the man in the Interpreter's house does, when he sweeps the room, so that Christian had been almost choked with the dust that flew about. Then (2) they teach that God makes use of just such sufferings, as Job's now are, in order to bring man to a knowledge of his hidden defects, and to bless him the more abundantly if he will be saved from them; that thus the sufferings of those who fear God are a wholesome medicine, disciplinary chastenings, and saving warnings; and that therefore true, not merely feigned, piety must be proved in the school of affliction by earnest self-examination, remorseful self-accusation, and humble submission.

Elihu therefore in this agrees with the rest of the book, that he frees Job's affliction from the view which accounts it the evil-doer's punishment (*vid.* ch. xxxii. 3). On the other hand, however, he nevertheless takes up a position apart from the rest of the book, by making Job's sin the cause of his affliction; while in the idea of the rest of the book Job's affliction has nothing whatever to do with Job's sin, except in so far as he allows himself to be drawn into sinful language concerning God by the conflict of temptation into which the affliction plunges him. For after Jehovah has brought Job over this his sin, He acknowledges His servant (ch. xlii. 7) to be in the right, against the three friends: his affliction is really not a merited affliction, it is not a result of retributive justice; it also had not chastisement as its design, it was an enigma, under which Job should have bowed humbly without striking against it—a decree, into the purpose of which the prologue permits us an insight, which however remains unexplained to Job, or is only explained to him so far as the issue teaches him that it should be to him the way to a so much the more glorious testimony on the part of God Himself.

With that criticism of Job, which the speeches of Jehovah consummate, the criticism which lies before us in the speeches of Elihu is irreconcilable. The older poet, in contrast with the false doctrine of retribution, entirely separates sin and punishment or chastisement in the affliction of Job, and teaches that there is an affliction of the righteous, which is solely designed to prove and test them. His thema, not Elihu's (as Simson[1] with Hengstenberg thinks), is *the mystery of the Cross*. For the Cross according to its proper notion is suffering ἕνεκεν δικαιοσύνης (or what in New Testament language is the same, ἕνεκεν Χριστοῦ). Elihu, however, leaves sin and suffering together as inseparable, and opposes the false doctrine of retribution by the distinction between disciplinary chastisement and judicial retribution. The Elihu section, as I have shown elsewhere,[2] has sprung from the endeavour to moderate the bewildering boldness with which the older poet puts forth his idea. The writer has felt in connection with the book of Job what every Christian must feel. Such a maintaining of his own righteousness in the face of friendly exhortations to penitence, as we perceive it in Job's speeches, is certainly not possible where " the dust of the room has flown about." The friends have only failed in this, that they made Job more and more an evil-doer deservedly undergoing punishment. Elihu points him to vainglorying, to carnal security, and in the main to those defects from which the most godly cannot and dare not claim exemption. It is not contrary to the spirit of the drama that Job holds his peace at these exhortations to penitence. The similarly expressed admonition to penitence with which Eliphaz, ch. iv. sq., begins, has not effected it. In the meanwhile, however, Job is become more softened and composed, and in remembrance of his unbecoming language concerning God,

---

[1] *Zur Kritik des B. Hiob*, 1861, S. 34.

[2] *Vid.* Herzog's *Real-Encyklopädie*, art. *Hiob*, S. 119.

he must feel that he has forfeited the right of defending himself. Nevertheless this silent Job is not altogether the same as the Job who, in ch. xl. and xlii., forces himself to keep silence, whose former testimony concerning himself, and whose former refusal of a theodicy which links sin and calamity together, Jehovah finally sets His seal to.

On the other hand, however, it must be acknowledged, that what the introduction to Elihu's speeches, ch. xxxii. 1–5, sets before us, is consistent with the idea of the whole, and that such a section as the introduction leads one to expect, may be easily understood really as a member of the whole, which carries forward the dramatic development of this idea ; for this very reason one feels urged to constantly new endeavours, if possible, to understand these speeches as a part of the original form. But they are without result, and, moreover, many other considerations stand in our way to the desired goal ; especially, that Elihu is not mentioned in the epilogue, and that his speeches are far behind the artistic perfection of the rest of the book. It is true the writer of these speeches has, in common with the rest of the book, a like Hebræo-Arabic, and indeed Hauranitish style, and like mutual relations to earlier and later writings ; but this is explained from the consideration that he has completely blended the older book with himself (as the points of contact of the fourth speech with ch. xxviii. and the speeches of Jehovah, show), and that to all appearance he is a fellow-countryman of the older poet. There are neither linguistic nor any other valid reasons in favour of assigning it to a much later period. He is the second issuer of the book, possibly the first, who brought to light the hitherto hidden treasure, enriched by his own insertion, which is inestimable in its relation to the history of the perception of the plan of redemption.

We now call to mind that in the last (according to our

view) strophe of Job's last speech, ch. xxxi. 35–37, Job desires, yea challenges, the divine decision between himself and
his opponents. His opponents have explained his affliction
as the punishment of the just God; he, however, is himself so
certain of his innocence, and of his victory over divine and
human accusation, that he will bind the indictment of his
opponents as a crown upon his brow, and to God, whose hand
of punishment supposedly rests upon him, will he render an
account of all his steps, and go forth as a prince to meet
Him. That he considers himself a צדיק is in itself not censurable, for he is such: but that he is מצדק נפשׁו מאלהים, i.e.
considers himself to be righteous in opposition to God, who
is now angry with him and punishes him; that he maintains
his own righteousness to the prejudice of the Divine; and
that by maintaining his own right, places the Divine in the
shade,—all this is explainable as the result of the false idea
which he entertains of his affliction, and in which he is
strengthened by the friends; but there is need of censure and
penitence. For since by His nature God can never do wrong,
all human wrangling before God is a sinful advance against
the mystery of divine guidance, under which he should rather
humbly bow. But we have seen that Job's false idea of God
as his enemy, whose conduct he cannot acknowledge as just,
does not fill his whole soul. The night of temptation in which
he is enshrouded, is broken in upon by gleams of faith, in
connection with which God appears to him as his Vindicator
and Redeemer. Flesh and spirit, nature and grace, delusion
and faith, are at war within him. These two elements are
constantly more definitely separated in the course of the controversy; but it is not yet come to the victory of faith over
delusion, the two lines of conception go unreconciled side by
side in Job's soul. The last monologues issue on the one side
in the humble confession that God's wisdom is unsearchable,
and the fear of God is the share of wisdom appointed to man;

on the other side, in the defiant demand that God may answer
for his defence of himself, and the vaunting offer to give Him
an account of all his steps, and also then to enter His presence
with the high feeling of a prince.   If now the issue of the
drama is to be this, that God really reveals Himself as Job's
Vindicator and Redeemer, Job's defiance and boldness must
be previously punished in order that lowliness and submission
may attain the victory over them.   God cannot acknowledge
Job as His servant before he penitently acknowledges as such
the sinful weakness under which he has proved himself to be
God's servant, and so exhibits himself anew in his true character which cherishes no known sin.   This takes place when
Jehovah appears, and in language not of wrath but of loving
condescension, and yet earnest reproof, He makes the Titan
quite puny in his own eyes, in order then to exalt him who is
outwardly and inwardly humbled.

THE UNRAVELMENT IN THE CONSCIOUSNESS.— CHAP. XXXVIII.–XLII. 6.

The First Speech of Jehovah, and Job's Answer.—
Chap. xxxviii.–xl. 5.

Schema : 4. 8. 8. 8. 12. 12. 6. 6. 10. 7. | 8. 8. 8. 12. 15. 10. | 2. 4.

[Then Jehovah answered Job out of the storm, and said:]
  2 *Who then darkeneth counsel*
    With words without knowledge?
  3 *Gird up now thy loins as a man :*
    I will question thee, and inform thou me!

" May the Almighty answer me!" Job has said, ch. xxxi. 35;
He now really answers, and indeed out of the storm (*Chethib,*
according to a mode of writing occurring only here and ch.
xl. 6, מנהסערה, arranged in two words by the *Keri*), which

is generally the forerunner of His self-manifestation in the world, of that at least by which He reveals Himself in His absolute awe-inspiring greatness and judicial grandeur. The *art.* is to be understood generically, but, with respect to Elihu's speeches, refers to the storm which has risen up in the meanwhile. It is not to be translated : Who is he who . . . , which ought to be הַמַּחְשִׁיךְ, but : Who then is darkening ; זֶה makes the interrogative מִי more vivid and demonstrative, Ges. § 122, 2 ; the *part.* מַחְשִׁיךְ (instead of which it might also be יַחְשִׁיךְ) favours the assumption that Job has uttered such words immediately before, and is interrupted by Jehovah, without an intervening speaker having come forward. It is intentionally עֵצָה for עֲצָתִי (comp. עַם for עַמִּי, Isa. xxvi. 11), to describe that which is spoken of according to its quality : it is nothing less than a decree or plan full of purpose and connection which Job darkens, *i.e.* distorts by judging it falsely, or, as we say : places in a false light, and in fact by meaningless words.[1]

When now Jehovah condescends to negotiate with Job by question and answer, He does not do exactly what Job wished (ch. xiii. 22), but something different, of which Job never thought. He surprises him with questions which are intended to bring him indirectly to the consciousness of the wrong and absurdity of his challenge—questions among which " there are many which the natural philosophy of the present day can frame more scientifically, but cannot satisfactorily solve."[2] Instead of כְּגֶבֶר (the received reading of Ben-Ascher), Ben-Naphtali's text offered כְּגַ (as Ezek. xvii. 10), in order not to allow two so similar, aspirated *mutæ* to come together.

---

[1] The correct accentuation is מחשיך with *Mercha*, עצה with *Athnach*, במלין with *Rebia mugrasch*, בלי (without *Makkeph*) with *Munach*.

[2] Alex. v. Humboldt, *Kosmos*, ii. 48 (1st edition), comp. Tholuck, *Vermischte Schriften*, i. 354.

4 *Where wast thou when I established the earth?*
  Say, if thou art capable of judging!
5 *Who hath determined its measure, if thou knowest it,*
  Or who hath stretched the measuring line over it?
6 *Upon what are the bases of its pillars-sunk in,*
  Or who hath laid its corner-stone,
7 *When the morning stars sang together*
  And all the sons of God shouted for joy?

The examination begins similarly to ch. xv. 7 sq. In opposition to the censurer of God as such the friends were right, although only negatively, since their conduct was based on self-delusion, as though they were in possession of the key to the mystery of the divine government of the world. יָדַע בִּינָה signifies to understand how to judge, to possess a competent understanding, 1 Chron. xii. 32, 2 Chron. ii. 12, or (ידע taken not in the sense of *novisse*, but *cognoscere*) to appropriate to one's self, Prov. iv. 1, Isa. xxix. 24. כִּי, ver. 5a, interchanges with אִם (comp. ver. 18b), for כִּי תֵדַע signifies: suppose that thou knowest it, and this *si forte scias* is almost equivalent to *an forte scis*, Prov. xxx. 4. The founding of the earth is likened altogether to that of a building constructed by man. The question: upon what are the bases of its pillars or foundations sunk (טבע, طبع, according to its radical signification, to press with something flat upon something, comp. طبق, to lay two flat things on one another, then both to form or stamp by pressure, *vid.* i. 377, note, and to press into soft pliant stuff, or let down into, *immergere*, or to sink into, *immergi*), points to the fact of the earth hanging free in space, ch. xxvi. 7. Then no human being was present, for man was not yet created; the angels, however, beheld with rejoicing the founding of the place of the future human family, and the mighty acts of God in accordance with the decree of His love (as at the building of the temple, the laying of the foundation, Ezra iii. 10, and the setting of the head-stone, Zech. iv. 7, were celebrated), for the angels were created before the visible world (*Psychol.* S. 63; *Genesis*, S. 105), as is indeed not taught here, but still (*vid.* on the other hand, Hofmann, *Schriftbew.* i. 400) is assumed. For בְּנֵי אֱלֹהִים are, as in ch. i. ii., the angels, who proceeded from God by a mode of creation which is likened to begetting, and who with Him form one πατριά (*Genesis*, S. 121). The "morning stars," however, are mentioned in connection with them, because between the stars and the angels, which are both comprehended in צְבָא הַשָּׁמַיִם (*Genesis*, S. 128), a mysterious connection exists, which is manifoldly attested in Holy Scripture (*vid.* on the other hand, Hofm. *ib.* S. 318). כּוֹכַב בֹּקֶר is the morning star which in Isa. xiv. 12 is called הֵילֵל (as extra-bibl. נֹגַהּ) from its dazzling light, which exceeds all other stars in brightness, and בֶּן־שַׁחַר, son of the dawn, because it swims in the dawn as though it were born from it. It was just the dawn of the world coming into being, which is the subject spoken of, that gave rise to the mention of the morning star; the *plur.*, however, does not mean the stars which came into being on that morning of the world collectively (Hofm., Schlottm.), but Lucifer with the stars his peers, as כְּסִילִים, Isa. xiii. 10, Orion and the stars his peers.

سهيل (Canopus) is used similarly as a generic name for stars of remarkable brilliancy, and in general *suhêl* is to the nomads and the Hauranites the symbol of what is brilliant, glorious, and beautiful;[1] so that even the beings of light of the first rank among the celestial spirits might be understood by כוכבי בקר. But if this ought to be the meaning, ver. 7*a*

[1] A man or woman of great beauty is called *suhêli, suhelije.* Thus I heard a Hauranitish woman say to her companion: *nahâr el-jôm nedâ, shuft ledsch* (لك) *wâhid Suhêli*, To-day is dew, I saw a *Suhêli*, *i.e.* a very handsome man, for thee.—WETZST.

and 7*b* would be in an inverted order. They are actual stars, whether it is intended of the sphere belonging to the earth or to the higher sphere comprehended in הַשָּׁמַיִם, Gen. i. 1. Joy and light are reciprocal notions, and the scale of the tones of joy is likened to the scale of light and colours; therefore the fulness of light, in which the morning stars shone forth all together at the founding of the earth, may symbolize one grandly harmonious song of joy.

8 *And [who] shut up the sea with doors,*
When it broke through, issued from the womb,
9 *When I put clouds round it as a garment,*
And thick mist as its swaddling clothes,
10 *And I broke for it my bound,*
And set bars and doors,
11 *And said: Hitherto come, and no further,*
And here be thy proud waves stayed!?

The state of תֹּהוּ וָבֹהוּ was the first half, and the state of תְּהוֹם the second half of the primeval condition of the forming earth. The question does not, however, refer to the תְּהוֹם, in which the waters of the sky and the waters of the earth were as yet not separated, but, passing over this intermediate condition of the forming earth, to the sea, the waters of which God shut up as by means of a door and bolt, when, first enshrouded in thick mist (which has remained from that time one of its natural peculiarities), and again and again manifesting its individuality, it broke forth (גִּיחַ of the fœtus, as Ps. xxii. 10) from the bowels of the, as yet, chaotic earth. That the sea, in spite of the flatness of its banks, does not flow over the land, is a work of omnipotence which broke over it, *i.e.* restraining it, a fixed bound (חֹק as ch. xxvi. 10, Prov. viii. 29, Jer. v. 22, = גְּבוּל, Ps. civ. 9), viz. the steep and rugged walls of the basin of the sea, and which thereby established a firm barrier behind which it should be kept.

Instead of וּפֹה, Josh. xviii. 8, ver. 11*b* has the *Chethib* וּפֹא. חֹק is to be understood with יָשִׁית, and "one set" is equivalent to the passive (Ges. § 137*) : let a bound be set (comp. יָשֵׁת, Hos. vi. 11, which is used directly so) against the proud rising of thy waves.

> 12 *Hast thou in thy life commanded a morning,*
> *Caused the dawn to know its place,*
> 13 *That it may take hold of the ends of the earth,*
> *So that the evil-doers are shaken under it?*
> 14 *That it changeth like the clay of a signet-ring,*
> *And everything fashioneth itself as a garment.*
> 15 *Their light is removed from the evil-doers,*
> *And the out-stretched arm is broken.*

The dawn of the morning, spreading out from one point, takes hold of the carpet of the earth as it were by the edges, and shakes off from it the evil-doers, who had laid themselves to rest upon it the night before. נָעַר, combining in itself the significations to thrust and to shake, has the latter here, as in the Arab. *nâ'ûra*, a water-wheel, which fills its compartments below in the river, to empty them out above. Instead of יָדַעְתָּה שַׁחַר with *He otians*, the *Keri* substitutes יָדַעְתָּ הַשַּׁחַר. The earth is the subj. to ver. 14*a*: the dawn is like the signet-ring, which stamps a definite impress on the earth as the clay, the forms which floated in the darkness of the night become visible and distinguishable. The subj. to ver. 14*b* are not morning and dawn (Schult.), still less the ends of the earth (Ew. with the conjecture: יתיבצו, "they become dazzlingly white"), but the single objects on the earth: the light of morning gives to everything its peculiar garb of light, so that, hitherto overlaid by a uniform darkness, they now come forth independently, they gradually appear in their variegated diversity of form and hue. In כְּמוֹ לְבוּשׁ, לבוש is conceived as accusative (Arab. *kemâ* *libâsan,* or *thauban*), while in כלבוש (Ps. civ. 6, *instar vestis*) it would be genitive. To the end of the strophe everything is under the logical government of the ל of purpose in ver. 13*a.* The light of the evil-doers is, according to ch. xxiv. 17, the darkness of the night, which is for them in connection with their works what the light of day is for other men. The sunrise deprives them, the enemies of light in the true sense (ch. xxiv. 13), of this light *per antiphrasin,* and the carrying out of their evil work, already prepared for, is frustrated. The ע of רשעים, vers. 13 and 15, is עֵין תלויה [*Ayin suspensum*], which is explained according to the Midrash thus: the רשעים, now עשירים (rich), become at a future time רשים (poor); or: God deprives them of the עין (light of the eye), by abandoning them to the darkness which they loved.

16 *Hast thou reached the fountains of the sea,*
   And hast thou gone into the foundation of the deep?

17 *Were the gates of death unveiled to thee,*
   And didst thou see the gates of the realm of shades?

18 *Hast thou comprehended the breadth of the earth?*
   Speak, in so far as thou knowest all this!

19 *Which is the way to where the light dwelleth,*
   And darkness, where is its place,

20 *That thou mightest bring it to its bound,*
   And that thou mightest know the paths of its house?

21 *Thou knowest it, for then wast thou born,*
   And the number of thy days is great!—

The root נב has the primary notion of obtruding itself upon the senses (*vid. Genesis,* S. 635), whence נבך in Arabic of a rising country that pleases the eye (*nabaka,* a hill, a hillside), and here (cognate in root and meaning נבע, Syr. Talmud. נְבַג, نبغ, نبط, *scaturire*) of gushing and bubbling water. Hitzig's conjecture, approved by Olsh., נבלי, sets aside a word that is perfectly clear so far as the language is concerned. On חֵקֶר *vid.* on ch. xi. 7. The question put to Job in ver. 17, he must, according to his own confession, ch. xxvi. 6, answer in the negative. In order to avoid the collision of two aspirates, the interrogative הֲ is wanting before הִתְבֹּנַנְתָּ, Ew. § 324, *b;* התבנן עד signifies, according to ch. xxxii. 12, to observe anything carefully; the meaning of the question therefore is, whether Job has given special attention to the breadth of the earth, and whether he consequently has a comprehensive and thorough knowledge of it. כֻּלָּהּ refers not to the earth (Hahn, Olsh., and others), but, as neuter, to the preceding points of interrogation. The questions, ver. 19, refer to the principles of light and darkness, *i.e.* their final causes, whence they come forth as cosmical phenomena. יִשְׁכָּן־אוֹר is a relative clause, Ges. § 123, 3, *c;* the noun that governs (the *Regens*) this virtual genitive, which ought in Arabic to be without the *art.* as being determined by the *regens*, is, according to the Hebrew syntax, which is freer in this respect, הַדֶּרֶךְ (comp. Ges. § 110, 2). That which is said of the bound of darkness, *i.e.* the furthest point at which darkness passes away, and the paths to its house, applies also to the light, which the poet perhaps has even prominently (comp. ch. xxiv. 13) before his mind: light and darkness have a first cause which is inaccessible to man, and beyond his power of searching out. The admission in ver. 21 is ironical: Verily! thou art as old as the beginning of crea- tion, when light and darkness, as powers of nature which are distinguished and bounded the one by the other (*vid.* ch. xxvi. 10), were introduced into the rising world; thou art as old as the world, so that thou hast an exact knowledge of its and thine own cotemporaneous origin (*vid.* ch. xv. 7). On the *fut.* joined with אָז regularly in the signification of the *aorist, vid.* Ew. § 134, *b.* The attraction in connection with מִסְפַּר is like ch. xv. 20, xxi. 21.

22 *Hast thou reached the treasures of the snow,*
   And didst thou see the treasures of the hail,
23 *Which I have reserved for a time of trouble,*
   For the day of battle and war?
24 *Which is the way where the light is divided,*
   Where the east wind is scattered over the earth?
25 *Who divideth a course for the rain-flood*
   And the way of the lightning of thunder,
26 *That it raineth on the land where no one dwelleth,*
   On the tenantless steppe,
27 *To satisfy the desolate and the waste,*
   And to cause the tender shoot of the grass to spring forth?

The idea in ver. 22 is not that—as for instance the peasants of *Menîn*, four hours' journey from Damascus, garner up the winter snow in a cleft of the rock, in order to convey it to Damascus and the towns of the coast in the hot months—God treasures up the snow and hail above to cause it to descend according to opportunity. אֹצְרוֹת (comp. Ps. cxxxv. 7) are the final causes of these phenomena which God has created—the form of the question, the design of which (which must not be forgotten) is ethical, not scientific, is regulated according to the infancy of the perception of natural phenomena among the ancients; but at the same time in accordance with the poet's task, and even, as here, in the choice of the agents of destruction, not merely hail, but also snow, according to the scene of the incident. Wetzstein has in his possession a writing of Muhammed el-Chatîb el-Bosrâwi, in which he describes a fearful fall of snow in Hauran, by which, in February 1860, innumerable herds of sheep, goats, and camels, and also many human beings perished.[1] עֵת־צָר might, according to ch.

---

[1] Since the Hauranites say of snow as of fire: *jahrik*, it burns (*brûlant* in French is also used of extreme cold), ch. i. 16 might also be understood of a fall of snow; but the tenor of the words there requires it to be understood of actual fire.

xxiv. 1, xix. 11, signify a time of judgment for the oppressor, *i.e.* adversary; but it is better to be understood according to ch. xxxvi. 16, xxi. 30, a time of distress: heavy falls of snow and tempestuous hail-storms bring hard times for men and cattle, and sometimes decide a war as by a divine decree (Josh. x. 11, comp. Isa. xxviii. 17, xxx. 30, Ezek. xiii. 13).

In ver. 24*a* it is not, as in ver. 19*a*, the place whence light issues, but the mode of the distribution of light over the earth, that is intended; as in ver. 24*b*, the laws according to which the east wind flows forth, *i.e.* spreads over the earth. אוֹר is not lightning (Schlottm.), but light in general: light and wind (instead of which the east wind is particularized, *vid.* p. 77) stand together as being alike untraceable in their courses. הֵפִיץ, *se diffundere*, as Ex. v. 12, 1 Sam. xiii. 8, Ges. § 53, 2. In ver. 25*a* the descent of torrents of rain inundating certain regions of the earth is intended—this earthward direction assigned to the water-spouts is likened to an aqueduct coming downwards from the sky—and it is only in ver. 25*b*, as in ch. xxviii. 26, that the words have reference to the lightning, which to man is untraceable, flashing now here, now there. This guiding of the rain to chosen parts of the earth extends also to the tenantless steppe. לֹא־אִישׁ (for בְּלֹא) is virtually an adj. (*vid.* on ch. xii. 24). The superlative combination שֹׁאָה וּמְשֹׁאָה (from שׁוֹא = שָׁאָה, to be desolate, and to give forth a heavy dull sound, *i.e.* to sound desolate, *vid.* on ch. xxxvii. 6), as ch. xxx. 3 (which see). Not merely for the purposes of His rule among men does God direct the changes of the weather contrary to human foresight; His care extends also to regions where no human habitations are found.

> 28 *Hath the rain a father,*
> *Or who begetteth the drops of dew?*
> 29 *Out of whose womb cometh the ice forth,*

And who bringeth forth the hoar-frost of heaven?
30　*The waters become hard like stone,*
　　And the face of the deep is rolled together.

Rain and dew have no created father, ice and hoar-frost no created mother. The parallelism in both instances shows that מִי הוֹלִיד asks after the one who begets, and מִי יָלַד the one who bears (*vid.* Hupfeld on Ps. ii. 7). בֶּטֶן is *uterus,* and meton. (at least in Arabic) *progenies uteri; ex utero cujus* is מבטן מי, in distinction from מֵאֵי־זֶה בטן, *ex quo utero.* אֶגְלֵי־טָל is excellently translated by the LXX., *Codd. Vat.* and *Sin.,* βώλους (with *Omega*) δρόσου; Ges. and Schlottm. correct to βόλους, but βῶλος signifies not merely a clod, but also a lump and a ball. It is the particles of the dew holding together (LXX., *Cod. Alex.*: συνοχὰς καὶ βω. δρ.) in a globular form, from אָגַל, which does not belong to גָּלַל, but to اجل, *retinere,* II. *colligere* (whence *agîl,* standing water, *ma"gal,* a pool, pond); אֶגְלֵי is *constr.,* like עֶגְלֵי from עֵגֶל. The waters "hide themselves," by vanishing as fluid, therefore: freeze. The surface of the deep (LXX. ἀσεβοῦς, for which Zwingli has *in marg.* ἀβύσσου) "takes hold of itself," or presses together (comp. Arab. *lekda,* crowding, synon. *hugûm,* a striking against) by forming itself into a firm solid mass (*continuum,* ch. xli. 9, comp. xxxvii. 10). Moreover, the questions all refer not merely to the analysis of the visible origin of the phenomena, but to their final causes.

31　*Canst thou join the twistings of the Pleiades,*
　　Or loose the bands of Orion?
32　*Canst thou bring forth the signs of the Zodiac at the right*
　　　time,
　　And canst thou guide the Bear with its children?
33　*Knowest thou the laws of heaven,*
　　Or dost thou define its influence on the earth?

That מַעֲדַנּוֹת here signifies the bindings or twistings (from
עָדַן = עָנַד, ch. xxxi. 36) is placed beyond question by the
unanimous translations of the LXX. (δεσμόν) and the Targ.
(שִׁירֵי = σειράς), the testimony of the Masora, according to
which the word here has a different signification from 1 Sam.
xv. 32, and the language of the Talmud, in which מעדנין,
Kêlim, c. 20, signifies the knots at the end of a mat, by
loosing which it comes to pieces, and *Succa*, 13b, the bands
(formed of rushes) with which willow-branches are fastened
together above in order to form a booth (*succa*); but מדאני,
Sabbat, 33a, signifies a bunch of myrtle (to smell on the
Sabbath). מעדנות כּימָה is therefore explained according to
the Persian comparison of the Pleiades with a bouquet of
jewels, mentioned on ch. ix. 9, and according to the comparison with a necklace (*'iqd-eth-thurajja*), *e.g.* in Sadi in his
Gulistan, p. 8 of Graf's translation : " as though the tops of
the trees were encircled by the necklace of the Pleiades."
The Arabic name *thurajja* (diminutive feminine of *tharwân*)
probably signifies the richly-adorned, clustered constellation.
But כִּימָה signifies without doubt the clustered group,[1] and
Beigel (in Ideler, *Sternnamen*, S. 147) does not translate
badly : " Canst thou not arrange together the rosette of

---

[1] The verb כום is still in general use in the *Piel* (to heap up, form a
heap, *part. mukauwam*, heaped up) and *Hithpa.* (to accumulate) in Syria,
and *kôm* is any village desolated in days of yore whose stones form a
desolate heap [comp. Fleischer, *De Glossis Habichtianis*, p. 41 sq.]. If,
according to Kamus, in old Jemanic *kîm* in the sense of *mukâwim* signifies
a confederate (synon. *chilt*, *gils*), the כִּימָה would be a confederation,
or a heap, assemblage (coetus) of confederates. Perhaps the כימה was
regarded as a troop of camels ; the Beduins at least call the star directly
before the seven-starred constellation of the Pleiades the *hâdi, i.e.* the
singer riding before the procession, who cheers the camels by the sound of
the *hadwa* (חִדְוָה), and thereby urges them on.—WETZST.

On πλειάδες, which perhaps also bear this name as a compressed group
(figuratively βότρυς) of several stars (ὅτι πλείους ὁμοῦ κατὰ συναγωγήν
εἰσι), *vid.* Kuhn's *Zeitschr.* vi. 282–285.

diamonds (chain would be better) of the Pleiades?" As to כְּסִיל, we firmly hold that it denotes Orion (according to which the Greek versions translate Ὠρίων, the Syriac *gaboro*, the Targ. נְפִלָא or נְפִילָא, the Giant). Orion and the Pleiades are visible in the Syrian sky longer in the year than with us, and there they come about 17° higher above the horizon than with us. Nevertheless the figure of a giant chained to the heavens cannot be rightly shown to be Semitic, and it is questionable whether כסיל is not rather, with Saad., Gecat., Abulwalíd, and others, to be regarded as the *Suhêl, i.e.* Canopus, especially as this is placed as a sluggish helper (כסיל, Hebr. a fool, Arab. the slothful one, *ignavus*) in mythical relation to the constellation of the Bear, which here is called עָיִשׁ, as ch. ix. 9 עָשׁ, and is regarded as a bier, נַעַשׁ (even in the present day this is the name in the towns and villages of Syria), with the sons and daughters forming the attendants upon the corpse of their father, slain by *Gedî*, the Pole-star. Understood of Orion, מִשְׁכוֹת (with which مسك, *tenere, detinere,* is certainly to be compared) are the chains (مسكة, *compes*), with which he is chained to the sky; understood of Suhêl, the restraints which prevent his breaking away too soon and reaching the goal.[1] מַזָּרוֹת is not distinct from מַזָּלוֹת,

---

[1] In June 1860 I witnessed a quarrel in an encampment of *Mo‘gil*-Beduins, in which one accused the others of having rendered it possible for the enemy to carry off his camels through their negligence; and when the accused assured him they had gone forth in pursuit of the marauders soon after the raid, and only turned back at sunset, the man exclaimed: Ye came indeed to my assistance as *Suhêl* to *Gedî* (פּזעתם לי פּזע סהיל ללגדי). I asked my neighbour what the words meant, and was informed they are a proverb which is very often used, and has its origin as follows: The *Gedî* (*i.e.* the Pole-star, called *mismâr*, מִשְׁמָר, in Damascus) slew the *Na‘sh* (נַעַשׁ), and is accordingly encompassed every night by the children of the slain *Nâ‘sh*, who are determined to take vengeance on the murderer. The sons (on which account poets usually say *benî* instead of *benât Na‘sh*) go first with the corpse of their father, and the daughters follow. One of the latter is called *waldâne*, a lying-in woman; she has

2 Kings xxiii. 5 (comp. מַזָּרוֹת, "Thy star of fortune," on Cilician coins), and denotes not the twenty-eight *menâzil* (from نَزَلَ, to descend, turn in, lodge) of the moon,[1] but the twelve signs of the Zodiac, which were likewise imagined as *menâzil*, *i.e.* lodging-houses or *burûg*, strongholds, in which one after another the sun lodges as it describes the circle of the year.[2] The usage of the language transferred מַזָּל also to the planets, which, because they lie in the equatorial plane of the sun, as the sun (although more irregularly), run through the constellations of the Zodiac. The question in ver. 32*a* therefore means: canst thou bring forth the appointed zodiacal sign for each month, so that (of course with the variation which is limited to about two moon's diameters by the daily progress of the sun through the Zodiac) it becomes visible after sunset and is visible before sunset? On ver. 33 *vid.* on Gen. i. 14–19. מִשְׁטָר is construed after the analogy of רָדָה בְּ, מָשַׁל, עָצַר; and שָׁמַיִם, as *sing.* (Ew. § 318, *b*).

only recently given birth to a child, and carries her child in her bosom, and she is still pale from her lying-in. (The clear atmosphere of the Syrian sky admits of the child in the bosom of the *waldâne* being distinctly seen.) In order to give help to the *Gedî* in this danger, the *Suhêl* appears in the south, and struggles towards the north with a twinkling brightness, but he has risen too late; the night passes away ere he reaches his goal. Later I frequently heard this story, which is generally known among the Hauranites.—WETZST.

We add the following by way of explanation. The Pleiades encircle the Pole-star as do all stars, since it stands at the axis of the sky, but they are nearer to it than to Canopus by more than half the distance. This star of the first magnitude culminates about three hours later than the Pleiades, and rises, at the highest, only ten moon's diameters above the horizon of Damascus—a significant figure, therefore, of ineffectual endeavour.

[1] Thus A. Weber in his *Abh. über die vedischen Nachrichten von den naxatra* (halting-places of the moon), 1860 (comp. *Lit. Centralbl.* 1859, col. 665), refuted by Steinschneider, *Hebr. Bibliographie*, 1861, Nr. 22, S. 93 f.

[2] The names "the Ram, the Bull," etc., are, according to Epiphanius, *Opp.* i. p. 34 sq. (*ed. Petav.*), transferred from the Greek into the Jewish astrology, *vid. Wissenschaft Kunst Judenthum*, S. 220 f.

34 *Dost thou raise thy voice to the clouds*
   That an overflow of waters may cover thee?
35 *Dost thou send forth lightnings, and they go,*
   And say to thee: Here we are?
36 *Who hath put wisdom in the reins,*
   Or who hath given understanding to the cock?
37 *Who numbereth the strata of the clouds with wisdom,*
   And the bottles of heaven, who emptieth them,
38 *When the dust flows together into a mass,*
   And the clods cleave together?

As ver. 25*b* was worded like ch. xxviii. 26, so ver. 34*b* is worded like ch. xxii. 11; the ך of תכסך is dageshed in both passages, as ch. xxxvi. 2, 18, Hab. ii. 17. What Jehovah here denies to the natural power of man is possible to the power which man has by faith, as the history of Elijah shows: this, however, does not come under consideration here. In proof of divine omnipotence and human feebleness, Elihu constantly recurs to the rain and the thunder-storm with the lightning, which is at the bidding of God. Most moderns since Schultens therefore endeavour, with great violence, to make מֻחוֹת and שֶׂכְוִי mean meteors and celestial phenomena. Eichh. (Hirz., Hahn) compares the Arabic name for the clouds, tachâ (tachwa), Ew. ضَحَا, sunshine, with the former; the latter, whose root is שָׂכָה (סָכָה), *spectare*, is meant to be something that is remarkable in the heavens: an atmospheric phenomenon, a meteor (Hirz.), or a phenomenon caused by light (Ew., Hahn), so that *e.g.* Umbr. translates: "Who hath put wisdom in the dark clouds, and given understanding to the meteor?" But the meaning which is thus extorted from the words in favour of the connection borders closely upon absurdity. Why, then, shall מֻחוֹת, from טוּחַ, طَلَّخَ, *oblinere, adipe obducere*, not signify here, as in Ps. li. 8, the reins (embedded in a cushion of fat), and in fact as the seat of the predictive faculty, like כְּלָיוֹת, ch. xix. 27, as the seat of the innermost longing for the future; and particularly since here, after the constellations and the influences of the stars have just been spoken of, the mention of the gift of divination is not devoid of connection; and, moreover, as a glance at the next strophe shows, the connection which has been hitherto firmly kept to is already in process of being resolved?

If טחות signifies the reins, it is natural to interpret שֶׂכְוִי also psychologically, and to translate the intellect (Targ. I., Syr., Arab.), or similarly (Saad., Gecat.), as Ges., Carey, Renan, Schlottm. But there is another rendering handed down which is worthy of attention, although not once mentioned by Rosenm., Hirz., Schlottm., or Hahn, according to which שׂכוי signifies a cock, *gallum*. We read in *b. Rosch ha-Schana*, 26*a*: "When I came to Techûm-Kên-Nishraja, R. Simeon b. Lakish relates, the bride was there called נינפי and the cock שׂכוי, according to which Job xxxviii. 36 is to be interpreted: שׂכוי = תרנגול." The Midrash interprets in the same way, *Jalkut*, § 905, beginning: "R. Levi says: In Arabic the cock is called סַכְוָא." We compare with this, *Wajikra rabba*, c. 1: "סוכו is Arabic; in Arabia a prophet is called סַכְיָא;" whence it is to be inferred that שׂכוי, as is assumed, describes the cock as a seer, as a prophet.

As to the formation of the word, it would certainly be without parallel (Ew., Olsh.) if the word had the tone on the *penult.*, but Codd. and the best old editions have the *Munach* by the final syllable; Norzi, who has overlooked this, at least notes שֶׂכְוִי with the accent on the *ult.* as a various reading. It is a secondary noun, Ges. § 86, 5, a so-called relative noun (De Sacy, *Gramm. Arabe*, § 768): שֶׂכְוִי, *speculator*, from שָׂכָה (שֶׂכוּ, שָׂכֹה), *speculatio*, as פִּלְאִי, Judg. xiii. 18 (comp. Ps. cxxxix. 6), *miraculosus*, from פֶּלֶא, a cognate form to the Chald. סַכְוִי (סָכְוָאה), of similar meaning. In connection with this primary signification, *speculator*, it is intelligible how סכוי in Samaritan (*vid.* Lagarde on Proverbs, S. 62) can signify the eye; here, however, in a Hebrew poet, the cock, of which *e.g.* Gregory says: *Speculator semper in altitudine stat, ut quidquid venturum sit longe prospiciat.* That this signification *speculator = gallus*[1] was generally accepted at least in the Talmudic age, the *Beracha* prescribed to him who hears the cock crow: "Blessed be He who giveth the cock (שֶׂכְוִי) knowledge to distinguish between day and night!" shows. In accordance with this, Targ. II. translates: who has given understanding לְתַרְנְגוֹל בָּרָא, *gallo sylvestri* (whereas Targ. I. לְלִבָּא, *cordi, scil. hominis*), to praise his Lord? and Jer.: (*quis posuit in visceribus hominis sapientiam*) *et quis dedit gallo intelligentiam.* This traditional rendering, condemned as *talmudicum commentum* (Ges.), we follow rather than the "phenomenon" of the moderns who guess at a meaning. What is questioned in Cicero, *de divin.* ii. 26: *Quid in mentem venit Callistheni dicere, Deos gallis signum dedisse cantandi, quum id vel natura vel casus efficere potuisset,* Jehovah here claims for Himself. The weather-prophet κατ᾽ ἐξοχήν among animals appropriately appears in this astrologico-meteorological connection by the side of the reins as, according to the Semitic view, a medium of augury (*Psychol.* S. 268 f.). The Koran also makes the cock the watchman who wakes up the heavenly hosts to their duty; and Masius, in his *Studies of Nature,* has shown how high the cock is placed as being prophetically (for divination) gifted. Moreover, the worship of cocks in the idolatry of the Semites was a service rendered to the stars: the Sabians offered cocks, probably (*vid.* Chwolsohn, ii. 87) as the white cock of Jezides,

---

[1] No Arab. word offers itself here for comparison: *tuchaj,* a cock, has different consonants, and if شكا in the sense of شالت, *fortem esse,* were to be supposed, שֶׂכְוִי would be a synon. of גֶּבֶר, which is likewise a name of the cock.

regarded by them as a symbol of the sun (*Deutsch. Morgen-länd. Zeitschr.* 1862, S. 365 f.).

In ver. 37b Jerome translates: *et concentum cœlorum quis dormire faciet;* נִבְלֵי, however, does not here signify harps, but bottles; and הִשְׁכִּיב is not: to lay to rest, but to lay down = to empty, pour out, which the *Kal* also, like the Arab. *sakaba,* directly signifies. בְּצֶקֶת might be taken actively: when it pours, but according to 1 Kings xxii. 35 the intransitive rendering is also possible: when the dust pours forth, *i.e.* flows together, לְמוּצָק, to what is poured out, *i.e.* not: to the fluid, but in contrast: to a molten mass, *i.e.* as cast metal (to be explained not according to ch. xxii. 16, but according to ch. xxxvii. 18), for the dry, sandy, dusty earth is made firm by the downfall of the rain (Arab. رصدت, *firmata est terra imbre,* comp. لَبِدَ, *pluviam emisit donec arena cohæreret*). רְגָבִים, *glebæ,* as ch. xxi. 33, from רֶגֶב, رجب, in the primary signification, which as it seems must be supposed: to bring together, from which the significations branch off, to thicken, become firm (*muraggab,* supported), and to be seized with terror.

> 39 *Dost thou hunt for the prey of the lioness*
> *And still the desire of the young lions,*
> 40 *When they couch in the dens,*
> *Sit in the thicket lying in wait for prey?*
> 41 *Who provideth for the raven its food,*
> *When its young ones cry to God,*
> *They wander about without food?*

On the wealth of the Old Testament language in names for the lion, *vid.* on ch. iv. 10 sq. לָבִיא can be used of the lioness; the more exact name of the lioness is לְבִיָּה, for לָבִיא is = לְבִי, whence לְבָאִים, lions, and לְבָאוֹת, lionesses. The lioness is mentioned first, because she has to provide for her young ones (גּוּרִים); then the lions that are still young, but yet are left to themselves, כְּפִירִים. The phrase מָלֵא חַיָּה (comp. חַיָּה of life that needs nourishment, ch. xxxiii. 20) is equivalent to מָלֵא נֶפֶשׁ, Prov. vi. 30 (*Psychol.* S. 204 *ad fin.*). The book of Psalms here furnishes parallels to every word: comp. on ver. 39*b*, Ps. civ. 21; on יִשֹׁחוּ, Ps. x. 10;[1] on מְעוֹנוֹת, *lustra*, Ps. civ. 22 (compared on ch. xxxvii. 8 already); on סֹךְ, סֻכָּה, which is used just in the same way, Ps. x. 9, Jer. xxv. 38. The picture of the crying ravens has its parallel in Ps. cxlvii. 9. כִּי, *quum*, is followed by the *fut.* in the signif. of the *præs.*, as Ps. xi. 3. As here, in the Sermon on the Mount in Luke xii. 24 the ravens, which by their hoarse croaking make themselves most observed everywhere among birds that seek their food, are mentioned instead of the fowls of heaven.

Ch. xxxix. 1 *Dost thou know the bearing time of the wild goats of the rock?*
Observest thou the circles of the hinds?

2 *Dost thou number the months which they fulfil,*
And knowest thou the time of their bringing forth?

3 *They bow down, they let their young break through,*
They cast off their pains.

4 *Their young ones gain strength, grow up in the desert,*
They run away and do not return.

The strophe treats of the female chamois or steinbocks, *ibices* (perhaps including the certainly different kinds of chamois), and stags. The former are called יְעֵלִים, from יָעַל,

---

[1] The Semitic is rich in such words as describe the couching posture of beasts of prey lying in wait for their prey, which then in general signify to lie in wait, lurk, wait (רצד, רבץ, ربص, لبد, وكّد); تعد له, *subsedit ei*, *i.e. insidiatus est ei*, which corresponds to יֵשְׁבוּ, ver. 40*b*, also belongs here, comp. *Psalter*, i. 500, note.

وَعِل (a secondary formation from עלה, عَلَا), to mount, there-fore: rock-climbers. חוֹלֵל is *inf. Pil.*: τὸ ὠδίνειν, comp. the *Pul.* ch. xv. 7. שֻׁמָּר, to observe, exactly as Eccl. xi. 4, 1 Sam. i. 12, Zech. xi. 11. In ver. 2 the question as to the expiration of the time of bearing is connected with that as to the time of bringing forth. תִּסְפּוֹר, *plene*, as ch. xiv. 16; לְדִתְּנָה (*littâna*, like עֵת = עֶדֶת, *vid.* p. 16, note) with an euphonic termination for לְדִתָּן, as Gen. xlii. 36, xxi. 29, and also out of pause, Ruth i. 19, Ges. § 91, 1, rem. 2. Instead of תְּפַלַּחְנָה Olsh. wishes to read תְּפַלֵּטְנָה, but this (synon. תמלטנה) would be : they let slip away; the former (synon. תבקענה) : they cause to divide, *i.e.* to break through (comp. Arab. *felâh*, the act of breaking through, freedom, prosperity). On בָּרַע, to kneel down as the posture of one in travail, *vid.* 1 Sam. iv. 19. "They cast off their pains" is not meant of an easy working off of the after-pains (Hirz., Schlottm.), but חֵבֶל signifies in this phrase, as Schultens has first shown, meton. directly the fœtus, as Arab. حَبْل, plur. *ahbâl*, and ὠδίν, even of a child already grown up, as being the fruit of earlier travail, *e.g.* in Æschylus, *Agam.* 1417 sq.; even the like phrase, ῥίψαι ὠδῖνα = *edere fœtum*, is found in Euripides, *Ion* 45. Thus born with ease, the young animals grow rapidly to maturity (חָלַם, *pinguescere, pubescere*, whence חֲלוֹם, a dream as the result of puberty, *vid. Psychol.* S. 282), grow in the desert (בַּבָּר, Targ. = בְּחוּן, *vid.* i. 329, note), seek the plain, and return not again לָמוֹ, *sibi h. e. sui juris esse volentes* (Schult.), although it might also signify *ad eas*, for the Hebr. is rather confused on the question of the distinction of gender, and even in חבליהם and בניהם the *masc.* is used ἐπικοίνως. We, however, prefer to interpret according to ch. vi. 19, xxiv. 16. Moreover, Bochart is right: *Non hic agitur de otiosa et mere speculativa cognitione, sed de ea cognitione, quæ Deo propria est, qua res omnes non solum novit, sed et dirigit atque gubernat.*

5 *Who hath sent forth the wild ass free,*
  And who loosed the bands of the wild ass,
6 *Whose house I made the steppe,*
  And his dwelling the salt country?
7 *He scorneth the tumult of the city,*
  He heareth not the noise of the driver.
8 *That which is seen upon the mountains is his pasture,*
  And he sniffeth after every green thing.

On the wild ass (not: ass of the forest), *vid.* p. 19, note.[1] In Hebr. and Arab. it is פֶּרֶא (*ferâ* or *himâr el-wahsh, i.e. asinus ferus*), and Aram. עֲרוֹד; the former describes it as a swift-footed animal, the latter as an animal shy and difficult to be tamed by the hand of man ; "Kulan" is its Eastern Asiatic name. LXX. correctly translates : τίς δέ ἐστιν ὁ ἀφεὶς ὄνον ἄγριον ἐλεύθερον. חָפְשִׁי is the *acc.* of the predi-

---

[1] It is a dirty yellow with a white belly, single-hoofed and long-eared ; its hornless head somewhat resembles that of the gazelle, but is much larger; its hair has the dryness of the hair of the deer, and the animal forms the transition from the stag and deer genus to the ass. It is entirely distinct from the *mahâ* or *baqar el-wahsh,* wild ox, whose large soft eyes are so much celebrated by the poets of the steppe. This latter is horned and double-hoofed, and forms the transition from the stag to the ox [distinct from the *ri'm,* ראם, therefore perhaps an antelope of the kind of the Indian *nîlgau,* blue ox, *Portax tragocamelus*]. I have not seen both kinds of animals alive, but I have often seen their skins in the tents of the *Ruwalâ.* Both kinds are remarkable for their very swift running, and it is especially affirmed of the *ferâ* that no rider can overtake it. The poets compare a troop of horsemen that come rushing up and vanish in the next moment to a herd of *ferâ.* In spite of its difficulty and hazardousness, the nomads are passionately given to hunting the wild ass, and the proverb cited by the Kâmûs : *kull es-sêd bigôf el-ferâ* (every hunt sticks in the belly of the *ferâ, i.e.* compared with that, every other hunt is nothing), is perfectly correct. When the approach of a herd, which always consists of several hundred, is betrayed by a cloud of dust which can be seen many miles off, so many horsemen rise up from all sides in pursuit that the animals are usually scattered, and single ones are obtained by the dogs and by shots. The herd is called *gemîle,* and its leader is called *'anûd* (עָנוּד), as with gazelles.—WETZST.

cate (comp. Gen. xxxiii. 2, Jer. xxii. 30). Parallel with
עֲרָבָה (according to its etymon perhaps, land of darkness,
terra incognita) is מְלֵחָה, salt [*adj.*] or (*sc.* אֶרֶץ) a salt land,
i.e. therefore unfruitful and incapable of culture, as the
country round the Salt Sea of Palestine: that the wild ass
even gladly licks the salt or natron of the desert, is a matter
of fact, and may be assumed, since all wild animals that feed
on plants have a partiality, which is based on chemical laws
of life, for licking salt.   On ver. 8*a* Ew. observes, to render
יְתוּר as " what is espied " is insecure, " on account of the structure of the verse " (*Gramm.* S. 419, Anm.). This reason is
unintelligible; and in general there is no reason for rendering
יְתוּר, after LXX., Targ., Jer., and others, as an Aramaic
3 *fut.* with a mere half vowel instead of Kametz before the
tone = יָתוּר, which is without example in Old Testament
Hebrew (for יְהוּא, Eccl. xi. 3, follows the analogy of יְהִי), but
יְתוּר signifies either *abundantia* (after the form יְבוּל, לְחוּם ch.
xx. 23, from יתר, وَتَر, p. 148) or *investigabile*, what can be
searched out (after the form יְקוּם, that which exists, from
תּוּר, تَار, to go about, look about), which, with Olsh. § 212,
and most expositors, we prefer.

9 *Will the oryx be willing to serve thee,*
  Or will he lodge in thy crib?
10 *Canst thou bind the oryx in the furrow with a leading rein,*
   Or will he harrow the valleys, following thee?
11 *Wilt thou trust him because his strength is great,*
   And leave thy labour to him?
12 *Wilt thou confide in him to bring in thy sowing,*
   And to garner thy threshing-floor?

In correct texts רֵים has a *Dagesh* in the *Resh*, and הֲיֹאבֶה
the accent on the *penult.*, as Prov. xi. 21 יִנָּקֶה רַע, and Jer.
xxxix. 12 מְאוּמָה רָע. The tone retreats according to the rule,
Ges. § 29, 3, *b;* and the *Dagesh* is, as also when the second

word begins with an aspirate,[1] *Dag. forte conj.*, which the *Resh* also takes, Prov. xv. 1 מַעֲנֶה־רַּךְ, exceptionally, according to the rule, Ges. § 20, 2, *a*.   In all, it occurs thirteen times with *Dagesh* in the Old Testament—a relic of a mode of pointing which treated the ר (as in Arabic) as a letter capable of being doubled (Ges. § 22, 5), that has been supplanted in the system of pointing that gained the ascendency.   רֵים (Ps. xxii. 22, רֵם) is contracted from רְאֵם (Ps. xcii. 11, *plene*, רְאֵים), which (= רְאֵם) is of like form with رِئْم (Olsh. § 154, *a*).[2]

Such, in the present day in Syria, is the name of the gazelle that is for the most part white with a yellow back and yellow stripes in the face (*Antilope leucoryx*, in distinction from عفري, '*ifrî*, the earth-coloured, dirty-yellow *Antilope oryx*, and حمري, *himrî*, the deer-coloured *Antilope dorcas*); the Talmud also (*b. Zebachim*, 113*b*; *Bathra*, 74*b*) combines ראימא and אורזילא or ארזילא, a gazelle (غَزَال), and therefore reckons the *reêm* to the antelope genus, of which the gazelle is a species; and

---

[1] The National Grammarians call this exception to the rule, that the *muta* is aspirated when the preceding word ends with a vowel, אתי מרחיק (*veniens e longinquo*), *i.e.* the case, where the word ending with a vowel is *Milel*, whether from the very first, or, when the second word is a monosyllable or has the tone on the *penult.*, on account of the accent that has retreated (in order to avoid two syllables with the chief tone coming together); in this case the aspirate, and in general the initial letter (if capable of being doubled) of the second monosyllabic or *penultima-*accented word, takes a *Dagesh*; but this is not without exceptions that are quite as regular.   Regularly, the second word is not dageshed if it begins with וּ, כְ, לְ, בְ, or if the first word is only a bare verb, *e.g.* עָשָׂה לֹּ, or one that has only וְ before it, *e.g.* וְעָשָׂה פֶּסַח; the tone of the first word in both these examples retreats, but without the initial of the second being doubled.   This is supplementary, and as far as necessary a correction, to what is said in *Psalter*, i. 392, Anm.

[2] Since *ra'ima*, inf. *ri'mân*, has the signification *assuescere*, רִים רָאם, רֵימָנא (Targ.) might describe the oryx as a gregarious animal, although all ruminants have this characteristic in common.   On רְאֵם, رِئْم, *vid.* Seetzen's *Reise*, iii. S. 393, Z 9ff., and also iv. 496.

the question, ver. 10*b*, shows that an animal whose home is on the mountains is intended, viz., as Bochart, and recently Schlottm. (making use of an academic treatise of Lichtenstein on the antelopes, 1824), has proved, the oryx, which the LXX. also probably understands when it translates μονοκέρως; for the Talmud. קרש, mutilated from it, is, according to *Chullin*, 59*b*, a one-horned animal, and is more closely defined as טביא דבי עילאי, "gazelle (antelope) of Be (Beth)-Illâi" (comp. Lewysohn, *Zoologie des Talmuds*, 1858, § 146). The oryx also appears on Egyptian monuments sometimes with two horns, but mostly with one variously curled; and both Aristotle[1] and Pliny describe it as a one-horned cloven-hoof; so that one must assent to the supposition of a one-horned variety of the oryx (although as a fact of natural history it is not yet fully established), as then there is really tolerably certain information of a one-horned antelope both in Upper Asia and in Central Africa;[2] and therefore there is sufficient ground for seeking the origin of the tradition of the unicorn in an antelope,—perhaps rather like a horse,—with one horn rising out of the two points of ossification over the frontal suture. The proper buffalo, *Bos bubalus*, cannot therefore

---

[1] *Vid.* Sundevall, *Die Thierarten des Aristoteles* (Stockholm, 1863), S. 64 f.

[2] J. W. von Müller (*Das Einhorn von gesch. u. naturwiss. Standpunkte betrachtet*, 1852) believed that in a horn in the Ambras Collection at Vienna he recognised a horn of the Monocerôs (comp. Fechner's *Centralblatt*, 1854, Nr. 2), but he is hardly right. J. W. von Müller, Francis Galton (*Narrative of an Explorer in Tropical South Africa*, 1853), and other travellers have heard the natives speak ingenuously of the unicorn, but without seeing it themselves. On the other hand, Huc and Gabet (*Journeyings through Mongolia and Thibet*, Germ. edition) tell us "a horn of this animal was sent to Calcutta: it was 50 centimetres long and 11 in circumference; from the root it ran up to a gradually diminishing point. It was almost straight, black, etc. . . . Hodgson, when English consul at Nepal, had the good fortune to obtain an unicorn. . . . It is a kind of antelope, which in southern Thibet, that borders on Nepal, is called *Tschiru*. Hodgson sent a skin and horn to Calcutta; they came from an unicorn that died in the menagerie of the Raja of Nepal." The

be intended, because it only came from India to Western Asia and Europe at a more recent date, but also not any other species whatever of this animal (Carey and others), which is recognisable by its flat horns, which are also near together, and its forbidding, staring, bloodshot eyes; for it is tameable, and is (even in modern Syria) used as a domestic animal. On the other hand there are antelopes which somewhat resemble the horse, others the ox (whence βούβαλος, βούβαλις, is a name for the antelope), others the deer and the ass. Schultens erroneously considers ראם to be the buffalo, being misled by a passage in the Divan of the Hudheilites, which gives the *ri'm* the by-name of *dhu chadam*, *i.e.* oxen-like white-footed, which exactly applies to the *A. oryx* or even the *A. leucoryx;* for the former has white feet and legs striped lengthwise with black stripes, the latter white feet and legs. Just as little reason is there for imagining the rhinoceros after Aquila (and in part Jerome); ῥινοκέρως is nothing but an unhappy rendering of the μονοκέρως of the LXX. The question in ver. 10*b*, as already observed, requires an animal that inhabits the mountains.

On אָבָה, to be willing = to take up, receive, *vid.* p. 125, detailed description follows, and the suggestion is advanced that this *Antilope Hodgsonii*, as it has been proposed to call the *Tschiru*, is the one-horned oryx of the ancients. The existence of one-horned wild sheep (not antelopes), attested by R. von Schlagintweit (*Zoologischer Garten*, 1st year, S. 72), the horn of which consists of two parts gradually growing together, covered by one horn-sheath, does not depreciate the credibility of the account given by Huc-Gabet (to which Prof. Will has called my attention as being the most weighty testimony of the time). Another less minute account is to be found in the Arabic description of a journey (communicated to me by Prof. Fleischer) by Selîm Bisteris (Beirût, 1856): In the menagerie of the Viceroy of Egypt he saw an animal of the colour of a gazelle, but the size and form of an ass, with a long straight horn between the ears, and (what, as he says, seldom go together) with hoofs, viz.—and as the expression حَافِرٌ, horse's hoof (not خُفٌّ, a camel's hoof), also implies—proper, uncloven hoofs,—therefore an one-horned and at the same time one-hoofed antelope.

note. The "furrow (תֶּלֶם, *sulcus*, not *porca*, the ridge between the furrows, *vid.* p. 198) of his cord" is that which it is said to break up by means of the ploughshare, being led by a rein. אַחֲרָיו refers to the leader, who goes just before or at the side; according to Hahn, to one who has finished the sowing which precedes the harrowing; but it is more natural to imagine the leader of the animal that is harrowing, which is certainly not left to itself.   On כִּי, ver. 12*a*, as an exponent of the obj., *vid.* Ew. § 336, *b*. The *Chethib* here uses the *Kal* שׁוּב transitively: to bring back (viz. that which was sown as harvested), which is possible (*vid.* ch. xlii. 10).   גָּרְנֶךָ, ver. 12*b*, is either a locative (into thy threshing-floor) or *acc.* of the obj. *per synecd. continentis pro contento,* as Ruth iii. 2, Matt. iii. 12. The position of the question from beginning to end assumes an animal outwardly resembling the yoke-ox, as the ראם is also elsewhere put with the ox, Deut. xxxiii. 17, Ps. xxix. 6, Isa. xxxiv. 7. But the conclusion at length arrived at by Hahn and in Gesenius' *Handwörterbuch,* that on this very account the buffalo is to be understood, is a mistake: *A. oryx* and *leucoryx* are both (for this very reason not distinguished by the ancients) entirely similar to the ox; they are not only ruminants, like the ox, with a like form of the hoof, but also of a plump form, which makes them appear to be of the ox tribe.

13 *The wing of the ostrich vibrates joyously,*
    Is she pious, wing and feather?
14 *No, she leaveth her eggs in the earth*
    And broodeth over the dust,
15 *Forgetting that a foot may crush them,*
    And the beast of the field trample them.
16 *She treateth her young ones harshly as if they were not hers;*
    In vain is her labour, without her being distressed.
17 *For Eloah hath caused her to forget wisdom,*
    And gave her no share of understanding.

18 *At the time when she lasheth herself aloft,*
She derideth the horse and horseman.

As the wild ass and the ox-like oryx cannot be tamed by man, and employed in his service like the domestic ass and ox, so the ostrich, although resembling the stork in its stilt-like structure, the colour of its feathers, and its gregarious life, still has characteristics totally different from those one ought to look for according to this similarity. רְנָנִים, a wail, prop. a tremulous shrill sound (*vid.* ver. 23), is a name of the female ostrich, whose peculiar cry (*vid.* p. 171) is called in Arabic *zimâr* (זְמָר). נֶעֱלָס (from עָלַס, which in comparison with עָלַץ, עָלַז, rarely occurs) signifies to make gestures of joy. אִם, ver. 13*b*, is an interrogative *an*; חֲסִידָה, *pia*, is a play upon the name of the stork, which is so called : *pia instar ciconiæ* (on this figure of speech, comp. Mehren's *Rhetorik der Araber*, S. 178). כִּי, ver. 14*a*, establishes the negation implied in the question, as *e.g.* Isa. xxviii. 28. The idea is not that the hen-ostrich abandons the hatching of her eggs to the earth (עֲזֹב לְ as Ps. xvi. 10), and makes them " glow over the dust " (Schlottm.), for the maturing energy compensating for the sitting of the parent bird proceeds from the sun's heat, which ought to have been mentioned ; one would also expect a *Hiph.* instead of the *Piel* תְּחַמֵּם, which can be understood only of hatching by her own warmth. The hen-ostrich also really broods herself, although from time to time she abandons the חַמֵּם to the sun.[1] That which contrasts with the φιλοστοργία of the stork, which is here made prominent, is that she lays her eggs in a hole in the ground, and partly, when the nest is full, above round about it, while חסידה ברושים ביתה, Ps. civ. 17. רננים is

---

[1] It does, however, as it appears, actually occur, that the female leaves the work of hatching to the sun by day, and to the male at night, and does not sit at all herself ; *vid.* Funke's *Naturgeschichte*, revised by Taschenberg (1864), S. 243 f.

construed in accordance with its meaning as *fem. sing.*, Ew.
§ 318, *a*. Since she acts thus, what next happens consistently
therewith is told by the not aoristic but only consecutive
וַתִּשְׁכַּח: and so she forgets that the foot may crush (זוּר, to
press together, break by pressure, as הַזּוּרָה, Isa. lix. 5 = הַזּוּרָה,
that which is crushed, comp. לָנֶה = לָנָה, Zech. v. 4) them (*i.e.*
the eggs, Ges. § 146, 3), and the beast of the field may
trample them down, crush them (דּוּשׁ as داس, to crush by
treading upon anything, to tread out).

Ver. 16. The difficulty of הִקְשִׁיחַ (from קָשָׁה, قسا, hardened
from קָשָׁה, قسا) being used of the hen-ostrich in the *masc.*,
may be removed by the pointing הַקְשִׁיחַ (Ew.); but this
alteration is unnecessary, since the Hebr. also uses the *masc.*
for the *fem.* where it might be regarded as impossible (*vid.*
ver. 3*b*, and comp. *e.g.* Isa. xxxii. 11 sq.). Jer. translates
correctly according to the sense: *quasi non sint sui*, but לְ is
not directly equivalent to כְּ (*vid.* vol. i. pp. 325, 398, note 1);
what is meant is, that by the harshness of her conduct she
treats her young as not belonging to her, so that they become
strange to her, Ew. § 217, *d*. In ver. 16*b* the accentuation
varies: in vain (לְרִיק with *Rebia mugrasch*) is her labour
that is devoid of anxiety; or: in vain is her labour (לריק with
Tarcha, יְגִיעָהּ with *Munach vicarium*) without anxiety (on her
part); or: in vain is her labour (לריק with *Mercha*, יגיעה with
Rebia mugrasch), yet she is without anxiety. The middle of
these renderings (לְרִיק in all of them, like Isa. xlix. 4 = לְרִיק, Isa.
lxv. 23 and freq.) seems to us the most pleasing: the labour
of birth and of the brooding undertaken in places where the
eggs are put beyond the danger of being crushed, is without
result, without the want of success distressing her, since she
does not anticipate it, and therefore also takes no measures to
prevent it. The eggs that are only just covered with earth,
or that lie round about the nest, actually become a prey to
the jackals, wild-cats, and other animals; and men can get

them for themselves one by one, if they only take care to
prevent their footprints being recognised; for if the ostrich
observes that its nest is discovered, it tramples upon its own
eggs, and makes its nest elsewhere (Schlottm., according to
Lichtenstein's *Südafrik. Reise*). That it thus abandons its
eggs to the danger of being crushed and to plunder, arises,
according to ver. 17, from the fact that God has caused it to
forget wisdom, *i.e.* as ver. 17*b* explains, has extinguished in
it, deprived it of, the share thereof (ב as Isa. liii. 12*a*, LXX.
ἐν, as Acts viii. 21) which it might have had. It is only one
of the stupidities of the ostrich that is made prominent here;
the proverbial *ahmaq min en-naʿáme*, " more foolish than the
ostrich," has its origin in more such characteristics. But if
the care with which other animals guard their young ones is
denied to it, it has in its stead another remarkable characteristic: at the time when (בָּעֵת here followed by an elliptical
relative clause, which is clearly possible, just as with בְּעֵת, ch.
vi. 17) it stretches (itself) on high, *i.e.* it starts up with
alacrity from its ease (on the radical signification of הִמְרִיא =
הִמְרָה, *vid.* p. 2, note), and hurries forth with a powerful flapping of its wings, half running half flying, it derides the
horse and its rider—they do not overtake it, it is the swiftest
of all animals; wherefore اعدى من الظليم (zalim, equivalent
to *delim* according to a less exact pronunciation, *supra*, p. 171,
note) and انفر من النعامة, fleeter than the ostrich, is just as
proverbial as the above احمق من النعامة; and " on ostrich's
wings " is equivalent to driving along with incomparable
swiftness. Moreover, on תַּמְרִיא and תִּשְׂחַק, which refer to
the female, it is to be observed that she is very anxious, and
deserts everything in her fright, while the male ostrich does
not forsake his young, and flees no danger.[1]

---

[1] We take this remark from Doumas, *Horse of the Sahara.* The following contribution from Wetzstein only came to hand after the exposition was completed: " The female ostriches are called רְנָנִים not from

19 *Dost thou give to the horse strength?*
   Dost thou clothe his neck with flowing hair?
20 *Dost thou cause him to leap about like the grasshopper?*
   The noise of his snorting is a terror!
21 *He paweth the ground in the plain, and boundeth about with*
       strength.
   He advanceth to meet an armed host.
22 *He laugheth at fear, and is not affrighted,*
   And turneth not back from the sword.
23 *The quiver rattleth over him,*
   The glittering lance and spear.
24 *With fierceness and rage he swalloweth the ground,*
   And standeth not still, when the trumpet soundeth.

the whirring of their wings when flapped about, but from their piercing
screeching cry when defending their eggs against beasts of prey (chiefly
hyænas), or when searching for the male bird.   Now they are called *rubd*,
from sing. *rubda* (instead of *rabdâ*), from the black colour of their long
wing-feathers ; for only the male, which is called חָיִק (pronounce hêtsh),
has white.   The ostrich-tribe has the name of בַּת הַיְּעָנָה (بِنْت الْوَعْنَة),
'inhabitant of the desert,' because it is only at home in the most lonely
parts of the steppe, in perfectly barren deserts.   *Neshwân* the Himjarite,
in his '*Shems el-'olûm*' (MSS. in the Royal Library at Berlin, *sectio
Wetzst. I.* No. 149, Bd. i. f. 110*b*), defines the word *el-wa'na* by : אָרֵץ
בִּיצָא לֹא תַנְבַת שִׂיא, a white (chalky or sandy) district, which brings
forth nothing ; and the Kâmûs explains it by אָרֵץ צַלְבָּה, a hard (unfruitful) district.   In perfect analogy with the Hebr. the Arabic calls the
ostrich *abu* (and *umm*) *es-sahârâ*, 'possessor of the sterile deserts.'   The
name יְעָנִים, Lam. iv. 3, is perfectly correct, and corresponds to the form

יְעָלִים (steinbocks) ; the form פָּעֵל (فَعِل) is frequently the *Nisbe* of פָּעַל
and פְּעָלָה, according to which בַּת הַיְּעָנָה = יָעֵן and בַּת הַיְּעָנָה = יָעֵל,
'inhabitant of the inaccessible rocks.'   Hence, says *Neshwân* (against
the non-Semite *Firûzâbâdi*, *wa'l* יָעֵל and *wa'la*) is exclusively the high
place of the rocks, and *wa'il* (יָעֵל) exclusively the steinbock.   The most
common Arabic name of the ostrich is *na'âme*, נְעָמָה, collective *na'âm*,
from the softness (*nu'ûma*, נְעוּמָה) of its feathers, with which the Arab
women (in Damascus frequently) stuff cushions and pillows.   *Umm*

25 *He saith at every blast of the trumpet: Ha, ha !*
And from afar he scenteth the battle,
The thundering of the captains and the shout of war.

After the ostrich, which, as the Arabs say, is composed of
the nature of a bird and a camel, comes the horse in its
heroic beauty, and impetuous lust for the battle, which is
likewise an evidence of the wisdom of the Ruler of the world
—a wisdom which demands the admiration of men.   This
passage of the book of Job, says K. Löffler, in his *Gesch.
des Pferdes* (1863), is the oldest and most beautiful description of the horse.   It may be compared to the praise of the
horse in Hammer-Purgstall's *Duftkörner ;* it deserves more

thelâthin, 'mother of thirty,' is the name of the female ostrich, because as
a rule she lays thirty eggs.   The ostrich egg is called in the steppe *dahwa,*
דַּחְוָה (coll. *dahû*), a word that is certainly very ancient.   Nevertheless the
Hauranites prefer the word *medha,* מַדְרָחָה.   A place hollowed out in the
ground serves as a nest, which the ostrich likes best to dig in the hot
sand, on which account they are very common in the sandy tracts of *Ard
ed-Dehânâ* (דַּהְנָא), between the *Shemmar* mountains and the *Sawâd*
(Chaldæa).   Thence at the end of April come the ostrich hunters with
their spoil, the hides of the birds together with the feathers, to Syria.
Such an unplucked hide is called *gizze* (גִּזֶּה).   The hunters inform us that
the female sits alone on the nest from early in the day until evening, and
from evening until early in the morning with the male, which wanders
about throughout the day.   The statement that the ostrich does not sit
on its eggs, is perhaps based on the fact that the female frequently, and
always before the hunters, forsakes the eggs during the first period of
brooding.   Even vers. 14 and 15 do not say more than this.   But when
the time of hatching (called *el-faqs,* פְּקֵץ) is near, the hen no longer
leaves the eggs.   The same observation is also made with regard to the
partridge of Palestine (*el-hagel,* חָגֵל), which has many other characteristics in common with the ostrich.   That the ostrich is accounted stupid
(ver. 17) may arise from the fact, that when the female has been
frightened from the eggs she always seeks out the male with a loud cry ;
she then, as the hunters unanimously assert, brings him forcibly back to
the nest (hence its Arabic name *zalîm,* ' the violent one').   During the
interval the hunter has buried himself in the sand, and on their arrival,
by a good shot often kills both together in the nest.   It may also be

than this latter the praise of majestic simplicity, which is
the first feature of classic superiority. Jer. falsely renders
ver. 19*b*: *aut circumdabis collo ejus hinnitum;* as Schlottm., who
also wishes to be so understood : Dost thou adorn his neck
with the voice of thunder ? The neck (צַוָּאר, prop. the twister,
as Persic *gerdân, gerdan,* from צוּר, صار, to twist by pressure,
to turn, bend, as Pers. from *gerdîden,* to turn one's self,
twist) has nothing to do with the voice of neighing. But
רַעְמָה also does not signify dignity (Ew. 113, *d*), but the
mane, and is not from רָם = רָאַם = רָעַם, the hair of the mane,
as being above, like λοφιά, but from רָעַם, *tremere,* the mane
as quivering, trembling (Eliz. Smith : the shaking mane) ;

accounted as stupidity, that, when the wind is calm, instead of flying
before the riding hunters, the bird tries to hide itself behind a mound or
in the hollows of the ground. But that, when escape is impossible, it is
said to try to hide its head in the sand, the hunters regard as an absurdity.
If the wind aids it, the fleeing ostrich spreads out the feathers of its tail
like a sail, and by constantly steering itself with its extended wings, it
escapes its pursuers with ease. The word הַמְרִיא, ver. 18, appears to be
a hunting expression, and (without an *accus. objecti*) to describe this
spreading out of the feathers, therefore to be perfectly synonymous with
the תַעְרִישׁ (تعريش) of the ostrich hunters of the present day. Thus
sings the poet *Râshid* of the hunting race of the S*ulubât*: ' And the
head (of the bride with its loosened locks) resembles the (soft and black)
feathers of the ostrich-hen, when she spreads them out (*'arrashannâ*). |
They saw the hunter coming upon them where there was no hiding-place,
| And stretched their legs as they fled.' The prohibition to eat the
ostrich in the Thora (Lev. xi. 16 ; Deut. xiv. 15) is perhaps based upon
the cruelty of the hunt ; for it is with the rarest exceptions always killed
only on its eggs. The female, which, as has been said already, does not
flee towards the end of the time of brooding, stoops on the approach of
the hunter, inclines the head on one side and looks motionless at her
enemy. Several Beduins have said to me, that a man must have a hard
heart to fire under such circumstances. If the bird is killed, the hunter
covers the blood with sand, puts the female again upon the eggs, buries
himself at some distance in the sand, and waits till evening, when the
male comes, which is now shot likewise, beside the female. The Mosaic
law might accordingly have forbidden the hunting of the ostrich from
the same feeling of humanity which unmistakeably regulated it in other
decisions (as Ex. xxiii. 19, Deut. xxii. 6 sq., Lev. xxii. 28, and freq.).

like φόβη, according to Kuhn, cogn. with σόβη; the tail, from φοβεῖν (σοβεῖν), to wag, shake, scare, comp. ἀΐσσεσθαι of the mane, *Il.* vi. 510.

Ver. 20*a*. The motion of the horse, which is intended by תַּרְעִישֶׁנּוּ (רָעַשׁ, رعس ,رعش, *tremere, trepidare*), is determined according to the comparison with the grasshopper : what is intended is a curved motion forwards in leaps, now to the right, now to the left, which is called the caracol, a word used in horsemanship, borrowed from the Arab. *hargala-l-farasu* (comp. חַרְגֹּל), by means of the Moorish Spanish ; moreover, رعس is used of the run of the ostrich and the flight of the dove in such "successive lateral and oblique motions" (Carey). נַחַר, ver. 20*b*, is not the neighing of the horse, but its snorting through the nostrils (comp. Arab. *nachîr*, snoring, a rattling in the throat), Greek φρύαγμα, Lat. *fremitus* (comp. Æschylus, *Septem c. Th.* 374, according to the text of Hermann : ἵππος χαλινῶν δ'ὡς κατασθμαίνων βρέμει) ; הוֹד, however, might signify pomp (his pompous snorting), but perhaps has its radical signification, according to which it corresponds to the Arab. *hawîd,* and signifies a loud strong sound, as the peal of thunder (*hawîd er-raʿd*), the howling of the stormy wind (*hawîd er-rijâ*h), and the like.[1] The substantival clause is intended to affirm that its dull-toned snort causes or spreads terror. In ver. 21*a* the

---

[1] A verse of a poem of Ibn-Dûchî in honour of Dôkân ibn-Gendel runs : Before the crowding (*lekdata*) of Taijâr the horses fled repulsed, | And thou mightest hear the sound of the bell-carriers (*hawîda mubershemât*) of the warriors (*el-menâir*, prop. one who thrusts with the lance). Here *hawîd* signifies the sound of the bells which those who wish to announce themselves as warriors hang about their horses, to draw the attention of the enemy to them. *Mubershemât* are the mares that carry the *burêshimân, i.e.* the bells. The meaning therefore is : thou couldst hear this sound, which ought only to be heard in the fray, in flight, when the warriors consecrated to death fled as cowards. Taijâr (Têjâr) is Sâlih the son of Canaʿan (died about 1815), mentioned in vol. i. p. 390, note 1, a great warrior of the wandering tribe of the ʿAneze.—WETZST.

plur. alternates with the *sing.*, since, as it appears, the representation of the many pawing hoofs is blended with that of the pawing horse, according to the well-known line,

Quadrupedante putrem sonitu quatit ungula campum
(VIRGIL, *Æn.* viii. 596) ;

or, since this is said of the galloping horse, according to the likewise Virgilian line,

Cavatque
Tellurem, et solido graviter sonat ungula cornu
(*Georg.* iii. 87 sq.).

חָפַר is, as the Arab. hâfir, hoof, shows, the proper word for the horse's impatient pawing of the ground (whence it then, as in ver. 29, signifies *rimari, scrutari*). עֵמֶק is the plain as the place of contest ; for the description, as now becomes still more evident, refers to the war-horse. The verb שִׂישׂ (שׂוּשׂ) has its radical signification *exsultare* (comp. شاص, σκιρτᾶν, of the fœtus) here; and since בְּכֹחַ, not בַּפֹּחַ, is added to it, it is not to be translated : it rejoices in its strength, but : it prances or is joyous with strength, LXX. γαυριᾷ ἐν ἰσχύϊ. The difference between the two renderings is, however, scarcely perceptible. נֶשֶׁק, armament, ver. 21b, is meton. the armed host of the enemy ; אַשְׁפָּה, "the quiver," is, however, not used metonymically for the arrows of the enemy whizzing about the horse (Schult.), but ver. 23 is the concluding description of the horse that rushes on fearlessly, proudly, and impetuously in pursuit, under the rattle and glare of the equipment of its rider (Schlottm. and others). רָנָה (cogn. of רָנַן), of the rattling of the quiver, as Arab. *ranna, ranima,* of the whirring of the bow when the arrow is despatched; to point it תִּרֻנֶּה (Prov. i. 20, viii. 3), instead of תִּרְנֶה, would be to deprive the language of a word supported by the dialects (*vid.* Ges. *Thes.*). On ver. 24a we may compare the Arab. *iltahama-l-farasu-l-arda,* the horse swallows up the ground, whence *lahimm, lahîm,* a swallower

= swift-runner; so here: with boisterous fierceness and
angry impatience (בְּרַעַשׁ וְרֹגֶז) it swallows up the ground, *i.e.*
passes so swiftly over it that long pieces vanish so rapidly
before it, as though it greedily sucked them up (גִּמֵּא intensive of גָּמָא, whence גֹּמֶא, the water-sucking papyrus); a somewhat differently applied figure is *nahab-el-arda*, *i.e.* according
to Silius' expression, *rapuit campum*. The meaning of ver.
24b is, as in Virgil, *Georg.* iii. 83 sq. :

> *Tum si qua sonum procul arma dedere,*
> *Stare loco nescit ;*

and in Æschylus, *Septem*, 375 : ὅστις βοὴν σάλπιγγος ὁρμαί-
νει (Hermann, ὀργαίνει) μένων (impatiently awaiting the call
of the trumpet). הֶאֱמִין signifies here to show stability (*vid.*
Genesis, S. 367f.) in the first physical sense (Bochart,
Rosenm., and others): it does not stand still, *i.e.* will not be
held, when (כִּי, *quum*) the sound of the war-trumpet, *i.e.*
when it sounds. שׁוֹפָר is the signal-trumpet when the army
was called together, *e.g.* Judg. iii. 27; to gather the army
that is in pursuit of the enemy, 2 Sam. ii. 28; when the
people rebelled, 2 Sam. xx. 1; when the army was dismissed
at the end of the war, 2 Sam. xx. 22; when forming for
defence and for assault, *e.g.* Amos iii. 6; and in general the
signal of war, Jer. iv. 19. As often as this is heard (בְּדֵי, in
sufficiency, *i.e.* happening at any time = *quotiescunque*), it
makes known its lust of war by a joyous neigh, even from
afar, before the collision has taken place; it scents (*præsagit*
according to Pliny's expression) the approaching conflict,
(scents even in anticipation) the thundering command of
the chiefs that may soon be heard, and the cry of battle
giving loose to the assault. "Although," says Layard (*New*
Discoveries, p. 330), "docile as a lamb, and requiring no
other guide than the halter, when the Arab mare hears the
war-cry of the tribe, and sees the quivering spear of her
rider, her eyes glitter with fire, her blood-red nostrils open

wide, her neck is nobly arched, and her tail and mane are
raised and spread out to the wind.　The Bedouin proverb
says, that a high-bred mare when at full speed should hide
her rider between her neck and her tail."

> 26 *Doth the hawk fly by thy wisdom,*
> *Doth it spread its wings towards the south?*
> 27 *Or is it at thy command that the eagle soareth aloft,*
> *And buildeth its nest on high?*
> 28 *It inhabiteth the rock, and buildeth its nest*
> *Upon the crag of the rock and fastness.*
> 29 *From thence it seeketh food,*
> *Its eyes see afar off.*
> 30 *And its young ones suck up blood;*
> *And where the slain are, there is it.*

The ancient versions are unanimous in testifying that,
according to the signification of the root, נֵץ signifies the
hawk (which is significant in the Hieroglyphics) : the soaring
one, the high-flyer (comp. نَصَّ, to rise, struggle forwards, and
نَصَّ, to raise the wings for flight).　The *Hiph.* יַאֲבֶר־ (jussive
form in the question, as ch. xiii. 27) might signify : to get
feathers, *plumescere* (Targ., Jer.), but that gives a tame
question; wherefore Gregory understands the *plumescit* of the
Vulgate of moulting, for which purpose the hawk seeks the
sunny side.　But הַאֲבִיר alone, by itself, cannot signify "to
get new feathers;" moreover, an annual moulting is common
to all birds, and prominence is alone given to the new feather-
ing of the eagle in the Old Testament, Ps. ciii. 5, Mic. i. 16,
comp. Isa. xl. 31 (LXX. πτεροφυήσουσιν ὡς ἀετοί).[1]　Thus,
then, the point of the question will lie in לְתֵימָן : the hawk is

---

[1] Less unfavourable to this rendering is the following, that אֶבְרָה
signifies the long feathers, and אֵבֶר the wing that is composed of them

a bird of passage, God has endowed it with instinct to migrate to the south as the winter season is approaching.

In vers. 27 sqq. the circle of the native figures taken from animal life, which began with the lion, the king of quadrupeds, is now closed with the eagle, the king of birds. It is called נֶשֶׁר, from נָשַׁר, نسر, vellere; as also vultur (by virtue of a strong power of assimilation = vultor) is derived from vellere, —a common name of the golden eagle, the lamb's vulture, the carrion-kite (Cathartes percnopterus), and indeed also of other kinds of kites and falcons. There is nothing to prevent our understanding the eagle κατ᾽ ἐξοχήν, viz. the golden eagle (Aquila chrysaëtos), in the present passage; for even to this, corpses, though not already putrified, are a welcome prey. In ver. 27b we must translate either: and is it at thy command that . . .? or: is it so that (as in הֲכִי) at thy command . . .? The former is more natural here. מְצוּדָה, ver. 28b, signifies prop. specula (from צוּד, to spy); then, however, as Arab. masâd (referred by the original lexicons to masada), the high hill, and the mountain-top. The rare form יַעְלְעוּ, for which Ges., Olsh., and others wish to read לַעְלְעוּ or יְלַעְלְעוּ (from לוּעַ, deglutire), is to be derived from עָלַע, a likewise secondary form out of עִלְעֵל (from עוּל, to suck, to give suck[1]), like שָׁרַשׁ out of שַׁרְשֵׁר (from שָׁרַר, سر, to make firm), Ew. § 118, a, comp. Fürst, Handwörterbuch, sub עוּל, since instances

(perhaps, since the Talm. אֲבָרִים signifies wings and limbs, artus, from אָבַר = הָבַר, هبر, to divide, furnish with joints), although נוֹצָה (from נָצָה, to fly) is the more general designation of the feathers of birds.

[1] The Arab. ʿalla does not belong here: it gains the signification iterum bibere from the primary signification of " coming over or upon anything," which branches out in various ways: to take a second, third, etc., drink after the first. More on this point on Isa. iii. 4.

Supplementary note: The quadriliteral עִלְעֵל to be supposed, is not to be derived from עָלַל, and is not, as it recently has been, to be compared with عل, "to drink." This Arab. verb does not signify "to drink" at all, are wanting in favour of עֲלֵי being formed out of לְעֲלֵי (*Jesurun*, p. 164). Schult. not inappropriately compares even גלל = נלגל in גָּלְגְּתָא, Γολγοθᾶ = גָּלְגָּלְתָּא. The concluding words, ver. 30*b*, are perhaps echoed in Matt. xxiv. 28. High up on a mountain-peak the eagle builds its eyrie, and God has given it a remarkably sharp vision, to see far into the depth below the food that is there for it and its young ones. Not merely from the valley in the neighbourhood of its eyrie, but often from distant plains, which lie deep below on the other side of the mountain range, it seizes its prey, and rises with it even to the clouds, and bears it home to its nest.[1] Thus does God work exceeding strangely, but wondrously, apparently by contradictions, but in truth most harmoniously and wisely, in the natural world.

[Then Jehovah answered Job, and said :]
Ch. xl. 2 *Will now the censurer contend with the Almighty?*
Let the instructor of Eloah answer it !

With ver. 1, ch. xxxviii. 1 is again taken up, because the speech of Jehovah has now in some measure attained the end which was assigned to it as an answer to Job's outburst of censure. רֹב is *inf. abs.*, as Judg. xi. 25; it is left to the hearer to give to the simple verbal notion its syntactic relation in accordance with the connection ; here it stands in the sense of the *fut.* (comp. 2 Kings iv. 43): *num litigabit*, Ges. § 131, 4, *b.* The *inf. abs.* is followed by יִסּוֹר as subj., which

but, among many other branchings out of its general primary signification, related to עלה, علّ, also signifies: "to take a second, third, etc., drink
after the first," concerning which more details will be given elsewhere.
עֲלֵעֵל goes back to עֵל, *lactare*, with the middle vowel, whence also עֲוִיל,
ch. xvi. 11, xii. 18, xxi. 11 (which see). The Hauran dialect has ʿâlâl
(plur. ʿawâlîl), like the Hebr. עֹלֵל (עוֹלָל = מְעוֹלָל), in the signification
juvenis, and especially *juvencus* (comp. *infra*, p. 359, note 1, "but they are
heifers," Arab. *illâ ʿawâlîl*).
[1] *Vid.* the beautiful description in Charles Boner's *Forest Creatures*, 1861.

(after the form שִׁכּוֹר) signifies a censurer and fault-finder,
μωμητής. The question means, will Job persist in this contending with God? He who sets God right, as though he
knew everything better than He, shall answer the questions
put before him.

> [Then Job answered Jehovah, and said:]
> 4 *Behold, I am too mean: what shall I answer Thee?*
>   *I lay my hand upon my mouth.*
> 5 *Once have I spoken, and will not begin again;*
>   *And twice—I will do it no more.*

He is small, *i.e.* not equal to the task imposed, therefore he
keeps his mouth firmly closed (comp. ch. xxi. 5, xxix. 9), for
whatever he might say would still not be to the point. Once
he has dared to criticise God's doings; a second time (שְׁתַּיִם =
שֵׁנִית, Ges. § 120, 5) he ventures it no more, for God's wondrous wisdom and all-careful love dazzle him, and he gladly
bows.

But how? Is not the divine speech altogether different
from what one ought to expect? One expects to hear from
the mouth of Jehovah something unheard of in the previous
course of the drama, and in this expectation we find ourselves
disappointed at the outset. For one need only look back and
read ch. ix. 4–10, where Job acknowledges and describes God
as a wise and mighty Lord over the natural world, especially
as an irresistible Ruler over everything great in it; ch.
xii. 7–10, where he refers to the creatures of the sky and
deep as proofs of God's creative power; ch. xii. 11–25, where
he sketches the grandest picture of God's terrible doings in
nature and among men; ch. xxvi. 5–14, where he praises
God as the Creator and Lord of all things, and describes
what he says concerning Him as only a faint echo of the
thunder of His might; ch. xxviii. 23 sqq., where he ascribes
absolute wisdom to Him as the Creator and Ruler of the

world. If one ponders these passages of Job's speeches, he will not be able to say that the speech of Jehovah, in the exhibition of the creative power and wisdom of God, which is its theme, would make Job conscious of anything which was previously unknown to him; and it is accordingly asked, What, then, is there that is new in the speech of Jehovah by which the great effect is brought about, that Job humbles himself in penitence, and becomes ready for the act of redemption which follows?

It has indeed never occurred to Job to desire to enter into a controversy with God concerning the works of creation; he is far from the delusion of being able to stand such a test; he knows in general, that if God were willing to contend with him, he would not be able to answer God one in a thousand, ch. ix. 3. And yet God closely questioned him, and thereby Job comes to the perception of his sin—how comes it to pass? Has the plot of the drama perhaps failed in this point? Has the poet made use of means unsuited to the connection of the whole, to bring about the needful effect, viz. the repentance of Job,—because, perhaps, the store of his thoughts was exhausted? But this poet is not so poor, and we shall therefore be obliged to try and understand the disposition of the speech of Jehovah before we censure it.

When one of Job's last words before the appearing of Jehovah was the word שׁדּי יענני, Job thereby desired God's decision concerning the testimony of his innocence. This wish is in itself not sinful; yea, it is even a fruit of his hidden faith, when he casts the look of hope away from his affliction and the accusation of the friends, into the future to God as his Vindicator and Redeemer. But that wish becomes sinful when he looks upon his affliction as a *de facto* accusation on the part of God, because he cannot think of suffering and sin as separable, and because he is conscious of his innocence, looks upon it as a decree of God, his opponent and his enemy, which is irreconcilable with the divine justice. This Job's condition of conflict and temptation is the prevailing one; his faith is beclouded, and breaks through the night which hangs over him only in single rays. The result of this condition of conflict is the sinful character which that wish assumes: it becomes a challenge to God, since Job directs against God Himself the accusation which the friends have directed against him, and asserts his ability to carry through his good cause even if God would enter with him into a judicial contention; he becomes a יסור and מוכיח אלוה, and raises himself above God, because he thinks he has Him for an enemy who is his best friend. This defiance is, however, not common godlessness; on the contrary, Job is really the innocent servant of God, and his defiant tone is only the result of a false conception which the tempted one indulges respecting the Author of his affliction. So, then, this defiance has not taken full possession of Job's mind; on the contrary, the faith which lays firm hold on confidence in the God whom he does not comprehend, is in conflict against it; and this conflict tends in the course of the drama, the nearer it comes to the catastrophe, still nearer to the victory, which only awaits a decisive stroke in order to be complete. Therefore Jehovah yields to Job's longing שדי יענני, in as far as He really answers Job; and even that this takes place, and that, although out of the storm, it nevertheless takes place, not in a way to crush and destroy, but to instruct and convince, and displaying a loving condescension, is an indirect manifestation that Job is not regarded by God as an evil-doer mature for judgment. But that folly and temerity by which the servant of God is become unlike himself must notwithstanding be destroyed; and before Job can realize God as his Witness and Redeemer, in which character his faith in its brighter moments has foreseen Him, his sinful censuring and blaming of God must be blotted out by penitence; and with it at the same time his foolish imagination, by which his faith has been almost overwhelmed, must be destroyed, viz. the imagination that his affliction is a *hostile* dispensation of God.

And by what means is Job brought to the penitent recognition of his gloomy judgment concerning the divine decree, and of his contending with God? Is it, perhaps, by God's admitting to him what really is the case: that he does not suffer as a sinner the punishment of his sin, but showing at the same time that the decree of suffering is not an unjust one, because its design is not hostile? No, indeed, for Job is not worthy that his cause should be acknowledged on the part of God before he has come to a penitent recognition of the wrong by which he has sinned against God. God would be encouraging self-righteousness if He should give Job the testimony of his innocence, before the sin of vainglory, into which Job has fallen in the consciousness of his innocence, is changed to *humility*, by which all uprightness that is acceptable with God is tested. Therefore, contrary to expectation, God begins to speak with Job about totally different matters from His justice or injustice in reference to his affliction. Therein already lies a deep humiliation for Job. But a still deeper one in God's turning, as it were, to the *abecedarium naturæ*, and putting the censurer of His doings to the blush. That God is the almighty and allwise Creator and Ruler of the world, that the natural world is exalted above human knowledge and power, and is full of marvellous divine creations and arrangements, full of things mysterious and incomprehensible to ignorant and feeble man, Job knows even before God speaks, and yet he must now hear it, because he does not know it rightly; for the nature with which he is acquainted as the herald of the creative and governing power of God, is also the preacher of humility; and exalted as God the Creator and Ruler of the natural world is above Job's censure, so is He also as the Author of his affliction. That which is new, therefore, in the speech of Jehovah, is not the proof of God's exaltation in itself, but the relation to the mystery of his affliction, and to his conduct towards God in this his affliction, in which Job is necessitated to place perceptions not in themselves strange to him. He who cannot answer a single one of those questions taken from the natural kingdom, but, on the contrary, must everywhere admire and adore the power and wisdom of God— he must appear as an insignificant fool, if he applies them to his limited judgment concerning the Author of his affliction.

The fundamental tone of the divine speech is the thought, that the divine working in nature is infinitely exalted above human knowledge and power, and that consequently man must renounce all claim to better knowledge and right of contention in the presence of the divine dispensations. But at the same time, within the range of this general thought, it is also in particular shown how nature reflects the goodness of God as well as His wisdom (He has restrained the destructive power of the waters, He also sendeth rain upon the steppe, though untenanted by man); how that which accomplishes the purposes for which it was in itself designed, serves higher purposes in the moral order of the world (the dawn of day puts an end to the works of darkness, snow and hail serve as instruments of divine judgments); how divine providence extends to all creatures, and always according to their need (He provides the lion its prey, He satisfies the ravens that cry to Him); and how He has distributed His manifold gifts in a way often paradoxical to man, but in truth worthy of admiration (to the steinbock ease in bringing forth and growth without toil, to the wild ass freedom, to the antelope untameable fleetness, to the ostrich freedom from anxiety about its young and swiftness, to the horse heroic and proud lust for the battle, to the hawk the instinct of

migration, to the eagle a lofty nest and a piercing sight).
Everywhere the wonders of God's power and wisdom, and
in fact of His goodness abounding in power, and His providence abounding in wisdom, infinitely transcend Job's knowledge and capacity. Job cannot answer one of all these
questions, but yet he feels to what end they are put to him.
The God who sets bounds to the sea, who refreshes the
desert, who feeds the ravens, who cares for the gazelle in
the wilderness and the eagle in its eyrie, is the same God
who now causes him seemingly thus unjustly to suffer. But
if the former is worthy of adoration, the latter will also be so.
Therefore Job confesses that he will henceforth keep silence,
and solemnly promises that he will now no longer contend
with Him. From the marvellous in nature he divines that
which is marvellous in his affliction. His humiliation under
the mysteries of nature is at the same time humiliation
under the mystery of his affliction; and only now, when he
penitently reveres the mystery he has hitherto censured, is
it time that its inner glory should be unveiled to him. The
bud is mature, and can now burst forth, in order to disclose
the blended colours of its matured beauty.

*The Second Speech of Jehovah, and Job's Second Penitent
Answer.*—Chap. xl. 6–xlii. 6.

Schema: 6. 10. 9. 12. 10. 9. | 4. 6. 6. 8. 8. 8. 10. | 6. 6.

[Then Jehovah answered Job out of the storm, and said:]
This second time also Jehovah speaks to Job out of the
storm; not, however, in wrath, but in the profound condescension of His majesty, in order to deliver His servant
from dark imaginings, and to bring him to free and joyous
knowledge. He does not demand blind subjection, but free
submission; He does not extort an acknowledgment of His
greatness, but it is effected by persuasion. It becomes manifest

that God is much more forbearing and compassionate than
men.   Observe the friends, the defenders of the divine
honour, these sticklers for their own orthodoxy, how they
rave against Job!   How much better is it to fall into the
hands of the living God, than into the hands of man!   For
God is truth and love; but men have at one time love without truth, at another truth without love, since they either
connive at one or anathematize him.   When a man who,
moreover, like Job, is a servant of God, fails in one point,
or sins, men at once condemn him altogether, and admit
nothing good in him; God, however, discerns between good
and evil, and makes the good a means of freeing the man
from the evil.   He also does not go rashly to work, but waits,
like an instructor, until the time of action arrives.   How
long He listens to Job's bold challenging, and keeps silence!
And then, when He does begin to speak, He does not cast
Job to the ground by His authoritative utterances, but deals
with him as a child; He examines him from the catechism
of nature, and allows him to say for himself that he fails in
this examination.   In this second speech He acts with him
as in the well-known poem of Hans Sachs with St Peter:
He offers him to take the government of the world for once
instead of Himself.   Here also He produces conviction; here
also His mode of action is a deep lowering of Himself.
It is Jehovah, the God, who at length begets Himself in
humanity, in order to convince men of His love.

7 *Gird up thy loins manfully :*
   I will question thee, and do thou answer me !
8 *Wilt thou altogether annul my right,*
   Condemn me, that thou mayest be righteous?
9 *And hast thou then an arm like God,*
   And canst thou with the voice thunder like Him?

The question with הַאַף stands to ch. xl. 2 in the relation of a climax: Job contended not alone with God, which is in itself wrong, let it be whatsoever it may; he went so far as to lose sight of the divine justice in the government of the world, and in order not to be obliged to give up his own righteousness, so far as to doubt the divine. וְאִם, ver. 9*a*, is also interrogative, as ch. viii. 3, xxi. 4, xxxiv. 17, comp. xxxix. 13, not expressive of a wish, as ch. xxxiv. 16. In the government of the world, God shows His arm, He raises His voice of thunder: canst thou perhaps—asks Jehovah—do the like, thou who seemest to imagine thou couldst govern the world more justly, if thou hadst to govern it? וּבְקוֹל כָּמֹהוּ are to be combined: of like voice to Him; the translation follows the accents (וּבקול with *Rebia mugrasch*).

> 10 *Deck thyself then with pomp and dignity,*
> *And in glory and majesty clothe thyself!*
> 11 *Let the overflowings of thy wrath pour forth,*
> *And behold all pride, and abase it!*
> 12 *Behold all pride, bring it low,*
> *And cast down the evil-doers in their place;*
> 13 *Hide them in the dust together,*
> *Bind their faces in secret:*
> 14 *Then I also will praise thee,*
> *That thy right hand obtaineth thee help.*

He is for once to put on the robes of the King of kings (עֲדָה, comp. עָטָה, to wrap round, Ps. civ. 2), and send forth his wrath over pride and evil-doing, for their complete removal. הֵפִיץ, *effundere, diffundere*, as Arab. *afâda*, vid. ch. xxxvii. 11. עֶבְרוֹת, or rather, according to the reading of Ben-Ascher, עַבְרוֹת, in its prop. signif. oversteppings, *i.e.* overflowings. In connection with vers. 11–13, one is directly reminded of the judgment on everything that is high and exalted in Isa. ii., where טָמְנֵם בֶּעָפָר also has its parallel (Isa. ii. 10). Not less, however, does ver. 14*b* recall Isa. lix. 16, lxiii. 5

(comp. Ps. xcviii. 1); Isaiah I. and II. have similar descriptions to the book of Job. The ἀπ λεγ. הָרַךְ is Hebræo-Arab.; *hadaka* signifies, like *hadama*, to tear, pull to the ground. In connection with טָמוּן (from טָמַן; Aram., Arab., טמר), the lower world, including the grave, is thought of (comp. Arab. *matmurât*, subterranean places); חָבַשׁ signifies, like حبس IV., to chain and to imprison. Try it only for once—this is the collective thought—to act like Me in the execution of penal justice, I would praise thee. That he cannot do it, and yet ventures with his short-sightedness and feebleness to charge God's rule with injustice, the following pictures of foreign animals are now further intended to make evident to him :—

15 *Behold now the behêmôth,*
   Which I have made with thee :
   He eateth grass like an ox.
16 *Behold now, his strength is in his loins,*
   And his force in the sinews of his belly.
17 *He bendeth his tail like a cedar branch,*
   The sinews of his legs are firmly interwoven.
18 *His bones are like tubes of brass,*
   His bones like bars of iron.

בְּהֵמוֹת (after the manner of the intensive *plur.* חָכְמוֹת, הוֹלֵלוֹת, which play the part of the abstract termination), which sounds like a *plur.*, but without the numerical plural signification, considered as Hebrew, denotes the beast κατ᾽ ἐξοχήν, or the giant of beasts, is however Hebraized from the Egyptian *p-ehe-mau*, (*muau*), *i.e.* the (*p*) ox (*ehe*) of the water (*mau* as in the Hebraized proper name מֹשֶׁה). It is, as Bochart has first of all shown, the so-called river or Nile horse, *Hippopotamus amphibius* (in Isa. xxx. 6, בַּהֲמוֹת נֶגֶב, as emblem of Egypt, which extends its power, and still is active in the interest of others), found in the rivers of Africa, but no longer found in the Nile, which is not inappropriately called a horse; the Arab. waterhog is better, Italian *bomarino*, Engl. sea-cow [?], like the Egyptian *p-ehe-mau*. The change of *p* and *b* in the exchange of Egyptian and Semitic words occurs also elsewhere, *e.g.* *pug'* and בּוּץ, *harpu* and חֶרֶב (ἅρπη), *Apriu* and עֲבָרִים (according to Lauth). Nevertheless *p-ehe-mau* (not *mau-t*, for what should the post-positive fem. art. do here?) is first of all only the בהמות translated back again into the Egyptian by Jablonsky; an instance in favour of this is still wanting. In Hieroglyph the Nile-horse is called *apet*; it was honoured as divine. Brugsch dwelt in Thebes in the temple of the *Apet*.[1] In ver. 15*b* עִמָּךְ signifies nothing but " with thee," so that thou hast it before thee. This water-ox eats חָצִיר, green grass, like an ox. That it prefers to plunder the produce of the fields—in Arab. *chadîr* signifies, in particular, green barley—is accordingly self-evident. Nevertheless, it has gigantic strength, viz. in its plump loins and in the sinews (שְׁרִירָי, properly the firm constituent parts,[2] therefore: ligaments and muscles) of its clumsy belly. The brush of a tail, short in comparison with the monster itself, is compared to a cedar (a branch of it), *ratione glabritiei, rotunditatis, spissi-*

---

[1] In the astronomical representations the hippopotamus is in the neighbourhood of the North Pole in the place of the dragon of the present day, and bears the name of *hes-mut*, in which *mut = t. mau*, "the mother." *Hes* however is obscure; Birch explains it by : raging.

[2] Starting from its primary signification (made firm, fast), سَرِير, שְׁרִירָא can signify *e.g.* also things put together from wood : a throne, a hand-barrow, bedstead and cradle, metaphor. the foundation. Wetzst. otherwise : " The שְׁרִירֵי הבטן are not the sinews and muscles, still less ' the private parts ' of others, but the four bearers of the animal body = *arkân el-batn*, viz. the bones of the מתנים, ver. 16*a*, together with the two shoulder-blades. The Arab. *sarîr* is that on which a thing is supported or rests, on which it stands firmly, or moves about. *Neshwân* (i. 280) says : ' *sarîr* is the substratum on which a thing rests,' and the *sarîr er-ra's*, says the same, is the place where the head rests upon the nape of the neck. The *Kâmûs* gives the same signification *primo loco*, which shows that it is general ; then follows in gen. مَضْطَجَع, " the support of a thing."

tudinis et firmitatis (Bochart); since the beast is in general almost without hair, it looks like a stiff, naked bone, and yet it can bend it like an elastic cedar branch; חָפֵץ is Hebræo-Arab., حفض [1] is a word used directly of the bending of wood (*el-'ûd*). Since this description, like the whole book of Job, is so strongly Arabized, פחד, ver. 17*b*, will also be one word with the Arab. *fachidh*, the thigh; as the Arabic version also translates: '*urûku afchâdhihi* (the veins or strings of its thigh). The Targ., retaining the word of the text here,[2] has פַּחֲדִין in Lev. xxi. 20 for אֶשֶׁךְ, a testicle, prop. *inguina*, the groins; we interpret: the sinews of its thighs or legs[3] are intertwined after the manner of intertwined vine branches, שׂרִיגִים.[4]   But

---

[1] Wetzst. otherwise: One may compare the Arab. خفض, *fut. i*, to hold, sit, lie motionless (in any place), from which the signification of desiring, longing, has been developed, since in the Semitic languages the figure of fixing (*ta'alluq*) the heart and the eye on any desired object is at the basis of this notion (wherefore such verbs are joined with the *præp.* בְּ). According to this, it is to be explained, "his tail is motionless like (the short and thick stem of) the cedar," for the stunted tail of an animal is a mark of its strength to a Semite.   In 1860, as I was visiting the neighbouring mountain fortress of *el*-Hosn with the octogenarian *Fêjâd*, the sheikh of *Fîk* in *Gôlân*, we rode past Fêjâd's ploughmen; and as one of them was letting his team go slowly along, the sheikh cried out to him from a distance: Faster! faster!   They (the steers, which thou ploughest) are not oxen weak with age, nor are they the dower of a widow (who at her second marriage receives only a pair of weak wretched oxen from her father or brother); but they are heifers (3–4 year-old steers) with stiffly raised tails (*wadhujûluhin muqashmare*, מְקַשְׁמָר an intensive קָשׁוּר or מְקֻשָּׁר [comp. שְׁלָאֲנָן, ch. xxi. 23]).

[2] Another Targ., which translates גבריה ושעבוזוהי, *penis et testiculi ejus*, vid. Aruch *s.v.* שעבז.

[3] According to Fleischer, *fachidh* signifies properly the thick-leg (= thigh), from the root *fach*, with the general signification of being puffed out, swollen, thick.

[4] In the choice of the word ישׂרגו, the *mushâgarat ed-dawâli* (from שׂרג = שׂנר), "the interweaving of the vine branches" was undoubtedly before the poet's eye; comp. *Deutsch. Morgenl. Zeitschr.* xi. 477: "On all sides in this delightful corner of the earth (the *Ghûta*) the vine left to itself, in diversified ramifications, often a dozen branches resembling so many huge snakes entangled together, swings to and fro upon the

why is פְּחָדָיו pointed thus, and not פַּחֲדָיו (as e.g. שְׂעָרָיו)? It is either an Aramaizing (with אַשְׁרָיו it has another relationship) pointing of the *plur.*, or rather, as Köhler has perceived, a regularly-pointed *dual* (like רַגְלָיו), from פַּחֲדַיִם (like פַּעֲמַיִם), which is equally suitable in connection with the signification *femora* as *testiculi.* מָטִיל, ver. 18*b*, is also Hebræo-Arab.; for مطل signifies to forge, or properly to extend by forging (hammering), and to lengthen, undoubtedly a secondary formation of טול, *tâla*, to be long, as *makuna* of *kâna*, *madana* of *dâna*, *massara* (to found a fortified city) of *sâra*, chiefly (if not always) by the intervention of such nouns as *makân*, *medîne*, *misr* (= מָצוֹר), therefore in the present instance by the intervention of this *metîl* (= *memtûl*[1]), whence probably μέταλλον (metal), properly iron in bars or rods, therefore metal in a wrought state, although not yet finished.[2] Its bones are like tubes of brass, its bones (גְּרָמָיו, the more Aram. word) like forged rods of iron—what an appropriate description of the comparatively thin but firm as iron skeleton by which the plump mass of flesh of the gigantic boar-like grass-eater is carried!

shining stem of the lofty white poplar." And *ib.* S. 491: " a twisted vine almost the thickness of a man, as though formed of rods of iron (comp. ver. 18)."

[1] The noun מָטִיל is also found in the Lexicon of *Neshwân*, i. 63: " מָטִיל is equivalent to מֶמְטוּל, viz. that which is hammered out in length, used of iron and other metals; and one says חَדִידָה מְטִילָה of a piece of iron that has been hammered for the purpose of stretching it." The verb *Neshwân* explains: " מָטַל said of iron signifies to stretch it that it may become long." The verb מטל can be regarded as a fusion of the root מדד (מטט, מוט, comp. מוֹטָה, and مطّ Beduin: to take long steps) with the root טול, to be long.—WETZST. The above explanation of the origin of the verb מטל seems to us more probable.

[2] Ibn-Koreisch in Pinsker, *Likkute*, p. קנא, explains it without exactness by *sebikat hadîd*, which signifies a smelted and formed piece of iron.

19 *He is the firstling of the ways of God;*
   He, his Maker, reached to him his sword.
20 *For the mountains bring forth food for him,*
   And all the beasts of the field play beside him.
21 *Under the lote-trees he lieth down,*
   In covert of reeds and marsh.
22 *Lote-trees cover him as shade,*
   The willows of the brook encompass him.
23 *Behold, if the stream is strong, he doth not quake;*
   He remaineth cheerful, if a Jordan breaketh forth upon his
   mouth.
24 *Just catch him while he is looking,*
   With snares let one pierce his nose!

God's ways is the name given to God's operations as the
Creator of the world in ver. 19a (comp. ch. xxvi. 14, where
His acts as the Ruler of the world are included); and the
firstling of these ways is called the Behêmôth, not as one of
the first in point of time, but one of the hugest creatures, *un
chef-d'œuvre de Dieu* (Bochart); רֵאשִׁית not as Prov. viii. 22,
Num. xxiv. 20, of the priority of time, but as Amos vi. 1, 6,
of rank. The *art.* in הָעֹשׂוֹ is, without the pronominal *suff.*
being meant as an accusative (Ew. § 290, *d*), equal to a
demonstrative pronoun (comp. Ges. § 109, *init.*): this its
Creator (but so that "this" does not refer back so much as
forwards). It is not meant that He reached His sword to
behêmoth, but (on which account לוֹ is intentionally wanting)
that He brought forth, *i.e.* created, its (behêmoth's) peculiar
sword, viz. the gigantic incisors ranged opposite one another,
with which it grazes upon the meadow as with a sickle:
ἀρούρῃσιν κακὴν ἐπιβάλλεται ἅρπην (Nicander, *Theriac.* 566),
ἅρπη is exactly the sickle-shaped Egyptian sword (*harpu* =
חֶרֶב). Vegetable food (to which its teeth are adapted) is
appointed to the behêmoth: "for the mountains produce

food for him;" it is the herbage of the hills (which is scanty
in the lower and more abundant in the upper valley of the
Nile) that is intended, after which this uncouth animal climbs
(*vid.* Schlottm.). בּוּל is neither a contraction of יְבוּל (Ges.),
nor a corruption of it (Ew.), but Hebræo-Arab. = *baul*, produce, from *bâla*, to beget, comp. *aballa*, to bear fruit (prop.
seed, *bulal*), root בל, to soak, wet, mix.[1] Ver. 20*b* describes
how harmless, and if unmolested, inoffensive, the animal is;
שָׁם there, viz. while it is grazing.

In ver. 21*a* Saadia correctly translates: تحت الضال ; and

ver. 22*a*, Abulwalid: يغطيه الضل مظلّلا له, *tegit eum lotus
obumbrans eum*, by interpreting الضل, more correctly الضال,
with *es-sidr el-berrî, i.e. Rhamnus silvestris* (*Rhamnus Lotus*,
Linn.), in connection with which Schultens' observation is to
be noticed: *Cave intelligas lotum Ægyptiam s. plantam Niloti-
cam quam Arabes* نوفر. The fact that the wild animals of the
steppe seek the shade of the lote-tree, Schultens has supported
by passages from the poets. The lotus is found not only in
Syria, but also in Egypt, and the whole of Africa.[2] The

---

[1] Whether בְּלִיל, ch. vi. 5, xxiv. 6, signifies mixed provender (*farrago*),
or perhaps ripe fruit, *i.e.* grain, so that *jabol*, Judg. xix. 21, in the signification " he gave dry provender consisting of barley-grain," would be
the opposite of the *jahushsh* (יְחֹשׁ) of the present day, " he gives green
provender consisting of green grass or green barley, h*ashîsh*," as Wetzst.
supposes, *vid.* on Isa. xxx. 24.

[2] The ضال or *Dûm*-tree, which likes hot and damp valleys, and hence
is found much on the northern, and in great numbers on the eastern, shores
of the Sea of Galilee, is called in the present day *sidra*, collect. *sidr;* and
its fruit, a small yellow apple, *dûma*, collect. *dûm*, perhaps " the not
ending, perennial," because the fruit of the previous year only falls from
the tree when that of the present year is ripe. Around Bagdad, as they
told me, the *Dûm*-tree bears twice a year. In Egypt its fruit is called
nebq (נְבֶק, not *nibq* as in Freytag), and the tree is there far stronger and
taller than in Syria, where it is seldom more than about four and twenty
feet high. Only in the *Wâdi 's-sidr* on the mountains of Judæa have I
seen several unusually large trunks. The *Kâmûs* places the signification

plur. is formed from the primary form צְאָל, as שִׁקְמִים from שֶׁקְם, Olsh. § 148, *b;* the single tree was perhaps called צְאֵלָה (= ضال), as שִׁקְמָה (Ew. § 189, *h*). Ammianus Marc. xxii. 15 coincides with ver. 21*b : Inter arundines celsas et squalentes nimia densitate hœc bellua cubilia ponit.* צֶלְלוֹ, ver. 22*a* (re-solved from צִלּוֹ, as גִּלְלוֹ, ch. xx. 7, from גִּלּוֹ[1]), is in apposition with the subj.: Lote-trees cover it as its shade (shading it). The double play of words in ver. 22 is [not] repro-duced in the [English] translation. הֵן, ver. 23*a*, pointing to something possible, obtains almost the signification of a con-ditional particle, as ch. xii. 14, xxiii. 8, Isa. liv. 15. The Arabic version appropriately translates ان طغى النهر, for طغى denotes exactly like עָשֵׁק, excessive, insolent behaviour, and is then, as also ظلم, عتا, and other verbs given by Schultens, transferred from the sphere of ethics to the over-flow of a river beyond its banks, to the rush of raging waters, to the rising and bursting forth of swollen streams. It does "the sweet *Dûm*-tree" first of all to ضال, and then "the wild D." In hotter regions there may also be a superior kind with fine fruit, in Syria it is only wild—*Neshwân* (ii. 192) says: "*dâla*, collect. *dâl*, is the wild *Dûm*-tree,"—yet I have always found its fruit sweet and pleasant to the taste.—WETZST.

[1] Forms like גִּלְל, צִלְל, are unknown to the language, because it was more natural for ease of pronunciation to make the primary form סָבַב into סַב than into סֶבַב; גִּלְלוֹ (*vid.* i. 377), צֶלְלוֹ, might more readily be referred to גִּלְל, צִלְל (in which the first *a* is a helping vowel, and the second a root vowel); but although the form קָטָל and the segolate forms completely pass into one another in inflection, still there does not exist a safe example in favour of the change of vowels of קָטָל into קְטָלִי; wherefore we have also derived אָגְלִי, ch. xxxviii. 28, from אָגֵל, not from אָגָל, although, moreover, *ĕ* fre-quently enough alternates with *ĭ* (*e.g.* יְשֶׁעֶךָ), and a transition into *ĕ* of the *ĭ* weakened from *ă* (*e.g.* יְדְכֶם) also occurs. But there are no forms like נְטֹפִי = נְטֹפִי from נָטֹף in reality, although they would be possible according to the laws of vowels. In Ges. *Handwörterb.* (1863) גִּלְלוֹ stands under גֵּלֶל (according to the form לֵבָב, which, however, forms לְבָבוֹ) and צֶלְלוֹ under צֵלֶל (a rare noun-form, which does not occur at all form verbs double *Ayin*).

not, however, terrify the behêmoth, which can live as well in
the water as on the land; לֹא יַחְפּוֹז, properly, it does not spring
up before it, is not disturbed by it. Instead of the Jordan,
ver. 23*b*, especially in connection with יָנִיחַ, the *'Gaihûn* (the
Oxus) or the *'Gaihân* (the Pyramus) might have been mentioned, which have their names from the growing force with
which they burst forth from their sources (גּוּחַ, גִּיחַ, comp.
'gâcha, to wash away). But in order to express the notion
of a powerful and at times deep-swelling stream, the poet
prefers the יַרְדֵּן of his fatherland, which, moreover, does not
lie so very far from the scene, according to the conception
at least, since all the wadis in its neighbourhood flow directly
or indirectly (as *Wâdi el-Meddân*, the boundary river between
the district of *Suwêt* and the *Nukra* plain) into the Jordan.
For יַרְדֵּן (perhaps from יָרַד[1]) does not here signify a stream
(rising in the mountain) in general; the name is not deprived
of its geographical definiteness, but is a particularizing expression of the notion given above.

The description closes in ver. 24 with the ironical challenge:
in its sight (בְּעֵינָיו as Prov. i. 17) let one (for once) catch
it; let one lay a snare which, when it goes into it, shall
spring together and pierce it in the nose; *i.e.* neither the
open force nor the stratagem, which one employs with effect
with other animals, is sufficient to overpower this monster.
מוֹקְשִׁים is generally rendered as equal to חַחִים, Isa. xxxvii. 29,
Ezek. xix. 4, or at least to the cords drawn through them, but
contrary to the uniform usage of the language. The description of the hippopotamus[2] is now followed by that of the crocodile, which also elsewhere form a pair, *e.g.* in Achilles Tatius,

---

[1] Certainly one would have expected יַרֵדְן like נֵרְדְן, while יַרְדֵּן like יַעְבֵּץ,
יַעְזֵר, appears formed from רָדַן; nevertheless יַרְדֵּן (with changeable *Ssere*)
can be understood as a change of vowel from יַרְדֵּן (comp. יֵשֵׁב for יִשַׁב).

[2] *Vid.* Brehm, *Aus dem Leben des Nilpferds*, *Gartenlaube* 1859, Nr.
48, etc.

iv. 2, 19. Behemoth and leviathan, says Herder, are the
pillars of Hercules at the end of the book, the *non plus ultra*
of another world [distant from the scene]. What the same
writer says of the poet, that he does not "mean to furnish
any contributions to Pennant's *Zoologie* or to Linnæus'
Animal Kingdom," the expositor also must assent to.

25 *Dost thou draw the crocodile by a hoop-net,*
 And dost thou sink his tongue into the line? !
26 *Canst thou put a rush-ring into his nose,*
 And pierce his cheeks with a hook?
27 *Will he make many supplications to thee,*
 Or speak flatteries to thee?
28 *Will he make a covenant with thee,*
 To take him as a perpetual slave?
29 *Wilt thou play with him as a little bird,*
 And bind him for thy maidens?

In ch. iii. 8, לִוְיָתָן signified the celestial dragon, that causes
the eclipses of the sun (according to the Indian mythology,
râhu the black serpent, and *ketu* the red serpent); in Ps.
civ. 26 it does not denote some great sea-saurian after the
kind of the hydrarchus of the primeval world,[1] but directly
the whale, as in the Talmud (Lewysohn, *Zoologie des Talm.*
§ 178 sq.). Elsewhere, however, the crocodile is thus named,
and in fact as תַּנִּין also, another appellation of this natural
wonder of Egypt, as an emblem of the mightiness of Pharaoh
(*vid.* on Ps. lxxiv. 13 sq.), as once again the crocodile itself is
called in Arab. *el-firʿaunu*. The Old Testament language
possesses no proper name for the crocodile; even the Talmudic
makes use of קְרוֹקְתָּא = κροκόδειλος (Lewysohn, § 271). לויתן
is the generic name of twisted, and תנין long-extended monsters. Since the Egyptian name of the crocodile has not
been Hebraized, the poet contents himself in תִּמְשֹׁךְ with

[1] *Vid.* Grässe, *Beiträge*, S. 94 ff.

making a play upon its Egyptian, and in تمساح, *timsâh*,[1]
Arabized name (Ew. § 324, *a*). To wit, it is called in Coptic
temsah, Hierogl. (without the *art*.) *msuh* (*emsuh*), as an animal
that creeps " out of the egg (*suh*)."[2] In ver. 25*b*, Ges. and
others falsely translate : Canst thou press its tongue down
with a cord ; הַשְׁקִיעַ does not signify *demergere* = *deprimere*,
but *immergere :* canst thou sink its tongue into the line, *i.e.*
make it bite into the hook on the line, and canst thou thus
draw it up ?   Ver. 25*b* then refers to what must happen in
order that the מְשִׁיךְ of the *msuh* may take place.   Herodotus
(and after him Aristotle) says, indeed, ii. 68, the crocodile
has no tongue ; but it has one, only it cannot stretch it out,
because the protruding part has grown to the bottom of the
mouth, while otherwise the saurians have a long tongue, that
can be stretched out to some length.   In ver. 26 the order of
thought is the same : for first the Nile fishermen put a ring
through the gills or nose of valuable fish ; then they draw a
cord made of rushes (σχοῖνον) through it, in order to put
them thus bound into the river.   " As a perpetual slave,"
ver. 28*b* is intended to say : like one of the domestic animals.

---

[1] Herodotus was acquainted with this name (χάμψαι = κροκόδειλοι) ;
thus is the crocodile called also in Palestine, where (as Tobler and Joh.
Roth have shown) it occurs, especially in the river *Damûr* near *Tantûra*.

[2] *Les naturalistes*—says Chabas in his *Papyr. magique*, p. 190—*comptent
cinq espèces de crocodiles vivant dans le Nil, mais les hieroglyphes rapportent
un plus grand nombre de noms déterminés par le signe du crocodile.*   Such
is really the case, apart from the so-called land crocodile or σκίγχος
(Arab. *isqanqûr*), the Coptic name of which, *hankelf* (according to Lauth
ha. n. kelf, ruler of the bank), is not as yet indicated on the monuments.
Among the many old Egyptian names for the crocodile, Kircher's *charuki*
is, however, not found, which reminds one of the Coptic *karus*, as κροκόδειλος of κρόκος, for κροκόδειλος is the proper name of the *Lacerta viridis*
(Herod. ii. 69).   Lauth is inclined to regard *charuki* as a fiction of
Kircher, as also the name of the phœnix, αλλοη (*vid*. p. 130).   The
number of names of the crocodile which remain even without *charuki*,
leads one to infer a great variety of species, and crocodiles, which differ
from all living species, have also actually been found in Egyptian tombs ;
vid. Schmarda, *Verbreitung der Thiere*, i. 89.

By צִפּוֹר, ver. 29a, can hardly be meant צִפֹּרֶת הַכְּרָמִים, the little
bird of the vineyard, *i.e.* according to a Talmud. usage of the
language, the golden beetle (*Jesurun*, p. 222), or a pretty
eatable grasshopper (Lewysohn, § 374), but, according to the
words of Catullus, *Passer deliciæ meæ puellæ*, the sparrow,
Arab. *'asfûr*—an example of a harmless living plaything
(שְׂחַק בְּ, to play with anything, different from Ps. civ. 26,
where it is not, with Ew., to be translated: to play with it,
but: therein).

> 30 *Do fishermen trade with him,*
>   *Do they divide him among the Canaanites?*
> 31 *Canst thou fill his skin with darts,*
>   *And his head with fish-spears?*
> 32 *Only lay thy hand upon him—*
>   *Remember the battle, thou wilt not do it again!*
> Ch. xli. 1 *Behold, every hope becometh disappointment:*
>   *Is not one cast down even at the sight of him?*

The fishermen form a guild (صَنَف, *sunf*), the associated
members of which are called חַבָּרִים (distinct from חֲבֵרִים).
On כָּרָה עַל, *vid.* on ch. vi. 27. "When I came to the towns
of the coast," says R. Akiba, *b. Rosch ha-Schana*, 26b,
"they called selling, which we call מכירה, כירה, there," according to which, then, Gen. 1. 5 is understood, as by the
Syriac; the word is Sanscrito-Semitic, Sanscr. *kri*, Persic
chirîden (*Jesurun*, p. 178). LXX. ἐνσιτοῦνται, according to
2 Kings vi. 23, to which, however, עָלָיו is not suitable. כְּנַעֲנִים
are Phœnicians; and then, because they were the merchant
race of the ancient world, directly traders or merchants.
The meaning of the question is, whether one sells the crocodile among them, perhaps halved, or in general divided up
(*vid.* i. 409). Further, ver. 31: whether one can kill it
בְּשֻׂכּוֹת, with pointed missiles (Arab. *shauke*, a thorn, sting,

dart), or with fish-spears (צִלְצָל, so called from its whizzing, צָלַל, *salla*). In ver. 32 the accentuation is the right indication: only seize upon him—remember the battle, *i.e.* thou wilt be obliged to remember it, and thou wilt have no wish to repeat it. זְכֹר is a so-called *imperat. consec.*: if thou doest it, thou wilt . . ., Ges. § 130, 2. תּוֹסַף is the pausal form of תּוֹסֶף (once *tôsp*, Prov. xxx. 6), of which it is the original form.

Ch. xli. 1. The *suff.* of תוֹחַלְתּוֹ refers to the assailant, not objectively to the beast (the hope which he indulges concerning it). נִכְזָבָה, ch. xli. 1, is 3 *præt.*, like נָאֶלְמָה, Isa. liii. 7 (where also the participial accenting as *Milra*, occurs in Codd.) ; Fürst's *Concord.* treats it as *part.*, but the participial form נִקְטָלָה, to be assumed in connection with it, along with נִקְטָלָה and נִקְטֶלֶת, does not exist. הֲגַם, ver. 1*b*, is, according to the sense, equivalent to הֲלֹא גַם; *vid.* on ch. xx. 4. מַרְאָיו (according to Ges., Ew., and Olsh., *sing.*, with the plural *suff.*, without a *plur.* meaning, which is natural in connection with the primary form מַרְאִי ; or what is more probable, from the *plur.* מַרְאִים with a *sing.* meaning, as פָּנִים) refers to the crocodile, and יֻטַל (according to a more accredited reading, יֻטַל = יוּטַל) to the hunter to whom it is visible.

What is said in ver. 30 is perfectly true ; although the crocodile was held sacred in some parts of Egypt, in Elephantine and Apollonopolis, on the contrary, it was salted and eaten as food. Moreover, that there is a small species of crocodile, with which children can play, does not militate against ver. 29. Everywhere here it is the creature in its primitive strength and vigour that is spoken of. But if they also knew how to catch it in very early times, by fastening a bait, perhaps a duck, on a barb with a line attached, and drew the animal to land, where they put an end to its life with a lance-thrust in the neck (Uhlemann, *Thoth*, S. 241): this was angling on the largest scale, as is not meant in ver. 25. If, on the other hand, in very early times they harpooned the crocodile, this would certainly be more difficult of reconcilement with ver. 31, than that mode of catching it by means of a fishing-hook of the greatest calibre with ver. 25. But harpooning is generally only of use when the animal can be hit between the neck and head, or in the flank; and it is very questionable whether, in the ancient times, when the race was without doubt of an unmanageable size, that has now died out, the crocodile hunt (ch. vii. 12) was effected with harpoons. On the whole subject we have too little information for distinguishing between the different periods. So far as the questions of Jehovah have reference to man's relation to the two monsters, they concern the men of the present, and are shaped according to the measure of power which they have attained over nature. The strophe which follows shows what Jehovah intends by these questions.

2 *None is so foolhardy that he dare excite him!*
   And who is it who could stand before Me?
3 *Who hath given Me anything first of all, that I must requite it?*
   Whatsoever is under the whole heaven is Mine.

One sees from these concluding inferences, thus applied, what is the design, in the connection of this second speech of Jehovah, of the reference to behêmoth and leviathan, which somewhat abruptly began in ch. xl. 15. If even the strength of one of God's creatures admits no thought of being able to attack it, how much more should the greatness of the Creator deter man from all resistance! For no one has any claim on God, so that he should have the right of appearing before Him with a rude challenge. Every creature under heaven is God's; man, therefore, possesses nothing that was not God's property and gift, and he must humbly yield, whether God gives or takes away. לֹא, ver. 2*a*, is not directly equivalent to אִין, but the clause is exclamatory. יְעוּרֶנּוּ *Chethîb,*

יעירנו Kerî, is the Palestine reading, the reverse the Baby-lonian ; the authorized text (chiefly without a Kerî) is יְעוּרֶנּוּ, from עוּר in a transitive signification (ἐγείρειν), as שׁוּב, ch. xxxix. 12, comp. xlii. 10. The meaning of הִקְדִּימַנִי is de-termined according to וָאֲשַׁלֵּם : to anticipate, viz. by gifts pre-sented as a person is approaching the giver (Arab. aqdama). הוּא, ver. 3b, is neutral, as ch. xiii. 16, xv. 9, xxxi. 11, 28. תַּחַת is virtually a subj. : that which is under . . . After these apparently epiphonematic verses (2 and 3), one might now look for Job's answer. But the description of the leviathan is again taken up, and in fact hitherto it was only the invincibility of the animal that was spoken of ; and yet it is not so described that this picture might form the exact pendent of the preceding.

4 *I will not keep silence about his members,*
   The proportion of his power and the comeliness of his struc-
      ture.
5 *Who could raise the front of his coat of mail?*
   Into his double teeth—who cometh therein?
6 *The doors of his face—who openeth them?*
   Round about his teeth is terror.

The Kerî לוֹ authorized by the Masora assumes an inter-rogative rendering: as to it, should I be silent about its members (לוֹ at the head of the clause, as Lev. vii. 7–9, Isa. ix. 2),—what perhaps might appear more poetic to many. הֶחֱרִישׁ (once, ch. xi. 3, to cause to keep silence) here, as usually : to be silent. בַּדָּיו, as ch. xviii. 13, vol. i. p. 323. דְּבַר signifies the relation of the matter, a matter of fact, as דִּבְרֵי, facts, Ps. lxv. 4, cv. 27, cxlv. 5. חִין (compared by Ew. with הִין, a measure) signifies grace, χάρις (as synon. חֶסֶד), here delicate regularity, and is made easy of pronunciation from חֵנְן, just as the more usual חֵן ; the language has avoided the form חֲנֶן, as observed above. לְבוּשׁ, clothing, we have translated "coat of mail," which the Arab. *libás* usually signifies ; פְּנֵי לְבוּשׁוֹ is not its face's covering (Schlottm.), which ought to be לְבוּשׁ פָּנָיו ; but פְּנֵי is the upper or front side turned to the observer (comp. Isa. xxv. 7), as Arab. وجه, (*wag'h*), *si rem desuper spectes, summa ejus pars, si ex adverso, prima* (Fleischer, *Glossæ*, i. 57). That which is the "doubled of its mouth" (רֶסֶן, prop. a bit in the mouth, then the mouth itself) is its upper and lower jaws armed with powerful teeth. The "doors of the face" are the jaws ; the jaws are divided back to the ears, the teeth are not covered by lips ; the impression of the teeth is therefore the more terrible, which the substantival clause, ver. 6*b* (comp. ch. xxxix. 20), affirms. שִׁנָּיו *gen. subjecti :* the circle, ἕρκος, which is formed by its teeth (Hahn).

> 7 *A pride are the furrows of the shields,*
> *Shut by a rigid seal.*
> 8 *One joineth on to the other,*
> *And no air entereth between them.*
> 9 *One upon another they are arranged,*
> *They hold fast together, inseparably.*

Since the writer uses אָפִיק both in the signif. *robustus,* ch. xii. 12, and *canalis,* ch. xl. 18, it is doubtful whether it must be explained *robusta (robora) scutorum* (as *e.g.* Ges.), or *canales scutorum* (Hirz., Schlottm., and others). We now prefer the latter, but so that "furrows of the shields" signifies the square shields themselves bounded by these channels ; for only thus is the סָגוּר, which refers to these shields, considered, each one for itself, suitably attached to what precedes. חוֹתָם צָר is an *acc.* of closer definition belonging to it : closed is (each single one) by a firmly attached, and therefore firmly closed, seal. LXX. remarkably ὥσπερ σμυρίτης λίθος, *i.e.* emery (*vid.* Krause's *Pyrogeteles,* 1859, S. 228). Six rows of knotty scales and four scales of the neck cover

the upper part of the animal's body, in themselves firm, and
attached to one another in almost impenetrable layers, as is
described in vers. 7 sq. in constantly-varying forms of expression (where יַפִּשׁ with *Pathach* beside *Athnach* is the correct
reading),—a גַּאֲוָה, *i.e.* an equipment of which the animal
may be proud. Umbr. takes גאוה, with Bochart, = גֵּוָה, the
back; but although in the language much is possible, yet
not everything.

> 10 *His sneezing sendeth forth light,*
>   *And his eyes are like the eyelids of the dawn;*
> 11 *Out of his mouth proceed flames,*
>   *Sparks of fire escape from him;*
> 12 *Out of his nostrils goeth forth smoke*
>   *Like a seething pot and caldron;*
> 13 *His breath kindleth coals,*
>   *And flames go forth out of his mouth.*

That the crocodile delights to sun itself on the land, and
then turns its open jaws to the sunny side, most Nile travellers since Herodotus have had an opportunity of observing;[1]
and in connection therewith the reflex action of sneezing
may occur, since the light of the sun produces an irritation
on the retina, and thence on the vagus; and since the sun
shines upon the fine particles of watery slime cast forth in
the act of sneezing, a meteoric appearance may be produced.
This delicate observation of nature is here compressed into
three words; in this concentration of whole, grand thoughts
and pictures, we recognise the older poet. עָטַשׁ is the usual

---

[1] Dieterici, *Reisebilder*, i. 194: " We very often saw the animal lying
in the sand, its jaws wide open and turned towards the warm sunbeams,
while little birds, like the slender white water-wagtail, march quietly
about in the deadly abyss, and pick out worms from the watery jaws."
Herodotus, ii. 68, tells exactly the same story; as the special friend of
the crocodile among little birds, he mentions τὸν τροχίλον (the sand-piper,
Pluvianus Ægyptius).

Semitic word for "sneezing" (synon. זֵרַר, 2 Kings iv. 35).
תָּהֶל shortened from תֵּהֶל, ch. xxxi. 26, *Hiph.* of הָלַל (comp.
p. 47). The comparison of the crocodile's eyes with עַפְעַפֵּי־שָׁחַר
(as ch. iii. 9, from עִפְעֵף, to move with quick vibrations, to
wink, *i.e.* tremble), or the rendering of the same as εἶδος
ἑωσφόρου (LXX.), is the more remarkable, as, according to
Horus, i. 68, two crocodile's eyes are the hieroglyph[1] for
dawn, ἀνατολή: ἐπειδήπερ (probably to be read ἐπειδὴ πρὸ)
παντὸς σώματος ζώου οἱ ὀφθαλμοὶ ἐκ τοῦ βυθοῦ ἀναφαίνονται.
There it is the peculiar brilliancy of the eyes of certain
animals that is intended, which is occasioned either by the
iris being furnished with a so-called lustrous substance, or
there being in the pupil of the eye (as *e.g.* in the ostrich)
that spot which, shining like metal, is called *tapetum lucidum.*
For ἀναφαίνεσθαι of the eyes ἐκ τοῦ βυθοῦ, is the lustre of
the pupil in the depth of the eye. The eyes of the crocodile,
which are near together, and slanting, glimmer through the
water, when it is only a few feet under water, with a red glow.

Nevertheless the comparison in ver. 10b might also be
intended differently. The inner (third) eyelid[2] of the croco-

---

[1] The eyes of the crocodile alone by themselves are no hieroglyph: how
could they have been represented by themselves as *crocodile's eyes?* But
in the Ramesseum and elsewhere the crocodile appears with a head pointing upwards in company with couching lions, and the *eyes* of the crocodile are rendered specially prominent. Near this group it appears again
in a curved position, and quite small, but this time in company with a
scorpion which bears a disc of the sun. The former (κροκοδείλου δύο
ὀφθαλμοί) seems to me to be a figure of the longest night, the latter
(κροκόδειλος κεκυφώς in Horapollo) of the shortest, so that consequently
ἀνατολή and δύσις do not refer to the rising and setting of the sun, but to
the night as prevailing against or succumbing to the day (communicated
by Lauth from his researches on the astronomical monuments). But since
the growth of the day begins with the longest night, and *vice versâ,* the
notions ἀνατολή and δύσις can, as it seems to me, retain their most
natural signification ; and the crocodile's eyes are, notwithstanding, a
figure of the light shining forth from the darkness, as the crocodile's tail
signifies black darkness (and Egypt as the black land).

[2] Prof. Will refers the figure not to the third eyelid or the *membrana*

dile is itself a rose red ; and therefore, considered in themselves, its eyes may also be compared with the "eyelids of
the dawn." What is then said, vers. 11–13, of the crocodile,
Achilles Tatius, iv. 2, says of the hippopotamus : μυκτὴρ ἐπὶ
μέγα κεχηνὼς καὶ πνέων πυρώδη καπνὸν ὡς ἀπὸ πηγῆς πυρός.
Bartram has observed on the alligator, that as it comes on the
land a thick smoke issues from its distended nostrils with a
thundering sound. This thick, hot steam, according to the
credible description which is presented here, produces the impression of a fire existing beneath, and bursting forth. The
subjective truth of this impression is faithfully but poetically
reproduced by the poet. On בִּידוֹד (root כד, *escudere*), *vid.*
i. 408. הִתְמַלֵּט signifies no more than to disentangle one's
self, here therefore : to fly out in small particles. אַגְמוֹן,
ver. 11*b*, is rendered by Saad., Gecat., and others, by *qumqum*
(קוּמְקוּם), a caldron ; the modern expositors derive it from אגם
= *agama*, to glow, and understand it of a "heated caldron."
But the word signifies either heat or caldron ; the latter signification, however, cannot be linguistically established ; one
would look for אַגָּן (Arab. *iggâne*, a copper [Germ. *Wasch-
kessel*]). The noun אַגְמוֹן signifies, ch. xl. 26, the reed σχοῖνος,
and in the Jerusalem Talmud, *Sota* ix. 12, some menial service (comp. Arab. *ugum*) ; Ew. rightly retains the former
signification, like a pot blown upon, *i.e.* fired, heated, and
beside it (in combination with it) reeds as fuel, which in
themselves, and especially together with the steaming water,
produce a thick smoke. The *Waw* is to be compared to the
Arabic *Waw concomitantiæ* (which governs the *acc.*).

nictitans, but to that spot on the *choroidea*, glistening with a metallic
lustre, which the crocodile has in common with most animals of the night
or the twilight, therefore to the brilliancy of its eye, which shines by
virtue of its lustrous coating ; *vid.* the magnificent head of a crocodile in
Schlegel's *Amphibien-Abbildungen* (1837-44).

14 *Great strength resteth upon his neck,*
   And despair danceth hence before him.
15 *The flanks of his flesh are thickly set,*
   Fitting tightly to him, immoveable.
16 *His heart is firm like stone,*
   And firm like the nether millstone.
17 *The mighty are afraid of his rising up;*
   From alarm they miss their aim.

Overpowering strength lodges on its neck, *i.e.* has its abiding place there, and before it despair, prop. melting away, dissolution (דְּאָבָה from דָּאַב, نَأَب = הוב *Hiph.*, نَاب II., to bring into a loose condition, synon. הֵמֵס), dances hence, *i.e.* springs up and away (יָדוּץ, Arab. *jadisu*, to run away), *i.e.* it spreads before it a despondency which produces terror, and deprives of strength. Even the pendulous fleshy parts (מַפְּלֵי), especially of its belly, hang close together, דָּבְקוּ, *i.e.* they are not flabby, but fit to it, like a metal casting, without moving, for the skin is very thick and covered with thick scales; and because the digestive apparatus of the animal occupies but little space, and the scales of the back are continued towards the belly, the tender parts appear smaller, narrower, and closer together than in other animals. יָצוּק here is not, as ch. xxviii. 2, xxix. 6, the *fut.* of צוּק, but the *part.* of יָצַק, as also ver. 16*ab*: its heart is firm and obdurate, as though it were of cast brass, hard as stone, and in fact as the nether millstone (פֶּלַח from פלח, *falacha*, to split, crush in pieces), which, because it has to bear the weight and friction of the upper, must be particularly hard. It is not intended of actual stone-like hardness, but only of its indomitable spirit and great tenacity of life: the activity of its heart is not so easily disturbed, and even fatal wounds do not so quickly bring it to a stand. מִשֵּׁתוֹ (from שֵׁת = שֵׁאת = שְׂאֵת), primary form שְׂאֵת, is better understood in the active sense: afraid of its rising, than the passive: of its exaltedness. אֵילִים (according

to another reading אֵלִים) is not, with Ew., to be derived from
אַיִל (Arab. *ijal*), a ram; but אֵילִים Ex. xv. 15, Ezek. xvii. 13
(comp. גְּיָרִים 2 Chron. ii. 16, נֵירִי 2 Sam. xxii. 29), אֵלִים Ezek.
xxxi. 11, xxxii. 21, and אוּלִים *Cheth.* 2 Kings xxiv. 15, are
only alternating forms and modes of writing of the participial adject., derived from אוּל (אֵיל) first of all in the primary form *awil* (as גֵּר = *gawir*). The signif. assigned to the
verb אוּל: to be thick = fleshy, which is said then to go
over into the signif. to be stupid and strong (Ges. *Handwörterb.*), rests upon a misconception: *âla* is said of fluids
"to become thick," because they are condensed, since they
go back, *i.e.* sink in or settle (Ges. correctly in *Thes.* : *notio
crassitiei a retrocedendo*). The verb *âla, ja'ûlu,* unites in
itself the significations to go backward, to be forward, and
to rule; the last two: *anteriorem* and *superiorem esse,* probably belong together, and אֵל signifies, therefore, a possessor
of power, who is before and over others. הִתְחַמֵּא, ver. 17*b*,
has the signif., which does not otherwise occur, to miss the
mark (from חטא, خَطِئَ, to miss, *opp.* صاب, to hit the mark),
viz. (which is most natural where אילים is the subject spoken
of) since they had designed the slaughter and capture of the
monster. שְׁבָרִים is intended subjectively, as תְּבִירָא = פַּחַד Ex.
xv. 16, Targ. II., and also as the Arab. *thubûr,* employed
more in reference to the mind, can be used of pain.

18 *If one reacheth him with the sword—it doth not hold;*
    Neither spear, nor dart, nor harpoon.
19 *He esteemeth iron as straw,*
    Brass as rotten wood.
20 *The son of the bow doth not cause him to flee,*
    Sling stones are turned to stubble with him.
21 *Clubs are counted as stubble,*
    And he laugheth at the shaking of the spear.

מַשִּׂיגֵהוּ, which stands first as *nom. abs.*, "one reaching him,"
is equivalent to, if one or whoever reaches him, Ew. § 357, *c*,
to which בְּלִי תָקוּם, it does not hold fast (בְּלִי with *v. fin.*, as
Hos. viii. 7, ix. 16, *Chethîb*), is the conclusion. חֶרֶב is instrumental, as Ps. xvii. 13. מַפָּע, from נָסַע, نزع, to move on,
hasten on, signifies a missile, as Arab. *minz'a*, an arrow,
manz'a, a sling. The Targ. supports this latter signification
here (*funda quæ projicit lapidem*) ; but since קֶלַע, the hand-
sling, is mentioned separately, the word appears to mean
missiles in general, or the catapult. In this combination of
weapons of attack it is very questionable whether שִׁרְיָה is a
cognate form of שִׁרְיוֹן (שִׁרְיָן), a coat of mail; probably it is
equivalent to Arab. *sirwe* (*surwe*), an arrow with a long
broad edge (comp. *serîje*, a short, round, as it seems, pear-
shaped arrow-head), therefore either a harpoon or a peculiarly formed dart.[1] "The son of the bow" (and of the אַשְׁפָּה,
pharetra) is the arrow. That the ἁπ. γεγρ. תוֹתָח signifies a
club (war-club), is supported by the Arab. *watacha*, to beat.
כִּידוֹן (*vid.* i. 408), in distinction from חֲנִית (a long lance),
is a short spear, or rather, since רַעַשׁ implies a whistling
motion, a javelin. Iron the crocodile esteems as תֶּבֶן, *tibn*,
chopped straw ; sling stones are turned with him into קַשׁ.
Such is the name here at least, not for stumps of cut stubble
that remain standing, but the straw itself, threshed and
easily driven before the wind (ch. xiii. 25), which is cut up
for provender (Ex. v. 12), generally dried (and for that
reason light) stalks (*e.g.* of grass), or even any remains of
plants (*e.g.* splinters of wood).[2] The *plur.* נֶחְשְׁבוּ, ver. 21*a*,

---

[1] On the various kinds of Egyptian arrows, *vid.* Klemm. *Culturgeschichte*,
v. 371 f.

[2] The Egyptio-Arabic usage has here more faithfully preserved the
ancient signification of the word (*vid.* Fleischer, *Glossæ*, p. 37) than
the Syro-Arabic ; for in Syria cut but still unthreshed corn, whether
lying in swaths out in the field and weighted with stones to protect it
against the whirlwinds that are frequent about noon, or corn already

does not seem to be occasioned by תותח being conceived collectively, but by the fact that, instead of saying תותח וכידון, the poet has formed וכידון into a separate clause. Parchon's (and Kimchi's) reading תוֹחָח is founded upon an error.

> 22 *His under parts are the sharpest shards,*
> *He spreadeth a threshing sledge upon the mire.*
> 23 *He maketh the deep foam like a caldron,*
> *He maketh the sea like a pot of ointment.*
> 24 *He lighteth up the path behind him,*
> *One taketh the water-flood for hoary hair.*
> 25 *Upon earth there is not his equal,*
> *That is created without fear.*
> 26 *He looketh upon everything high,*
> *He is the king over every proud beast.*

Under it, or, תַּחְתָּיו taken like תַּחַת, ch. xli. 3, as a virtual subject (*vid.* ch. xxviii. 5, p. 98): its under parts are the most pointed or sharpest shards, *i.e.* it is furnished with exceedingly pointed scales. חַדּוּד is the intensive form of חַד (Arab. hadîd, sharpened = iron, p. 94, note), as חַלּוּק, 1 Sam. xvii. 40, of חָלָק (smooth),[1] and the combination חַדּוּדֵי חָרֶשׂ (equal the combination חדודי הֲחֲרָשִׂים, comp. ch. xxx. 6) is moreover superlative: in the domain of shards standing prominent as sharp ones, as Arab. *chairu ummatin,* the best people, prop. *bon en fait de peuple* (Ew. § 313, *c, Gramm. Arab.* § 532). LXX. ἡ στρωμνὴ αὐτοῦ ὀβελίσκοι ὀξεῖς, by drawing יְרַפֵּד to ver. 22*a,* and so translating as though it were רְפִידָתוֹ (Arab. *rifâde, stratum*). The verb רָפַד (*rafada*),

---

brought to the threshing-floors but not yet threshed, is called *qashsh.*— WETZST.

[1] In Arabic also this substantival form is intensive, *e.g. lebbûn,* an exceedingly large kind of tile, dried in the open air, of which farm-yards are built, nearly eight times larger than the common tile, which is called *libne* (לְבֵנָה).

cogn. רָבַד, signifies *sternere* (ch. xvii. 13), and then also *fulcire*; what is predicated cannot be referred to the belly of the crocodile, the scales of which are smooth, but to the tail with its scales, which more or less strongly protrude, are edged round by a shallow cavity, and therefore are easily and sharply separated when pressed; and the meaning is, that when it presses its under side in the morass, it appears as though a threshing-sledge with its iron teeth had been driven across it.

The pictures in ver. 23 are true to nature; Bartram, who saw two alligators fighting, says that their rapid passage was marked by the surface of the water as it were boiling. With מְצוּלָה, a whirlpool, abyss, depth (from צוּל = צָלַל, to hiss, clash; to whirl, surge), יָם alternates; the Nile even in the present day is called *bahr* (sea) by the Beduins, and also compared, when it overflows its banks, to a sea. The observation that the animal diffuses a strong odour of musk, has perhaps its share in the figure of the pot of ointment (LXX. ὥσπερ ἐξάλειπτρον, which Zwingli falsely translates *spongia*); a double gland in the tail furnishes the Egyptians and Americans their (pseudo) musk. In ver. 24*a* the bright white trail that the crocodile leaves behind it on the surface of the water is intended; in ver. 24*b* the figure is expressed which underlies the descriptions of the foaming sea with πολιός, *canus*, in the classic poets. שֵׂיבָה, hoary hair, was to the ancients the most beautiful, most awe-inspiring whiteness. מָשְׁלוֹ, ver. 25*a*, understood by the Targ., Syr., Arab. version, and most moderns (*e.g.* Hahn: there is not on earth any mastery over it), according to Zech. ix. 10, is certainly, with LXX., Jer., and Umbr., not to be understood differently from the Arab. *mithlahu* (its equal); whether it be an inflexion of מֹשֶׁל, or what is more probable, of מְשֹׁל (comp. ch. xvii. 6, where this *nomen actionis* signifies a proverb = word of derision, and הִתְמַשֵּׁל, to compare one's self, be equal, ch. xxx. 19). עַל־עָפָר

is also Hebr.-Arab.; the Arabic uses *turbe*, formed from *turâb* (*vid.* on ch. xix. 25), of the surface of the earth, and *et-tarbâ-u* as the name of the earth itself. הֶעָשׂוּ (for הֵעָשׂוּי, as צָפוּ, ch. xv. 22, *Cheth.* = צָפוּי, resolved from עָשׂוּי, *'asûw*, 1 Sam. xxv. 18, *Cheth.*) is the confirmatory predicate of the logical subj. described in ver. 25a as incomparable; and לִבְלִי־חָת (from חַת, the *ă* of which becomes *ĭ* in inflexion), *absque terrore* (comp. ch. xxxviii. 4), is virtually a nom. of the predicate: the created one (becomes) a terrorless one (a being that is terrified by nothing). Everything high, as the לבלי־חת, ver. 25a, is more exactly explained, it looketh upon, *i.e.* remains standing before it, without turning away affrighted; in short, it (the leviathan) is king over all the sons of pride, *i.e.* every beast of prey that proudly roams about (*vid.* on ch. xxviii. 8).

[Then Job answered Jehovah, and said:]
Ch. xlii. 2 *Now I know that Thou canst do all things,*
     And no plan is impracticable to Thee.
   3 *" Who then hideth counsel—*
     Without knowledge?"
     Thus have I judged without understanding,
     What was too wonderful for me, without knowing.

He indeed knew previously what he acknowledges in ver. 2, but now this knowledge has risen upon him in a new divinely-worked clearness, such as he has not hitherto experienced. Those strange but wondrous monsters are a proof to him that God is able to put everything into operation, and that the plans according to which He acts are beyond the reach of human comprehension. If even that which is apparently most contradictory, rightly perceived, is so glorious, his affliction is also no such monstrous injustice as he thinks; on the contrary, it is a profoundly elaborated מְזִמָּה, a well-digested, wise עֵצָה of God. In ver. 3 he repeats to himself the chastening word of Jehovah, ch. xxxviii. 2, while he chastens himself with it; for he now perceives that his judgment was wrong, and that he consequently has merited the reproof. With לָכֵן he draws a conclusion from this confession which the chastening word of Jehovah has presented to him: he has rashly pronounced an opinion upon things that lie beyond his power of comprehension, without possessing the necessary capacity of judging and perception. On the mode of writing יָדַעְתִּ, *Cheth.*, which recalls the Syriac form *jed'et* (with the pronominal *suff.* cast off), *vid.* Ges. § 44, rem. 4; on the expression ver. 2*b*, comp. Gen. xi. 6. The repetition of ch. xxxviii. 2 in ver. 3 is not without some variations according to the custom of authors noticed in *Psalter*, i. 330. הִגַּדְתִּי, "I have affirmed," *i.e.* judged, is, ver. 3*c*, a closed thought, which, however, then receives its object, ver. 3*d*, so that the notion of judging goes over into that of pronouncing a judgment. The clauses with וְלֹא are circumstantial clauses, Ew. § 341, *a*.

> 4 *O hear now, and I will speak:*
>   *I will ask Thee, and instruct Thou me.*
> 5 *I had heard of Thee by the hearing of the ear,*
>   *And now mine eye hath seen Thee.*
> 6 *Therefore I am sorry, and I repent*
>   *In dust and ashes.*

The words employed after the manner of entreaty, in ver. 4, Job also takes from the mouth of Jehovah, ch. xxxviii. 3, xl. 7. Hitherto Jehovah has interrogated him, in order to bring him to a knowledge of his ignorance and weakness. Now, however, after he has thoroughly perceived this, he is anxious to put questions to Jehovah, in order to penetrate deeper and deeper into the knowledge of the divine power and wisdom. Now for the first time with him, the true, living perception of God has its beginning, being no longer

effected by tradition (לְ of the external cause: in consequence of the tidings which came to my ears, comp. Ps.
xviii. 45, comp. Isa. xxiii. 5), but by direct communication
with God. In this new light he can no longer deceive himself concerning God and concerning himself; the delusion
of the conflict now yields to the vision of the truth, and only
penitential sorrow for his sin towards God remains to him.
The object to אֶמְאַס is his previous conduct. נִחַם is the exact
expression for μετανοεῖν, the godly sorrow of repentance not
to be repented of. He repents (sitting) on dust and ashes
after the manner of those in deep grief.

If the second speech of Jehovah no longer has to do with
the exaltation and power of God in general, but is intended
to answer Job's doubt concerning the justice of the divine
government of the world, the long passage about the hippopotamus and the crocodile, ch. xl. 15–xli. 26, in this second
speech seems to be devoid of purpose and connection. Even
Eichhorn and Bertholdt on this account suppose that the
separate portions of the two speeches of Jehovah have fallen
into disorder. Stuhlmann, Bernstein, and De Wette, on the
other hand, explained the second half of the description of the
leviathan, ch. xli. 4–26, as a later interpolation; for this part
is thought to be inflated, and to destroy the connection between
Jehovah's concluding words, ch. xli. 2, 3, and Job's answer,
ch. xlii. 2–6. Ewald forcibly rejected the whole section,
ch. xl. 15–xli. 26, by ascribing it to the writer of Elihu's
speeches,—an opinion which he has again more recently
abandoned. In fact, this section ought to have had a third
poet as its writer. But he would be the double (Doppel-
gänger) of the first; for, deducting the somewhat tame לֹא
אַחֲרִישׁ בַּדָּיו, ch. xli. 4,—which, however, is introduced by
the interrupted description being resumed, in order now to
begin in real earnest,—this section stands upon an equally
exalted height with the rest of the book as a poetic production

and lofty description; and since it has not only, as also Elihu's speeches, an Arabizing tinge, but also the poetic genius, the rich fountain of thought, the perfection of technical detail, in common with the rest of the book; and since the writer of the book of Job also betrays elsewhere an acquaintance with Egypt, and an especial interest in things Egyptian, the authenticity of the section is by no means doubted by us, but we freely adopt the originality of its present position.

But before one doubts the originality of its position, he ought, first of all, to make an earnest attempt to comprehend the portion in its present connection, into which it at any rate has not fallen from pure thoughtlessness. The first speech of Jehovah, moreover, was surprisingly different from what was to have been expected, and yet we recognised in it a deep consistency with the plan; perhaps the same thing is also the case in connection with the second.

After Job has answered the first speech of Jehovah by a confession of penitence, the second can have no other purpose but that of strengthening the conviction, which urges to this confession, and of deepening the healthful tone from which it proceeds. The object of censure here is no longer Job's contending with Jehovah in general, but Job's contending with Jehovah on account of the prosperity of the evil-doer, which is irreconcilable with divine justice; that contending by which the sufferer, in spite of the shadow which affliction casts upon him, supported the assertion of his own righteousness. Here also, as a result, the refutation follows in the only way consistent with the dignity of Jehovah, and so that Job must believe in order to perceive, and does not perceive in order not to be obliged to believe. Without arguing the matter with Job, as to why many things in the government of the world are thus and not rather otherwise, Jehovah challenges Job to take the government of the world into his own hand, and to give free course to his wrath, to cast down everything that is exalted, and to render the evil-doer for ever harmless. By thus thinking of himself as the ruler of the world, Job is obliged to recognise the cutting contrast of his feebleness and the divine rule, with which he has ventured to find fault; at the same time, however, he is taught, that—what he would never be able to do—God really punishes the ungodly, and must have wise purposes when, which He indeed might do, He does not allow the floods of His wrath to be poured forth immediately.

Thus far also Simson is agreed; but what is the design of the description of the two Egyptian monsters, which are regarded by him as by Ewald as out of place here? To show Job how little capable he is of governing the world, and how little he would be in a position to execute judgment on the evil-doer, two creatures are described to him, two unslain monsters of gigantic structure and invincible strength, which defy all human attack. These two descriptions are, we think, designed to teach Job how little capable of passing sentence upon the evil-doer he is, who cannot even draw a cord through the nose of the behêmoth, and who, if he once attempted to attack the leviathan, would have reason to remember it so long as he lived, and would henceforth let it alone. It is perhaps an emblem that is not without connection with the book of Job, that these בהמות and לויתן (תנין), in the language of the Prophets and the Psalms, are the symbols of a worldly power at enmity with the God of redemption and His people. And wherefore should Job's confession, ch. xlii. 2, not be suitably attached to the completed description of the leviathan, especially as the description is divided into two parts by the utterances of Jehovah, ch. xli. 2, 3, which retrospectively and prospectively set it in the right light for Job?

THE UNRAVELMENT IN OUTWARD REALITY.—
CHAP. XLII. 7 SQQ.

Job's confession and tone of penitence are now perfected. He acknowledges the divine omnipotence which acts according to a wisely-devised scheme, in opposition to his total ignorance and feebleness. A world of divine wisdom, of wondrous thoughts of God, now lies before him, concerning which he knows nothing of himself, but would gladly learn a vast amount by the medium of divine instruction. To these mysteries his affliction also belongs. He perceives it now to be a wise decree of God, beneath which he adoringly bows, but it is nevertheless a mystery to him. Sitting in dust and ashes, he feels a deep contrition for the violence with which he has roughly handled and shaken the mystery,— now will it continue, that he bows beneath the enshrouded mystery? No, the final teaching of the book is not that God's rule demands *faith* before everything else; the final teaching is, that sufferings are for the righteous man the way to glory, and that his faith is the way to sight. The most craving desire, for the attainment of which Job hopes where his faith breaks forth from under the ashes, is this, that he will once more behold God, even if he should succumb to his affliction. This desire is granted him ere he yields. For he who hitherto has only heard of Jehovah, can now say: עתה עיני ראתך; his perception of God has entered upon an entirely new stage. But first of all God has only borne witness of Himself to him, to call him to repentance. Now, however, since the rust of pollution is purged away from Job's pure soul, He can also appear as his Vindicator and Redeemer. After all that was sinful in his speeches is blotted out by repentance, there remains only the truth of his innocence, which God Himself testifies to him, and the

truth of his holding fast to God in the hot battle of temptation, by which, without his knowing it, he has frustrated the
design of Satan.

> Ver. 7. *And it came to pass, after Jehovah had spoken these*
> *words to Job, that Jehovah said to Eliphaz the Temanite,*
> *My wrath is kindled against thee and thy two friends: for*
> *ye have not spoken what is correct in reference to Me, as*
> *My servant Job.*

In order that they may only maintain the justice of God,
they have condemned Job against their better knowledge
and conscience; therefore they have abandoned truth in
favour of the justice of God,—a defence which, as Job has
told the friends, God abhors. Nevertheless He is willing to
be gracious.

> Ver. 8. *And now take unto you seven bullocks and seven*
> *rams, and go to My servant Job, and offer an offering for*
> *yourselves, and Job My servant shall pray for you; only*
> *his person will I accept, that I recompense not unto you*
> *your folly: for ye have not spoken what is correct in*
> *reference to Me, as My servant Job.*

Schlottm., like Ew., translates נְכוֹנָה what is sincere, and
understands it of Job's inward truthfulness, in opposition to
the words of the friends contrary to their better knowledge
and conscience. But נכן has not this signification anywhere:
it signifies either *directum* = *rectum* or *erectum* = *stabile,* but
not *sincerum.* However, objective truth and subjective truthfulness are here certainly blended in the notion "correct."
The "correct" in Job's speeches consists of his having denied
that affliction is always a punishment of sin, and in his holding fast the consciousness of his innocence, without suffering
himself to be persuaded of the opposite. That denial was
correct; and this truthfulness was more precious to God than

the untruthfulness of the friends, who were zealous for the honour of God.

After Job has penitently acknowledged his error, God decides between him and the friends according to his previous supplicatory wish, ch. xvi. 21. The heavenly Witness makes Himself heard on earth, and calls Job by the sweet name of עַבְדִּי. And the servant of Jehovah is not only favoured himself, but he also becomes the instrument of grace to sinners. As where his faith shone forth he became the prophet of his own and the friends' future, so now he is the priestly mediator between the friends and God. The friends against whom God is angry, but yet not as against רְשָׁעִים, but only as against those who have erred, must bring an offering as their atonement, in connection with which Job shall enter in with a priestly intercession for them, and only him (כִּי אִם, non alium sed = non nisi), whom they regarded as one punished of God, will God accept (comp. Gen. xix. 21)— under what deep shame must it have opened their eyes!

Here also, as in the introduction of the book, it is the עוֹלָה which effects the atonement. It is the oldest and, according to its meaning, the most comprehensive of all the blood-offerings. Bullocks and rams are also the animals for the whole burnt-offerings of the Mosaic ritual; the proper animal for the sin-offering, however, is the he-goat together with the she-goat, which do not occur here, because the age and scene are strange to the Israelitish branching off of the חטאת from the עולה. The double seven gives the mark of the profoundest solemnity to the offering that was to be offered. The three also obey the divine direction; for although they have erred, God's will is above everything in their estimation, and they cheerfully subordinate themselves as friends to the friend.[1]

---

[1] Hence the Talmudic proverb (vid. Fürst's Perlenschnüre, S. 80) : אוֹ חברא כחברי איוב או מיתותא, either a friend like Job's friends or death!

Ver. 9. *Then Eliphaz of Teman, and Bildad of Shuach,*
[and] Zophar of Naamah, went forth and did as Jehovah
had said to them; and Jehovah accepted the person of Job.

Jehovah has now risen up as a witness for Job, the spiritual
redemption is already accomplished ; and all that is wanting
is, that He who has acknowledged and testified to Job as His
servant should also act outwardly and visibly, and in mercy
show Himself the righteous One.

Ver. 10. *And Jehovah turned the captivity of Job, when he*
prayed for his friends; and Jehovah increased everything
that Job had possessed to the double.

רֵעֵהוּ is to be understood generally, as ch. xvi. 21, and the בְּ
signifies not " because," but " when." The moment in which
Job prayed for his friends became, as the climax of a life
that is well-pleasing with God, the turning-point of glory to
him. The Talmud has borrowed from here the true proverb :
כל־המתפלל בעד חברו נענה תחלה, *i.e.* he who prays for his fellow-
men always finds acceptance for himself first of all. The
phrase שׁוּב שְׁבוּת (שְׁבִית) signifies properly to turn captivity,
then in general to make an end of misery; also in German,
elend, old High Germ. *elilenti*, originally signified another,
foreign country (*vid. Psalter*, ii. 192), since an involuntary
removal from one's native land is regarded as the emblem of
a lamentable condition. This phrase does not exactly stamp
Job as the *Mashal* of the Israel of the Exile, but it favoured
this interpretation. Now when Job was recovered, and doubly
blessed by God, as is also promised to the Israel of the
Exile, Isa. lxi. 7 and freq., sympathizing friends also appeared
in abundance.

Ver. 11. *Then came to him all his brothers, and all his sisters,*
and all his former acquaintances, and ate bread with him

in his house, and expressed sympathy with him, and com-
forted him concerning all the evil which Jehovah had
brought upon him ; and each one gave him a Kesitá, and
each a golden ring.

Prosperity now brought those together again whom calamity
had frightened away; for the love of men is scarcely anything
but a number of coarse or delicate shades of selfishness. Now
they all come and rejoice at Job's prosperity, viz. in order to
bask therein.   He, however, does not thrust them back ; for
the judge concerning the final motives of human love is God,
and love which is shown to us is certainly more worthy of
thanks than hatred.   They are his guests again, and he
leaves them to their own shame.   And now their tongues,
that were halting thus far, are all at once become eloquent :
they mingle congratulations and comfort with their expressions of sorrow at his past misfortune.   It is now an easy
matter, that no longer demands their faith.   They even bring
him each one a present.   In everything it is manifest that
Jehovah has restored His servant to honour.   Everything is
now subordinated to him, who was accounted as one forsaken
of God.   קְשִׂיטָה is a piece of metal weighed out, of greater
value than the shekel, moreover indefinite, since it is nowhere
placed in the order of the Old Testament system of weights
and measures, adapted to the patriarchal age, Gen. xxxiii. 19,
in which Job's history falls.[1] נְזָמִים are rings for the nose
and ear ; according to Ex. xxxii. 3, an ornament of the women
and men.

The author now describes the manner of Job's being
blessed.

---

[1] According to *b. Rosch ha-Schana*, 26a, R. Akiba found the word קשיטה
in Africa in the signification מעה (coin), as a Targ. (*vid.* Aruch, *s.v.*
קשיטה) also translates ; the Arab. *qist* at least signifies balances and
weight.

Ver. 12. *And Jehovah blessed Job's end more than his begin-*
ning; and he had fourteen thousand sheep and six thousand
camels, and a thousand yoke of oxen and a thousand she-
asses.

The numbers of the stock of cattle, ch. i. 3,[1] now appear
doubled, but it is different with the children.

Ver. 13. *And he had seven sons and three daughters.*

Therefore, instead of the seven sons and three daughters
which he had, he receives just the same again, which is also
so far a doubling, as deceased children also, according to the
Old Testament view, are not absolutely lost, 2 Sam. xii. 23.
The author of this book, in everything to the most minute
thing consistent, here gives us to understand that with men
who die and depart from us the relation is different from
that with things which we have lost. The pausal שִׁבְעָנָה
(instead of שִׁבְעָה), with paragogic *âna*, which otherwise is a
fem. suff. (Ges. § 91, rem. 2), here, however, standing in a

---

[1] Job, like all the wealthier husbandmen in the present day, kept she-
asses, although they are three times dearer than the male, because they
are useful for their foals; it is not for the sake of their milk, for the
Semites do not milk asses and horses. Moreover, the foals are also only
a collateral gain, which the poor husbandman, who is only able to buy a
he-ass, must forego. What renders this animal indispensable in husbandry
is, that it is the common and (since camels are extremely rare among the
husbandmen) almost exclusive means of transport. How would the husbandman, *e.g.*, be able to carry his seed for sowing to a field perhaps six
or eight miles distant? Not on the plough, as our farmers do, for the
plough is transported on the back of the oxen in Syria. How would he
be able to get the corn that was to be ground (*tachne*) to the mill, perhaps a day's journey distant; how carry wood and grass, how get the
manure upon the field in districts that require to be manured, if he had
not an ass? The camels, on the other hand, serve for harvesting (*ragâd*),
and the transport of grain (*ghalle*), chopped straw (*tibn*), fuel (*hatab*),
and the like, to the large inland towns, and to the seaports. Those
village communities that do not possess camels for this purpose, hire them
of the Arabs (nomads).—WETZST.

prominent position, is an embellishment somewhat violently brought over from the style of the primeval histories (Gen. xxi. 29; Ruth i. 19): a septiad of sons. The names of the sons are passed over in silence, but those of the daughters are designedly given.

Ver. 14. *And the one was called Jemîma, and the second Kezia, and the third Keren ha-pûch.*

The subject of וַיִּקְרָא is each and every one, as Isa. ix. 5 (comp. *supra*, ch. xli. 25, *existimaverit quis*). The one was called יְמִימָה (Arab. *jemâme*, a dove) on account of her dove's eyes; the other קְצִיעָה, cassia, because she seemed to be woven out of the odour of cinnamon; and the third קֶרֶן הַפּוּךְ, a horn of paint (LXX. Hellenizing: κέρας ἀμαλθείας), which is not exactly beautiful in itself, but is the principal cosmetic of female beauty (*vid.* Lane, *Manners and Customs of the Modern Egyptians*, transl.): the third was altogether the most beautiful, possessing a beauty heightened by artificial means. They were therefore like three graces. The writer here keeps to the outward appearance, not disowning his Old Testament standpoint. That they were what their names implied, he says in

Ver. 15. *And in all the land there were not found women so fair as the daughters of Job: and their father gave them inheritance among their brothers.*

On נִמְצָא, followed by the *acc.*, vid. Ges. § 143, 1, *b.* לָהֶם, etc., referring to the daughters, is explained from the deficiency in Hebrew in the distinction of the genders. Ver. 15*b* sounds more Arabian than Israelitish, for the Thora only recognises a daughter as heiress where there are no sons, Num. xxvii. 8 sqq. The writer is conscious that he is writing an extra-Israelitish pre-Mosaic history. The equal distribution of the property again places before our eyes the pleasing picture of family concord in the commencement of the history; at the same time it implies that Job will not have been wanting in sons-in-law for his fair, richly-dowried daughters,—a fact which ver. 16 establishes:

> *And Job lived after this a nundred and forty years, and saw his children and his children's children to four generations.*

In place of וַיְרָא, the *Keri* gives the unusual Aorist form וַיִּרְאֶה, which, however, does also occur elsewhere (*e.g.* 1 Sam. xvii. 42). The style of the primeval histories, which we here everywhere recognise, Gen. l. 23 (comp. Isa. liii. 10), is retained to the last words.

Ver. 17. *And Job died, old, and weary of life.*

In the very same manner Genesis, xxv. 8, xxxv. 29, records the end of the patriarchs. They died satiated of life; for long life is a gift of God, but neither His greatest nor His final gift.

A New Testament poet would have closed the book of Job differently. He would have shown us how, becoming free from his inward conflict of temptation, and being divinely comforted, Job succumbs to his disease, but waves his palm of victory before the throne of God among the innumerable hosts of those who have washed their robes and made them white in the blood of the Lamb. The Old Testament poet, however, could begin his book with a celestial scene, but not end it with the same. True, in some passages, which are like New Testament luminous points in the Old Testament poem, Job dares to believe and to hope that God will indeed acknowledge him after death. But this is a purely individual aspiration of faith—the extreme of hope, which comes forth against the extreme of fear. The unravelment does not correspond to this aspiration. The view of heaven which a Christian poet would have been able to give at the close of the book is only rendered possible by the resurrection and ascension of Christ. So far, what Oehler in his essay on the Old Testament Wisdom (1854, S. 28) says, in opposition to those who think the book of Job is directed against the Mosaic doctrine of retribution, is true: that, on the contrary, the issue of the book sanctions the present life phase of this doctrine anew. But the comfort which this theologically and artistically incomparable book presents to us is substantially none other than that of the New Testament. For the final consolation of every sufferer is not dependent upon the working of good genii in the heavens, but has its seat in God's love, without which even heaven would become a very hell. Therefore the book of Job is also a book of consolation for the New Testament church. From it we learn that we have not only to fight with flesh and blood, but with the prince of this world, and to accomplish our part in the conquest of evil, to which, from Gen. iii. 15 onwards, the history of the world tends; that faith and avenging justice are absolutely distinct opposites; that the right kind of faith clings to divine love in the midst of the feeling of wrath; that the incomprehensible ways of God always lead to a glorious issue; and that the suffering of the present time is far outweighed by the future glory—a glory not always revealed in this life and visibly future, but the final glory above. The nature of faith, the mystery of the cross, the right practice of the care of souls,—this, and much besides, the church learns from this book, the whole teaching of which can never be thoroughly learned and completely exhausted.

MAP OF THE COUNTRY
round the **MONASTERY OF JOB** in the Nukra.

el-Gubêtje

el-Gâbië

Umm Haurân

el-Haggägije

Tülûl el-Hishsh

Tell el-Gâbië

Nawâ

Sinn Nawâ

Bet Genn

Jâbis

Tell el Gumú'

Road from Chisfin

Es-Sâdîje

Tesîl

to Shemuskin

Dêr el-Lebwe

Makâm Ejûb

'Atawân

Dêr Éjûb

Wâdi el-Horîr

Dêr el-Harîr

Tell 'Ashtarâ

Tajibet el-Ism

Kufr es-igân

W. el. Ghar

Tell es-sêf

Wâdi Hît

Chirbet 'Ashtarâ or Ruins of the Nïla Springs

Sinnin

Sahem Geïtun

Ijûn en Nîl

Shepherd Encampment

el-Firâ

Tell es Sonïn

Wâdi Dâil

el-Mnzerib

Wâdi Jâbis

Es-Sîra

Ancient Bridge of Sira with 9 Arches

Dâîl

Kufr es-Sâmir

Gibbin

Tulûl Hân el-Mjîle

Tafas

Wâdi el-Jarmuk

Pilgrim Caravan Route

El-Ashari

Samach

Depth of Gorge about 250 feet

'Ain el-bâride

es-Sa'âde

Bendek

'Ain esh-Shâchne

Tell esh-Shihâb Ruins

Castle of el-Muzêrîb

el-Kasaba (Pilgrim fair)

Lake of Kês

Springs

el-'Mankûle

Gur'hâ

Ancient Temple

Kanât Zêzûn

Kanât Bolak

Chirbet Kês

el-'Auuâôwije (Mill)

el-'Bashawije (Mill)

'Owêrib

Bridge el-Charjân

el ō Kabu

el 5 Chan

Thâlith

Zêzûn

River

Wâdi el Charjân

or

Wâdi el-Jedûde

Ataman

Dr. Wetzstein's Route

Extinct Volcanic Mounds

Scale in Miles (English)

NB. The places underlined are inhabited

W.H. Macfarlane. Edinr

Drawn by Wetzstein.

GOLAN

GEDUR

HAURÂN

APPENDIX

—•—

THE MONASTERY OF JOB IN HAURAN, AND THE TRADITION OF JOB.

(WITH A MAP OF THE DISTRICT.)

By J. G. WETZSTEIN.

THE oral tradition of a people is in general only of very subordinate value from a scientific point of view when it has reference to an extremely remote past; but that of the Arabs especially, which is always combined with traditions and legends, renders the simplest facts perplexing, and wantonly clothes the images of prominent persons in the most wonderful garbs, and, in general, so rapidly disfigures every object, that after a few generations it is no longer recognisable. So far as it has reference to the personality of Job, whose historical existence is called in question or denied by some expositors, it may be considered as altogether worthless, but one can recognise when it speaks of Job's native country. By the אֶרֶץ עוּץ the writer of the book of Job meant a definite district, which was well known to the people for whom he wrote; but the name has perished, like many others, and all the efforts of archæologists to assign to the land its place in the map of Palestine have been fruitless. Under these circumstances the matter is still open to discussion, and the tradition respecting Job has some things to authorize it.

True, it cannot of itself make up for the want of an historical testimony, but it attains a certain value if it is old, *i.e.* if it can be traced back about to the time of the destruction of Jerusalem by the Romans, when reliable information was still obtainable respecting that district, although its name was no longer in use.

In all the larger works of travel on Palestine and Syria, we find it recorded that Haurân is there called Job's fatherland. In Hauran itself the traveller hears this constantly; if any one speaks of the fruitfulness of the whole district, or of the fields around a village, he is always answered: Is it not the land of Job (*bilâd Êjûb*)? Does it not belong to the villages of Job (*diâ' Êjûb*)? Thus to Seetzen[1] *Bosrâ* was pointed out as a city of Job; and to Eli Smith[2] even the country lying to the east of the mountains was called the land of Job. In *Kanawat*, a very spacious building, belonging to the Roman or Byzantine period, situated in the upper town, was pointed out to me as the summer palace of Job (the inscription 8799 in *Corp. Inscr. Græc.* is taken from it). The shepherds of *Dâ'il*, with whom I passed a night on the *Wâdi el-Lebwe*, called the place of their encampment Job's pasture-ground. In like manner, the English traveller Buckingham, when he wandered through the *Nukra*, was shown in the distance the village of *Gherbi* (*i.e.* *Chirbet el-ghazale*, which from its size is called *el-chirbe* κατ' ἐξοχήν) as the birthplace and residence of Job,[3] and it seems altogether as though Hauran and the Land of Job are synonymous. But if one inquires partioularly for that part of the country in which Job himself dwelt, he is directed to the central point of Hauran, the plain of Hauran (*sahl*

[1] Seetzen, *Reisen durch Syrien*, etc., i. 66.
[2] Ed. Robinson, *Palästina*, iii. 911 [Germ. edit.].
[3] C. Ritter, *Geogr. von Syr. u. Pal.* ii. 842 [= *Erdkunde*, xv. Pt. 2, p. 842].

Haurân),[1] and still more exactly to the district between the towns of *Nawâ* and *Edre'ât*, which is accounted the most fertile portion of the country, covered with the ruins of villages, monasteries, and single courts, and is even now comparatively well cultivated. Among the nomads as well as among the native agricultural population, this district is called from its formation *Nukra* or *Nukrat esh-Shâm*,[2] a name by which this highly-favoured plain is known and celebrated by the poets in the whole Syrian desert, as far as 'Irâ*k* and *H*igâz.

But even the national writers are acquainted with and frequently make mention of the Hauranitish tradition of Job; yet they do not call Job's home *Nukra*,—for this word, which belongs only to the idiom of the steppe, is unknown to the literature of the language,—but *Bethenîje* (*Batanœa*). It is so called in a detailed statement of the legends of Job:[3] After the death of his father, Job journeyed into Egypt[4] to marry *Rahme* (רִחְמָה) the daughter of Ephraim, who had inherited from her grandfather Joseph the robe of beauty; and after he had brought her to his own country, he received from God a mission as prophet to his countrymen, viz. to the inhabitants of Haurân and Batanæa (بعثه اللّه رسولا الى قومه وهم اهل حوران والبثنية تبع). The historian of Jerusalem, Mugîr ed-dîn el-*H*ambeli, in the chapter on the legends of the prophets, says: "Job came from *el-'Ês*,

---

[1] Whether the word מִישֹׁר, Deut. iii. 10, only signifies the plain of Hauran or its southern continuation, the eastern *Belkâ*, may be doubtful, because in that passage both the Amorite kingdoms are spoken of. But since it is the "cities" of the plain, of which the eastern Belkâ can have had but few or none, that are spoken of, מִישֹׁר will surely exclude the latter.

[2] On this name, which belongs to the modern geography of the country, comp. my *Reisebericht über Hauran u. d. Trachonen*, S. 87.

[3] Catalogue of Arab. MSS. collected in Damascus by J. G. Wetzstein. Berlin 1863, No. 46, p. 56.

[4] [The connection with Egypt, in which these legends place Job, is worthy of observation.—DEL.]

and the Damascene province of B a t a n æa was his property."
In like manner, in the *Geography* of J â k û t el-*H*amawi,[1]
under the art. *Bethenîje*, it is said: "and in this land lived
Job (*wakân Êjûb minhâ*)."

Modern exegetes, as is known, do not take the plain of
Hauran, but the mountain range of Hauran with its eastern
slope, as the *Provincia Batanæa*. I have sought elsewhere[2] to
show the error of this view, and may the more readily confine
myself to merely referring to it, as one will be convinced of
the correctness of my position in the course of this article.
One thing, however, is to be observed here, that the supposition
that Basan is so called as being the land of basalt rocks, is an
untenable support of this error. The word b a s a l t may be
derived from $B\alpha\sigma\acute{\alpha}\nu\tau\iota\varsigma$, or a secondary formation, $B\alpha\sigma\acute{\alpha}\lambda\tau\iota\varsigma$,
because Basan is exclusively volcanic;[3] but we have no more
right to reverse the question, than to say that Damascus may
have received its name from the manufacture of damask.[4]

---

[1] Orient. MSS. in the Royal Library in Berlin, Sect. Sprenger, No.
7–10.

[2] *Reisebericht*, S. 83–87.

[3] *Vid*. vol. ii. p. 91, comp. p. 93, note 2, of the foregoing Commentary.

[4] In the fair at *Muzêrîb* we again saw the sheikh of the *Wêsîje*-Beduins,
whose guest we had been a week before at the S p r i n g s of J o s e p h in
western *Gôlân*, where he had pitched his tent on a wild spot of ground
that had been traversed by lava-streams. In answer to our question
whether he still sojourned in that district, he said: "No, indeed! *Nâzilîn
el-jôm bi-ar*d *bethêne shêle* (we are now encamped in a district that is
completely *bethêne*)." I had not heard this expression before, and inquired what it meant. The sheikh replied: *bethêne* (بَثَيْنَة) is a stoneless plain covered with rich pasture. I often sought information
respecting this word, since I was interested about it on account of the
Hebrew word בַּשֶׁן, and always obtained the same definition. It is a
diminutive form, without having exactly a diminutive signification, for
in the language of the nomads it is an acknowledged fact that such a
form takes the place of the usual form. The usual form is either *bathne*
or *bathane*. The *K*âmûs gives the former signification, "a level country."
That the explanation of the Kamus is too restricted, and that of the
Sheikh of Wêsîje the more complete, may be shown from the Kamus

The home of Job is more definitely described in the following passages. Mu*h*ammed el-Ma*k*deshi[1] says, p. 81 of his geography: " And in *H*aurân and Batanæa lie the villages of Job and his home (diâ῾ Êjûb wa-diâruh). The chief place (of the district) is Nawâ, rich in wheat and other cereals." The town of Nawâ is still more definitely connected with Job by Jâ*k*ût el-*H*amawi under the article *Nawâ:* "Between Nawa and Damascus is two days' journey; it belongs to the district of *H*auran,[2] and is, according to some, the

itself. In one place it says, The word moreover signifies (*a*) the thick of the milk (cream); (*b*) a tender maiden; (*c*) repeated acts of benevolence. These three significations given are, however, manifestly only figurative applications, not indeed of the signification which the Kamus places *primo loco*, but of that which the Sheikh of the Wêsije gave; for the likening of a " voluptuously formed maiden," or of repeated acts of benevolence, to a luxurious meadow, is just as natural to a nomad, as it was to the shepherd Amos (ch. iv. 1) to liken the licentious women of Samaria to well-nourished cows of the fat pastures of Basan. Then the Kamus

brings forward a collective form *buthun* (بُثْن, perhaps from the sing.

bathan = בְּשָׁן, like أَسَد from *asad*) in the signification pastures (رِياض);

pastures, however, that are damp and low, with a rich vegetation. That the word is ancient, may be seen from the following expression of Châlid ibn el-Welîd, the victor on the Jarmûk: " 'Omar made me governor of Damascus; and when I had made it into a *buthêne, i.e.* a stoneless fertile plain (easy to govern and profitable), he removed me." Jâkût also mentions this expression under *Bethenîje.* Châlid also uses the diminutive as the nomads do (he was of the race of Machzûm); probably the whole word belongs only to the steppe, for all the women who were called *buthêne, e.g.* the beloved of the poet Gemîl, and others mentioned in the "Dîwân of Love" (*Dîwân es-sabâbe*), were Beduin women.

After what has been said, we cannot assign to the Hebr. בְּשָׁן any other signification than that of a fertile stoneless plain or low country. This appellation, which was given, properly and originally, only to the heart of the country, and its most valuable portion, viz. the Nukra, would then *a potiori* be transferred to the whole, and when the kingdom of Basan was again destroyed, naturally remained to that province, of which it was the proper designation.

[1] Orient. MSS. in the Royal Library at Berlin; Sect. Sprenger, No. 5.

[2] If writers mention *H*aurân alone, they mean thereby, according to the usage of the language of the Damascenes, and certainly also of the

chief town of the same. Nawâ was the residence (*menzil*) of Job;" and Ibn er-Râbi says, p. 62 of his essay on the excellences of Damascus:[1] "To the prophets buried in the region of Damascus belongs also Job, and his tomb is near Nawâ, in the district of Hauran." Such passages prove at the same time the identity of the Nukra with Batanæa; for if the latter is said to be recognisable from the fact of Job's home being found in it, and we find this sign in connection with the Nukra in which Nawâ with its surrounding country is situated, both names must denote one and the same district.

That, according to the last citation, Job's tomb is also shown in the Nukra, has been already observed in my *Reisebericht*, S. 121. Jâkût, under *Dêr Êjûb*, thus expresses himself: "The Monastery of Job is a locality in Hauran, a Damascene province, in which Job dwelt and was tried of God. There also is the fountain which he made to flow with his foot, and the block of rock on which he leant. There also is his tomb." What Kazwîni says in his *Wonders of Creation* ('*agâib el-machlûkât*), under *Dêr Êjûb*, accords with it: "The Monastery of Job lies in one of the Damascene provinces, and was the place of Job's residence, in which God tried him. There

prophet Ezekiel (ch. xlvii. 16, 18), the plain of Haurân as far as the borders of the Belkâ, including the mountains of Haurân, the Legâ, and Gêdûr; it is only in the district itself, where special divisions are rendered necessary, that the three last mentioned parts are excluded. If writers mention Haurân and *Bethenîje* together, the context must determine whether the former signifies the whole, and the latter the part, as in the above quotation from Makdeshi, or whether both are to be taken as coordinate, as in a passage of Istachri (edited by Möller, Gotha 1839): "And Haurân and Bethenîje are two provinces of Damascus with luxuriant corn-fields." Here the words are related to one another as Auranitis (with the chief town Bostra) to Batanæa (with the chief town Adratum, *i.e. Edre'ât*), or as the Haurân of the Beduins and the Nukra of the same. The boundary between both is the *Wâdi 'Irâ*, which falls into the *Zêdi* south of *Edre'ât*.

[1] Catalogue of Arab. MSS. collected in Damascus, No. 26.

also is the fountain which sprang forth at the stamping of his foot, when at the end of his trial God commanded him, and said: Strike with thy foot—(thus a fountain will spring forth, and) this shall be to thee a cool bath and a draught (*Korân*, xxxviii. 41 sqq.). There is also the rock on which he sat, and his tomb." Recurring to the passage of the Koran cited, we shall see that the stone of Job, the fountain and the tomb, are not situated in the Monastery itself, but at some little distance from it.

I came with my *cortége* out of Gôlân, to see the remarkable pilgrim fair of *Muzérîb*, just when the Mekka caravan was expected; and since the Monastery of Job, never visited by any one now-a-days, could not lie far out of the way, I determined to seek it out, because I deluded myself with the hope of finding an inscription of its founder, 'Amr ɪ., and in fact one with a date, which would have been of the greatest importance in reference to the history of the Ghassanides,—a hope which has remained unfulfilled. In the evening of the 8th of May we came to *Tesîl*. Here the Monastery was for the first time pointed out to us. It was lighted up by the rays of the setting sun,—a stately ruin, which lay in the distance a good hour towards the east. The following morning we left Tesîl. Our way led through luxuriant corn-fields and fields lying fallow, but decked with a rich variety of flowers in gayest blossom, to an isolated volcanic mound, *Tell el-Gumû*,[1] from which we intended to reconnoitre the surrounding country. From this point, as far as the eye could reach, it swept over fields of wheat belonging to the communities of *Sahm*, *Tell Shihâb*, *Tesîl*, *Nawâ*, and *Sa'dîje*, which covered a region which tradition calls the home of Job. True, the volcanic chaos (*el-wa'r*) extended in the west to the distance

---

[1] "Hill of the heaps of riders." The hill is said to have been named after a great engagement which took place there in ancient days. Among the 'Aneze the *gem'*, גֶּמַע, plur. *gumû'*, is a division of 400–600 horsemen.

of some three miles up the hill on which we stood, and on the north the plain was bounded partly by *Tell el-Gâbïa* and the " tooth of Nawâ" (*sinn Nawâ*), a low ridge with a few craters; but towards the E. and S. and S.W. the plain was almost unbounded, for isolated eminences, as *Tell 'Ashtarâ, T. Ash'arî, T. Shihâb, T. el-Chammân*, and others, rose above the level of the plain only like mole-hills; and the deep gorges of the *Meddân, Jarmûk*, Hît, and *Muchêbi*, were sudden and almost perpendicular ravines, either not seen at all, or appeared as dark marks. The plain slopes gently and scarcely perceptibly towards *Kufr el-mâ, Kufr es-sâmir, Zêzûn*, and *Bendek;* and the *Naher el-'Owêrid*, a river abounding in water in its level bed, resembles a glistening thread of silver. If this district had trees, as it once had,—for among the ruins one often discovers traces of vineyards and garden walls, which it can have no longer, since the insecurity and injustice of the country do not admit of men remaining long in one and the same village, therefore not to take hold upon the soil and establish one's self, and become at home anywhere,—it would be an earthly paradise, by reason of its healthy climate and the fertility of its soil. That even the Romans were acquainted with the glorious climate of Hauran, is proved by the name *Palæstina salutaris*, which they gave to the district.[1] The inhabitants of Damascus say there is no disease whatever in Haurân; and as often as the plague or any other infectious disease shows itself in their city, thousands flee to Hauran, and to the lava-plateau of the Legâ. This healthy condition may arise from the volcanic formation of the country, and from the sea-breeze, which it always has in connection with

---

[1] This appellation is erroneously given to the province of Petra (*Palæstina tertia*) in Burckhardt's Travels (Gesenius' edition, S. 676). Böcking also, *Not. dign. or.* pp. 139, 345, and 373, is guilty of this oversight. Comp. thereon, Mommsen, *Verzeichniss der röm. Provinzen aufgesetzt um*, 297, in the *Transactions of the Berlin Acad. der Wissensch.* 1862, S. 501 f.

its position, which is open towards the west. Even during
the hottest days, when *e.g.* in the *Ghûta* a perfect calm prevails, so that no breeze is felt, this cool and moist sea-breeze
blows refreshingly and regularly over the plain; and hence
the Hauranitish poet never speaks of his native country
without calling it the "cool-blowing N*u*k*ra*" (*en-nukra el-
'adîje*). But as to the fertility of the district, there is indeed
much good arable land in the country east of the Jordan, as
in *Irbid* and *Suwêt*, of the same kind as between S*a*lt and
'*Ammân*, but nowhere is the farming, in connection with a
small amount of labour (since no manure is used), more productive than in Hauran, or more profitable; for the trans-
parent "Batanæan wheat" (h*i*nta *bethenîje*) is always at least
25 per cent. higher in price than other kinds. Hence the
agriculture of that region also, in times of peace and security
(during the first six centuries after Christ), produced that
fondness for building, some of the magnificent memorials of
which are our astonishment in the present day; and, in fact,
not unfrequently the inscriptions testify that the buildings
themselves owe their origin to the produce of the field. Thus,
in the locality of *Nâhite* in the N*u*k*ra*, I found the following
fragment of an inscription : ... Μασαλέμου Ράββου κτίσμα ἐξ
ἰδίων κόπων γεωργικῶν ἐν ἔτι σπ, Masalemos son of Rabbos
set up (this memorial) out of the produce of his farming in
the year 280. Of a like kind is the following remains of
two distichs in Murduk: ... δρός τε σαόφρων | ... μεγαρόν
| ... ισ ἀνάπαυμα μέγιστον | ... γεωπονίης. In *Shakkâ*
the longer inscription of a mausoleum in a state of good preservation begins :

Βάσσος ἑῆς πάτρης μεγακύδεος ἀγλαὸν ὄμμα
'Εκ σφετέρου καμάτοιο γεωπονίης τέ μ' ἔδειμεν.

Bassos, beaming eye of the honourable city of his birth,
Has built me out of the produce of his own tillage.

Similar testimonies are to be found in the inscriptions in Burckhardt.

After a long sojourn on the hill, which was occasioned by the investigation of some interesting plants in the crater of the mound, we set out for *Sa'dije*, which is built on the slope of a hill. After a good hour's journey we arrived at the *Makâm Êjûb*, "the favoured tomb of Job," situated at the southern base of the hill, and rendered conspicuous by two white domes, and there we dismounted. The six attendants and alumni of the Makâm, or, as the Arabs thoughtfully call them, "the servants of our master Job" (*châdimîn séjidna Êjûb*), received us, with some other pilgrims, at the door of the courtyard, and led us to the basin of the fountain of Job, by the side of which they spread out their mantles for us to rest upon under the shade of a walnut tree and a willow. While the rest were engaged in the duties of hospitality, the superior of the Makâm, the Sheikh Sa'îd el-Darfûri (from Darfûr) did not leave us, and made himself in every way obliging. Like him, all the rest of the inhabitants of the place were black, and all unmarried; their celibacy, however, I imagine, was only caused by the want of opportunity of marrying, and the limited accommodation of the place. Sheikh Sa'îd believed himself to be fifty years of age; he left his home twenty years before to go on pilgrimage to Mekka, where he "studied" four years; the same length of time he sojourned in Medîna, and had held his present office ten years. Besides his mother tongue, he spoke Arabic and a little Turkish, having been in Constantinople a few years before. His judgment of the inhabitants of that city is rather harsh: he charges them with immorality, drunkenness, and avarice. In one year, said he, I could hardly save enough to travel by the steamer to Chôdscha Bêk (Odessa). How different was my experience of the inhabitants of this city! I was there three months, during which time I had nothing to provide for, and left with ninety *Mânôt* (imperials), which just sufficed to set up these dilapidated relics again. A Russian ship brought me to Smyrna, whence I travelled by the *Nemsâwi* (Austrian Lloyd steamer) to Syria.

According to the account given by the inhabitants of Sa'dîje, the Makâm has been from ancient times a negro hospice. These Africans, commonly called *'Abîd* in Damascus, and in the country *Tekârine*, come chiefly from Tekrûr in Sûdân; they first visit Mekka and Medîna, then Damascus, and finally the Makâm of Job. Here they sojourn from twenty to thirty days, during which time they wash themselves daily in Job's fountain, and pray upon Job's stone; and the rest of the day they either read or assist the dwellers in the Makâm in their tillage of the soil. When they are about to leave, they receive a testimonial, and often return home on foot across the Isthmus of Suez, often by water, chiefly from Jâfâ, by the Austrian Lloyd ship to Egypt, and thence to their native country. These pilgrims, so far as the requirements of their own country are concerned, are *literati;* and it appears as though by this journey they obtained their highest degree. I have frequently met them in my travels. They are known by their clean white turban, and the white broad-sleeved shirt, which reaches to the ankles, their only garment. They carry a small bundle over the shoulder upon a strong staff, which may serve as a weapon of defence in case of need. In this bundle they carry a few books and other effects, and above this their cloak. They are modest, taciturn men, who go nimbly onward on their way, and to whom one always gladly gives a supper and a night's lodging.

We visited the holy places in the company of the Sheikh Sa'îd. The Makâm, and the reservoir, which lies fifty paces to the front of it, are surrounded by a wall. This reservoir is filled by a strong, rapid, and cold stream of water, which comes from the fountain of Job, about 400 paces distant. The fountain itself springs up by the basalt hill on which the village and the Job's stone are situated; and it is covered in as far as the reservoir (called *birke*), in order to keep the water fresh, and to guard against pollution. Between the fountain and the Ma*k*âm stand a half-dozen acacias and a pomegranate, which were just then in full bloom. The Ma*k*âm itself, on which the wretched habitations for the attendants and pilgrims adjoin, is a one-storey stone building, of old material and moderate circumference. The first thing shown us was the stone trough, called *gurn*, in which Job bathed at the end of his trial. The small space in which this relic stands, and over which, so far as I remember, one of the two domes is raised, is called *wadjet sêjidnâ* Êjûb, "the lavatory of our lord Job." Adjoining this is the part with the tomb, the oblong mound of which is covered with an old torn green cloth. The tomb of *Sa'd* was more carefully tended. Our Damascene travelling companions were divided in their opinions as to the person whose tomb was near that of Job, as in Syria it is hardly possible to find and distinguish the ma*k*âms of the many men of God (*rigâl Allâh*) or favoured ones of God (*auliâ*) who bear the same names; but a small white flag standing upon the grave informed us, for it bore the inscription: "This is the military emblem (*râje*) of our lord *Sa'd abû Merzûka*."

Perhaps the preservation of the Ma*k*âm of Job is due to the tomb of Sa'd, as its endowments have long since disappeared, while the tomb of Sa'd still has its revenues. From 'Aglûn it receives tribute of oil and olives yearly. And several large vegetable gardens, which lie round about the Ma*k*âm, and are cultivated by its attendants, must also contribute something considerable towards its maintenance. In these gardens they grow *dura* (maize), tobacco, turnips, onions, and other things, for their own use and for sale.

The plants, which can be freely watered from the fountain of Job, are highly esteemed. The government levies no taxes on the Maḵâm, and the Arabs no tribute; and since, according to the popular belief, the Beduin horse that is watered from the *birke* dies, the Beduins do not even claim the rights of hospitality,—a fortunate circumstance, the removal of which would speedily cause the ruin of the hospice. From nightly thieves, who not unfrequently break through the walls of the stables in the villages of the plain, and carry off the smaller cattle, both the Maḵâm and the village are secure; for if the night thieves come, they see, as every one in Hauran testifies, a surging sea around the place, which prevents their approach.

From the Maḵâm we ascended the hill of the village, on the highest part of which is the stone of Job (*Sachrat Êjûb*). It is inside a small Mussulman hall of prayer, which in its present form is of more modern origin, but is undoubtedly built from the material of a Christian chapel, which stood here in the pre-Muhammedan age. It is an unartistic structure, in the usual Hauranitish style, with six or eight arches and a small dome, which is just above the stone of Job. My Mussulman attendants, and a Hauranite Christian from the village of Shemiskîn, who had joined us as we were visiting the *Sachra*, trod the sacred spot with bare feet, and kissed the rock, the basaltic formation of which is unmistakeable. Against this rock, our guide told us, Job leaned "when he was afflicted by his Lord" (hîn *ibtelâ min rabbuh*).[1] While these people were offering up their *ʿAsr* (afternoon) prayer in this place, Saʿîd brought me a handful of small long round

[1] As is generally known, the black stone in Mekka and the *Sachra* in Jerusalem are more celebrated than the stone of Job; but less revered are the *Mebrak en-nâka* in Boṣrâ, the thievish stone of Moses in the great mosque at Damascus, the *doset en-nebî* on the mountain of el-Hîgâne, and others.

stones and slag, which the tradition declares to be the worms that fell to the ground out of Job's sores, petrified. "Take them with thee," said he, "as a memento of this place; let them teach thee not to forget God in prosperity, and in misfortune not to contend with Him." The frequent use of these words in the mouth of the man might have weakened them to a set phrase: they were, however, appropriate to the occasion, and were not without their effect. After my attendants had provided themselves with Job's worms, we left the Sachra. These worms form a substantial part of the Hauranitish tradition of Job, and they are known and revered generally in the country. Our Christian attendant from Shemiskîn bound them carefully in the broad sleeve of his shirt, and recited to us a few verses from a kasîde, in which they are mentioned. The poem, which a member of our company, the dervish Regeb, wrote down, is by a Hauranite Christian, who in it describes his unhappy love in colours as strong as the bad taste it displays. The lines that are appropriate here are as follows:—

> Min 'azma nârî nâra jôm el-qijâma,
> Tûfâna Nûha 'dmû' a 'ênî 'anuh zôd.
> Ja' qûba min hoznî hizânuh qisâma
> Min belwetî Ejûba jertâ' bihe 'd-dûd.[1]

The fire of hell at the last day will kindle itself from the glow of my pain,
　　And stronger than the flood of Noah are the tear-streams of mine eyes.
The grief of Jacob for his son was but a small part of my grief;
　　And, visited with my misery, Job was once the prey of worms.[2]

The village, which the peasants call Shêch Sa'd, and the nomads Sa'dîje, is, as the name implies, of later origin, and perhaps was founded by people who fled hither when oppressed elsewhere, for the sake of being able to live more peacefully under the protection of the two tombs. That the

[1] The metre forms two spondeo-iambics and trochæo-spondaics.
[2] Comp. vol. ii. p. 158 of the foregoing Commentary.

place is not called Êjûbîje, is perhaps in order to distinguish
it from the Monastery of Job. In less than a quarter of an hour we rode up to the Dêr
Êjûb, a square building, standing entirely alone, and not surrounded by ruins. When the Arabian geographers call it a
village, they reckon to it the neighbouring Saʿdîje with the
Makâm. It is very extensive, and built of fine square blocks
of dolerite. While my fellow-traveller, M. Dörgens, was
engaged in making a ground-plan of the shattered building,
which seemed to us on the whole to have had a very simple
construction, I took some measurements of its sides and
angles, and then searched for inscriptions. Although the
ground-floor is now in part hidden in a mezbele,[1] which has
been heaped up directly against the walls, on the east side,
upon the architrave, not of the chief doorway, which is on
the south, but of a door of the church, is found a large Greek
inscription in a remarkable state of preservation. The architrave consists of a single carefully-worked block of dolerite,
and at present rests almost upon the ground, since the rubbish has filled the whole doorway. The writing and sculp-
ture are hollowed out.

In the centre is a circle, and the characters inscribed at
each side of this circle are still undeciphered; the rest of the
inscription is easy to be read: αὕτη ἡ πύλη κ(υρίο)υ δίκαιοι
εἰσελεύσοντε ἐν αὐτῇ· τοῦτο τὸ ὑπέρθυρον ἐτέθη ἐν χρόνοις
Ἡλίου εὐλαβεστ(άτου) ἡγουμ(ένου) μ(ηνί) Ἰουλίῳ κε̄ ἰνδ(ι)κ-
(τίωνος) ιε τοῦ ἔτους πηντακοσιοστοῦ τρικοστοῦ ἔκτου κ(υρί)ου
Ἰ(ησ)οῦ Χ(ριστ)οῦ βασιλεύοντος. The passage of Scripture,
Ps. cxviii. 20, with which this inscription begins, is frequently found in these districts in the inscriptions on church
portals.

This inscription was an interesting discovery; for, so far
as I know, it is the oldest that we possess which reckons

[1] On the word and subject, vid. vol. ii. 152 of the foregoing Commentary.

according to the Christian era, and in the Roman indiction (*indictio*)[1] we have an important authority for determining its date. Now, since there might be a difference of opinion as to the beginning of the "kingdom of Christ," I was anxious to have the judgment of an authority in chronology on the point; and I referred to Prof. Piper of Berlin, who kindly furnished me with the following communication:—" . . . The inscription therefore furnishes the following data: July 25, indict. xv., year 536, κυρίου Ἰοῦ Χοῦ βασιλεύοντος. To begin with the last, the Dionysian era, which was only just introduced into the West, is certainly not to be assumed here. But it is also by no means the birth of Christ that is intended. Everything turns upon the expression βασιλεύοντος. The same expression occurs once in an inscription from Syria, *Corp. Inscr. Græc.* 8651: βασιλεύοντος Ἰουστινιανοῦ τῷ ια ἔτει. The following expression, however, occurs later concerning Christ on Byzantine coins: *Rex regnantium* and Βασιλεὺς Βασιλέων (after Apoc. xvii. 14, xix. 16), the latter under John Zimiszes (died 975), in *De Saulcy, Pl.* xxii. 4. But if the βασιλεία of Christ is employed as the era, we manifestly cannot refer to the epoch of the birth of Christ, but must take the epoch of His ascension as our basis: for with this His βασιλεία first began; just as in the West we sometimes find the calculation begins *a passione.* Now the fathers of the Western Church indeed place the death (and therefore also the ascension) of Christ in the consulate of the two *Gemini*, 29 A.D. Not so with the Greek fathers. Eusebius takes the year of His death, according to one supposition, to be the 18th year of Tiberius, *i.e.* 785 A.U.C. = 32 A.D. Supposing we take this as the first year *regnante Jesu Christo*, then the year 536, of the inscription of the Monastery of Job, is reduced to our era, after the birth of Christ, by adding 31. Thus we have the

---

[1] *Vid.* Gibbon, ed. Smith, ii. 333.—Tr.

number of the year 567, to which the accompanying xv.
indictio corresponds, for $567 + 3 = 570$; and $\frac{570}{15}$ has no remainder. XV. is therefore the indiction of the year 567,
which more accurately belongs to the year from 1st Sept.
566 to 31st Aug. 567. And since the day of the month is
mentioned in the inscription, it is the 25th July 567 that is
indicated. For it appears to me undoubted that the indic-
tions, according to the usual mode of computation among the
Greeks, begin with the 1st Sept. 312. Thus a Sidonian
inscription of Dec. 642 A.D. has the I. indiction (*Corp.
Inscr. Gr.* 9153). . . . "

Thus far Prof. Piper's communication. According to this
satisfactory explanation of its date, this inscription is perhaps
not unqualified to furnish a contribution worth notice, even
for the chronology of the life of Jesus, since the Ghassinides,
under whom not only the inscription, but the Monastery
itself 300 years earlier, had its origin, dwelt in Palestine, the
land of Christ; and their kings were perhaps the first who
professed Christianity.

The "festival of the Monastery of Job," which, according
to *Kazwînî's* Syrian Calendar,[1] the Christians of the country
celebrated annually on the 23d April, favours the pre-
Muhammedan importance of the Monastery. This festival
in *Kazwînî's* time, appearing only by name in the calendar,
had undoubtedly ceased with the early decline of Christianity
in the plain of Hauran, for the historically remarkable exodus
of a large portion of the Ghassinides out of the cities of
Hauran to the north of Georgia had taken place even under
the chalifate of Omar. The Syrian Christians of the present
day celebrate the festival of Mâr Gorgius (St George), who
slew the dragon (*tennîn*) near Beirût, on the 23d April. A
week later (the 1st May, oriental era) the Jews of Damascus
have the *sôm Êjûb* (the fast of Job), which lasts twenty-

[1] *Calendarium Syriacum Cazwinii*, ed. Guil. Volck, Lips. 1859, p. 15.

four hours. In *Kazwînî's* calendar it is erroneously set down to the 3d May.

Moreover, with reference to the Monastery, it must be mentioned that, according to the history of *Ibn Kethîr*,[1] the great Greco-Ghassinide army, which, under the leadership of Theodoric, a brother of the Emperor Heraclius, was to have repulsed the attack of the Mussulmans on Syria, revolted in its neighbourhood in the 13th year of the Hegira (*Higra*), while the enemy was encamped on the south bank of the *Meddân*, and was drawn up near *Edre'ât*. After several months had passed came the battle known as the "battle of the *Jarmûk*," the issue of which cost the Byzantines Syria. The volcanic hollows of the ground, which for miles form a complex network of gorges, for the most part inaccessible, offer great advantages in defensive warfare; and here the battle near *Edre'î*, in which 'Og king of Bashan lost his kingdom, was probably fought.

According to the present division of the country, the Monastery of Job and the Ma*k*âm are in the southern part of *Gêdûr*, an administrative district, which is bounded on the north by the *Wâdi Bêrût*, on the east by the *W. el-Horêr* and the high road, on the south by the *Jarmûk*, and on the west by the *W. Hit* and by a range of volcanic mounds, which stretch to the south-east corner of the Snow-mountain (*el-Hermón*); this district, however, has only a nominal existence, for it has no administration of its own. Either it is added to *Haurân*, or its revenues, together with those of Gôlân, are let out to the highest bidder for a number of years. *Gêdûr* is the natural north-western continuation of the plain of *Haurân*; and the flat bed of the *Horêr*, which does not form a gorge until it comes to the bridge of *Sîra*, forms no boundary proper. Moreover, the word is not found in ancient geography; and the Arabian geographers, even

[1] Comp. A. v. Kremer, *Mittelsyrien*, etc., Vienna 1853, S. 10.

the later ones, who recognised the idea of *Gêdûr*, always
so define the position of a locality situated in Gêdûr, that
they say it is situated in the *H*aurân.　Thus Jâ*k*ût describes
the town of el-Gâbïa, situated in western Gêdûr, and in like
manner, as we have seen above, Nawâ and the Monastery of
Job, etc.[1]　There is no doubt that, as the Gêdûr of the
present day is reckoned in the *Nukra*, so this country also
in ancient days, at least as far as its northern watershed, has
belonged to the tetrarchy of *Batanæa*.

The Monastery of Job is at present inhabited.　A certain
sheikh, *Ahmed el-Kâdirî*, has settled down here since the
autumn of 1859, as partner of the senior of the Damascene
'Omarîje (the successors of the Chalif 'Omar), to whose
family endowments (*waqf*) the Monastery belongs, and with
his family he inhabits a number of rooms in the inner court,
which have escaped destruction.　He showed us the decree
of his partner appointing him to his position, in which he is
styled Sheikh of the *Dêr Êjûb*, *Dêr el-Lebwe*, and *'Ashtarâ*.
Dêr el-Lebwe, "the monastery of the lion," [2] was built by the
Gefnide *Eihem ibn el-Hârith;* and we shall have occasion to
refer to *'Ashtarâ*, in which Newbold,[3] in the year 1846,
believed he had found the ancient capital of Basan, *'Ashtarôt*,
further on.　But the possessor of all these grand things was
a very unhappy man.　While we were drinking coffee with
him, he related to us how the inhabitants of Nawâ had left

---

[1] Jâ*k*ût says under *Gêdûr*, " It is a Damascene district, it has villages,
and lies in the north of *H*aurân ; according to others, it is reckoned
together with *H*aurân as one district."　The last words do not signify
that *Gêdûr* and *H*aurân are words to be used without any distinction ; on
the contrary, that Gêdûr is a district belonging to *H*aurân, and comprehended in it.

[2] The name of this monastery, which is about a mile and a half north-
east of the Dêr Ejûb, is erroneously called D. el-lebû in Burckhardt's
Travels in Syria (ed. Gesenius, S. 449).　The same may be said of D.
en-nubuwwe in *Annales Hamzæ*, ed. Gottwaldt, p. ǁ٨.

[3] C. Ritter, *Geogr. v. Syr. u. Pal.* ii. 821 [*Erdk.* xv. Pt. 2, p. 821].

him only two yoke (*feddân*) of arable land from the territory assigned to him, and taken all the rest to themselves. The harvest of that year, after the deduction of the *bedhâr* (the new seed-corn), would hardly suffice to meet the demands of his family, and of hospitality; and for his partner, who had advanced money to him, there would be nothing left. In Damascus he found no redress; and the Sheikh of Nawâ, *Dhiâb el-Medhjeb*, had answered his last representation with the words, "He who desires Job's inheritance must look for trials." Here also, as in Arabia generally, I found that intelligence and energy was on the side of the wife. During our conversation, his wife, with one of her children, had drawn near; and while the child kissed my hand, according to custom, she said: "To-morrow thou wilt arrive at *Muzêrîb;* Dhiâb will also be going thither with contributions for the pilgrims. We put our cause in thy hands, arrange it as seems thee best; this old man will accompany thee." And as we were riding, the Sheikh A*h*med was also obliged to mount, and his knowledge of the places did us good service on *Tell Ashtarâ* and *Tell el-Ash'arî*. In Muzêrîb, where the pilgrim fair and the arriving caravans for Mekka occupied our attention for five days, we met Dhiâb and the *Ichtiârîje* (elders of the community) of Nawâ; and, after some opposition, the sheikh of the Monastery of Job obtained four *feddân* of land under letter and seal, and returned home satisfied.

The case of this man is no standard of the state of the Hauranites, for there are so many desolated villages that there is no lack of land; only round about *Nawâ* it is insufficient, since this place is obliged to take possession of far outlying fields, by reason of its exceedingly numerous agricultural population.[1] The more desolate a land exposed to

---

[1] That the Sheikh A*h*med was permitted to take up his abode in the Monastery, was owing to a religious dread of his ancestor (*gidd*), '*Abdel-Kâdir el-Gîlâni*, and out of courteousness towards his partner.

plunder becomes, the more populous must its separate towns become, since the inhabitants of the smaller defenceless villages crowd into them. Thus the inhabitants of the large town of *Kenâkir* at the present time till the fields of twelve neighbouring deserted villages; and *Salt*, the only inhabited place in the *Belkâ*, has its corn-fields even at a distance of fifteen miles away. The poet may also have conceived of Job's domain similarly, for there were five hundred ploughmen employed on it; so that it could not come under the category of ordinary villages, which in Syria rarely have above, mostly under, fifty yoke of oxen. According to the tradition, which speaks of "Job's villages" (*diâ' Êjûb*), these ploughmen would be distributed over several districts; but the poet, who makes them to be overwhelmed by one ghazwe, therefore as ploughing in one district, will have conceived of them only as dwelling in one locality.

It might not be out of place here to give some illustration of the picture which the poet draws of Job's circumstances and position as a wealthy husbandman. *H*aurân, the scene of the drama (as we here assume), must at that period, as at present, have been without protection from the government of the country, and therefore exposed to the marauding attacks of the tribes of the desert. In such a country there is no private possession; but each person is at liberty to take up his abode in it, and to cultivate the land and rear cattle at his own risk, where and to what extent he may choose. Whoever intends doing so must first of all have a family, or as the Arabs say, "men" (*rigâl*), *i.e.* grown-up sons, cousins, nephews, sons-in-law; for one who stands alone, "the cut off one" (*maktû'*), as he is called, can attain no position of eminence among the Semites, nor undertake any important enterprise.[1] Then he has to make treaties with all the nomad

---

[1] In the present day the household is called *'ashîra*, and all families of importance in Haurân are and call themselves *'ashâir* (عشاير); but the

tribes from which he has reason to fear any attack, *i.e.* to pledge himself to pay a yearly tribute, which is given in native produce (in corn and garments). Thus the community of *el-Higâne*, ten years since, had compacts with 101 tribes; and that Job also did this, seems evident from the fact that the poet represents him as surprised not by neighbouring, but by far distant tribes (Chaldæans and Sabæans), with whom he could have no compact.[1] Next he proceeds to erect a *chirbe, i.e.* a village that has been forsaken (for a longer or shorter period), in connection with which, excepting the relations, slaves, and servants of the master, all those whom interest, their calling, and confidence in the good fortune of the master, have drawn thither, set about

ancient word *batn* does also occur, and among the Semitic tribes that have migrated to Mauritania it is still in use instead of the Syrian *'ashíra*. *Batn*, collect. *butûn*, is the fellowship of all those who are traced back to the בֶּטֶן of one ancestral mother. Thus even in Damascus they say : *nahn ferd batn*, we belong to one family; in like manner in the whole of Syria: this foal is the *batn* of that mare, *i.e.* its young one; or : I sold my mare without *batn*, or with one, two, three-fourths of her *batn, i.e.* without her descendants, or so that the buyer has only 6 or 12 or 18 *kîrât* right of possession in the foals she will bear. In all these applications, *batn* is the *progenies uteri*, not the *uterus* itself; and, according to this, בְּנֵי בִטְנִי, ch. xix. 17, ought to be explained by "all my relations by blood."

[1] These sudden attacks, at any rate, do not say anything in favour of the more southernly position of *Ausitis*. If the Beduin is but once on his horse or *delûl*, it is all the same to him whether a journey is ten days longer or shorter, if he can only find water for himself and his beast. This, however, both bands of marauders found, since the poet distinctly represents the attacks as having been made in the winter. The general ploughing of the fallow-lying *wâgiha* of a community (it is called *shiqâq el-wâgiha*), ready for the sowing in the following autumn, always takes place during January and February, because at this time of the year the earth is softened by the winter rains, and easy to plough. While engaged in this work, the poet represents Job's ploughmen as being surprised and slain. Hence, for the destruction of 500 armed ploughmen—and they were armed, because they could only have been slain with their weapons in their hands in consequence of their resistance—at least 2000 horsemen were necessary. So large a *ghazwe* is, however, not possible in the summer,

the work. Perhaps ch. xv. 28 has reference to Job's settlement.[1] With reference to the relation of the lord of a village (*ustâd beled,* or *sâhib dé'a*) to his work-people, there are among the dependants two classes. The one is called *zurrá'*, " sowers," also *fellâhin kism,* " participating husbandmen," because they share the produce of the harvest with the *ustâd* thus: he receives a fourth while they retain three-fourths, from which they live, take the seed for the following season, give their quota towards the demands of the Arabs, the village shepherds, the field watchmen, and the scribe of the community (*chatîb*); they have also to provide the farming implements and the yoke-oxen. On the other hand, the *ustâd* has to provide for the dwellings of the people, to pay the land-tax to the government, and, in the event of a failure of the crops, murrain, etc., to make the necessary advances, either in money or in kind at the market price, and without

but only in the winter, because they could not water at a draw-well, only at the pools (*ghudrân*) formed by the winter rains. For one of these raids of the Chaldæans, Haurân, whither marauding bands come even now during the winter from the neighbourhood of Babylon in six or seven days, lay far more convenient than the country around *Ma'ân* and *'Akaba*, which is only reached from the Euphrates, even in winter, by going a long way round, since the *Nufûd* (sandy plains) in the east, and their western continuation the *Hâlât,* suck in the rain without forming any pools. On the other hand, however, this southern region lay nearer and more convenient for the incursions of the Sabæans, viz. the Keturæan (Gen. xxv. 3), *i.e.* Petræan tribe of this name. The greater or less distance, however, is of little consequence here. Thus, as the *Shemmar* of *Negd* from time to time make raids into the neighbourhood of Damascus, so even the tribes of *Wâdi el-Korâ* might also do the same. Moreover, as we observed above, the poet represents the sudden attacks as perpetrated by the Sabæans and Chaldæans, probably because *they only,* as being foreign and distant races which never had anything to do with Job and his men, and therefore were without any consideration, could practise such unwonted barbarities as the robbery of ploughing heifers, which a *ghazwe* rarely takes, and the murder of the ploughmen.

[1] [Verbally, ch. iii. 14*b*, which we, however, have interpreted differently, accords with this.—DEL.]

any compensation. This relation, which guarantees the maintenance of the family, and is according to the practice of a patriarchal equity, is greatly esteemed in the country; and one might unhesitatingly consider it therefore to be that which existed between Job and his ploughmen, because it may with ease exist between a single *ustâd* and hundreds, indeed thousands, of country people, if ch. i. 3 did not necessitate our thinking of another class of country people, viz. the *murâbi'în*, the "quarterers." They take their name from their receiving a fourth part of the harvest for their labour, while they have to give up the other three-fourths to the *ustâd*, who must provide for their shelter and board, and in like manner everything that is required in agriculture. As Job, according to ch. i. 3 (comp. on ch. xlii. 12), provided the yoke-oxen and means of transport (asses and camels), so he also provided the farming implements, and the seed for sowing. We must not here think of the paid day-labourer of the Syrian towns, or the servants of our landed proprietors; they are unknown on the borders of the desert. The hand that toils has there a direct share in the gain; the workers belong to the *aulâd*, "children of the house," and are so called; in the hour of danger they will risk their life for their lord.

This rustic labour is always undertaken simultaneously by all the *murâbi'în* (it is so also in the villages of the *zurrâ'*) for the sake of order, since the *ustâd*, or in his absence the village sheikh, has the general work of the following day announced from the roof of his house every evening. Thus it is explained how the 500 ploughmen could be together in one and the same district, and be slain all together.

The *ustâd* is the sole judge, or, by deputy, the *sheikh*. An appeal to the government of the country would be useless, because it has no influence in Hauran; but the servant who has been treated unjustly by his master, very frequently turns as *dachîl fi 'l-haqq* (a suppliant concerning his right) to his powerful neighbour, who is bound, according to the customs of the country, to obtain redress for him (comp. ch. xxix. 12–17). If he does not obtain this by persuasion, he cries for force, and such a demand lies at the root of many a bloody feud.

Powerful and respected also as the position, described in ch. xxix., of such a man is, it must, according to the nature of its basis, fall in under strokes of misfortune, like those mentioned in ch. i. 14–19, and change to the very opposite, as the poet describes it in ch. xxx.

After these observations concerning the agricultural relations of Hauran, we return to the tradition of Job. As we pursue the track of this tradition further, we first find it again in some of the Christian writers of the middle ages, viz. in Eugesippus (*De distanc. loc. terr. sanct.*), in William of Tyre (*Histor. rerum a Francis gest.*), and in Marino Sanuto (*De secretis fid. cruc.*). The passages that bear upon the point are brought together in Reland (*Palest.* pp. 265 sq.) ; and we would simply refer to them, if it were possible for the reader to find his way among the fabulous confusion of the localities in Eugesippus and Sanuto.

The oldest of these citations is from Eugesippus, and is as follows: One part of the country is the land of *Hus*, out of which Job was; it is also called *Sueta*, after which Bildad the Suhite was named. Sanuto tells us where this locality is to be sought. "*Sueta* is the home of Baldad the Suite. Below this city (*civitas*), in the direction of the Kedar-tribes, the Saracens are accustomed to assemble out of Aram, Mesopotamia, Ammon, Moab, and the whole Orient, around the fountain of *Fiale ;* and, on account of the charms of the place, to hold a fair there during the whole summer, and to pitch their coloured tents." In another place he says: *fontem Fialen Medan, i.e. aquas Dan, a Saracenis nuncupari.*

Now, since according to an erroneous, but previously prevalent etymology, "the water of Dan" (מֵי דָן = יְאֹר דָן) denoted the Jordan, and since we further know from Josephus (*Bell.* iii. 10, 7) that the *Phiala* is the small lake of *Râm*, whose subterranean outflow the tetrarch Philip is said to have shown to be the spring of the Jordan, which comes to light deeper below, we should have thought the country round about the lake of Râm, at the south foot of Hermôn, to be the home of Job and Bildad. This discovery would be confirmed by the following statement of Eugesippus (in Reland, *loc. cit.*): "The river *Dan* flows under ground from its spring as far as the plain of Meldan, where it comes to light. This plain is named after the fair, which is held there, for the Saracens call such an one *Meldan*. At the beginning of the summer a large number of men, with wares to sell, congregate there, and several Parthian and Arabian soldiers also, in order to guard the people and their herds, which have a rich pasture there in the summer. The word *meldan* is composed of *mel* and *dan.*" It is indeed readily seen that the writer has ignorantly jumbled several words together in the expression *meldan*, as *mê Dan*, "water of Dan," and *mêdân* or *mîdân*, "market-place;" perhaps even also *leddân*, the name of the great fountain of the Jordan in the crater of the *Tell el-*Kâdi. In like manner, the statement that the neighbourhood of *Phiala*, or that of the large fountain of the Jordan, might formerly have been a fair of the tribes, is false, for the former is broken up into innumerable craters, and the latter is poisoned by the swamp-fevers of the Hûle; but as to the rest, both Eugesippus and Sanuto seem really to speak of a tradition which places Job's or Bildad's home in that region. And yet it is not so: their tradition is no other than the Hauranitish; but ignorance of the language and geography of the country, and some accidental circumstances, so confused their representations, that it is difficult to find out what is right. The first clue is given us by the history of William of Tyre, in which (l. xxii. c. 21) it is said that the crusaders, on their return from a marauding expedition in the Nu*k*ra, wished to reconquer a strong position, the *Cavea Roob*, which they had lost a short time before. "This place," says the historian, "lies in the province of *Suite*, a district distinguished by its pleasantness, etc.; and that Baldad, Job's friend, who is on that account called the Suite, is said to have come from it." This passage removes us at once into the neighbourhood of *Muzêrîb* and the Monastery of Job, for the province of Suete is nothing but the district of *Suwêt* (صويت),[1] the north-western boundary of which is formed by the gorge of the *Wâdî Rahûb*. The *Cavea Roob*, which was first of all again found out by me on my journey in 1862, lies in the middle of the steep bank of that wadi, and is at present called *maghâret Rahûb*, "the cave of R.," or more commonly *mu'allakat Rahûb*, "the swinging cave of R.," and at the time of the Crusades commanded the dangerous pass which the traveller, on ascending from the south end of the Lake of Galilee to *Edre'ât* by the nearest way, has to climb on hands and feet. In another passage (xvi. 9), where the unhealthy march to *Bosrâ* is spoken of, Will. of Tyre says: "After we had come through the gorge of *Roob*, we reached the plain which is called *Medan*, and where every year the Arabs and other oriental tribes are accustomed to hold a large fair." This plain is in the vicinity of *Muzêrîb*, in which the great pilgrim-fair is held annually. We find something similar in xiii. 18: "After having passed Decapolis[2] we came to the pass of *Roob*, and further on into the plain of *Medan*, which stretches far and wide in every direction, and is intersected

---

[1] *Reisebericht*, S. 46; comp. Ritter, *Syr. u. Pal.* ii. 1019 [*Erdk.* xv. Pt. 2, p. 1019].

[2] Here in the more contracted sense, the district of *Gadara*, *Kefârât*, and *Irbid*.

by the river *Dan,* which falls into the Jordan between
Tiberias and *Scythopolis* (*Bîsân*)." This river, the same as
that which Sanuto means by his *aquæ Dan* (*Mê Dân*), is
none other than the *Wâdi el-Meddân,* called "the overflow-
ing one," because in the month of March it overflows its
banks eastward of the *Gezzâr*-bridge. It is extremely strange
that the name of this river appears corrupted not only in all
three writers mentioned above, but also in Burckhardt; for,
deceived by the ear, he calls it *Wâdi Om el-Dhan.*[1] The
Meddân is the boundary river between the *Suwêt* and *Nukra*
plains; it loses its name where it runs into the *Makran;* and
where it falls into the valley of the Jordan, below the lake
of Tiberias, it is called *el-Muchêbi.*

We have little to add to what has been already said. The
Fiale of Sanuto is not the Lake Râm, but the round *begge,* the
lake of springs of Muzêrîb, the rapid outflow of which, over
a depth of sixty to eighty feet, forms a magnificent waterfall,
the only one in Syria, as it falls into the Meddân near the
village of *Tell Shihâb.*

The unfortunate confusion of the localities was occasioned
by two accidental circumstances: first, that both, the springs
of the Jordan below *Bâniâs* and the lake of *Muzêrîb,* have a
village called *Rahûb* (רחוב) in their vicinity, of which one is
mentioned in Judg. xviii. 28 sq., and the other, about a mile
below the *Cavea Roob,* is situated by a fountain of the same
name, from which village, cavern, and wadi derive their
names; secondly, that there, as here, there is a village *Abil*
(אָבֵל): that near Dan is situated in the "meadow-district of
'Ijôn" (*Merg 'Ijûn*); and that in the *Suwêt* lies between
Rahûb and the *Makran,* and was visited by Seetzen as well
as by myself. Perhaps the circumstance that, just as the
environs of *Muzêrîb* have their *Midân,*[2] so the environs of

---

[1] Burckhardt, *Travels in Syr. and Pal.* (ed. Gesenius, S. 392).
[2] The word *el-mîdân* and *el-mêdân* signifies originally the hippodrome,

Bâniâs have their *Ard el-Mejâdin*, "region of battle-fields,"
may also have contributed to the confusion; thus, for example,
the country sloping to the west from the *Phiala* towards the
Hûle, between *Gubbâtâ ez-zêt* and *Za'ûra*, is called, perhaps
on account of the murderous encounters which took place
there, both in the time of the Crusades and also in more
ancient times. It is certainly the ground on which the battle
narrated in the book of Joshua, ch. xi., took place, and also
the battle in which Antiochus the Great slew the Egyptian
army about 200 B.C.

What we have gained for our special purpose from this
information (by which not a few statements of Ritter, K. v.
Raumer, and others, are substantiated), is not merely the fact
that the tradition which places Job's home in the region of
Muzêrîb existed even in the middle ages (which the quotation given above from *Makdeshî*, who lived before the time
of the Crusades, also confirms), and even came to the ears of
the foreigners who settled in the country as they then passed
through the land, but also the certainty that this tradition
was then, as now, common to the Christians and the Mussulmans, for the three writers previously mentioned would hardly
have recorded it on the testimony of the latter only.[1]

then the arena of the sham-fight, then the place of contest, the battle-
field, and finally a wide level place where a large concourse of men are
accustomed to meet. In this sense the Damascenes have their *el-mîdân*,
the Spanish cities their *almeidân*, and the Italians their *corso*.

[1] [Estôri ha-Parchi, the most renowned Jewish topographer of Palestine, in his work *Caftor wa-ferach*, completed in 1322 (newly edited by
Edelmann, published by Asher, Berlin, 1852, S. 49), says דאר איוב lies
one hour south of נבו, since he identifies *Nawâ* with the Reubenitish
Nebô, Num. xxxii. 38, as *Zora'* with יעזר, Num. xxxii. 35 ; so that he
explains ארץ עוץ by ארץ יעזר, although he at the same time considers
the name, according to Saadia, as one with אלגוטה (*el-Ghuta*). His
statements moreover are exact, as one might expect from a man who
had travelled for seven years in all directions in Palestine; and his conclusion, ארץ עוץ היא ארץ קדם לארץ ישראל כנגד טבריא, perfectly accords
with the above treatise.—DEL.]

There can be no doubt as to which of these two religions
must be regarded as the original mother of this tradition.
The Hauranite Christians, who, from their costume, manners, language, and traditions, undoubtedly inherited the
country from the pre-Muhammedan age, venerate the Makâm
perhaps even more than the Muhammedans; which would be
altogether impossible in connection with the hostile position
of the two religious sects towards one another, and in connection with the zealous scorn with which the Syrian Christians regard the religion of Islam, if the Hauranitish tradition
of Job and the Makâm were of later, Muhammedan origin.
It is also possible that, on a closer examination of the Makâm
and the buildings about the Sachra, one might find, besides
crosses, Greek inscriptions (since they are nowhere wanting
in the Nukra), which could only have their origin in the time
before the occupation of Islam (635 A.D.); for *after* this the
Hauranite Christians, who only prolong their existence by
wandering from *chirbe* to *chirbe*, have not even built a single
dwelling-house, much less a building for religious worship,
which was forbidden under pain of death in the treaty of
Omar. But in connection with the pre-Islam Monastery of
Job, which owed its origin only to the sacred tradition that
held its ground in that place, are monumental witnesses that
this tradition is pre-Islamic, and has been transferred from
the Christians to the Mussulmans, required? We may go
even further, and assert that Muhammed, in the Sur. xxxviii.
41 sqq. of the Korân, had the Hauranitish tradition of Job
and the localities near Sa'dîje definitely before his mind.

We must regard the merchandise caravans which the
inhabitants of *Tehâma* sent continuously into the "north
country," *esh-shâm*,[1] and the return freight of which consisted chiefly of Hauranitish corn, as proof of a regular

[1] In Jemen and *Higâz*, Syria may have been called *Shâm* in the earliest
times. The name was taken into Syria itself by the immigration of the

intercourse between the east Jordanic country and the west
of the Arabian peninsula in the period between Christ and
Muhammed. Hundreds of men from Mekka and Medina
came every year to *Bosrâ;* indeed, when it has happened
that the wandering tribes of Syria, which were, then also
as now, bound for Hauran with the *kêl, i.e.* their want of
corn, got before them, and had emptied the granaries of
Bosrâ, or when the harvests of the south of Hauran had
been destroyed by the locusts, which is not unfrequently the
case, they will have come into the *Nukra*[1] as far as Nawâ,
sometimes even as far as Damascus, in order to obtain their
full cargo.

If commerce often has the difficult task of bringing together
the most heterogeneous peoples, and of effecting a reciprocal
interchange of ideas, it here had the easy work of sustaining
the intercourse among tribes that were originally one people,
spoke one idiom, and regarded themselves as all related; for

Jemanic tribes of Kudâ'a, and others, because they brought with them
the name of Syria that was commonly used in their native land.

[1] The remarkable fair at *Muzêrîb* can be traced back to the earliest
antiquity, although Bosrâ at times injured it; but this latter city, from its
more exposed position, has been frequently laid in ruins. It is probable
that the merchants of Damascus pitched their tents for their Kasaba,
i.e. their moveable fair, twice a year (in spring and in autumn) by the
picturesque lake of Muzêrîb. If, with the tradition, we take the *Nukra*
to be the home of Job, of the different ways of interpreting ch. vi. 19
there is nothing to hinder our deciding upon that which considers it as
the greater caravan which came periodically out of southern Arabia to
Hauran (Bosrâ or Muzêrîb). *Têmâ* with its well, *Heddâg* (comp. Isa.
xxi. 14), celebrated by the poets of the steppe, from which ninety camels
(*sâniât*) by turns raise a constantly flowing stream of clear and cool
water for irrigating the palms and the seed, was in ancient times, perhaps, the crossing point of the merchant caravans going from south to
north, and from east to west. Even under the Omajad Chalifs the
Mekka pilgrim-route went exclusively by way of *Têmâ*, just as during the
Crusades so long as the Franks kept possession of *Kerak* and *Shôbak*.
An attempt made in my *Reisebericht* (S. 93–95) to substitute the
Hauranitish *Têmâ* in the two previously mentioned passages of Scripture, I have there (S. 131) given up as being scarcely probable.

the second great Sabæan migration, under ʿ*Amr* and his son
Taʿlabe, had taken possession of Mekka, and left one of their
number, *Rabîʿa ibn Hâritha,* with his attendants (the Chuzâ-
ites), behind as lord of the city. In the same manner they
had become possessed of *Jathrib* (*el-Medîna*), and left this
city to their tribes *Aus* and *Chazreg:* the remainder of the
people passed on to Peræa and took possession of the country,
at that time devastated, as far as Damascus, according to *Ibn
Saʿîd,* even including this city. By the reception of Christianity, the Syrian Sabæans appear to have become but slightly
or not at all estranged from their relatives in the Higâz, for
Christianity spread even here, so that the Cæsars once ventured to appoint a Christian governor even to the city of
Mekka. This was during the lifetime of the Gefnite king
ʿ*Amr ibn Gebele.* At the time of Muhammed there were
many Christians in Mekka, who will for the most part have
brought their Christianity with the Syrian caravans, so that
at the commencement of Islâm the Hauranitish tradition of
Job might have been very well known in Mekka, since many
men from Mekka may have even visited the Ma*k*âm and
the *S*achra, and there have heard many a legend of Job like
that intimated in the *K*orân xxxviii. 43. Yea, whoever will
give himself the trouble to investigate minute commentaries
on the Koran, especially such as interpret the Koran from
the tradition (ha*d*îth), *e.g.* the *Kitâb ed-durr el-muchtâr,* may
easily find that not merely *K*az*w*înî, *Ibn el-Wardî,* and *Jâkût,*
whose observations concerning the Monastery of Job have
been given above, but also much older authorities, identify
the Koranish fountain of Job with the Hauranitish.

A statement of Eusebius, of value in connection with this
investigation, brings us at one stride about three hundred
years further on. It is in the *Onomastikon,* under Καρναείμ,
and is as follows: " *Astaroth Karnaim* is at present (about
310 A.D.) a very large village (κώμη μεγίστη) beyond the

Jordan, in the province of Arabia, which is also called *Bata-nœa*. Here, according to tradition (ἐκ παραδόσεως), they fix the dwelling (οἶκος) of Job." On the small map which accompanies these pages, the reader will find in the vicinity of the Ma*k*âm the low and somewhat precipitous mound, not above forty feet in height, of *Tell 'Ashtarâ*, the plateau of which forms an almost round surface, which is 425 paces in diameter, and shows the unartistic foundations of buildings, and traces of a ring-wall. Here we have to imagine that *'Astarot Karnaim*. Euseb. here makes no mention whatever of the city of *Astaroth*, the ancient capital of *Basan*, for this he does under Ἀσταρὼθ; the hypothesis of its being the residence of king 'Og, which Newbold[1] set up here, consequently falls to the ground. The κώμη μεγίστη of Eusebius must, in connection with the limited character of the ground, certainly be somewhat contracted; but the identity of the localities is not to be doubted in connection with the great nearness of the οἶκος (the Ma*k*âm).[2] Let us compare another statement that belongs here; it stands under Ἀσταρὼθ Καρναείμ, and is as follows: "There are at the present time two villages of this name in Batanæa, which lie nine miles distant from one another, μεταξὺ ΑΔΑΡΩΝ καὶ ΑΒΙΛΗϹ." Jerome has *duo castella* instead of two villages, by which at

---

[1] C. Ritter, *Geogr. v. Syr. u Pal.* ii. 819 sqq. [*Erdk.* xv. 2, p. 819 sqq.]. The information of Newbold, which is printed in the *Zeitschr. d. Deutsch. Morgenl. Gesellschaft*, i. 215 sq., is unfortunately little to be relied on, and is to be corrected according to the topography of the mound given above.

[2] A small, desolated stone village, situated a quarter of an hour's journey from the mound of '*Ashtarâ*, which however has not a single house of any importance, has two names among the inhabitants of that region, either *Chirbêt 'Ijûn en-Nîle* (the ruins near the Nila-springs) or *Chirbêt 'Ashtarâ*, which can signify the ruins of '*Ashtarâ* and the ruins near '*Ashtarâ*. Since it is, however, quite insignificant, it will not be the village that has given the name to the mound, but the mound with its buildings, which in ancient days were perhaps a temple to Astarte, surrounded by a wall, has given the name to the village.

least the κώμη μεγίστη is somewhat reduced; for that it is one of these two castles[1] can be the less doubtful, since they also regulate the determining of the respective localities. If the reading *ABIΛHC* is correct, only *Abil* (אָבֵל) in the north of *Suwêt* can (since, without doubt, the Arabian names of the places in Hauran existed in Eusebius' day) be intended; and *ΑΔΑΡΩΝ* ought then to be changed into *ΑΛΑΡΩΝ*, in order to denote the large village of *El-hârâ*, on the lofty peak of the same name in the plain of Gêdûr. *El-hârâ* lies to the north, and *Abil* to the south of *'Ashtarâ*. If, however, as is most highly probable, instead of *ABIΛHC* (which form Euseb. does not use elsewhere, for he calls the town of *Abil* ᾿Αβέλ, and the inscription in Turra has the form πόλεως ᾿Αβέλις), *ABIΔHC* is to be read, which corresponds to the ᾿Αβιδᾶ of Ptolemy (*ed. Wilberg*, p. 369) and the modern *'Abidîn* near *Bêtirrâ*, thus the name of the other village is to be changed from *ΑΔΑΡΩΝ* to *ΑΡΑΡΩΝ* (for which the *Cod. Vat.* erroneously has *ΔΡΑΡΩΝ*), the modern *'Arâr*.[2] *'Abîdîn*, however, lies nine miles west, and *'Arâr* nine miles east of *'Ashtarâ*.

Now, as to the second village, and its respective castle, which is mentioned in the second citation from the *Onomastikon*, I believe that both Euseb. and Jerome intend to say there are two villages, of which the one has the byname of the other; consequently the one is called *Astarôt* (*Karnaim*), and the other *Karnaim* (*Astarôt*). Twelve miles west of *'Ashtarâ* lies

[1] [The meaning of "castle," as defined by Burckhardt, *Travels in Syr.* etc. p. 657, should be borne in mind here. "The name of Kala'at or *castle* is given on the Hadj route, and over the greater part of the desert, to any building walled in and covered, and having, like a *Khan*, a large courtyard in its enclosure. The walls are sometimes of stone, but more commonly of earth, though even the latter are sufficient to withstand an attack of Arabs."—Tr.]

[2] Some, in connection with this word, have erroneously thought of the city of *Edre'ât*, which Eusebius calls ᾿Αδρά in the immediately preceding article ᾿Αδραά, and in the art. ᾿Εδραεί.

the Golanite village of Kornîje (קָרְנָיָה), which in old Kanêtra
I have taken up in my trigonometrical measurements.

We find also a third passage in the *Onomast.* which belongs
here; it is under 'Ιαβώκ in *Cod. Vat.*, under 'Ιδουμαία in
Cod. Leid. and *Vallarsi*, and runs: " According to the view
of a certain one (κατά τινος), this region is the land of *Asitis*
(*Ausitis*), the home of Job, while according to others it is
Arabia (ἡ 'Αραβία); and again, according to others, it is the
Land of Sîhôn." Whether genuine or not, this passage
possesses a certain value. If it is genuine, Jerome would
have left it accordingly untranslated, because he would not
be responsible for its whole contents, for he not unfrequently
passes over or alters statements of Eusebius where he believes
himself to be better informed; but, taken exactly, he could
only have rejected the views of those who seek Job's native
country on the *Jabbo*k (if the passage belongs to the art. 'Ιαβώκ) or in Edom (if it belongs to 'Ιδουμαία), or in the *Belkâ*,
the land of Sîhôn; but not the view of those who make Arabia
(*Batanœa*) to be *Ausitis*, for the statement of Eusebius with
reference to this point under Καρναείμ he translates faithfully. If the passage is not genuine, it at any rate gives the
very early testimony of an authority distinct from Eusebius
and Jerome in favour of the age of the Hauranitish tradition
concerning Job, while it has only a single (κατά τινος) authority for the view of those who make Edom to be Ausitis, and
even this only when the passage belongs to 'Ιδουμαία.

By means of these quotations from the *Onomastikon,* that
passage of Chrysostom (*Homil. V. de Stud.* § 1, tom. ii. p.
59), in which it is said that many pilgrims from the end of
the earth come to Arabia, in order to seek for the dunghill
on which Job lay, and with rapture to kiss the ground where
he suffered (— — ἀπὸ περάτων τῆς γῆς εἰς τὴν 'Αραβίαν
τρέχοντες, ἵνα τὴν κοπρίαν ἴδωσι, καὶ θεασάμενοι καταφιλή-
σωσι τὴν γῆν), appears also to obtain its right local refer-

ence. This Arabia is certainly none other than that which Eusebius explains by ἡ καὶ Βαταναία, and that κοπρία or *mezbele* to be sought nowhere except near the *Makâm Êjûb.* And should there be any doubts upon the subject, ought they not to be removed by the consideration that the proud structure of the Monastery of Job, with its spring festivals mentioned above, standing like a Pharos casting its light far and wide in that age, did not allow either the Syrian Christians or the pilgrims from foreign parts to mistake the place, which tradition had rendered sacred, as the place of Job's sufferings?

There is no monastery whose origin, according to an unimpeachable testimony, belongs to such an early date as that of the Monastery of Job. According to the chronicles of the peoples (*ta'rîch el-umem*), or the annals of Hamze el-Isfahâni (died about 360 of the Hegira), it was built by 'Amr I., the second Gefnide. Now, since the first Ghassanitish king (*Gefne* I.) reigned forty-five years and three months, and 'Amr five years, the Monastery would have been in existence about 200 A.D., if we place the beginning of the Gefnide dynasty in the time 150 A.D. Objections are raised against such an early date, because one is accustomed on good authority to assign the origin of monasteries to about the year 300 A.D. In the face of more certain historical dates, these objections must remain unheeded, for hermit and monastery life (*rahbanîja*) existed in the country east of Jordan among the Essenes and other societies and forms of worship, even before Christianity; so that the latter, on its appearance in that part, which took place long before 200 A.D., received the monasteries as an inheritance: but certainly the chronology of the Gefnide dynasty is not reliable. *Hamze* fixes the duration of the dynasty at 616 years; *Ibn Sa'îd*,[1] in his history of the pre-Islamic Arabs, at

[1] Wetzstein, Catal. Arab. MSS. collected in Damascus, No. 1, p. 89.

601 years; and to the same period extends the statement of *Mejânishi*,[1] who, in his topography of the *Ka'be*, says that between the conquest of Mekka by *Ta'lebe* and the rule of the Kosî in this city was 500 years. On the contrary, however, *Ibn Jusef*[2] informs us that this dynasty began " earlier " than 400 years before Islamism. With this statement accord all those numerous accounts, according to which the " rupture of the dyke " (*sêl el-'arim*), the supposed cause of the Jemanic emigration, took place rather more than 400 years before Islamism. If therefore, to content ourselves with an approximate calculation, we make Islamism to begin about 615 (the year of the "Mission" was 612 A.D.), and the Gefnide dynasty, with the addition of the " earlier," 415 years previous, then the commencement of the reign of Gefne I. would have been 200 A.D., and the erection of the Monastery shortly before 250.

When the tribe whose king later on built the Monastery migrated from Jemen into Syria, the Trachonitis was in the hands of a powerful race of the Kudâ'ides, which had settled there in the first century of our era, having likewise come out of Jemen, and become tributary to the Romans. This race had embraced Christianity from the natives; and some historians maintain that it permitted the *Gefnides* to settle and share in the possession of the country, only on the condition that they likewise should embrace Christianity. In those early times, these tribes, of course, with the new religion received the tradition of Job also from the first hand, from the Jews and the Jewish Christians, who, since the battle of the Jewish people with the Romans, will have found refuge and safety to a large extent in Petræa, and especially in the hardly accessible Trachonitis. The Nukra also, as the most favoured region of Syria and Palestina, will have had its

---

[1] Wetzst. Catal. Arab. MSS. collected in Damascus, No. 24, p. 16.
[2] *Hamzæ Isfahan. Annales, ed. Gottwald*, Vorrede, p. xi.

native population, among which, in spite of the frequent massacres of Syrians and Jews, there will have been many Jews. Perhaps, moreover, the protection of the new Jemanic population of Hauran again attracted Jewish settlers thither; Nawâ[1] at least is a place well known in the Talmud and Midrash, which is mentioned, as a city inhabited by the Jews among those who are not Jews, and as the birth-place of several eminent teachers.[2] Moreover, in Syria the veneration of a spot consecrated by religious tradition is independent of its being at the time inhabited or desolate. The supposed tombs of Aaron near *Petra*, of Hud near *Gerash*, of Jethro (*Suʿêb*) in the valley of *Nimrîn*, of Ezekiel in *Melîhat Hiskîn*, of Elisha on the *el-Jeshaʿ* mountains, and many other *mezâre* (tombs of the holy, to which pilgrims resort), are frequently one or more days' journey distant from inhabited places, and yet they are carefully tended. They are preserved from decay and neglect by vows, by the spring processions, and especially by the piety of the Beduins, who frequently deposit articles of value near the *mezâre*, as property entrusted to the care of the saint. The Makâm of Job may also have been such a consecrated spot many centuries before the erection of the Monastery, and perhaps not merely to the Jews, but also to the Aramæan and Arab population. The superstitious veneration of such places is not confined among the Semites to a particular religious sect, but is the common heritage of the whole race; and the tra-

---

[1] If *Nawâ* is not also of Jewish origin, its name is nevertheless the old Semitic נָוֶה, "a dwelling" (ch. v. 3, 24, viii. 6, xviii. 15), and not, as *Jâkût* supposes, the collective form of *nawât*, "the kernel of a date."

[2] [No less than three renowned teachers from *Nawâ* appear in the Talmud and Midrash: ר' שִׁילָא דְנוה, *Schila* of *Nawa* (*jer. Sabbath* cap. ii., *Wajikra rabba* cap. xxxiv., *Midrasch Ruth* on ii. 19a), ר' פלטיא דנוה (*Midr. Koheleth* on i. 4b) and ר' שָׁאוּל דנוה (*ib.* on xii. 9a). נוה is mentioned as an enemy of the neighbouring town of חלמיש in *Wajikra rabba* c. xxiii., *Midr. Echa* on i. 17a, and *Midr. Schir* on ii. 1.—DEL.]

dition of Job in particular was, originally, certainly not Israelitish, but Aramæan.

Job is not mentioned in the writings of Josephus, but we do find there a remarkable passage concerning Job's native country, the land of the Usites, viz. *Ant.* i. 6 : "*Aram*, from whom come the *Aramœans*, called by the Greeks *Syrians*, had four sons, of whom the first was named Οὔσης, and possessed *Trachonitis* and *Damascus*." The first of these two, Trachonitis, has usually been overlooked here, and attention has been fixed only on Damascus. The word *el-Ghûta* (الغوطة), the proper name of the garden and orchard district around Damascus, has been thought to be connected in sound with ʿ*Us*, and they have been treated as identical : this is, however, impossible even on philological grounds. *Ghûta* would certainly be written עוּטָה in Hebrew, because this language has no sign for the sound *Gh* (غ) ; but Josephus, who wrote in Greek, ought then to have said Γούσης, not Οὔσης, just as he, and the LXX. before him and Eusebius after him, render the city עזה by Γάζα, the mountain עיבל by Γαιβάλ, the village עי by Γαί, etc. In the same manner the LXX. ought to have spoken of a Γαυσῖτις, not Αυσῖτις, if this were the case. Proper names, also, always receive too definite and lasting an impress for their consonants, as ע and ט, to be easily interchanged, although this is possible with the roots of verbs. Moreover, if the word עוץ had had the consonant צ (ض), Josephus must have reproduced it with τ or θ, not with σ, in accordance with the pronunciation (especially if he had intended to identify עוץ and *Ghûta*). And we see from Ptolemy and Strabo, and likewise from the Greek mode of transcribing the Semitic proper names in the Haurânite inscriptions of the Roman period, *e.g.* Μάθιος and Νάταρος for ماضى and نضر, that in the time of Josephus the sound of צ had already been divided into ص and ض ; comp. *Abhandl. der Berlin. Acad. d. Wissenschaft*, 1863,

S. 356 f. Hence it is that Josephus manifestly speaks only of one progenitor Οὔσης, therefore of one tribe; while the word *Ghûta,* often as a synonym of *buq'a* (בִּקְעָה), denotes a low well-watered country enclosed by mountains, and in this appellative signification occurs as the proper name of several localities in the *most widely separated parts of Arabia* (comp. *Jâkût, sub voce*), which could not be the case if it had been = עִיץ אֶרֶץ.[1] The word *Ausitis* used by the LXX. also has no formation corresponding to the word *Ghûta,* but shows its connection with אֶרֶץ עִיץ by the termination; while the word *Ghûta* rendered in Greek is Γουθατά (in Theophanes Byzant. Γουθαθά), in analogy *e.g.* with the form Ῥεβλαθά for *Ribla* (Jos. *Ant.* x. 11).[2]

But why are we obliged to think only of Damascus, since Josephus makes *Trachonitis* also to belong to the land of the *Usites?* If we take this word in its most limited signification, it is (apart from the eastern *Trachon*) that lava plateau, about forty miles long and about twenty-eight broad, which is called the *Legâ* in the present day. This is so certain, that one is not obliged first of all to recall the well-known inscription of the temple of *Mismîa,* which calls this city situated in the *Legâ,* Μητροκώμη τοῦ Τράχωνος. From the western border of this *Trachon,* however, the Monastery of Job is not ten miles distant, therefore by no means outside the radius that was at all times tributary to the Trachonites (*Arab el-wa'r*), a people unassailable in their habitations in the clefts of the

---

[1] On the name '*Us,* as the name of men and people, may be compared the proper names '*As* and '*Aus,* together with the diminutive '*Owês,* taken from the genealogies of the Arabs, since the Old Testament is wanting in words formed from the root עִיץ, and none of those so named was a Hebrew. In Hebr. they might be sounded עִיץ, and signify the "strong one," for the verbal stems عَصَى ,عَوَص ,عَصّ (comp. عَصَب ,عَصَر, عَصَم, and others) have the signif. "to be compressed, firm, to resist."

[2] On this word-formation comp. *Reisebericht, S.* 76.

rocks.[1]   According to this, the statement of Josephus would at least not stand in open contradiction to the Hauranitish tradition of Job.   But we go further, and maintain that the Monastery of Job lies exactly in the centre of *Trachonitis.* This word has, viz. in Josephus and others, a double signification—a more limited and a wider one.   It has the more limited where, together with *Auranitis, Batanœa, Gamalitica,* and *Gaulonitis,* it denotes the separate provinces of the ancient kingdom of *Basan.*   Then it signifies the *Trachonitis* κατ' ἐξοχήν, *i.e.* the wildest portion of the volcanic district, viz. the *Legâ,* the H*aurân* mountain range, the S*afâ* and H*arra* of the *Râgil.*   On the other hand, it has the wider signification when it stands alone; then it embraces the whole volcanic region of Middle Syria, therefore with the more limited Trachonitis the remaining provinces of Basan, but with the exception, as it seems, of the no longer volcanic *Galadine* (North Gilead).   In this sense, therefore, as a geographical notion, Trachonitis is almost synonymous with Basan.

Since it is to the interest of this investigation to make the assertion advanced sure against every objection, we will not withhold the passages in support of it.   Josephus says, *Ant.* xv. 10, 3, the district of H*ûle* (Οὐλαθά) lies between Galilee and Trachonitis.   He might have said more accurately, " between Galilee and Gaulonitis," but he wished to express that the great basaltic region begins on the eastern boundary of the H*ûle.*   The word Trachonitis has therefore the *wider* signification.   In like manner, in *Bell.* iii. 10 it is said the lake of *Phiala* lies 120 stadia east of Paneion (*Bâniâs*) on the way to the Trachonitis.   True, the Phiala is a crater, and therefore itself belongs to Trachonitis, but between it and Bâniâs the lava alternates with the chalk formation of the H*ermôn,* whereas to the south and east of the Phiala it is

---

[1] Comp. Jos. *Ant.* xv. 10, 3; *Zeitschr. für allg. Erdkunde,* New Series, xiii. 213.

everywhere exclusively volcanic; Trachonitis has therefore
here also the *wider* signification. *Ant.* xvii. 2, it is said
Herod had the castle of *Βαθύρα* built in Batanæa (here, as
often in Josephus, in the signification of Basan), in order to
protect the Jews who travel from Babylon (*viâ* Damascus) to
Jerusalem against the Trachonite robbers. Now, since this
castle and village (the *Bêtirrâ* mentioned already), which is
situated in the district of *Gamalitica* on an important ford of
the *Muchêbi* gorge between 'Abidin and *Sebbûte*, could not be
any protection against the robbers of Trachonitis in the more
limited sense, but only against those of Golan, it is manifest
that by the Trachonites are meant the robbers of Trachonitis
in the *wider* sense. Aurelius Victor (*De Hist. Cæs.* xxvii.)
calls the Emperor M. Julius Philippus, born in *Bosrâ*, the
metropolis of Auranitis, quite correctly *Arabs Trachonites;*
because the plain of Hauran, in which Bosra is situated, is
also of a basaltic formation, and *therefore* is a part of the
Trachonitis. The passage of Luke's Gospel, iii. 1, where it
says Herod tetrarch of Galilee, and Philip tetrarch of Ituræa
and Trachonitis, also belongs here. That Philip possessed not
perhaps merely the Trachonitis (similar to a province assigned
to a man as banishment rather than for administration, pro-
ducing little or no revenue) in the more *limited* sense, but
the whole Basanitis, is shown by Josephus, who informs us,
Ant. xvii. 11, 4 and freq., that he possessed Batanæa (in the
more restricted sense, therefore the fruitful, densely popu-
lated, profitable Nuḳra), with Auranitis, Trachonitis, etc. We
must therefore suppose that in the words τῆς Ἰτουραίας καὶ
Τραχωνίτιδος χώρας in Luke, one district is meant, which
by Ἰτουραίας is mentioned according to the marauding portion of its population, and by Τραχωνίτιδος more generally,
according to its trachonitic formation.[1] Ioannes Malalas

---

[1] Eusebius in his *Onomast.* also correctly identifies the two words, at
one time under Ἰτουραία, and the other time under Τραχωνῖτις. After

(*Chronogr.* ed. *Dindorf,* p. 236), who, as a Syrian born, ought to be well acquainted with the native usage of the language, hence calls Antipas, as a perfectly adequate term, only toparch of Trachonitis; and if, according to his statement (p. 237), the official title of this Herod was the following: Σεβαστὸς Ἡρώδης τοπάρχης καὶ θεσμοδότης Ἰουδαίων τε καὶ Ἑλλήνων, βασιλεὺς τῆς Τραχωνίτιδος, it is self-evident that "king of Trachonitis" here is synonymous with king of Basan. In perfect harmony with this, Pliny says (*H. N.* v. 18) that the ten cities of Decapolis lay within the extensive tetrarchies of Trachonitis, which are divided into separate kingdoms. Undoubtedly Pliny adds to these tetrarchies of Trachonitis in the wider sense, which are already known to us, *Galadine* also, which indeed belonged also to the pre-Mosaic *Basan,* but at the time of Josephus is mostly reckoned to *Peræa* (in the more limited sense).

On the ground of this evidence, therefore, the land of the Usites of Josephus, with the exception of the Damascene portion, was Trachonitis in the wider sense; and since the Maḳâm Êjûb is in the central point of this country, this statement accords most exactly with the Syrian tradition. It is clear that the latter remains untouched by the extension of

what we have said elsewhere (*Reisebericht,* S. 91 ff.) on the subject, surely no one will again maintain that the peaceful villages of the plain of Gêdûr were the abodes of the Ituræans, the wildest of all people (Cic. *Phil.* ii. 11; Strabo, xvi. 2). Their principal hiding-places will have been the Trachonitis in the more restricted sense, but one may seek them also on the wooded mountains of *Gôlân* and in the gorges of the *Makran.* That Ptolemy and Josephus speak only of the Trachonites and never of the Ituræans (in the passage *Ant.* xiii. 11, 3, Ἰδουμαία is to be read instead of Ἰτουραία), and Strabo, on the other hand, speaks only of the latter, favours the identity of the two; of like import is the circumstance, that Pliny (*H. N.* v. 23) makes the inhabitants of the region of Bætarra (Bêtirrâ) Ituræans, and Josephus (*Ant.* xvii. 2) Trachonites. But in spite of the identity of the words *Trachonitis* and *Ituræa,* one must not at the same time overlook the following distinction. If the Trachonites are called after the country, it must be the description of all the inhabit-the geographical notion in Josephus, for without knowing anything more of a "land of the Usites," it describes only a portion of the same as the "native country of Job;" and again, Josephus had no occasion to speak of Job in his commentary on the genealogies, therefore also none to speak of his special home within the land of the Usites. Eusebius, on the other hand, in his *De Originibus* (ix. 2, 4), refers to this home, and says, therefore limiting Josephus' definition: *Hus, Traconitidis conditor, inter Palæstinam et Cœlesyriam tenuit imperium; unde fuit Iob.*

With this evidence of agreement between two totally independent witnesses, viz. the Syrian tradition and Josephus, the testimony of the latter in particular has an enhanced value; for, although connected with the Bible, it nevertheless avails as extra-biblical testimony concerning the Usites, it comes from an age when one might still have the historical fact from the seat of the race, and from an authority of the highest order. True, Josephus is not free from disfigurements, where he has the opportunity of magnifying his people, himself, or his Roman patrons, and of depreciating an enemy; but here he had to do with nothing more than the statement of the residence of a people; and since the word Οὔσης also

ants of the country, whereas the Ituræans, if they gave the name to the country, are not necessarily its exclusive population. The whole of the district of which we speak has a twofold population in keeping with its double character (rugged rock and fruitful plain), viz. cattle-rearing freebooters in the clefts of the rocks, and peaceful husbandmen in the plain; the former dwelling in hair tents (of old also in caves), the latter in stone houses; the former forming the large majority, the latter the minority of the population of the district. If writers speak of the *Ituræans*, they mean exclusively that marauding race that hates husbandry; but if they speak of the *Trachonites*, the connection must determine, whether they speak of both classes of the population, or only of the marauding Trachonites (the Ituræans), or of the husbandmen of the plain (of the provinces of *Batanæa* and *Auranitis*). The latter are rarely intended, since the peaceful peasant rarely furnishes material for the historian.

has no similarity in sound with the words *Damascus* and *Trachonitis*, that might make a combination with them plausible, we may surely have before us a reliable historical notice here, or at least a tradition which was then general (and therefore also for us important), while we may doubt this in connection with other parts of the genealogies, where Josephus seems only to catch at that which is similar in sound as furnishing an explanation.

But that which might injure the authority of Josephus is the contradiction in which it seems to stand to a far older statement concerning *Ausitis*, viz. the recognised postscript of the LXX. to the book of Job, which makes Job to be the Edomitish king Jobab. The identification, it may be said, can however only have been possible because *Ausitis* was in or near Edom. But the necessity of this inference must be disputed. It is indeed unmistakeable that that postscript is nothing more than a combination of the Jews beyond Palestine (probably Egyptio-Hellenistic), formed, perhaps, long before the LXX.,—such a vagary as many similar ones in the Talmud and Midrash. From the similarity in sound of Ἰωβάβ with Ἰώβ, and the similarity in name of Ζαρά, the father of *Jobab*, with a son of Reʿûël and grandson of Esau (Gen. xxxvi. 13), Job's descent from Esau has been inferred. That Esau's first-born was called *Eliphaz* and his son *Temân*, seemed to confirm this combination, since (in accordance with the custom[1] of naming the grandson as a rule after his grandfather) *Eliphaz* the Temanite might be regarded as grandson of that *Eliphaz*, therefore like Job as great-grandson of Esau and πέμπτος ἀπὸ Ἀβραάμ. The apparent and certainly designed advantages of this combination were: that Job, who had no pedi-

---

[1] From this custom, which is called the grandfather's "living again," the habit, singular to us, of a father calling his son *jâ abî*, "my father!" or *jâ bêjî*, "my little father," as an endearing form of address, is explained.

gree, and therefore was to be thought of as a non-Israelite, was brought into the nearest possible blood-relationship to the people of God, and that, by laying the scene in the time of the patriarchs, all questions which the want of a Mosaic colouring to the book of Job might excite would be met. Now, even if the abode of Job were transferred from the land of 'Us to Edom, it would be only the consequence of his combination with *Jobab*, and, just as worthless as this latter itself, might lead no one astray. But it does not seem to have gone so far; it is even worthy of observation, that מבצרה (from *Bosra*, the Edomite city[1]), being attached to the misunderstood υἱὸς Ζαρά ἐκ Βοσόρρας, Gen. xxxvi. 33, is reproduced in the LXX. by μητρὸς Βοσόρρας, as also that Job's wife is not called an Edomitess, but a γυνὴ 'Αράβισσα. And it appears still far more important, that Ausitis lies ἐν τοῖς ὁρίοις τῆς 'Ιδουμαίας καὶ 'Αραβίας, so far as the central point of 'Ιδουμαία is removed by the addition καὶ τῆς 'Αραβίας, and Job's abode is certainly removed from the heart of Idumæa. The *Cod. Alex.* exchanges that statement of the place, even in a special additional clause, for ἐπὶ τῶν ὁρίων τοῦ Εὐφράτου, therefore transfers Ausitis to the vicinity of the Euphrates, and calls the father of Jobab (= Job) Ζαρὲθ ἐξ ἀνατολῶν ἡλίου (מבני קדם). Nevertheless we attach no importance to this variation of the text, but rather offer the suggestion that the postscript gives prominence to the observation: οὗτος (viz. 'Ιώβ) ἑρμηνεύεται ἐκ τῆς Συριακῆς βίβλου.[2]

---

[1] It need hardly be mentioned that one is not to think of the Hauranitish *Bosrâ* (بصرى), since this name of a city only came into use some centuries after Christ.

[2] [It is indeed possible that the Hebrew text is meant here, for Philo usually calls the Hebrew Χαλδαϊστί, and the Talmud describes the Jewish country-dialect as סורסי ; it is possible, and even more probable, that it is a Syrian, *i.e.* Aramæan Targum—but not less possible that it is a Syrian original document. According to Malalas (*ed. Dindorf*,

If we compare the postscript of the LXX. with the legend
of Islam, we find in both the Esauitish genealogy of Job;
the genealogy of the legend is: Êjûb ibn Zârih (זֶרַח) ibn
Reû'îl ibn el-'Ais ibn Ishâk ibn Ibrâhîm; and we may suppose that it is borrowed directly from the LXX., and that it
reached Arabia and Mekka even in the pre-Islamic times by
means of the (Arabian) Christians east of Jordan, who had
the Old Testament only in the Greek translation.   Even the
Arabic orthography of the biblical proper names, which can
be explained only on the supposition of their transfer from the
Greek, is in favour of this mode of the transmission of the
Christian religion and its legends to the people of the Higaz.
Certainly there can be no doubt as to an historical connection
between the postscript and the legend, and therefore it would
be strange if they did not accord respecting the home of Job.
The progenitor el-'Ais (עִיץ), in the genealogy of the legend, is
also a remarkable counterpart to the Ausitis ἐν τοῖς ὁρίοις τῆς
'Ιδουμ. καὶ 'Αρ., for it is a blending of עֵשָׂו and עוּץ, and it has
to solve the difficult problem, as to how Job can be at the
same time an *Usite* and an *Esauite;* for that Job as an Aisite
no longer belongs to Idumæa, but to the district of the more
northern Aramæans, is shown *e.g.* from the following passage
in *Mugîr ed-dîn's* History of Jerusalem : " Job belonged to
the people of the Romans (*i.e.* the *Aisites*[1]), for he sprang

p. 12), Origen understands ἐκ τῆς Συριακῆς βίβλου elsewhere of a Hebrew
original, but in *c. Celsum* iii. 6 he describes the Hebrew language in
relation to the Syriac and Phœnician as ἑτέρα παρ' ἀμφοτέρας, and the
Homilies on Job in *Opp. Origenis,* ed. *Delarue,* ii. 851, say : *Beati Iob
scriptura primum quidem in Arabia Syriace scripta, ubi et habitabat.*
—DEL.]

[1] We will spare ourselves the ungrateful task of an inquiry into the
origin of this 'Ais and his Protean nature.   Biblical passages like Lam.
iv. 21, or those in which the readings אֲרָם and אֱדוֹם are doubtful,
or the erroneous supposition (Jos. *Ant.* viii. 7) that the *Ben-Hadad*
dynasty in Damascus is of Edomitish origin, may have contributed to his
rise.   Moreover, he is altogether one and the same with the *Edom* of the

from *el-'Ais*, and the Damascene province of *Batancæa* was his property."

The κοπρία of the LXX., at ch. ii. 8, leads to the same result; that it is also found again as *mezbele* in the later legend, is a further proof how thoroughly this accords with the LXX., and how it has understood its statement of the position of *Ausitis*. It may also be maintained here, that it was only possible to translate the words בתוך־האפר by ἐπὶ τῆς κοπρίας ἔξω τῆς πόλεως when "heap of ashes" and "dung-hill" were synonymous notions. This, however, is the case only in Hauran, where the dung, as being useless for agricultural purposes, is burnt from time to time in an appointed place before the town (*vid.* ii. p. 152[1]), while in every other part of Syria it is as valuable and as much stored up as among us. If the LXX. accordingly placed the κοπρία of Job in Hauran, it could hardly represent *Ausitis* as *Edom*.

But how has the Ausitis of the LXX. been transferred hither? Certainly not as the "land of *'Us*" (in the sense of the land of *Basan*, land of *Haurân*), for without wasting a word about it, there has never been such an one in the country east of the Jordan: but as "the land of the Usites" in the sense of the Arabic *diâr 'U*s (dwelling-place of the Usites) or *ard benî 'U*s. A land receives designations of

Jewish tradition: he is called the father of *Rûm*, *Aṣfar*, *Sôfar*, *Sîfûn* (מֶלֶךְ הצפון), and *Nidr* (*Hamz. Iṣfah. Ann.* p. ٧٩, l. 18, read نصر for نصر, and *Zeitschr. d. d. m. Gesellsch.* ii. 239, 3, 6, read *ennidr* for *ennefer*), *i.e.* of the Messiah of the Christians (according to Isa. xi. 1).

[1] Comp. ii. p. 158, note, of the foregoing Commentary. [The Arabic version of Walton's Polyglot translates after the Peschito in accordance with the Hebr. text: "on the ashes (*er-remâd*)," whereas the Arabic translation, of which Tischendorf brought back fifteen leaves with him from the East, and which Fleischer, in the *Deutsch. Morgenl. Zeitschr.* 1864, S. 288 ff., has first described as an important memorial in reference to the history of MSS., translates after the *Hexapla* in accordance with the LXX.: "on the dunghill (*mezbele*) outside the city."—DEL.]

this kind with the settlement of a people in it; they run
parallel with the proper name of the country, and in the rule
vanish again with that people. These designations belong,
indeed, to the geography of the whole earth, but nowhere
have they preserved their natural character of transitoriness
more faithfully than in the lands where the Semitic tongue
is spoken. It is this that makes the geographical knowledge
of these countries so extremely difficult to us, because we
frequently take them to be the names of the countries, which
they are not, and which—so far as they always involve a
geological definition of the regions named—can never be displaced and competently substituted by them. In this sense
the *land of the Usites* might, at the time of the decay of both
Israelitish kingdoms, when the ארם דמשׂק possessed the whole
of Peræa, very easily extend from the borders of Edom to
the gates of Damascus, and even further northwards, if the
Aramæan race of 'Us numbered many or populous tribes (as
it appears to be indicated in כל מלכי ארץ העוץ, Jer. xxv. 20),
in perfect analogy with the tribe of *Ghassân*, which during
five hundred years occupied the country from the Ælanitic
Gulf to the region of *Tedmor*, at one time settling down, at
another leading a nomadic life, and Hauran was the centre
of its power. By such a rendering the 'Αραβία of the postscript would not be different from the later *provincia Arabiœ*,
of which the capital was the Trachonitish *Bostra*, while it
was bounded on the south end of the Dead Sea by Edom
(*Palœstina tertia*).

But should any one feel a difficulty in freeing himself from
the idea that *Ausitis* is to be sought only in the *Ard el-Hâlât*
east of *Maʿân*, he must consider that the author of the book
of Job could not, like that legend which places the miraculous
city of *Iram* in the country of quicksands, transfer the corn-
fields of his hero to the desert; for there, with the exception
of smaller patches of land capable of culture, which we may

not bring into account, there is by no means to be found that
husbandman's Eldorado, where a single husbandman might
find tillage for five hundred (ch. i. 3), yea, for a thousand
(ch. xlii. 12) yoke of oxen. Such numbers as these are not
to be depreciated; for in connection with the primitive agriculture in Syria and Palestine,—which renders a four years'
alternation of crops necessary, so that the fields must be
divided into so many portions (called in Hauran *wâgihât*, and
around Damascus *auguh*, أوجه), from which only one portion
is used annually, and the rest left fallow (*bûr*),—Job required
several square miles of tillage for the employment of his
oxen. It is all the same in this respect whether the book of
Job is a history or poem : in no case could the *Ausitis* be a
country, the notorious sterility of which would make the statement of the poet ridiculous.

Our limited space does not admit of our proving the worth
which we must acknowledge to the tradition, by illustrating
those passages of the Old Testament scriptures which have
reference to עוּץ and אֶרֶץ עוּץ. But to any one, who, following
the hints they give, wishes again to pursue the investigations,
elsewhere useless, concerning the position of the land of the
Usites, we might indicate : (1) that עוּץ the first-born of
Aram (Gen. x. 23) is the tribe sought, while two others of
this name—a Nahorite, ch. xxii. 21, and a Horite, ch.
xxxvi. 28—may be left out of consideration ; the former
because the twelve sons of Nahor need not be progenitors of
tribes, and the latter because he belongs to a tribe extermi-
nated by the Edomites in accordance with Deut. ii. 12, 22 :
(2) that אֶרֶץ הָעוּץ, Jer. xxv. 20, is expressly distinguished
from אֱדוֹם in the 21st verse, and—if one compares the round
of the cup of punishment, Jer. ch. xxv., with the detailed
prophecies which follow in ch. xlvi.–li., to which it is a pro-
œmium that has been removed from its place—corresponds to
דַּמֶּשֶׂק (with Ḥamât and Arpad), ch. xlix. 23 : (3) that there-

fore Lam. iv. 21, where יֹשֶׁבֶת בְּאֶרֶץ עוּץ would be devoid of purpose if it described the proper habitable land of Edom, must
describe a district extending over that, in which the Edomites had established themselves in consequence of Assyria
having led away captive the Israelitish and Aramæan population of the East Jordanic country and Cœle-Syria. In
connection with Jer. xxv. 20 one must not avoid the question
whether עוּץ is the name of the אֲרַם דַּמֶּשֶׂק that has been
missed. Here the migration of the Damascene Aramæans
from Kîr (Am. ix. 7) ought to be considered, the value of
the Armenian accounts concerning the original abode of the
Usites tested, what is erroneous in the combination of קִיר
with the river Kur shown and well considered, and in what
relations both as to time and events that migration might
have stood to the overrunning of Middle Syria by the
Aramæan Sôbæan tribes (from Mesopotamia) under Hadad-
ezer, and to the seizure and possession of the city of
Damascus by Rezon the Sôbæan? Finally, one more tradition might be compared, to which some value may perhaps
be attached, because it is favoured by the stone monuments,
whose testimony we are not accustomed otherwise to despise
in Palestine and Syria. The eastern portal of the mosque of
Benî Uméja in Damascus, probably of the very temple, the
altar of which king Ahaz caused to be copied (2 Kings
xvi. 10), is called Gêrûn or the Gerun gate: the portal in
its present form belongs to the Byzantine or Roman period.
And before this gate is the Gêrûnîje, a spacious, vaulted
structure, mostly very old, which has been used since the
Mussulman occupation of the city as a méda'a, i.e. a place for
religious ablutions. The topographical writings on Damascus
trace these two names back to a Gêrûn ibn Sa'd ibn 'Ad ibn
'Aus (עוּץ) ibn Iram (אֲרַם) ibn Sâm (שֵׁם) ibn Nûh (נוֹחַ), who
settled in Damascus in the time of Solomon (one version of
the tradition identifies him with Hadad, Jos. Ant. viii. 7),

and built in the middle of the city a castle named after him, in which a temple to the planet (*kôkeb*) *Mushteri*, the guardian-god of the city, has been erected. That this temple, which, as is well known, under Theodosius, at the same time with the temple of the sun at Ba'lbek, passed over to the Christians, was actually surrounded with a strong, fortified wall, is capable of proof even in the present day. In this tradition, which has assumed various forms, a more genuine counterpart of the biblical עוץ appears than that '*A*is which we have characterized above as an invention of the schools, viz. an '*A*us (عوص), father of the Adite-tribe which is said to have settled in the Damascene district under that *Gêrûn*, and also ancestor of the prophet *Hûd*, lost to the tradition, whose *makâm* on the mountains of *Suêt* rises far above *Gerash* the city of pillars, this true *Iram dhât el-'imâd*, the valley of the Jabbok and the *Sawâd* of Gilead.

It is with good reason that we have hitherto omitted to mention the Ἀίσῖται of Ptolemy v. 18 (19). The Codd. have both Ἀίσεῖται and Ἀίσῖται; different Semitic forms (*e.g.* the name of the بنى حَيس, which, according to Jâkût, once dwelt in the *Harra* of the *Ragil*) may lie at the basis of this name, only not the form עוץ, which ought to be Οὐσῖται, or at least Αὐσῖται (which no Cod. reads). As to the abodes of the Ἀίσῖται, Ptolemy distributes them under nine greater races or groups of races, which in his time inhabited the Syrian steppe. Three of these had their settlements in the eastern half of the Syrian steppe towards the Euphrates or on its western banks: the Καυχαβηνοί in the north, the Ἀίσῖται in the middle, and the Ὀρχηνοί in the south. According to this the Ἀίσῖται would have been about between *Hît* and *Kûfa*, or in that district which is called by the natives *Ard el-Wudjan*, and in which just that race of the Chaldæans might have dwelt that plundered Job's camels.

There we are certainly not to seek the scene of the drama of Job; and if the Edomites were dispersed there (Lam. iv. 21), they were not to be envied on account of their fortune. But if the Αἰσῖται are to be sought there, we may not connect the Καυχαβηνοί with the village of *Cochabe* (كوكبا) on the Hermon (Epiphan. *Hær.* x. 18), in order then to remove the Αἰσῖται, dwelling " below them," to Batanæa.

And now, in concluding here, I have still to explain, that in writing these pages I was not actuated by an invincible desire of increasing the dull literature respecting the ארץ עוץ by another tractate, but exclusively by the wish of my honoured friend that I should furnish him with a contribution on my visit to the *Makâm Êjûb*, and concerning the tradition that prevails there, for his commentary on the book of Job.

As to the accompanying map, it is intended to represent the hitherto unknown position of the Makâm, the Monastery, and the country immediately around them, by comparing it with two localities marked on most maps, *Nawâ* and the castle of *Muzêrîb*. The latter, the position of which we determined in 1860 as 32° 44' north lat. and 35° 51' 45" east long. (from Greenwich), lies three hours' journey on horseback south of the Monastery. The *Wâdi Jarmûk* and *Wâdi Hît* have the gorge formation in common with all other wadis that unite in the neighbourhood of *Zêzûn* and form the *Makran*, which is remarkable from a geological point of view : a phenomenon which is connected with the extreme depression of the valley of the Jordan. For the majority of the geographical names mentioned in this essay I refer the reader to Carl Ritter's *Geographie von Syrien und Palästina ;*[1] others will be explained in my *Itinerarien*, which will be published shortly.

---

[1] Translated by W. L. Gage, and published by T. and T. Clark, Edinburgh, 1866, 4 vols.

THE MODE OF TRANSCRIBING THE ARABIC WORDS.

t = ת, ت; th = ת, ث; 'g [soft, the ' *over* the g has been generally omitted, as liable to be mistaken for an accent in connection with vowels], or, in accordance with the predominant pronunciation, g = ج; h or hh = ح; ch = خ; dh = ذ; z = ז, j; sh or sch = ش; s or ss = צ, ص; d or dd = ض; t or tt = ט, ظ; z = ظ; ' = ע, ع, *e.g.* '*Ain* = עין, *Gumû'* = גמוע; gh = غ; k (k) or q = ק, ق; k (c) = ك. The exact transcription is sometimes omitted where the word occurs more frequently, *e.g.* Haurân, Makâm. Instead of *ijj* and *uww* are written *îj* and *ûw*. The vowels a and e correspond to the *Fath* (פתח), and u and o to the *Damm;* nevertheless the use of o is limited to the emphatic and guttural consonants, including r, while a, according to rule, is subject to this limitation only in nominal forms,—in verbal forms it is also combined with the rest of the consonants; $â, ê$ (*ei, ai*), and $ô$ (*au*) are = *Fath* followed by *Elif, Jod,* or *Waw,* $û$ = *Damm* followed by *Waw*.

The sign for *Hamza* is ', *e.g. mala'a* = ملا (מלא). The *Tenwîn* (Nunation) is only expressed exceptionally, *e.g.* '*gelle* = גּלֵּה as it is generally pronounced, especially when the word stands out of its connection as the root form, not '*gellat-un* (the nunized nominative). Perfect consistency has not been attainable in a book, the printing of which, together with the working in of constantly accumulating material, has occupied nearly two years.

[The consonantal notation is given above according to the variation that has been rendered necessary by the want of casts for printing according to the system adopted by Dr Delitzsch. We were obliged to have recourse to the old notation, which is clumsy and confusing, *e.g.* *hh* = ﺡ, *tt* = ﻁ, ﻝ, and in one or two instances a · has been used in the *tt* thus, *t·t*, to represent ﻝ̄ (with *Teshdîd*). This applies to the first volume; but in the second I have adopted a change, which occurred to me later, viz. to use Roman letters among the Italics to represent the stronger consonants, or *vice versâ*, Italics among Roman letters. The advantage of this will be seen more especially in the exact reproduction of geographical names, as by means of it the spelling is not affected, and at the same time the Arabic letters are fairly distinguished. Suffice it to remind the student that the *j* is to be pronounced as Engl. *y*, being = ﻱ.

ABBREVIATIONS

Have been rarely used in the translation, and those used are mostly familiar and self-evident. The names of critics are given in full in the earlier part, and though abbreviated, as constantly recurring, need no explanation here. "The Arabic Version referred to is that of the London Polyglot; the Syriac, the ancient Syrian version. *b.* and *j.* in connection with Talmud citations signify respectively the Babylonian and Jerusalem Talmuds; *b.* with the names of persons, *ben* (*bar*), son." The Biblical references are according to the *Hebrew* divisions, *e.g.* Ps. xcii. 11 (10), as also the division of ch. xl. xli.

INDEX OF TEXTS

END OF VOL. II.